Imperial Intimacies

Imperial Intimacies

A Tale of Two Islands

Hazel V. Carby

VERSO
London • New York

First published by Verso 2019
© Hazel V. Carby 2019

1 3 5 7 9 10 8 6 4 2

Verso
UK: 6 Meard Street, London W1F 0EG
US: 20 Jay Street, Suite 1010, Brooklyn, NY 11201
versobooks.com

Verso is the imprint of New Left Books

ISBN-13: 978-1-78873-509-4
ISBN-13: 978-1-78873-511-7 (UK EBK)
ISBN-13: 978-1-78873-512-4 (US EBK)

British Library Cataloguing in Publication Data
A catalogue record for this book is available from the British Library

Library of Congress Cataloging-in-Publication Data

Names: Carby, Hazel V., author.
Title: Imperial intimacies : a tale of two islands / Hazel V. Carby.
Description: London ; Brooklyn, NY : Verso, 2019. | Includes bibliographical
 references.
Identifiers: LCCN 2019017193| ISBN 9781788735094 (hardback : alk. paper) |
 ISBN 9781788735117 (UK EBK) | ISBN 9781788735124 (US EBK)
Subjects: LCSH: Carby, Hazel V.—Family. | Carby family. | Historians—Great
 Britain—Biography. | Women historians—Great Britain—Biography. |
 Racially mixed women—Great Britain—Biography. | Racially mixed
 families—Great Britain—History—20th century. | Blacks—Great
 Britain—History—20th century. | Jamaicans—Great Britain—History—20th
 century. | Welsh—Migrations. | Great Britain—Colonies—America—History.
 | Great Britain—Colonies—Emigration and immigration—History. |
 Jamaica—Emigration and immigration—History. | Slavery—Jamaica—History.
 | Jamaica—History—To 1962.
Classification: LCC DA3.C37 A3 2019 | DDC 929.20941—dc23
LC record available at https://lccn.loc.gov/2019017193

Typeset in Sabon LT by Hewer Text UK Ltd, Edinburgh
Printed and bound by CPI Group (UK) Ltd, Croydon CR0 4YY

For Ian
Nicholas, April,
Nicole and Chloe

Identity is not only a story, a narrative which we tell ourselves about ourselves, it is stories which change with historical circumstances. And identity shifts with the way in which we think and hear them and experience them. Far from only coming from the still small point of truth inside us, identities actually come from outside, they are the way in which we are recognized and then come to step into the place of the recognitions which others give us. Without the others there is no self, there is no self-recognition.

Stuart Hall

Contents

CONTENTS

Family Registers

Part Four: Accounting

Part Five: Legacies

Preface

Every story is, by definition, unfaithful. Reality ... can't be told or repeated. The only thing that can be done with reality is to invent it again.

Tomás Eloy Martínez,
Santa Evita

I can read poetry and plays, and things of that sort, and do not dislike travels. But history, real solemn history, I cannot be interested in ...

I read it a little as a duty but it tells me nothing that does not either vex or weary me. The quarrels of popes and kings, with wars or pestilences, in every page; the men all so good for nothing, and hardly any women at all – it is very tiresome: and yet I often think it odd that it should be so dull, for a great deal of it must be invention. The speeches that are put into the heroes' mouths, their thoughts and designs – the chief of all this must be invention, and invention is what delights me in other books.

Jane Austen, *Northanger Abbey*

Imperial Intimacies is a very British story. It is a story of the everyday ties, relations and intricate interdependencies of empire and colonialism. It does not conform to the way in which most stories of empire have been told and it questions what we think we know about our shared colonial past. I incorporate stories of my Welsh mother, my Jamaican father and their ancestors into

I

material drawn from colonial archives and histories to show how they were shaped by the times and places in which they lived. But family stories and historical accounts sit uneasily side by side. When I assembled the various pieces I found that rather than cohere into a unified narrative their juxtaposition revealed the shards of conflict and contradiction that familial, national and imperial ideologies work to conceal. I used family memories as a guide to navigate material in the National Archives of Jamaica and the UK, but when I stumbled I had to put aside the voices of my relatives because they hindered my ability to see what they had disguised, hidden, or had no intention of passing on.

Imperial Intimacies is an account written from the perspective of someone of Jamaican Welsh ancestry who does not take for granted definitions of *being* British but rather is interested in how subjects *become* British and how people are inscribed into ideologies of empire and beliefs of whiteness that enable them to feel superior even when desperately poor. The story of imperial relations is as restless as the Atlantic surging between the islands of Britain and Jamaica as I follow currents that draw me into the mid-eighteenth century. But it is also anchored, temporarily, in the particular places in which people in my family lived and died: the urban centres of London, Bath, Bristol, Cardiff and Kingston and the rural landscapes of Devon, Somerset, Lincolnshire and Portland. It is not an exceptional story about becoming British but asserts that Britishness harbours the deepest interconnections of class and race and gender: trying to find your way as the white mother of a black child; trying to survive as a black child in a colony and a black man in the metropole; being a girl regarded as an oxymoron when she claimed she was both black and British.

In the concluding pages of *My Brother*, Jamaica Kincaid alludes to her ideal reader, a particular person, her father-in-law and former editor of *The New Yorker*, recently deceased. Kincaid's words form a memorial to an ideal reader, one who no longer exists. Before I read Kincaid's memorial, before I realized that for Kincaid an ideal reader was someone who disagreed with and argued against what she wrote and disapproved of the style in which she wrote it, before reading *My Brother*, I had considered myself an ideal reader of Jamaica Kincaid's work. That was because I assumed that an ideal reader would be full of admiration for a writer, that an ideal reader would be knowledgeable about and sympathetic towards the people and places a writer renders into prose. An ideal reader, I believed, would surely feel empathy for the intellectual and political contours of the worlds a writer created. I was wrong; Jamaica Kincaid is wise. I too, will attempt to disconcert, to challenge and to confront the assumptions that any reader may bring to these pages.

Is it possible to produce a reckoning of movement between and among places, spaces and peoples, the scattering that results in racialized encounters and the violent transactions that produce racialized subjects? Pitting memory, history and poetics against each other in a narrative of racial encounters is intended to undermine the binary thinking that opposes colonial centre to colonized margin, home to abroad, and metropole to periphery. Does it matter *where* encounters between Africans and Europeans, between those constructed as 'black' and as 'white' take place: in an African or English village, town, or city; if they occur in the impenetrable darkness of the dungeon of a coastal fort, or in the claustrophobic hold of a slave ship, or take place, face to face, in the glaring light reflected from the Atlantic Ocean; if they are confrontations on the shores of a Caribbean island or on the streets of a metropolitan imperial city? Perhaps it is not, in fact, only the place that is significant but also the manner of the journey and arrival, the eager walking, or manacled stumble, the panicked flight, or forced or voluntary sailing toward and away from each other.

The architecture of this tale has the tensile strength of a spider's web spun across the Atlantic: spinnerets draw threads from archives, histories and memories, joining the movement of men from Britain during the Revolutionary and Napoleonic Wars to the flood of volunteers that left the Caribbean to travel to Britain during the Second World War; the radial fibres that hold rural England and rural Jamaica in tension link the Atlantic port cities of Bristol and Kingston. Orphan threads have been left broken because I do not know how they should connect. Though I am unable to make these repairs the web weathers and holds. It is a story of imperial intimacies, of geographies of pain, of the continuing aftermath of enslavement, a story of land, of sea and of war.

Part One:

Inventories

The starting point of critical elaboration is the consciousness of what one really is, and is 'knowing thyself' as a product of the historical process to date which has deposited in you an infinity of traces, without leaving an inventory. Such an inventory must therefore be made at the outset.

Antonio Gramsci

Where Are You From?

During the first bitterly cold month of 1948 in Britain, a girl was born. Attending primary school at the tail-end of the postwar baby boom, she was one of forty-eight children in her classroom. By the time she was old enough to be aware of her surroundings she lived in Mitcham, then in the county of Surrey, a large part of which lay in the metropolitan green belt. Surrey was famous for the beauty of its North Downs, had more woods than any other county in the UK, and was home to the wealthiest population in Britain. The girl's mother, Iris, loved having an address in a 'posh' county, as if the mere reputation of Surrey could burnish their lives. Iris's ambition was to move south, deeper into Surrey, to achieve middle-class status and the security it promised, but she never did rub shoulders with the residents of the stockbroker belt. Mitcham was a part of Surrey in name only and her neighbourhood was the last gasp of the working-class estates of South London, the boundary *before* gracious living began. It was ugly and soulless and, as with similar South London estates, a nursery for white supremacist hatred. In 1965, Mitcham was finally cast out of Surrey and incorporated into the London Borough of Merton. With the change of address Iris's hopes of class mobility were dashed.

As an adult I can compile an inventory of the history and design of this environment, but to the girl it was as if an incomprehensible higher power had delivered hunks of concrete and steel complete, unexpected and unwelcome. She knew the buildings that materialized around her didn't grow, that they weren't organic like trees or animals, but she did not know that the residential suburb in which she lived was the product of a human vision, that it had been planned and developed by people in offices. The four major arteries of the neighbourhood of Pollards Hill radiated outwards from a concrete roundabout, with grass and a signpost in the middle. The girl would throw open her bedroom window. Elbows on the window sill, chin resting on hands, she leant into the long twilight of summer evenings, face lit by the moon as she looked out across a grid of carefully tended squares of grass and narrow beds of flowers partitioned by rows of wooden fences which culminated in a shed or garage. Through a gap between the corner of the Baptist Church and the end of a row of brick terraced houses she could glimpse the roundabout and listen to combustion engines lower in tone as a car, lorry, or motorbike slowed and entered the circle, then rise sharply and suddenly in pitch as the vehicle sped away. Sights, sounds and smells of the night were exalting. Breathing the night deep into lungs it was possible to believe that the roundabout was organic, pliable, a living creature with tentacles drawing vehicles in toward its heart. Abruptly changing its mind, the creature loosened its grip and flung them out screaming into the distance.

At night people were tucked away indoors and the landscape became soft-edged, filled with the shadowy shapes and noises of nonhuman residents: the low guttural warnings of felines stalking each other; squeaks and snuffles from rootling hedgehogs; an 'urgent sweaty-smokey reek' and a rustling of undergrowth announcing the presence of a red fox. The girl longed to bring the magic and promise of the outside indoors. One evening she crawled under the shrubbery, trapped a hedgehog in a shoe box, smuggled it into her room and into bed to keep as a friend.

This girl was a wanderer. Her parents worked long hours and the neighbour Iris paid to take care of her children was inattentive. The girl would check to see if her younger brother was contentedly playing with his toys before she crept through the neighbour's kitchen, scampered down the back-garden path, lifted the latch on the tall wooden gate, closed it behind her and ran.

Once outside she could explore at will; inside the walls of her house she was a girl who was cowed, a shrunken being who worked to render herself invisible. The streets were important avenues of escape, but if the sights, sounds and smells of the night were magical, what the daylight revealed was crass and mundane. She explored streets between rows of modest two-story terraced houses. She scurried across the field of 'prefabs' – two-bedroom, prefabricated aluminium, asbestos-clad bunga-lows resting on slabs of concrete, hastily erected as a solution to the postwar housing crisis. It was dangerous to linger there because the inhabitants registered their disapproval of brown children by throwing stones. The prefabs were meant to be temporary structures but remained for twenty years. As the girl stood staring at the huge estate of six-story maisonettes, she was disoriented by its scale and uniformity. She despaired when the council built a high-density 'low-rise' estate of three-story houses and flats because it blocked her route to the hill she loved to climb and roll down.

She traversed an area which stretched from the hill, rising directly behind the roundabout, and fanning out southwest until reaching more than 400 acres of ancient common land. The girl avoided the main roads in favour of walking or biking the network of streets which connected them. She was nearly always headed to the common, where she could breathe and roam, or sit under trees and dream, or dig into the silt of ponds just to see what lived or was buried there. Having crossed the length of the common the girl arrived at the town centre, in which stood the library; the common and the library saved her, but it was many years before she would learn how to draw a map of what she could not see.

The apple trees she climbed, the fragrant wild marjoram and sweet woodruff she brushed past in exploring her favourite places, the open green space of the common and the hill – these were traces of the farms, fields and woodland that for the most part had been paved over. Lying, dreaming, in the long grass of the hill, listening intently to crickets, and creating chains of buttercups, the girl could not imagine the remains of the Celtic fort that lay beneath the soil. In the flora of the landscape there was still evidence of the eighteenth-century physic gardeners who had cultivated 250 acres of lavender, wormwood, chamomile, aniseed, rhubarb, liquorice, peppermint and other medicinal plants.

When her brother was old enough the girl took him to play in the park at the end of Sherwood Park Avenue, site of the vanished Sherwood Farm which had been demolished to build homes for heroes from the First World War. An act of bureaucratic wizardry had replaced local history with national mythology in the district; overlaid onto bricks and mortar was a thin veneer of enchantment evoking the ancient woodlands and footpaths of legend. Three centuries after the actual Sherwood Forest in Nottinghamshire had been enclosed, its commons turned into private estates, and its various communities dispossessed and dispersed, someone in Mitcham Town Hall had decided that war heroes deserved to walk down roads named after the outlaw Robin Hood and his companions.

Once upon a time, after the war to end all wars, a town planner, sitting at a desk in the council offices, pored over the designs for the future Pollards Hill, racking their brains for names that would enable the residents to erase the horrors of war with fantasies of a medieval world of courtliness while waiting for the bus to take them to work. Robin Hood had already been used twice, once for a Close and again for a Lane. The map was also filling up with references to Abbots, Manors and the Greenwood. Scanning the drawings, the planner came across a small unnamed cul-de-sac protruding from the side of Holly Way. Perhaps this wizard of street names was musing about medieval architecture, or perhaps they consulted one of their architectural colleagues; either way, the shape of the cul-de-sac reminded someone of an oriel, a medieval bay window designed to bring sunlight and fresh air into the interior of a building. A projection into light, an outlook, a turn away from the darkness of war and brutality, a name selected in a moment of hope before another war loomed on the horizon. Oriel was the name given to the Close where the girl would eventually live, a name bequeathed when there were still open green vistas. By the time her family moved in the view was grim: housing estates and prefabs spread to the horizon. But for this girl the world of Robin Hood was living all around her, and, for a while, that was sufficient.

She was content to explore, until she encountered people in shops, the library, the park, at school, or those who quite rightly chased her from their apple trees – people who wanted to know where she was from. The question may appear innocuous, but she came to dread it. Her parents had taught her to hold her head erect, to look directly, without guile, at adults who addressed her, to smile with her eyes not just her teeth, to speak clearly, to be conspicuously open, transparent and honest. Her dad told her that if she did not follow this advice she would be regarded as 'shifty', duplicitous and unworthy of attention. The girl absorbed every word because she was eager to be considered a 'good' girl, polite and deferential. Not until she was a teenager did she realize that her father had been coaching her on the art of being a 'good' black girl, acceptable to white people.

The girl was surprised and disconcerted by the increasingly insistent demands to respond to what she came to think of as *The Question!* Her father had not prepared her for such intense cross-examination. At first she was confused about what was being asked of her, because she lived in the same neighbourhood as her interrogators. The girl took pride in her navigational skills, which she honed by following the pathways of the medieval land of *Robin Hood*, her favourite illustrated story book. She could provide anyone who asked with directions to her house via Abbots, Sherwood and Greenwood Roads, but that was not what people wanted from her.

The challenge was to find a satisfactory response to *The Question!*, for the girl was deceived by the apparent simplicity of the answer. If a child at school wanted to know where she was from she would, as a gesture of friendship, embellish the bare bones of street names with tantalizing scraps of tales from the adventures of Robin Hood, Maid Marian and Friar Tuck: outlaws who robbed from the rich to give to the poor. When it became clear that *The Question!* demanded a more detailed response than simply giving her current address, the girl offered the name of the village in Devon – Folly Gate – where she was born, and stories of Exmoor extracted from the novel *Lorna Doone*. This information only confirmed the fears and anxiety that prompted *The Question!* in the first place. The fact that she was born in England rendered her paradoxical. Adults and children

There is, it seems to me, an overwhelming tendency to abstract questions of race from what one might call their internal social and political basis and contexts in British society – that is to say, to deal with 'race' as if it has nothing intrinsically to do with the present 'condition of England'. It's viewed rather as an 'external' problem, which has been foisted to some extent on English society from the outside: it's been visited on us, as it were, from the skies. To hear problems of race discussed in England today, you would sometimes believe that relations between British people and the peoples of the Caribbean or the Indian sub-continent began with the wave of black immigrants in the late forties and fifties . . .

[Neither right nor left] can nowadays bring themselves to refer to Britain's imperial and colonial past, even as a contributory factor to the present situation. The slate has been wiped clean.'

Stuart Hall

alike considered the possibility of her Englishness derisory and dismissed her accounts as deliberately perverse and misleading. Classmates reproduced, verbatim, the words of their parents: 'Anyone can see that she is the wrong colour to be from around here, no matter what she says!' The girl was declared a fool and a liar. Her suggestion that she was native, that she belonged, was an audacious claim in postwar Britain.

As I wrote this girl into being I saw that her dread of *The Question!* haunts the woman the girl became. *The Question!* is still posed whenever I am regarded as being out of place, seen as an enigma, an incongruity, or a curiosity. The girl was confronted by a bewildering array of contesting national and racialized definitions of self and subject. She was being asked to provide a reason for her being which she did not have. It was sobering to realize that 'where' and 'from' did not reference geography but the fiction of race in British national heritage. The girl was cautious as she sought to find her way through this cultural maze, but eventually, when all the answers she could invent were rejected, she reluctantly acknowledged that she was being rebuffed for what she was. When she was dismissed, disregarded and disparaged, when she was treated as less than the human she knew herself to be, her chin sunk into her chest, she mumbled and looked sideways out of the corner of her eyes. She became the uncooperative black girl her father did not wish her to be.

Her classmates grew bored with her petulant refusal to reveal a difference their pinches and punches tried to expose. The girl's body reddened and bruised under fingers poking and squeezing as if unravelling a dense series of knots; knuckles vented their frustration on her brown skin. I can still see this girl refusing to let anyone see her cry. All tears were suppressed until, back at her desk, she concealed her face with a book and let them trickle in silence down her cheeks. In this way books became her refuge.

Far more fearsome than leaving classmates dissatisfied was irritating a teacher, or any curious adult, who asked *The Question!* They interpreted her silence and shrugs as deliberate perversity, an outright refusal to cooperate. This girl discovered that the adoption of a posture of timidity with a hint of speech impairment was likely to end the interrogation. Answers were mumbled incoherently, with eyes lowered to feet neatly encased in white cotton socks and brown leather Clarks T-bar sandals. Honesty was best avoided in these circumstances: muttering about being born in England condemned her to utter disapproval and the exasperated demand, 'but *where* did you come from *before* that?' Some adults were convinced she was not telling the truth. Others believed her, an outcome which was far, far worse because then she was accused of being a monstrosity, a 'half-caste': the issue of a black father and a white mother. Facts failed her so she turned to fiction.

In this unstable landscape Robin Hood's adventures were too earth-bound. When the girl was too young to imagine, let alone assert, that she was not accountable to anyone, she invented alternative figures of authority to whom she would account for herself. She concocted a place on earth with the help of DC

Comics, where she had found a short story about a scientist in a laboratory examining drops of water through his microscope. In one drop he discovered a universe and, by gradually increasing the magnification, located the Milky Way and eventually planet Earth. The girl's fantasy involved travelling from another, kinder, galaxy to South London in order to observe the human species in its natural habitat. The mode of travel by which she was transported constantly changed in her head. The girl saw herself as a scientist who, at an unspecified time and place in the future, would be called upon to report the observations recorded in her journals. The plot was short on detail – she had no idea on whose behalf she watched, listened and wrote – but the girl knew that she must not share the nature of her mission with anyone in her family or at school. Standing on her bed leaning out of her window she wondered if the creature inhabiting the roundabout was also an alien, the tall signpost at its centre a transmitter for communication with the mothership. But was it a friend or a foe? Could it read her mind? The girl grew adept living in anticipation of *The Question!*, which crouched in the shadows waiting to challenge her right to belong. If only those around her knew what she really was!

Resurrecting the world of this girl is risky for my sense of self, a self which has been carefully assembled out of a refusal to acknowledge or remember. I do not wish to provide justifications for my present or past self-creations. The demand that the girl account for her racial self was contemptable. She stumbled for many years before she learnt the difficult lesson that she was not accountable to those who questioned her right to belong. *The Question!* destabilizes my world still because there is no answer that can satisfy racist conjectures about the shades of brown in skin.

As an adult, living in the United States, I find that unexpressed assumptions determine the terms, conditions and boundaries within which any answer provided will be accepted or dismissed. When I wish to be agreeable, I expend effort analysing which conjectures are in play and attempt to provide an answer which will satisfy expectations and avoid a miserable sense of failure.

Failure to be satisfyingly *read* places the questioner in the awkward position of having to repeat *The Question!*, which is then patiently re-articulated in a louder and more forceful tone of voice, as if I was hard of hearing:

'*Where are you from?*'

Meaning, of course, are you black or white?

Like a cat with its paw on the tail of a hapless mouse, I glean pleasure from watching an interrogator flounder. However, I have to exercise caution in my selection of prey: it is unseemly to torment one's professional colleagues; it is dangerous to play mind games with British immigration personnel, or with police in the UK; it is asking for serious trouble to joke with officials from Homeland Security or cops in the US of A.

As a result of this lifetime of negotiation, observation and reporting, I am armed with a series of suitable explanations for my various selves. I have fictional and factual justifications for the when, where and why of their being, and carry a potted history for all occasions – such as when a distinguished black professor asked me, 'How did a nice white girl like you come to study African American literature?' As a woman, a writer and an academic I am assumed to be out of place: too black to be British, too white, or too West Indian, to be a professor of African American Studies. *The Question!*, of course, is the wrong question. If I am asked to identify the origin of the selves I have become, without hesitation I describe the various libraries in which the girl I no longer recognize, the girl I have long since left behind, the girl I discarded and rejected, found sanctuary.

My father, of course, was always asked *The Question!* too. It was a constant hum in the background of our lives, white noise, a condition of our existence in England. We only spoke of it once. In 1962, my father and his younger brother, who also lived in the UK, had two very different reactions to Jamaican Independence. My uncle immediately applied for a Jamaican passport and urged my father to do so. They had a serious disagreement about nationality and allegiance. My father was determined to retain his British nationality, reasoning that he was born a British citizen, in a British territory, and had lived in the UK for two decades before Jamaica became independent. He was very proud of being British and had no plans to live anywhere else.

Sixteen years later, my father wished to travel to the United States to visit his younger siblings and their families. Like most people, he had not constantly renewed his British passport because he hadn't travelled outside of the country since being demobilized from the RAF in 1950. Being a very methodical man, he assembled the paperwork necessary for his application for a new passport. He wrote to the Ministry of Defence requesting documentation of his service in the Royal Air Force and, when it arrived, placed it in a file with his original British passport which had expired on 8 April 1948. The application process required an interview at the headquarters of the Immigration and Nationality Directorate in Croydon. It was on this occasion that my father confronted *The Question!* in its most aggressive and antagonistic form: a situation where disbelief had nasty consequences. I regret not being a witness to what occurred in that immigration room. I know that if I had been there I would have lost my temper and my father would have been ashamed of such behaviour from his daughter. He would have deemed it undignified.

When my father described how he had been treated in this interview I shared his humiliation. As I sat by his side, he held fast to my hand, his grasp as tight as that of a man who was drowning. He seemed to be forcing air into his lungs through a throat constricted with the effort not to cry, not to scream in frustration. His need to tell his story fought against his distress; he could barely speak. I felt as if I was manipulating mental forceps to extract word by word what had happened.

My father, then fifty-seven, was interviewed by a young woman who not only insulted and intimidated him but also accused him of lying, of being 'an illegal immigrant', one of those who had 'sneaked into the country, landing at night on the

Essex coast with a boatload of other illegals'. This representative of the British immigration service declared that all his records, including his RAF record and original passport, were probably forgeries. This was an absurd accusation. I knew that in the face of this racist rant my father would have maintained his dignity, making no demands to see a superior official, not complaining or raising his voice. He just bent to pick up his papers, which the interviewer had swept off her desk onto the floor in a wild gesture of incredulity. Once gathered, he did not look at her again but stood with his head held high, turned his back on her, walked out of her office and left the building.

Evidently the interview was just an exercise in humiliation, since my father was not issued with any official documentation of application denial, nor were any procedures instigated against him as an illegal immigrant. When he walked out of the room I imagine the interviewer felt smug and self-satisfied, believing 'he wouldn't be back, as she had given another one of *them* a hard time'. The aim of this performance was to dissuade my father from pursuing his claim to Britishness any further, because *she had shown him* he was not welcome. Such are the pleasures reaped by Home Office bureaucrats in the course of their day. Respectability, honesty, loyalty and duty were ingrained in my father and he regarded himself as a British gentleman in every aspect of his being. He carried all his records to the Jamaican High Commission where, in order to be issued with a Jamaican passport, he had to formally renounce his British citizenship, an act which deeply pained him.

I have kept all my father's papers. Gathered from the floor of the office in Croydon is his first British passport, issued on 8 April 1943, which declares the National Status of Carl Collin Carby to be a 'British Subject by Birth' and his profession 'Royal Air Force Recruit', alongside the letter of confirmation of service from the Ministry of Defence. I have his three Jamaican passports, all of which carry entry visas to the USA, his birth certificate, and handwritten copies of every letter that my father wrote to the Immigration and Nationality Directorate, part of the Home Office, over a period of more than two decades. Each letter is formally addressed, 'Dear Sirs, Madam'; each is stapled and labelled 'copy'. Taken together these papers form an archive of the shifting racist terrain of the rules and regulations of British immigration.

One of the letters, dated 10 February 2003, addresses the 'recent restrictions on Jamaicans travelling to England'. In it my father asks if these restrictions will affect his return to the UK after attending the graduation of his grandson from high school in the USA. Most poignant is a letter written later that same year, which declares, 'I am now 82 years of age and wish to complete my affairs by reverting to a British Subject.' He details every aspect of his life in the RAF, explains that he is the recipient of an award for long service from Westminster City Council and an owner of properties in Streatham and Mitcham in London and, at the time of writing, in the city of York. This letter, accompanied by extensive documentation, concludes 'I shall be most grateful for your kind consideration.' The process took eighteen months. On 19 July 2004, 'Issued on the direction of the Secretary of State, Home Office, London', my father was granted a Certificate of Naturalization as a British Citizen under the British Nationality Act of 1981.

Becoming British: Iris

On the 3rd of September 1939, when Britain and France declared war on Germany, my mother, Iris, was nineteen and my father, Carl, had just turned eighteen. The Second World War not only sutured them together, it left an indelible imprint on the adults they became. As their first child, born into a bleak, scrupulously rationed, postwar world, I also lived in the shadow of war. Like other members of their generation my parents processed their experiences of war through storytelling, and thus constantly relived it; as children, my generation claimed and recycled our parent's memories, reproducing them in the classroom as well as at play. Gradually, I realized that my stories were received as being different from those of other children and from the version of British history and the workings of empire that we were being taught. So I fell silent.

... historical authenticity resides not in the fidelity to an alleged past but in an honesty vis-á-vis the present as it re-presents that past.
Michel-Rolph Trouillot

Both of my parents grew up poor on islands more than 4,000 nautical miles apart from each other: Iris experienced the poverty of agricultural life in a neglected rural outback of the imperial metropole; while Carl suffered the poverty of colonial neglect of the imperial periphery. But they were not strange to each other when they met. The distance between Britain and Jamaica cannot take the measure of their Britishness, realized as a structure of ethics and values made coherent through shared ideas about empire. Iris and Carl were conscripted as subjects belonging to and within the British Empire, conscripted before either could fully comprehend how the circumstances of their becoming might have been otherwise. As children, each had celebrated Empire Day by waving Union Jacks with patriotic enthusiasm, wearing starched shirts and a spotless school uniform; as young adults both had volunteered to serve and save the empire. They each had distinct perspectives and a sense of self anchored in the people and places that nurtured them, but both Carl and Iris considered themselves British without equivocation and were unhesitatingly loyal to whatever Britishness meant to them. When war drew them into its orbit they eagerly embraced the upheavals in their lives, dusted off the dreams and ambitions they had previously considered unattainable, and ran toward the possibility of infinitely expanded futures.

Iris was born in Wales in 1920 and grew up in a series of English villages in the counties of Somerset and Devon. She was the daughter of Charles and Beatrice Leaworthy: Charles was an agricultural labourer, Beatrice a seamstress. In December of 1935, just before Iris's sixteenth birthday and six months before she was due to sit her Oxford School Certificate examination, Beatrice was diagnosed with tuberculosis. Iris shelved her ambition to go to college, left the Bridgwater County School for Girls, and nursed her mother until she died, in March 1938.

Immediately after burying Beatrice in Bristol, Charles installed his mistress in their cottage to replaced his dead wife. Iris, grieving, felt betrayed and fled. Like most young women from a poor, rural background and lacking a school certificate, she felt she had no option but to go into domestic service. By the time my mother told me this story she had rationalized her decision, but was she aware that I also longed to leave her and my home? I imagined a young Iris escaping at any cost, seeking complete independence. What she found was domestic drudgery in a village outside of Brighton. This period of servitude was transmitted to me in a series of revelations and warnings about

I try to invent you for myself.
Virginia Woolf to Vita Sackville-West

the perils of domestic service. Although I empathized with the resentment and pain of Iris as a young woman, I also knew her as my mother, who constantly made impulsive decisions and was full of resentment toward everyone in her life.

Iris's duties as a parlour maid in a large house began at 4 a.m. each morning. She rose from her bed in an unheated attic room to begin the tasks necessary to ensure her mistresses rose from their beds in comfort and warmth. Before the fires were lit she would scrape and sweep the hearths, carrying the ashes in buckets downstairs and the coals in buckets back upstairs. She would then return to the kitchen where she had previously fired up the cast-iron range, hauled water, filled large kettles and placed them on the hot plates. She was exhausted even before she carried warm water back upstairs and into the rooms of her employers, two middle-aged, wealthy sisters who had never married. At the close of a long working day, before she could retire to her bed, it was Iris's responsibility to find the cat and bring it indoors before the house was locked for the night. This task she dreaded above all others because the cat, out hunting in the neighbourhood cemetery, did not want to be found. Iris was afraid of the dead and the dark, so scrambling over and around the gravestones terrified her. There were many dawns in which Iris had to retrieve a damp, cold, mewling cat from the doorstep before either of the sisters discovered that she had been left outside all night.

I don't think my mother's career as a domestic servant lasted longer than a few months before she went to live in the home of her aunt Maud, Beatrice's older sister, in a village in South Wales. Wondering what to do next, Iris remembered the advice offered in the November 1933 edition of the Bridgwater County School for Girls Magazine: under the heading

There is an increasing demand for women in connection with the rapidly developing care and training of Mental Defectives – a class of persons who differ entirely from the insane, and may be suitably cared for by young people for whom they have a real affection. 'Nurse attendant' posts may be held by girls of seventeen and upwards, and afford excellent preliminary training for General or Mental Nursing posts. Many colonies for Mental Defectives are springing up in beautiful country surroundings with excellent buildings and large staffs, where an active, intelligent girl can obtain a good salary and thorough training.

'Careers for Girls', Bridgwater County School for Girls Magazine, 1933

'Careers for Girls', mention was made of the opportunities available in the 'rapidly developing care and training of Mental Defectives', in the disdainful terminology of the period.

As an 'active, intelligent girl', Iris applied to the Glamorgan County Council, which in 1930 had acquired Hensol Castle in Pontyclun to establish such 'a home'. Originally planned to hold a hundred men with learning disabilities, it expanded to accommodate 460 inmates, men, women and children. Iris soon went to work at Hensol as a Nurse Attendant. In contrast to her many stories of life in domestic service, my mother was subdued when asked about her days there. I learnt that she harboured both rational and irrational fears of Hensol: incidents of physical violence could explode without warning; and ghosts, she was warned, could be encountered during the night shift in the supposedly haunted gothic castle.

In September 1939, the nation was mobilized by war; gendered patterns of work were reorganized, and women were recruited into jobs from which they had previously been excluded. During the First World War, women had been asked to volunteer for work in order to allow men to enter the armed forces. When another war appeared inevitable, the government realized that volunteering would not produce sufficient numbers of women and that it would be necessary to introduce some form of conscription: single women between eighteen and sixty years of age had to be registered by 1941.

Iris did not wait to be conscripted: war offered her the opportunity to obtain a decent job and reignited her ambition to attain middle-class respectability and security, if not through college then via the Civil Service. In South Wales, the choices available to her were joining the land army or working in the munitions factories built underground nearby. Iris didn't hesitate. In the fall of 1939, eighteen months after the death of her mother, she secured a position in London as a civil servant in the Air Ministry and was placed in the rapidly expanding department that dealt with family allowances. I am unsure how she accomplished this because matriculation was a requirement for entry to the Civil Service, but it must have been evident to the person who interviewed her that she was a candidate of 'special talent'. The young Iris was smart and audacious; perhaps she told the interviewer that she had matriculated when she hadn't; perhaps, in a time of war, no one checked to see if her school record had been received by their office.

> The Civil Service Posts are much sought after, and are reserved for persons of special talent. In the Government Departments, only girls of great ability are likely to obtain the better posts.
>
> 'Careers for Girls', Bridgwater County School for Girls Magazine, 1933

Iris was in London for just a short time. Air Ministry departments were relocated to a number of different sites. As early as 1936, the government had developed secret plans to secure the machinery of governance from the disruption that would be caused by air raids in the event of another war: government departments and ministries were to be moved out of London and dispersed throughout the provinces. By January 1940, Iris was working for the Family Allowance Branch temporarily based in

Tetbury, a small market town in the Cotswold district of Gloucestershire. But the dispersed departments of the Air Ministry were quickly reassembled fifty miles further north in the city of Worcester, the site chosen to house the prime minister and parliament if they had to be evacuated from London in the face of an invasion.

The young Iris loved Worcester, a beautiful medieval city on the banks of the River Severn overlooked by a twelfth-century cathedral. When she described living in the YWCA with the other young single women recruited by the Air Ministry she was radiant, and I beheld the young vivacious woman my mother used to be. In our life together, my mother always felt unappreciated, but she spoke with obvious pride when she told the story of how highly she was praised and how rapidly she was promoted in the Air Ministry when she found an accounting error in the family allowance records. As a child, Iris had been withdrawn and lived a lonely, solitary life; as a young woman, she learnt how to cultivate friends. My mother treasured the years she spent in Worcester, the most exciting of her entire life because of, and in spite of, the war.

One evening Iris went with her friends to a dance organized as a social event for men from the local RAF stations. My mother told me she saw an airman from Jamaica standing alone and that she was the only woman who would dance with him. What did this young Iris actually see when she saw this brown-skinned man? When she related the circumstances of their encounter my mother spoke in great detail of how brave she was to defy convention but said little about the person she met.

Many people use the terms English and British as if they were synonymous, though my mother never did. Integral to Iris's sense of being British was her insistence on being Welsh. Being born in Wales was more significant than growing up in the county of Somerset and residing in England for most of her life. I do not know at what point in her life Iris decided to stress her Welsh roots; perhaps she chose to be Welsh when she left domestic service and went to live in South Wales with her aunts and her cousins. After the war, when we all lived in London, my mother would assert her allegiance to Wales, regaling her children with tales of the heroic Owain Glyndwr, born in 1359, declared Prince of Wales in 1400, and crowned Owain IV King of Wales in 1404. I am amazed at how much Welsh history and mythology I have retained. Glyndwr raised a Welsh army in revolt against English domination and for years successfully fought the armies of the English King, Henry IV, but he was destined to be the last native Prince of Wales. My mother's stories focused on his triumphs: we did not hear how Glyndwr suffered a final indignity at the hands of his English oppressors. We were left to discover the history of the defeat of the Welsh in a library.

By the time we were teenagers my brother and I identified as Londoners, but as children we believed we were being raised on the wrong side of the Welsh border. In 1969, it seemed as if the entire nation was glued to television sets to watch the spectacular ceremony of the formal investiture of Prince Charles, son of Queen Elizabeth II, as Prince of Wales, within the medieval walls of Caernarfon Castle. Although my mother would express the requisite respect for the Royal Family, particularly her admiration for the Queen Mother, I never heard her refer to Prince Charles as the Prince of Wales, a title he had carried since his birth.

This refusal to be English did not compromise her Britishness in the least. Iris had vivid memories of everyone in her school and community participating in the annual celebrations of Empire Day on 24 May, occasions when even the most marginal members of small rural communities felt themselves connected to, and part of, a much larger colonial world. Empire Day celebrations were significant sites for producing multiple meanings of Britishness. Whatever my mother learnt about Britishness through this schooling formed the core of an ethical code and a basis for judgement, which, although never explicitly articulated as a coherent whole, punctuated her attempts to provide her offspring with guidelines for living.

My mother was distressed to find that 24 May was increasingly becoming a day of anti-imperialist protest rather than celebration. I can see her pacing as she mines her memories to reproduce the sense of inclusion, communal ethics and values she found lacking in her offspring. Her vivid descriptions of Empire Day celebrations tumble out until she stops pacing, turns, lifts her head and recites as if she was addressing her school assembly . . .

> If you can keep your head while all about you
> Are losing theirs and blaming it on you

This scene became so familiar, so predictable that I had to restrain myself from screaming in frustration, 'I know, I know!'

I shut down, switched off all sensation. I became so successful at closing my mind that now I have no memory of my mother's recitations of the middle verses of Rudyard Kipling's poem, *If*. Perhaps she skipped large chunks of it or perhaps the opening verse of this imperialist diatribe is sufficient to trigger mental erasure.

A quick turn of my mother's head, her frown, her glare, is all it takes to recapture my full attention for the last lines, delivered slowly and with great deliberation, now etched in my mind:

> Yours is the earth and everything that's in it
> And – which is more – you'll be a Man my son!

These words, learnt by rote in my mother's elementary school classroom, were passed on as a valued and valuable legacy, knowledge to aid my brother and I in negotiating the present and preparing for the future. The words were offered, but not received, as gifts. I hated the poem then. I still loathe each word.

The childhood of Iris's generation was saturated with the imperialism and class divisions of the Edwardian Age. Empire Day had been instituted in schools in 1902, when 'textbooks focused increasingly on the benefits of spreading trade and civilization'. Imperialism, as it was experienced 'at home', worked to glue together a society otherwise sharply divided by class. As

Bill Woods, a working-class labourer from Bristol who was the same age as Iris, described his childhood:

> They used to encourage us to be proud of the flag, salute the flag when we was at school.
>
> Yes, I was proud of being British. We was always taught to be proud of the Queen and King.
>
> We was the people of the world wasn't us?

P. D. James, the mystery writer, also belonged to the same generation but, unlike my mother and Bill Woods, was a child of the middle class. James's father, a middle-level civil servant, had served as an officer in the Great War; Iris's father also served in it but as a private in the infantry. When my grandfather left the army he returned to the life of an agricultural labourer. P. D. James may have been raised within the same national borders as Iris but the material conditions of her life separated and insulated her from the poverty that characterized the rural world of Iris's childhood, or the urban England of Bill Woods's Bristol working class. Nevertheless, James, looking back on her childhood from her eighties, also describes the shared imaginary of a British community as 'people of the world', a global imaginary visually realized on the walls of her Ludlow school. P. D. James, Bill James and Iris would never have been reminded of blood-soaked cane fields and factories when they stirred a spoonful of sugar into their cups of tea.

> A map, permanently displayed in the largest double classroom, with its splurges of red – Canada, India, Australia, New Zealand – its small islands like splashes of blood in all the oceans of the world, enabled our teacher to point out that this was, in truth as well as legend, an empire on which the sun never set. Empire Day was a notable event celebrated with a march round the playground and a salute to the flag.
>
> P. D. James

Celebrations of Empire Day predominate in memories of schooling in the 1920s: the wearing of 'rosettes of red, white and blue', the singing of 'I Vow to Thee My Country' or 'Blake's "Jerusalem"', or the national songs of 'Scotland, Ireland, Wales and England'; readings from the Bible and patriotic speeches by a Lord Mayor 'counselling' his listeners 'to be wise rulers of men in [the] far-flung Empire'. While children in Britain were wearing red, white and blue, marching around their respective playgrounds, singing anthems and saluting the Union Jack, the boy in Jamaica who would become Iris's husband was also marching, singing the same songs, wearing the same colours, and pledging allegiance on the exact same day. Children all over the British West Indies were being schooled to be 'Little Black Englishmen'.

Becoming British: Carl

My father grew up in Kingston, Jamaica, in what he characterized as 'difficult times' – a phrase he did not explain. As a child
I had no reference point for what he meant by 'difficult', or even
when those 'times' had been, because in our house the usual
reference point for the past was the Second World War, which
was summoned into being with such animation and emotion
that I felt I had lived through it too. My parents hoped that it
would possible for them to be, once again, the people they imagined themselves to be during the war: young people with promising futures ahead of them. In the good times, their memories
allowed them to relive those years, to recover their youthful
dreams, and they smiled and laughed despite there being little
cause for smiles and laughter in their postwar present.

My father told me little about Jamaica; it was as if he had
been born an airman in the Royal Air Force. I do not know
exactly when, on hearing him utter the words 'difficult times', I
was prompted me to see him as a man who had his own history
before the war, a time before he met and married Iris. I was
unsure if I even *wanted* to hear my father explain exactly how
difficult those times were; I feared the anguish that might escape
through the crack I could sometimes hear in his voice. I was a
cautious, distant observer of my father's battles to contain his
emotions. Living with him was like living within the radius of a
sleeping volcano. As a volcanologist studies the tiniest changes
in the volcano's surface, I was alert to the signs of my father's

restraint, the danger signals of an imminent explosion: a furrowed brow, narrowed eyes, the jaw tightening as his chin lifted and neck muscles stretched taut, the rapid swallowing that caused his prominent Adam's apple to bob up and down.

For many years, 'difficult times' was a phrase sufficient unto itself. Uttered as a word of closure, it not only indicated that no more need be said but also constituted a warning to me that on no condition was I to pursue the subject. A preliminary intake of breath – a hint that a question was forming – would produce a withering glare and my curiosity would die in my throat. It took me years to unravel and make sense of 'difficult times', to create even a partial portrait of my father's life in Jamaica and his passage into war. For a black girl and young black woman who spent so much of her life in libraries, to remain unaware of the historical conditions that shaped the man her father was to become is shocking. My ignorance was hidden under a superficial veneer of what I thought I knew of Jamaica from reading, from listening to the music of Robert Nesta Marley, and from inhabiting the vibrant, if precarious, black culture of the UK, shaped as much by black cultural forms from North America as from the Caribbean.

Perhaps it was a kind of wilful blindness, a blindness shared with others of my generation who focused our political and intellectual energies on the demand to be regarded as black Britons, as black citizens, while relegating to the back of our minds how much information about our colonial pasts our Caribbean parents had deliberately withheld from us. I acknowledged, eventually, how little I really knew, and assembled a history for my father, taking his partial memories and enigmatic references with me into libraries. There I learnt how to undertake systematic research, from which I learnt enough to ask my father the right questions.

His story emerged in fragments over a decade during which I had to teach myself to listen not only to his words but also to his silences. I saw the word JAMAICA pass across the television screen, superimposed on the bodies of women, on white sand beaches, turquoise seas, palm trees and bushes covered in the most brilliant red flowers I have ever seen, and I turned to look at him. I saw actors in nineteenth-century plantation dress beckoning, promising a return to the island 'as it used to be', a visual realization of a modern form of indenture and indebtedness produced by tourism. Walking together down Croydon High Street my father stops and stares at similar images reproduced on large posters in the travel agent's window. He considers the information about British Overseas Airways flights to Kingston. My father begins to talk. At home he rummages around in his wardrobe, finds a red shoebox and brings it to me. The corners are torn and the box is held together with rubber bands, but from the way he holds it I know that it is not just fragile but precious. On the torn lid, the gold lettering has faded so I cannot read the name of the shop, but I can just barely read the word, Kingston. Inside are postcards, letters and photographs; inside is Jamaica. Unfamiliar names – Castleton Gardens, Dunn's River Falls, Swift River – fall from his lips. When I hear 'we used to dive and swim in Kingston Harbour together', I realize I am listening to stories of my father and his brother, my uncle Dudley, as boys. I had never imagined them as children before.

I anticipated that my father would confirm the romance of the landscapes and beautiful bodies used to tantalize and entice tourists. I was wrong. At first, I saw his postcards through the eyes of a young black woman who had grown up in Europe; I saw through the eyes of the metropole. London had bestowed on me an imperial gaze, the gaze of a potential tourist who sees only scenes of lush vegetation and the luxury of abundance. Listening closely, though, I heard my father's memories as a critical commentary on what I saw, and only then did I grasp his becoming. He gave me the gift of a counter history which revealed the enormous distance and dissonance between the advertising campaigns and what my father knew of Jamaica, 'as it used to be'. I came to understand the images as both a backdrop and a stage for a drama of contradiction.

Through my father's stories I became more than the daughter of a Jamaican; I became both historian and colonial subject. I learnt what it meant to live in Jamaica as a Crown Colony, under the rule of the Colonial Office, 4,680 miles away; I learnt about massive unemployment and the starvation wages paid to those who had jobs; I learnt of the complete and utter immiseration of a population; and I learnt about the hunger marches of the 1930s.

These stories, and the accounts of Jamaican historians, seemed very distant from the lives we were living in London; I did not immediately place my father, or his family, among those who were hungry. Gradually, I recognized that I had a relation to these starving people, that they were my family too, as aunts and uncles, as grandparents, as great uncles and aunts, as cousins, and that there was a wider community to which I belonged and which had a claim on me. For the first time, I encountered the particular social, economic and political conditions in Jamaica in the context of unrest throughout the British West Indies and I confronted colonialism in the aftermath of enslavement. I was a daughter beginning to understand her father.

Many decades later, on Father's Day, June 2013, I was holding my father's thin cold hands between mine. We were alone, a father and daughter together in one of the few rooms of his residential care home without a television. We relished a rare moment of quiet, away from the main rooms which, despite their cheerful and sunny aspect, felt like warehouses for aged and decaying bodies, rooms in which I experienced a constriction in my chest.

We were looking through large windows onto a lovely garden. All of a sudden, my father's grasp tightened around my hand and I turned to look at him, startled: 'I must tell you', he said, with extraordinary urgency, 'how terrible, how very, very terrible it was.' As his memories tumbled out we were no longer in Yorkshire but on the streets of Kingston in May 1938, where mass protests immediately followed the burning of cane fields. Strikes that began on Tate and Lyle's Frome sugar estate and factory in Westmoreland had spread to other estates across the island and onto the banana and coal wharves of the Kingston dockyards, where one of my father's uncles was a wharf manager.

I had taught courses on the Caribbean so was all too familiar with the details of the unrest in 1937 and 1938. A hundred years after the supposed emancipation, men, women and children still lived and worked under the regimes of power, poverty and punishment associated with enslavement. Protesting workers at Frome had been shot by the police.

We are the Sons of slaves who have been paying rent to the landlords for fully many decades[,] we want better wages, we have been exploited for years and we are looking to you to help us.

We want a minimum wage law. We want freedom in this the hundredth year of our Emancipation. We are still economic Slaves, burdened in paying rent to Landlords who are sucking out our vitalities.

'Petition to the Governor of Jamaica', 23 April 1938

The British company Tate & Lyle garnered enormous profits during the 1930s. Seeking sources of investment for this excess capital they bought land and developed sugar estates in Jamaica. Frome was purchased in 1937, and run through a subsidiary, the West Indies Sugar Company (WISCO). With the acquisition of plantations and the building of a new factory at Frome, rumours spread among labourers across the island that Tate & Lyle would increase worker's wages. When these expectations were not met, bitter disappointment was followed by explosions of anger. The rallying cry of the workers was 'A Dollar a Day', but Tate & Lyle preferred to pay generous dividends to its investors rather than invest in a labour force that toiled on starvation wages.

I was startled by the sudden urgency in my father's voice, and puzzled by his tugging at my hand to force me to pay attention. I heard a warning to be careful, an admonition to learn from what happened in Jamaica and what it meant to protest in the streets, to confront political authority directly, to be brutally beaten by the police and the military. I realized that my father no longer saw a grey-haired, middle-aged woman in front of him, but was addressing his rebellious young daughter, the daughter who marched and protested in the streets of London, the daughter who needed to *listen* to him.

The doctors had explained that in addition to his autoimmune disease my father suffered from dementia, but I had more time to be attentive to the details of what he wanted to say and his manner of speaking than the medical staff. While his short-term memory was impaired, his long-term memory was clear and sharp. What he could grasp and hang onto in the present, what preserved his sense of self, was a vivid reliving of the past through story.

That afternoon in York, in his residential care home, I was not having a conversation with my father or listening to his stories but receiving fragments of his memories which confused riots in Jamaica in 1938 with incidents of rebellion and police brutality in the UK: times when he was forced to confront the British racism he was reluctant to acknowledge; times when he was deeply afraid for his daughter; times when he feared for the future of black life in Britain. I was totally confused by what I was hearing, but then I realized that my father was simultaneously recalling many marches and protests that had occurred between 1968 and 1981: the mounted police during anti–Vietnam War protests in front of the American Embassy in Grosvenor Square, black protest marches in Lewisham and Newham, the Black People's Day of Action, rebellion on the streets of Brixton and Liverpool. I was shaken and disoriented by how intensely I could feel the fear and sense of urgency radiating from my father as he talked about all those places and times. All I could do was try to reassure and calm him, to calm myself.

The crisis my father experienced in June 2013 replays in my mind like a film loop, and I am unable to provide any simple explanation for its eruption. The television was always on in the main lounge of his care home so perhaps the trigger was the images of hundreds of riot police in full battle mode against G8 summit protesters in London that saturated the media in the days immediately prior to my visit. What remains with me most vividly is the memory of a father issuing a warning to a young daughter he is afraid is in danger, while also calling upon me as a teacher and a mother, urging me to pass on his stories to my students, to his grandson, to the next generation.

I write about a father who no longer lives except through my words; I try to remember the point in time when his stories about difficult times in Jamaica connected to my life in London, when I was able to see a Jamaica I had never previously imagined. From the time I left home for college in 1967, I was deeply involved in British anti-racist and black political life, and this was when my father must have recognized and feared for the rebel in me. From 1987 onwards, he read everything I published on race and racism and we had the conversations about Britain that we should have had when I was growing up.

In April 2014, three months after the death of my father, I am on a research trip in Jamaica. A taxi driver takes me to 19 Potter's Row, in Rae Town. The driver, who grew up in the city of Kingston, states baldly and somewhat warily that he has never been to this poverty-stricken neighbourhood before. The poverty in Potter's Row is economic, not cultural: in the 1930s, Don Drummond, who would become the world's finest trombonist, lived at 26 Potter's Row, and in the 1950s Mutabaruka, poet and deejay from Irie FM, lived on the street.

Before I left the hotel, I had stared at my reflection in the bathroom mirror. I was trying to steel myself against grief by fully inhabiting the dispassionate mode of the scholar. My attempt to adopt a professional exterior had little staying power and my facade crumbled when I stood, as a bereaved daughter, rooted to the spot, outside the house where my father was born in 1921. I was barely aware that my driver had explained our presence to the young people gathered on the corner, that the eldest boy had peeled off from the group and, as he ran up the steps into the house, said 'I will ask . . .'. Ask who? Did he say, 'My sister', did he say 'My Mother'? The name of the person he went to find was lost as he turned away, his voice barely audible above the sound system at the other end of the street.

The small single-story weatherboard house with a zinc roof nestled underneath a large frangipani tree. The boy ran up concrete steps and pushed open the door. The metal grills which had once enclosed the windows had been removed and the openings boarded over. The grills lay, neatly stacked, in the corner. A pink and black child's bicycle leant on its stand under the tree. The yard had been swept clean. The door and plywood window boards were painted a light yellow, the walls and removed window grills light blue, the concrete foundation and steps the turquoise of the Caribbean Sea.

A young woman, possibly the children's elder sister, came down the steps to meet the stranger at her front door. She listened patiently. I told her that my father had been born in the house in 1921 and she raised her eyebrows. I asked permission to photograph the outside of the building, and this was instantly granted. It was one of Kingston's very, very hot days, the air was heavy and still, and neither she nor I wanted to stand in the full glare of the sun for too much longer. Without entering the yard, I rapidly took two photographs.

The young woman was courteous and polite but I felt impertinent, an intruder into the lives of those who lived there, and I wanted to vanish. If only I could find the words to explain to her that I am a daughter grieving for her father, that I am overwhelmed by a deluge of his memories of poverty. I stutter my thanks but am mortified to realize that in my haste to not be a nuisance I have neglected to introduce myself properly or to ask her name. I yearn to say more to her retreating back, but by then it's too late and she has already re-entered her home. No one seemed discomforted by my visit except me – I feel I behaved like an intrusive, imperialistic anthropologist.

Potter's Row lies in the shadow of the notorious General Penitentiary. The maximum-security prison covers eleven acres of the south side of the street for three blocks west and three blocks south, all the way to the water. You can see the back of the penitentiary from the Palisadoes and Norman Manley International airport. Built in the nineteenth century by the British, the prison has a sinister and daunting aspect. Designed to generate awe, and fear, it resembles both a fortress and the Tower of London. The brick walls are twenty-two-feet high and five-feet, six-inches thick, with round watch towers on each corner. In the centre of the street is a massive tower with crenelated battlements housing the main gate. The entire outer perimeter is adorned with razor wire.

This is the prison of one of my father's stories. The General Penitentiary remains notorious for the cruelty and brutality of its systems of discipline and punishment, for its overcrowding, for the gross inadequacy of the nutritional quality and quantity of its food, and for its unsanitary conditions that 'beggar the imagination'. But in the 1930s, people felt that conditions were better inside the prison than outside of it. The starving and unemployed organized marches to be admitted to the General Penitentiary in order to be fed. 'We knew someone inside', my father said, 'I went to the back door of the prison where a guard would pass out loaves of bread baked in the prison ovens.' So many were inside because of their poverty that, as I listened to my father's stories, I wondered how he managed to avoid imprisonment in the penitentiary that cast such a shadow over his birthplace.

My father was his grandmother's child. Marie Munroe was left with five children, Ferdinand, Madline, Ivy, Rose and Massa, when her husband, Edward George Munroe, a commercial clerk, died in the Kingston earthquake which struck on 14 January 1907 just after 3:30 in the afternoon. The commercial and residential sections of the city were utterly destroyed and there were over a thousand fatalities. Marie and Edward lived in Franklin Town and after Edward left for work that morning he was never seen again. His body was never recovered. He was

employed in the business district which caught fire and could not be saved because the fire station had collapsed. White residents fled Kingston, and over 10,000 black and coloured survivors found themselves living on the racecourse where a tent city was eventually erected. I do not know if Marie and her children were among them.

The depth of Marie's grief and shock at such an incomprehensible disaster are palpable in the story she told my father – and that my father passed on to me – of my great grandfather walking along a road when it suddenly opened up and he fell into the crevice. The attempt to explain this inexplicable sudden destruction and disappearance drew upon embedded cultural memories of the earthquake of 7 June 1692, when huge fissures appeared in the ground, land

During the quake, bricks were seen everywhere as walls and edifices fell, and almost immediately after the quake, fire broke out in Kingston. The fire destroyed fifty-six acres of commercial Kingston – it engulfed South Parade on the north, Mark Lane on the east and Orange Street on the west. Nearly every building on Harbour Street, Port Royal Street and Water Lane had been demolished. Newspapers such as the Jamaican Daily Telegraph and Anglo-American Herald reported that stores collapsed, covering 'hundreds of persons of all classes of the community.' The Gleaner Company's offices were demolished and they could only resume printing on January 18, 1907 at the Government Printing Office. In the Gleaner's January 18 publication, it was reported that hundreds were killed instantly; omnibuses and streetcars were overturned, a number of churches, and banks and other business places were severely damaged.

'History of Earthquakes in Jamaica', National Library of Jamaica slipped from the mountains, and over a thousand acres of the capital of Port Royal sank and was submerged under the sea. The earth literally opened up and swallowed thousands. In 1907 the initial 35 seconds of tremors from the massive 9.5 magnitude earthquake toppled buildings, overturned omnibuses and street cars and caused fires. Residents were crushed, buried under rubble and burnt to death.

Weeks later, the Colonial Office put in place a complex accounting system for issuing financial assistance to 'worthy recipients'. As a widow with children, Marie was entitled to support, but only if she could produce documentation to prove that she had been legally married and that her children were legitimate. The Colonial Office correspondence from 1907 reveals the stunning callousness of imperial calculation. The British government demanded that Jamaicans produce extensive documentation, even though they were traumatized by a major earthquake, grieving the loss of partners, parents, children and friends, and their dwellings had been destroyed along with all their possessions. All district relief committees were under strict instructions to compensate only reputable widows and orphans they deemed worthy. Exceptions were made for 'special cases': widows, for example, who were considered 'genteel' (which translates into white or light skinned and middle class). Marie would not have received such a designation. The amount of annuity awarded to widows was calculated at one eighth of the deceased husband's annual income over the previous three years, evidence of which would also have to be provided. I have no idea what Edward earned as a commercial clerk but I assume he would have been in the lowest category of £120–200 per annum, which would have allowed Marie to be awarded a £25 annuity, as long as she did not remarry. Children, if the mother was living, received one thirty-second of their father's income, which would have amounted to £6.5s.0d. The category below this was 'pauper'. Marie did not remarry and perhaps the annuity was the reason. Edward's death brought both anguish and financial insecurity.

Marie had grown up on Potter's Row, living with her parents at number 8. Her father, John Craddock, repaired sewing machines in a small shop around the corner on Tower Street, directly opposite the main gate of the penitentiary. Marie must have moved back when the area was re-inhabited, and possibly owned 19 Potter's Row. Although her daughter Rose gave birth to her first child, Carl, in that house, my father had no memory of his mother ever living there. Carl was happy with his grandmother Marie, his uncle Massa, and his uncle Ferdinand who served in the First World War and suffered from shell shock. In addition to the annuity she would have received if she qualified, Marie received a small monthly sum of money, in dollars, from her daughter Ivy who had emigrated to New York City.

Carl had a peripatetic life with his grandmother, moving between various addresses in Rae Town and the adjacent neighbourhoods of Franklyn Town and Rollington Pen, now Rollington Town. His parents, Wilfred Carby, who maintained the trucks for the Kingston Ice Making Company, and Rose, a seamstress, and his younger siblings Joyce, Dudley, Dustin and Avis, were usually close by. Carl saw them frequently, except for a period when Wilfred was promoted to manage a Rae Brothers garage on the north side of the island in Montego Bay. My father grew up essentially as an only child, his life shaped by his grandmother and uncles.

Ferdinand was an autodidact, speaking French, Spanish, some Chinese and a smattering of Latin; he 'was never without a book in his hand in English, Spanish or French'. Carl hungered not only for food but also for education; he longed to attend one of the prestigious secondary schools that prepared Jamaica's elite for entry into professions and universities in Europe and North America, but their doors were open only to the wealthy. Instead, he was sent to a small kindergarten class for just eight to ten children, run by two women in their house, before attending Franklyn Town elementary until he and his grandmother moved too far away for him to walk there each day, after which he went to Rollington Pen school.

It was Ferdinand and Marie who encouraged Carl to value education. Ferdinand was evidently an important role model, but he contracted pneumonia and died when his nephew was at

Rollington Pen. This meant that Carl had to assume increasing responsibility for his family when he was still in elementary school, caring for his ill uncle before he died, looking after his grandmother, and managing his uncle Massa's alcoholism.

In 1936, now aged fifteen, Carl was going to work every day at N. A. Taylor's Hardware Store on Orange Street. In the evenings he attended Kingston Technical College, first to obtain his school certificate, and then for courses in bookkeeping which earned him promotion at N. A. Taylor's to the post of book-keeper's assistant. On my visit to downtown Kingston eighty years later, N. A. Taylor's had long gone, so instead I made a pilgrimage to the legendary Rocker's International Records on Orange Street, where I sat with my partner, surrounded by vinyl. Mitchie Williams spun tales and turntables, inducting us into the musical history of the street when it was the heart and soul of Ska, Rocksteady and Reggae – the music to which I was devoted in the 1960s and '70s in London.

Noel Anthony Taylor was the fifth son of R. W. Taylor, merchant, politician and founder of R. W. Taylor & Co., which developed into one of the largest wholesale and retail businesses in the island. As a member of the Jamaican elite, Noel Taylor was educated at Wolmer's, the school of Carl's dreams. My father respected Noel Taylor as an employer because he wrote a recommendation for him to attend Kingston Technical College but I believe that Taylor may also have paid the college fees. Perhaps Noel Taylor had a paternalistic interest in my father and saw him as a striver, a young man worthy of investment.

Carl's diligence was rewarded with a promotion to the position of a clerk; the average wage for a clerk was between 8 and 9 shillings a week, and with this he had to support an extended family. His hard work, however, was not the only reason Carl was promoted – having lighter skin, coffee-coloured as opposed to dark brown, was an advantage. As a clerk, he was trying to climb out of poverty and reach the lowest rungs of the Jamaican middle class – a precarious position. Shades of skin colour are foundational to the composition of class formation in Jamaica: Stuart Hall referred to it as a pigmentocracy. In the 1930s

and '40s, only those of the very lightest hue were employed by merchants as shop assistants, for they were, like the goods, on display in the front of the stores. Brown Jamaicans like Carl were employed in the back rooms, while manual labourers on the sugar estates or the docks were overwhelmingly dark-skinned.

In the words of Ken Hill, an activist in the movement for union representation for workers, life during this period 'was intolerable . . . Life wasn't worth living. Jamaica was flat on her back. She had no hope before 1938.' In May that year, in the wake of the unrest and agitation against starvation wages on Tate & Lyle's estate at Frome, the wharf workers employed by the United Fruit Company staged a general walkout. But what happened at Frome was just a prelude to rebellion across the island – among urban and rural workers, banana growers in Portland and St Mary, field and factory cane workers, Public Works Department labourers, and militant ex-servicemen who had been settled on government land grants. In Kingston it included not just dockers but also waged workers in private and public sectors, with the exception of shop assistants and clerks, among whom was my father.

Noel Taylor had moved his store from Orange Street to 31 West Parade and given it a new name, Taylor's Notion, Hardware and Furniture Dealer. The store was located on one of the roads that bordered what was then Victoria Park, since renamed after Sir William Grant, a labour activist in the dock-workers' strike. The park was an important site for political meetings and street orators, for agitation for increased wages, labour rights and rights to land ownership, and for the genera-tion of hope and belief in a future that Ken Hill noted was absent before 1938. William Grant's political speeches attracted large crowds. My father described the vast numbers of people that would gather on Sundays to listen to the rousing speeches from regulars like Grant, Barrington Williams and the Rev. Ethland Gordon. During May 1938, the gatherings increased in frequency. Did Carl just hurry past all this political activity to take care of his grandmother, or attend an evening class, or did he overhear a word, a phrase, a sentence, an appeal for justice that made him hesitate, linger and join the throngs of people?

The unrest and strikes across the island that continued throughout the month of May were met by force. In addition to the police there were six platoons of the Sherwood Foresters Regiment of the British Army, almost 5,000 armed special constables, and two Royal Navy cruisers standing offshore. By 23 May a general strike was underway in Kingston. Carl would have gone to work as usual, but as strikers and protesters marched down King Street, toward Parade, early in the day, all the stores closed. There are reports that clerks and shop assistants, gathering on the tops of buildings, clapped their hands for the police as they chased and harassed protestors. Could my father have clapped? The city was brought to a standstill as strikes by manual workers and tram drivers erupted throughout the capital. Street cleaners had been on strike since the day before so there was garbage everywhere.

What did my father witness in 1938 that made him so afraid for the safety of his daughter marching in London decades later? What memories of those events still haunted him in the last months of his life, lessons he wanted his daughter to know and to pass on? On the first day of the Kingston strike, police beat protestors with their batons. By the next day, May 24, Empire Day, a public holiday, military trucks patrolled Kingston and the police were using bullets that killed and wounded civilians. Residents of Kingston had to face 400 police officers, eighty troops, 250 special constables and the Kingston Infantry Volunteers. In Carl's neighbourhood a woman and her nine-year-old son were killed by police in Matthew Lane, both of them shot in the head. The police clubbed anyone who gathered around. On Hanover Street, a youth was bayonetted in the leg, and on North Street two girls and a man were shot by military patrols. The violence continued and increased. On 25 May, Kingston shop assistants joined the strikers.

Nothing my father ever told me or wrote in his letters led me to believe that he participated in the protests, though he did say that the strikes 'tore the family apart'. I spent a long time trying to figure out what he meant by that. One of Wilfred Carby's brothers was a wharf manager, which would have made him one of bosses and thus opposed to the strike and the strikers on the wharves. I knew there was a contentious history between the two different branches of Carbys over the issue of skin colour, my family being darker than the other branch of Carbys, many of whom now consider themselves 'white'. This breach was apparently widened in 1938, by the different branches of the family being on opposing sides of the political rebellion. Ken Post has noted that along with 'the emergence of big stores in Kingston ... came a growing consciousness on the part of shop assistants of the need to organize'. The Jamaica United Clerks Association was formed in 1937. Did Carl join or, being a very cautious man, did he consider it too much of a risk? I will never know the answer.

The British government, more concerned with their imperial adventures in Africa and India, relegated their Crown Colony of Jamaica to the status of an 'imperial backwater', and regarded it as a 'financial burden'. Poverty and pain were constant companions on the island. Decades of colonial neglect, and the starvation wages and malnutrition that inevitably followed, lay not just on the surface of the skin in the beaded sweat of rebels, but hollowed out the bodies of adults and children, softening bones, inflaming joints, penetrating livers, spleens, kidneys and hearts, attacking lungs and bowels. The effects of this neglect can be seen in the high death rate among infants. Marie and Edward, like many Jamaicans, just registered the births of their children as male or female. Naming took place when it was thought the child would survive. It is also evident in the diseases suffered by many members of Carl's family, like Ferdinand's death from pneumonia at a young age. Marie's health deteriorated, and she developed difficulty breathing. A doctor recommended they move closer to the water where the sea air might help. Carl became desperate and searched for weeks to find somewhere on or near the sea front that he could afford, moving Marie in two stages. First, he rented an apartment in Rae Street, around the corner from the house where he was born, which was slightly closer to the water. Eventually, he moved with his grandmother to 12 Water Lane, where they shared a house with other tenants. Poor working people always have to work multiple jobs and for Carl it was no different: he was employed as the caretaker for the Water Lane premises in return for a reduction in rent; he was responsible for the other tenants, for the house, and for maintaining its beach. His caretaker duties were added to his full-time job at Taylor's, attending evening classes, and nursing his grandmother.

I suspect Marie suffered from pulmonary tuberculosis. My father always became vague when asked about his grandmother's symptoms, as if he had to conceal what he knew and felt. There was such stigma attached to the disease that he would have been ashamed to admit to it, if it was true. In the metropole, the 1911 National Insurance Act and the Public Health Acts of 1921 and 1936 laid the groundwork for legislation that would provide a National Health Service after the

Second World War. In the UK a complex network of sanatoria, hospitals, dispensaries and medical specialists devoted to the free treatment of tuberculosis was built through direct state intervention. In Jamaica, though, the state abdicated responsibility. Colonial subjects had to pay a fee for each use of the underfunded and frequently inadequate medical services. There was a system of Medical Relief Tickets for subjects earning less than 12 shillings a week, but to be eligible one had to be on the 'pauper roll' or deemed 'worthy' by a parochial board responsible for the distribution of tickets, and a separate ticket had to be obtained for each medical visit. The ticket system became the most criticized aspect of the colony's medical services.

In present-day Kingston, I was unable to stand where 12 Water Lane used to be. It proved impossible to imagine what the area was like when my father brought his grandmother there to nurse her through the final months of her life. I followed the trail of an old map to the correct location, stopped and looked around. I was close to the water but where Water Lane used to be was now the centre of the city's urban transportation hub: I was surrounded by buses, concrete, tarmac and a major road. Marinas for expensive boats owned by the transatlantic super-rich dominated the shoreline. *Private Access Only* signs prevented me from walking beyond the bus terminal. I had to resort to Google Earth to see that there is still a small beach out of sight of the bus terminal. This beach, with trees and loungers, is in front of an exclusive apartment complex. I wonder who looks after the beach now?

Carl was able to ease the final days, weeks and months of Marie's life but he could not prevent her death on the 6 of May 1941. I heard my father speak many times of the depth of his loss and, always, tears filled his eyes, even into his old age. His grandmother was the love of his life and her death devastated him. His responsibilities toward his family did not end here, however, for his care-work multiplied. His aunt Madline arranged for him to stay with a friend of hers but then became very ill herself. Carl went to see his ex-headmaster at Franklyn

Town school, whose son was a doctor at the best hospital, and he succeeded in gaining Madline admission for treatment. After a brief stay in the hospital she too died, apparently destitute, since Carl arranged and paid for her funeral with an advance on his wages from Noel Taylor.

Carl's father Wilfred walked out of his marriage to Rose and away from any further responsibility for his children. He 'abandoned them' – the term my father always used to explain and justify to his daughter why she had no relationship with her paternal grandfather; why, from that point in time, he refused to talk to Wilfred, or even respond to his letters. As the eldest son, Carl contributed to the welfare of his siblings and of his mother Rose, who, like her uncle, suffered from alcoholism.

My father's stories and memories revealed the emergence of a man whose sense of self coalesced around the concept of dignity, a dignity maintained in relation to conditions of personhood, deportment and employment: wearing shirts with a collar and tie, a suit, polished shoes; working in a clean and orderly environment; being trusted to tend to the accounts of a business; becoming a person who could gain and retain respect. In the face of desperate poverty my father adopted the clerical garb and manners of accountancy as a counterweight to the terrible conditions of his life; his clothes were part of keeping it together, a demonstration of restraint and self-respect. As he buttoned his collar and knotted his tie he swallowed the bile of poverty and kept in check the emotions that surged when he was being treated as less than human.

My father did little else than go to work in the back room of the hardware store during the day and take classes at the Technical College in the evenings. He never mentioned a social life. The immediate effect of the outbreak of war in September 1939 was that the price of food, firewood, kerosene, men's trousers, boots and imported cloth soared. Although no one escaped the effect of rampant inflation, this was a disaster for the poor who were barely surviving even before the price increases. By 1942, Jamaica was in a dire economic crisis with massive unemployment. No fuel was being delivered because

German U-boats were operating throughout the Caribbean, destroying shipping and oil storage tanks. Crime in Kingston rose dramatically. One ironic comment on the state of wartime Jamaica was made by street gangs who chose to operate under the name 'RAF', conjuring the image of the Royal Air Force, but actually meaning 'Rob And Flee'.

Recruitment for the Royal Air Force began in Jamaica in April of 1942, and my father was always proud to say that he was among the first to volunteer. He explained his regret at not being able to afford to join the RAF at the beginning of the war. What he omitted to say was that the RAF did not accept black recruits until 1940, and then they had to volunteer from within the UK. The earliest Jamaican RAF volunteers came either from wealthy or middle-class families, white or brown, who could afford the cost of travel to Britain, or whose travel was financed by English businessmen in the island as their contribution to the war effort. I can still hear the echo of regret in my father's voice, and I imagine that when he asked for Noel Taylor's sponsorship he was refused. In 1942, after a series of rigorous medical and educational tests, Carl was accepted into the RAF to train as aircrew. He made a special point of saying that he was issued with two sets of tropical uniform. I never understood the significance of this remark until I discovered how extremely expensive clothes had become in wartime Jamaica.

After initial training in wireless telegraphy, navigation and military exercises, Carl left the island on 18 June 1943, unaware that he would never live there again. It was a four-week journey that began on a Canadian National Steamship, the SS Colborne, to New York. Upon arrival in New York the Jamaican and Trinidadian recruits were instructed in the racial codes and conventions of the United States, which they were expected to observe. Next, they travelled by rail to New Brunswick, Canada, on Canadian Pacific Rail which ran a service to and from New York City in those days.

It was not at home but at school that the child who was to become this airman's daughter was told that Britain in 1940 stood alone, facing invasion after the fall of Europe to Hitler's armies and the evacuation of the British Expeditionary Force from Dunkirk. In my school, many of Churchill's speeches were read out loud by the teachers, the poetic phrases becoming ingrained in the minds of the pupils who, in turn, were able to recite: 'And now it has come to us to stand alone in the breach, and face the worst that the tyrant's might and enmity can do . . . We are fighting by ourselves alone; but we are not fighting for ourselves alone.'

Once more unto the breach, dear friends, once more;
Or close the wall up with our English dead . . .

And you, good yeoman,
Whose limbs were made in England, show us here
The mettle of your pasture; let us swear
That you are worth your breeding; which I doubt not;
For there is none of you so mean and base,
That hath not noble lustre in your eyes.

Henry V, Act 3, Scene 1

Churchill's words were used as a pedagogic mantra throughout my childhood to instil British character, the preeminent qualities of which, we were told, were manifest during the war years. His phrases and cadence were resonant with Shakespearean language, meter and imagery, particularly the speeches of Henry V, which we were also taught to recite. In this way Englishness was situated as the dominant feature of Britishness; British character was made synonymous with English character, and seamlessly threaded into English history through its literature.

The question that dogged me as a schoolgirl was how the peculiarities of English character, evident during the Second World War when *they* 'stood alone', related to the framed portrait of my father in his RAF uniform which stood on our piano. Even if he could be characterized as 'a good yeoman', his 'limbs' were not 'made in England'. I was unable to resolve this contradiction when only a girl, but it was my first lesson in historical amnesia. Not until many years later did I understand that the might of the British Empire and its powerful imperial economy rendered the meaning of 'standing alone' an absurd if efficacious claim. Britain could and did mobilize vast resources, including people, from around the globe and assembled them into a formidable war machine.

The RAF's wartime expansion was embodied in the British Commonwealth Air Training Plan, the most ambitious aviation training program in history. Recruits came from many other nations, including the United States, in addition to the Commonwealth countries. Because of the fear of invasion the UK was not a suitable site for training and Canada became the primary location of 'The Plan', as it was known. Carl and the other twenty-two recruits from Jamaica and Trinidad were transported to No. 31 Personnel Depot in Moncton, Canada, built specifically for RAF personnel. The depot was a city within a city, built out of swamps at the northwest end of Moncton to accommodate 10,000 men, with its own churches, department store, movie theatres, fire department and police force, on streets named Oxford Street, Piccadilly, Lambeth Walk, Tottenham Court and other roads recalling London.

Moncton was home to the Royal Canadian Air Force and the location of the empire's largest training and transit camp for the Commonwealth Air Training Plan. In Canada there was no need for the instruction in racial codes that had been necessary in New York, and Canadian families opened their doors to all members of the RAF. I heard many stories of the hospitality and friendship offered to my father and the other recruits from the West Indies. There were thousands of allied personnel in training with the RAF and the RCAF, and waiting in the embarkation centre until they could be sent on to Halifax, Nova Scotia. My father's amazement was evident in his voice when he described arriving in Moncton as being like 'a holiday'. What he remembered most vividly was the food: 'lots of excellent meals and as much as one could devour'. He was no longer hungry.

After approximately six weeks in Moncton, Carl began the next stage of his journey in Halifax, where he and the other RAF recruits from the Caribbean joined a large North Atlantic convoy consisting of cargo vessels protected by battleships and frigates. Recruits were 'packed four to a bunk on a troopship . . . It was like pushing animals together because they really had the ships all cramped to make sure they got as many as they could to fight for England.'

It was in this convoy that Carl entered the battle of and for the Atlantic, a battle he would continue when his RAF crew joined Coastal Command. I was only able to extract very thin threads of memory from my father, which easily became tangled, and only gradually could I loosen them in the archive of Admiralty records. Reading RAF operational log books, and deciphering the codes allocated to North Atlantic convoys, the calculus of war and brutal reasonings of expendability became evident.

In his usual restrained, understated manner, my father described his journey across the Atlantic as being 'more eventful [than life at Moncton] because the convoy was attacked by German submarines'. Sound travels underwater much faster than through the air, so I realized that he and the other recruits, lying in the bowels of their ship, probably seasick, would have heard the explosions before the crew on deck. Shock waves would have rocked the ship. Was this the time and place I wondered, when Carl began to feel fear, when the feeling of adventure, the 'holiday', ended and war began? My father told me he did not know until he landed in the UK that 'two of the ships in the convoy were lost in that attack', but he never spoke about what happened to the crew aboard those ships.

Such silences distance the self from disaster and danger, as does the language of war: it was ships that were 'lost', not human beings. My father's careful word choice rendered invisible the fact that 186 people died and dozens were wounded when the *Orkan*, flying under the flag of Poland, was torpedoed and sank within five minutes on October 8th, and a cargo vessel, the US *Yorkmar*, was torpedoed and sank the following day. What Carl did not know, what he could not have known, and what none of those who made that journey knew, was that their convoy, SC143, was used as bait in the battle for control of the North Atlantic. Enigma had broken the German codes and the British knew that Rossbach, a Wolfpack of U-boats, was lying in wait for SC143. Western Approaches Command seized the opportunity to attack the Wolfpack, diverting another convoy,

HX259, to the south. SC143 was reinforced with four destroyers, including the *Orkan*, and sent directly toward Rossbach. But it was not only such calculations of expendability that I discovered in the records.

I knew not only that my father's training in the RAF involved the acquisition of skills that he described in detail – flying, wireless telegraphy and military drills – but that there were also multiple realities and equations of war that he did not pass on. He was silent about his role in a war machine determined to exercise its maximum destructive capacity. No longer a clerk in the back room of Taylor's Notion, Hardware and Furniture Dealer, whose horizons were confined by the columns of account books and the endless battles to fend off despair and destitution for his family, Carl was now mapping a space for his existence that must have appeared vast with possibility. He talked in great detail of being a member of Coastal Command, the maritime arm of the RAF which flew over 500,000 miles every week. He was proud of having been part of a successful mission to locate the crew of a plane lost in the Italian Alps. Carl found flying exhilarating, and revelled in being part of a meteorological squadron on trips that lasted between eight and ten hours, and sometimes over twelve, ranging over the North Pole, Greenland, Iceland and the North Atlantic. He loved the challenging, absorbing work of sending very lengthy weather reports in code, while simultaneously obtaining the positions and bearings of the aircraft from radio stations.

Though my father acknowledged the tension, anxiety and stress that began before a mission and lasted until you had landed and been debriefed, he said time and time again that the crew had complete confidence in each other and therefore *knew* that no harm would come to them, and that they all they relied on the gunners' constant look out for attacks from enemy aircraft. He would talk for hours about the special bond the crew had with each other, a warmth and affection that bolstered their confidence in their invulnerability. Over time my father's crew gained the reputation of being the luckiest in the entire squadron, so lucky that the Wing Commander would choose their aircraft for his flights.

The wages and apparent benefits offered by the war machine only serve to conceal its fundamental inhumanity. If my father was scarred by what he saw of the violence of the imperial state perpetrated against people just like him on the streets of Kingston, if he found such violence terrible, he had nothing to say about the allied policy of 'massacre by aerial bombardment', perpetrated by the RAF on German cities. In addition to serving with Coastal Command, Carl and his crew served in Bomber Command 50 Squadron based at RAF Waddington, in Lincolnshire. He said only that they took part in 'the bombing of Essen, an industrial town', but nothing else.

When they were flying in formation among a fleet of advancing bombers, I wonder if my father and his crew ever saw themselves as W. G. Sebald described them: 'teeming messengers of death . . . striking like the apocalypse'. Did they ever attempt to account for the destruction they unleashed or recognize that the 'war in the air was war pure and undisguised?'

When I first heard about Bomber Command and about Essen, described by my father as 'an industrial town', I imagined the destruction of factories and machinery. I was unable to comprehend the full horror: the deliberate annihilation of people, their dwellings, their history and their natural environment. I do not know what my father thought he, his crew, and his squadron left behind in Essen after their bombs were dropped. I believe he thought about it, for he was at great pains to repeat, many times, that in Coastal Command 'we carried extra petrol instead of bombs'.

My father's 'most difficult and painful experience of the war' was the breakup of his crew and their demobilization. I will always remember his words: 'After spending so much time together and sharing various experiences *as one* a very strong bond developed, and breaking off this bond suddenly was far from being easy.' He treasured being '*as one*', and for him, for the first time in his life, that meant being regarded as an absolute equal. Carl was mistaken to think that such comradery, once forged, would last forever. What he was to face in postwar Britain were more 'difficult times'.

A decade ago, on a visit to my parent's house, I found my father reading a collection of nineteenth-century English poetry. He had been delving into the piles of books I had acquired as an undergraduate, books I was unable to take with me when I left to live on the other side of the Atlantic, and which my parents had carefully transported to the city of York when they moved from South London. He was reading what he said were two of his favourite poems, Thomas Gray's 'Elegy Written in a Country Graveyard' and Oliver Goldsmith's 'The Deserted Village'. I had no idea that these were his favourite poems, and I don't remember ever having a conversation with him about English poetry, not even during the years I was reading English at college. I was always mailing him books about 'race' and biographies of black lives from the US. He read each one and would tell me what he thought. Through such gifts I was persistently dragging my father into my North American educator's world of racialized subjects and subjectivities while, at home, he was reading and re-reading Thomas Gray. This poetry was always next to his chair, and later next to his bed. I didn't ask him why it was important to him, why he loved it, or what connections he was making as he read the poems over and over. I don't know why I did not ask.

Those born in Jamaica in the 1920s were at the tail-end of the second generation of freemen and many, including Carl, volunteered to fight in two world wars, before they had the right to vote. If you consult histories of the Commonwealth Air Training Plan you will find stories of brave white Canadians, New Zealanders, Australians and South Africans who willingly risked their lives to rally to Britain's aid in her 'darkest hour'. But you will not find any reference to anyone from the Caribbean, whose arrival is barely noted in the Operational Record book for the Depot.

Nevertheless, West Indian volunteers, schooled as British subjects, were in Moncton training as pilots, navigators and wireless operators who would go on to defend the North Atlantic and fly bombers and fighter planes from the UK into the heart of Europe. The erasure of their presence in New Brunswick is layered upon other erasures from the same soil: the erasure of the broken promises made by the defeated British to 3,500 black loyalists evacuated to Nova Scotia in 1783 at the end of the American Revolutionary War; and to the more than 2,000 African Americans during the War of 1812–1815 who were "summarily liberated by British forces, in field operations in the Chesapeake Bay region" and shipped to Nova Scotia – whether they wanted to go there or not. All of them 'came with nothing to nowhere, were landed with indifference' in the Maritime Provinces without money or provisions, 'plunked on rocky, thorny land (soon laced with infant's skeletons) ... so poor, they supposedly didn't even have history'.

As my father's mind fragmented, much of his sixty-five years since the war and all sense of the present dissolved, while the years of his youth in Jamaica and his service in the RAF returned for us both. Until his last days he could recite his RAF number. One day, trying to locate the books my father had read in his Kingston classrooms, I found copies of the *Royal Reader* he remembered so clearly, texts which were used to school imperial subjects all over the empire. In *Royal Reader* no. 5 is 'Elegy Written in a Country Churchyard', by Thomas Gray, and 'The Deserted Village', by Oliver Goldsmith.

Lost

In the late 1950s, in Mitcham, a girl was lost. I do not mean that she was incapable of finding her way, but that I had to let her go.

Sometimes, as she wandered around Pollards Hill, the girl would visit someone from her elementary class or Sunday school. She paid attention to the distinguishing features of different types of housing as she negotiated various ways in and out of them. Prefabs were built very close together and had only tiny rectangular patches of ground in front, on which residents spread grass seed and planted rose bushes. Despite their efforts to brighten daily life, behind the unruly splotches of crimson and gold stood serried ranks of identical dun metallic buildings. The metal front doors had large glass panels at their centre, through which the girl could peer inside to see who was home before she knocked, unless the doors and windows were draped with net curtains. Then she would wait patiently on a doorstep while the curtains twitched, a signal that she was being inspected before her visit was either answered or ignored.

She disliked the maisonettes, large blocks of concrete without individual gardens, because no one was allowed to set foot on the communal squares of grass surrounded by rickety wooden fencing. After skirting the forbidden zone, the girl had to climb an exterior stairway and then walk down an interior concrete

> It will be a long time still, I think, before a woman can sit down to write a book without finding a phantom to be slain, a rock to be dashed against.
>
> Virginia Woolf

balcony to reach one of the front doors, all of which were identical. To access terraced houses meant unlatching a gate and walking down a short path to doors that were infinitely varied, canvases that portrayed the level of middle-class aspiration. Some were intimidating: solid and sombre wood with two small panes of glass too high to see through, even on tiptoe. These doors reeked of respectability. Others were flamboyant, enticing the girl with their variety of sizes and shapes of windows and frosted glass. She stood outside all of these different doors and always flinched when some were slammed in her face. Occasionally a door would remain open, just a crack, while someone called out to the child she had come to see, 'That nigger (or 'wog' – 'wog' was a common form of address) from your school is here.'

One day, when she was nine years old, she was finally invited into one of the respectable terraced houses. A male teenager opened the door and stared at her while she asked for his sister. She had seen him before, waiting outside of her school for his younger sibling. He told her to come inside. Pleasantly surprised, the girl eagerly stepped over the threshold. In the hallway, the young man closed the door and stood in front of it, blocking the light. He seemed much taller when he was standing over her.

He pushed her, hard. Body twisting, tumbling backwards, reaching out, falling, pain as her head hit the stairs, lifted, tossed, lying face down, gasping, barely able to breathe through rust coloured carpet. She turned her head and stared at a metal carpet clip jammed against her nose. A weight fell on her, the young man's hands tugged at her school uniform reached under her skirt grasped the elastic of her underwear ragged nails scraped her skin. Searing pain inside, radiating up and out. A hand clamped over her mouth, a scream died in her throat as her body convulsed. On her side she fought to bring her knees up to her chest and wrapped her arms around herself lying on rough carpet that rubbed and burned the skin. She knew how to turn inward. I can no longer watch the girl. I am teetering on the edge of a cliff; a small trembling body falls and I take flight after her. Our bodies land, beached, but then I look and I am alone. The girl I carry inside me is different, she changed. We changed.

My attempts to forget, fail. I retain memories I thought I had erased long ago: the weight of a body; being the target of absolute fury, unassuageable anger and disgust; a bewildered girl hauled like a rag doll up off the floor; him spitting into her face, 'you don't even know what just happened to you, do you?' She was deposited outside the front door and discarded, on the path, like he was carrying out the rubbish. Before the front door slammed shut, he issued a warning, 'Just don't tell anyone.' She never did.

For the first time she was unsure of her way home. Rather than acknowledge abuse the girl believed she had been very bad, and I carried the burden of guilt. A creeping paralysis stifled the fear of comprehending the meaning of that weight, of the words echoing in the chamber of memory. She withdrew into interior spaces where some sort of I survived, and became a self-sustaining being. She gave up making house calls.

Part Two:

Calculations

Fictions of Racial Logic

As dusk fell on 21 June 1948, launches packed with sightseers circled a British troopship in the Thames estuary; fog was beginning to form in the marshes but the passengers on board the *Empire Windrush* eagerly returned the waves of those below. Formerly German and bearing the name the *Monte Rosa*, the ship had transported German troops into battle, borne prisoners from Norway to concentration camps, and evacuated German refugees fleeing the advance of the Red Army. In 1945 the *Monte Rosa* was seized as a prize of war by the British, converted once more into a troopship, and renamed in January 1947.

The names of British troopships began with the word *Empire* followed by the name of a river. The River Windrush begins in the Cotswold Hills, and meanders through Oxfordshire before its confluence with the Thames, but only those who have lived along its banks, or in the village named after it, think of a river when its name is spoken. Sailing regularly on the Southampton-Gibraltar-Suez-Aden-Colombo-Singapore-Hong Kong route, the *Empire Windrush* made just one journey to the Caribbean, but it was this journey that inscribed it into British history.

> Nineteen forty-eight was ... the year of the arrival at Tilbury Docks in the UK of the SS *Empire Windrush*, the troopship, with its cargo of West Indian volunteers, returning from home leave in the Caribbean, together with a small company of civilian migrants. This event signaled the start of post-war Caribbean migration to Britain and stands symbolically as the birthdate of the Afro-Caribbean black diaspora.
>
> Stuart Hall, 2005

If ships are haunted by the voices of the passengers they have carried it is only certain sounds that are heard when the name *Empire Windrush* is evoked: silent are the anxious whispers of German troops as they crouched on its decks, gone are the sighs of relief from rescued evacuees mounting its gangplanks, eradicated are the cries of despair from the Norwegian Jews who huddled in its hold and would not return to the land of their birth. What remains is the voice of a Calypsonian, Aldwyn Roberts, better known as Lord Kitchener, whose music captured the hopes, dreams and disappointments of a generation of West Indians who came home to Britain, the 'Mother Country'.

On 22 June, Roberts and 491 other passengers from Jamaica carrying British passports disembarked at Tilbury with the intention of being part of the labour force needed to rebuild the devastated metropolitan heart of empire. Most of the passengers on the *Empire Windrush* were returning servicemen, many of them former RAF personnel, but their service to Britain during the war was quickly forgotten, their claims to being as British as anyone else denied.

Outside of my immediate family it seemed as if the ship was remembered only as the first of many ships that carried racial problems into the country. My father, a flight sergeant in the RAF, was sent to Jamaica to escort servicemen returning from leave on one of those ships, and he was one of these problems. As were his two children and his wife, who, in addition to being a traitor to her race, must be a slut because no respectable white woman would associate with, let alone marry, a Jamaican.

Anti-immigration sentiment flourished as I grew from infant to teenager, and in the increasingly antagonistic atmosphere evocations of the *Windrush* became a burden to bear. It was as if the ship represented a cultural and political break in time. A mythological system of beliefs developed, marking a before and after in British history: before the *Windrush* Britain was white; black bodies contaminated traditional British values; the heartbeat of the nation was regulated by the rhythms of 'fair play' until black people arrived from the colonies and cancerous traces of race and racism appeared in the nation's bloodstream; before boatloads of ungrateful immigrants landed and taxed the natural tolerance of its domestic citizens to unacceptable limits, the British Empire had been a benevolent force for good in its colonies. In short, the *Windrush* symbolized the beginning of the end of empire and Britain's demise from the status of being a great power.

At school, the girl suffered the consequences of this historical amnesia. When the boy who sat at the desk to her right – the one who used to pinch her arm whenever the teacher's back was turned – had finished talking about heat and flies and deserts and driving tanks across Egypt, he looked at her smugly as if to say 'beat that'. It was her turn to describe her father's contribution to the war effort. She stood and stated clearly that her father served in the RAF. On the piano at home stood a photograph of a young man in RAF uniform, with an enigmatic smile, head titled at a slightly rakish and dare-devil angle, holding a pipe in his hand. In the eyes of his daughter her father was the epitome of wartime British heroism.

Before the girl could describe the photograph to her classmates, she was abruptly interrupted by the teacher. In a loud, sharp voice she was told to sit back down and listen carefully. She sat. The entire class was stunned. Silenced by their teacher's angry glare, they stared at the girl who cowered in shock and humiliation as the teacher warned her about the dire consequences of telling lies and insisted that there were no 'coloured' people in Britain during the war, that no coloured people served in any of the armed services, and certainly not in the RAF, the most elite branch of the British military. The eyes of the teacher swept like searchlights over the class, scanning the rows of desks behind which the children sat rigid. There was nowhere to hide. Speaking in the slow and deliberate tone of voice that she adopted when she would brook no opposition, the teacher declared that *coloured people were not British but immigrants who arrived on these shores after the war had been fought and won.* All the children shifted back in their seats. This was the girl's formal introduction to British history as taught in the 1950s at her primary school. She had previously absorbed the fact that she was a 'nigger', a 'wog', 'coloured' and 'half-caste', and now she learnt that she was not considered British.

In 1998, the fiftieth anniversary of the arrival of the *Empire Windrush* was the occasion for a rash of publications and events that reclaimed the story for the more positive purpose of celebrating 'the irresistible rise of multi-racial Britain'. Probably the most important intervention by the media was the BBC's four-part television series, *Windrush*, which documented the formation of a vibrant black British community. The documentary engrossed Iris and Carl. It was the first public acknowledgement of the difficulties they had had to confront because of their marriage, and my mother told me that as they sat in their living room watching other black and white couples recount their stories they both wept. Their enthusiasm for the television series was unbounded. They both stressed its historical importance and told me to use it in my teaching, but as I listened I could see that the programme held deep personal and emotional significance for each of them. In the face of their joy I was unable to describe my reservations, to explain how troubled I was that the *Windrush* remained a dominant icon, apparently the only model for understanding issues of race in modern Britain. There were many publications marking the anniversary, each striving to define the modern, black British subject and community, all telling the story of the emergence of an 'authentic' and singular British 'blackness' that had its roots in the arrival of the *Windrush* in June 1948. The girl, five months old when the ship entered the Thames Estuary, had already been classified as a statistic in a very different narrative of British racialized history, a narrative with its roots in the war and its legacy of 'brown babies'.

Racial calculations that weighed and assessed what black residence would mean for postwar Britain did not originate with the docking of the *Empire Windrush*. Though its arrival initiated a new phase in the formation of a Caribbean diaspora in Britain, it did not usher in a new racial state. Laura Tabili argues that 'racial categories and racial subordination were reconstituted on British soil' in the 1920s and '30s. In the 1940s the British government adopted racialized policies and practices to manage black civilian and military personnel. When the British confronted a black presence at home it challenged their previous idea of themselves as rulers of colonies who resided at a geographical distance from those they colonized. The encounter within the borders of this island nation – an encounter between a parochial metropolitan population and an international constituency consisting of black Americans and black volunteers from the Caribbean – led to the creation of new formulations of being and becoming a national subject relating to the ways in which people became racialized. Race is not a material object, a thing; it has to do not with what people are but with how they are classified. It is a practice or series of practices, a technology that calculates and assigns differences to peoples and communities and then institutionalizes these differences. It is a verb not a noun. The only way to understand the complex configurations and connotations of 'race' is in the context of particular times and places. I use the word racialization to capture the practices and processes involved in the calculations and impositions of difference, all of which have their own logic but are not eternally fixed.

The racialization that took place during the Second World War in Britain was related to the fears, anxieties and desires that shaped ideas about 'race' in the colonies and in pre-war British port cities, the sites of the oldest black communities in the country. The mobilization of women in the homeland and of troops and civilians from the Caribbean resulted in encounters between young women, like my mother, from the colonial heartland and young men, like my father, from its colonized periphery. These fears, anxieties and desires circulated around these two sets of bodies – black men and white women – which became marked as racially antithetical. Many of these wartime encounters between racialized bodies flourished into sexual relationships, with some, despite the overwhelming opposition, culminating in marriage and increasing what officials regarded as the 'problem' of 'half-caste children'. The racial calculations that defined the girl were rooted in this unease about the threat to national cultural identity represented by these children.

What became defined as the black presence in wartime was actually a very diverse population. My father was one of approximately 12,500 volunteers from the Caribbean serving in the armed forces: the vast majority came from Jamaica and served in the RAF. The Ministry of Labour recruited civilians: a thousand technicians and trainees worked in the Merseyside and Lancashire munitions factories, and 1,200 British Hondurans toiled as foresters in Scotland, for example. If the presence of West Indians disappeared from postwar memory, the 3 million American troops stationed in Britain from 1942 onwards, 130,000 of whom were black, left an indelible impression.

American servicemen regarded their British hosts as a kind but not a modern people. One early American volunteer for the RAF said he liked English people well enough but was frustrated because he saw them as tied to 'ancient restrictions', suffering from an inertia produced by Britain's 'Old School Tie' class consciousness. He looked at Britain and saw a society governed by the forces of 'tradition and precedent', forces so strong that 'thinking in politics, business and religion seems to have congealed'. He considered the British 'the most economically backward people' he had met, a people who heartily resisted 'labor-saving devices and short-cut direct business methods'. If Britain resisted becoming modern in the ways described by this North American airman, the country's politicians were worried about the future, particularly the possible consequences of the presence of black colonial and US personnel on British soil. The government instituted policies and practices to control and discipline military personnel which sought to appease Britain's most powerful ally, making concessions to its dominant racial ideas and practices of segregation. But these policies were also influenced by ideas of race that circulated throughout the British Empire, by actual and imagined relations to Britain's colonial subjects.

The recruitment of civilian workers from the Caribbean into Britain began in February 1941, and they were sent to areas of previous black settlement in the northwest because that is where officials thought they would be 'most easily absorbed'. Schemes for industrial workers were designed to prevent any further black settlement and were linked to programmes for postwar colonial development: limited terms of employment to be followed by immediate repatriation. As early as January 1942, dismay about black servicemen being based in Britain was recorded in a Foreign Office memo: 'the recruitment to the United Kingdom of Coloured British subjects, whose remaining in the United Kingdom after the war might create a social problem, was not considered desirable'. In the Colonial Office archives there are records of discussions about expanding repatriation to include the already long-established black populations of British ports at the war's end: '"the great coloured social problem" in Liverpool and other port towns would be "greatly eased by the resettlement of African peoples in West Africa where they could obtain proper and adequate employment"'.

Although the British government was already deeply concerned about its homegrown black residents and about the increasing presence of black colonial subjects, histories of the response to the presence of black American soldiers in Britain propose that an American 'racial problem' was imported into the UK with US troops and that the UK had no experience of how to deal with it. On the contrary, although Winston Churchill had been urging President Roosevelt to send American troops to Britain since the Autumn of 1941, when Roosevelt announced to Congress on 6 January 1942 that US forces were to be stationed in the UK, the British government immediately sought to dissuade the Americans from sending black GIs. The British Chiefs of Staff explicitly asked for the maximum number of *white* engineering regiments.

Throughout that spring and summer, British officials pressured the US government to 'reduce as far as possible the number of coloured troops . . . sent to this country'. In a pathetic attempt to represent this exclusionary British policy as altruistic, Foreign Secretary Anthony Eden told American Ambassador Winant that the British 'climate was badly suited to negroes'. The British did not need North Americans to teach them about racism.

Black GIs arrived and continued to arrive despite British protests: US military command insisted that they were needed to service and supply their European Theatre of Operations (ETO). The occupants of Whitehall, along with the commanders of the ETO, resolved that these black troops would have to be managed, and being managed meant instituting practices of segregation. On a visit to Britain, Arthur Sulzberger, the publisher of the *New York Times*, recognizing that Britain already had a long-standing resident black population, made what he considered 'a gesture of sympathy' for Whitehall's dilemma when he suggested that black American troops 'be moved out of rural areas and concentrated in ports like Liverpool', because it was in places like these that the British were 'used to all kinds of foreigners, including negroes'.

What evolved were government, military, national and local practices that produced racialized subjects as not conforming to acceptable conventions of British citizenship. These practices policed and tried to prevent very specific kinds of encounters – sexual encounters between black men and white women. Black male and white female bodies became subject to spatial management on the cultural, political and social terrain of British society.

Commanders in the US military were worried about violent confrontations between black and white troops if black soldiers were seen with white women. General Eisenhower suggested a solution: a rotation of leave passes which would guarantee that white and coloured troops were never in the same town on the same day. The War Office and the Home Office were more than happy to oblige their white American 'cousins' (black Americans have never been embraced by this familial term). Managing the issue by instituting forms of segregation relieved the British government's fears and anxieties about the consequences of sexual relations between white women and black men. The Colonial Office was eager to suppress knowledge of the British role in instituting American-style racial segregation because of its concern that such revelations would cause anger, frustration and possible rebellion in British colonies.

It would have been impossible for the British government to institute widespread practices of segregation without the cooperation of its regional commissioners, many of whom were ex-colonial officials, and without the participation of local police forces and local government officials. Covert racial segregation became the practice in Southern Command from July 1942 on.

Wherever possible a new black unit in SOS [Services of Supply] was 'quarantined on base to allow time to 'indoctrinate' it about British conditions and to coordinate arrangements with local officials ... liaison officers working with British Southern Command made arrangements in towns like Yeovil and Chard for separate blocks of cinema seats or separate rooms in pubs for black troops. The aim ... was to prevent 'white and colored soldiers from attending the same activities simultaneously', while giving each race 'an equal opportunity of attending the same [kind of] functions as the other.' But, to avoid imputations of racial discrimination, everything was to be done 'on an organizational basis' – in other words, a dance would be held for a company of the '98th Engineer Regiment' (which happened to be black) or for a company of the 16th Infantry Regiment (which happened to be white). As [Gen. J. C. H.] Lee himself put it: 'While color lines are not to be announced or even mentioned, entertainments such as dances should be "by organization." The reason, if any, given for such an arrangement should be "limitation of space and personnel."'

At the military depot at Ashchurch three miles outside of Tewkesbury, a town just sixteen miles from Worcester where Iris worked for the Air Ministry, white troops were issued passes for

Tuesdays, Thursdays and Saturdays, while black troops were given passes for Mondays, Wednesdays and Fridays. They alternated Sundays. A day club was established for black troops at Tewkesbury, and clubs at Worcester and Cheltenham for white troops. My mother maintained she had not known that black and white American troops were segregated in the region but she must have done. Could she not admit such knowledge to me, her black daughter? Did she feel culpable? There was ambivalence and some dissension among the civilian population about such policies, but was it easier to live with if you just denied its existence? Officially, segregation was always denied: these policies and practices were explained away as required for organizational efficiency. While in public the British government distanced itself from the racial segregation instituted by the US Army it could not have been maintained without British authorization, cooperation and acquiescence.

The leaders of the British armed forces were not opposed to segregation. The War Office believed that 'British officers should lecture their troops, including women soldiers of the Auxiliary Territorial Service (ATS), on the need to minimize contact with black GIs but they would not put anything on paper, because of the sensitive nature of the subject'. Ignoring such qualms, General Arthur Dowler, the senior administrative officer in Southern Command, went ahead and issued his 'Notes on Relations with Coloured Troops', on 7 August 1942. Dowler wanted British men and women not only to recognize the presence of a problem but to conform to the attitudes of white American citizens.

The National Association for the Advancement of Colored People (NAACP) complained to the ARC [American Red Cross] on several occasions about 'segregated recreational centers in London and other English cities for Negro soldiers' and its executive secretary, Walter White, cabled Churchill in November about reports that the British government had asked Washington to send no more black troops to Britain. (After long consultation the Foreign Office decided discretely to ignore the telegram because it was doubted 'whether we could honestly give a categorical denial.')

Dowler stated that the 'generality' of blacks 'were of simple mental outlook' and lacked 'the white man's ability to think and act to a plan ...' British soldiers ... 'should not make intimate friends with them, taking them to cinemas and bars ...' 'white women should not associate with colored men ...' they 'should not walk out, dance or drink with them'.

'Notes on Relations with Coloured Troops', 7 August 1942

There was no objection, not even from the Colonial Office, 'to the double standard policy of covertly supporting US Army segregation, as long as the British authorities were not implicated in its enforcement'.

At what point in 1942, I wonder, did Iris realize that she was being addressed as a racialized citizen, advised explicitly as a woman who was white? She loved to tell the story of the courage it took to walk across the ballroom floor and stand in front of Carl, the pride she felt because she was the only woman to ask him to dance. To feel brave, to be proud, means that she must have considered herself white, that her whiteness had a value and she was willing to risk her worth.

In 1942, Nancy Cunard and George Padmore jointly authored a pamphlet entitled *The White Man's Duty* to publicize how 'the coloured soldier of the USA over here in very large numbers ... may be the same as a white American soldier in democracy, when democracy is a battlefield, [but] he is not the same in daily relations with the people of Great Britain, because some of his chiefs have requested that this be not so'. And, as Cunard and Padmore went on to stress, 'the colour issue in Britain was part of the wider question of racial discrimination within the empire as a whole'.

The anxieties and fears, the frantic exchange of covert memos and circulation of not so covert 'Notes', the endless wrangling and manoeuvring among the ministries, the Foreign Office and the Colonial Office about the spatial management and control of white and black bodies, the 'what on earth to do' nature of it

Although the Home Office stated a clear policy of opposing caste patterns, the armed forces of Great Britain never made any such clear statement. In fact, the letters ... indicate that women personnel were advised not to consort with Negroes, and interviews made by the writer have not only confirmed this, but also reveal that similar advice was given to British male troops. There was a great tendency on the part of the British government to avoid admitting that any such orders were given, but an air council letter written in September of 1945 indicates that such an order was in existence in 1942. The 1945 letter was written to clear up certain complaints by Jamaican RAF men that the RAF sanctioned discrimination against them. The RAF made clear that the 1942 directive against consorting with colored men was to apply to American colored men only and that a directive of 1944 had specifically stated that no pressure was to be used against the women's associating with Jamaican personnel – on the bases. The latter qualification was restressed in the 1945 letter.

St. Clair Drake Papers

all, swirled and coalesced around men and women like Iris and Carl. Mechanisms of the state policed and attempted to prevent their relationship. As a couple they were caught in the entanglement of race, its skeins threading into their actions, attitudes and beliefs, ultimately governing even the smallest details of their lives.

Carl was a member of the first wave of volunteers from Jamaica. He described his arrival in the UK in 1943 as an airman recently transported from training in Canada: when he and the other Jamaican volunteers reached their destination, RAF Padgate, Bridgnorth, before they were even taken to their billets the sergeant receiving them 'took us to the ablutions where we received instructions in meticulous detail on how to use the shower, the wash basins and the toilets, as if to say we had never seen or used a bathroom before'.

Racist beliefs about the past and present of subject peoples in the colonies and black settlements in the UK were marshalled by members of the Cabinet to predict what Britain might face in its future. The Home Secretary, Herbert Morrison, stated that he was 'fully conscious that a difficult sex problem might be created . . . if there were a substantial number of cases of sex relations between white women and coloured troops and the procreation of half-caste children'. Morrison's articulation of what he called a 'sex problem' did not arise from the recognition of 'an "external" problem' which had been 'foisted to some extent on English society from the outside', or imported into Britain with the arrival of the bodies of black GI's or personnel from the Caribbean. On the contrary, it was a 'home-grown' composite racialized consciousness, drawing upon past official responses to the existence of black communities in Britain and upon the racialization of bodies in colonial territories, a consciousness that gave English national culture its character, meaning, substance and resonance. Before the war this consciousness had been nurtured, given form and realized in the policing and disciplining of colonial subjects and the black residents of Bristol, Cardiff, London and Liverpool.

West Indians who served in the RAF during the war tell their own stories of humiliation. They remember British women groping their bottoms in order locate the tails that they imagined West Indian men hid in their trousers, and of children running from them in fear. They tell stories about the Paramount dance hall on Tottenham Court Road and the brutality they suffered at the hands of those British and American white men who resented West Indians dancing with English women. Antagonism to this 'intimate socializing' was also expressed in the newspapers, who had a 'field day talking about "ill-timed and unwanted fraternizing" and protesting that blacks and whites be allowed to mix in such a way'. One West Indian remembers reading an article headlined, 'Don't Let this Go On', in which the author suggested that the Paramount should be bombed. It was 'a concerted attempt', he concluded, 'to besmirch the name of the Paramount [that] dared to permit black servicemen to pass through its doors'.

> Women who befriended the West Indian servicemen were a much-maligned body of people, being objects of derision, jibes and taunts. Yet most never wavered in their allegiance and loyalty when the going was toughest and no amount of praise could be too high for them. In the very early days they remained a tower of strength and were among the few to extend a hand of welcome to the lads.

Another Jamaican ex-serviceman tells the story of being refused service in a pub after a game of cricket, adding that in the more than fifty years since, he has never forgotten the humiliation. He told his interviewer that he walked back to his base in floods of tears. There he weighed the bitter irony of his situation: at the beginning of the war Jamaica had presented

> I had to take myself, my little case containing my cricket kit, my unquenched thirst and walk slowly home ... I was taking stock of myself and, for the first time in my life, I was asking myself: Why have I travelled thousands of miles to be on the receiving end of such treatment? I was as British, nay I considered myself more British than the British ... and more patriotic than the most fanatic Anglophile.

a squadron of Spitfires to Britain as a gift, yet here he was, an airman willing to risk his life for that same country in which he was not even allowed purchase a pint.

It was not only black men who had to be policed and disciplined; historians record the 'intensive efforts [that] were made to guide the conduct of British women'. For women in the armed service, 'military discipline was invoked' to discourage them from fraternizing with black soldiers and, in January 1944, these policies hardened when 'the Women's Territorial Auxiliary issued an order "forbidding its members to speak to coloured American soldiers except in the presence of a white [person]"'.

These systems of surveillance were not only instituted and regulated by the military, they were also enabled and maintained by members of local constabularies, who 'routinely reported women soldiers found in the company of black GIs to their superiors'. Even civilian women were persecuted and prosecuted by local police, who evoked 'a variety of laws' to take them into custody when they were found in the company of black soldiers. David Reynolds has provided us with examples drawn from the records of constabularies in different parts of the country: racially mixed couples were prosecuted for damaging crops when were they found in fields, and women were prosecuted and subsequently jailed for trespass when found with black GIs on US military bases.

WOMEN TRAMPS MENACE SOCIAL LIFE IN WALES

Girl tramps have become a menace to Wales. Aged between 15 and 20 they have been sleeping rough and camp-following in the tradition of the Napoleonic days, spreading disease and immorality.

At least 50 per cent of these women have followed American troops from station to station ever since they landed in this country. They live on what the troops provide for them and are constantly in and out of the Police-courts.

Their complete loss of self-respect has put their behaviour with troops on the plane of exhibitionism and parents in the districts concerned complain of the dangerous effect it must have on their own children.

One of the black spots is Maindy Barracks, Cardiff and residents in the area have petitioned and complained to the police.

Extract from *Western Mail and South Wales News*, 12 September 1945, St. Clair Drake Papers

If 'loose lips sank ships', women who were condemned as having 'loose' morals were regarded as a direct threat to the health and safety of the nation. Amid the panic 'about the declining morals of girls and young women in British cities and towns', white women who became the escorts of, or married, black servicemen faced scorn, contempt and scathing abuse. As Sonya Rose has written, definitions of the nation during the war 'could not incorporate within it pleasure-seeking, fun-loving, and sexually expressive women and girls. The women and girls who could not, or would not, put aside their "foolish world" to rescue the nation were constructed as anti-citizens – in contrast to those who were self-sacrificing.' Women who crossed the boundaries of conventional behaviour, particularly in wartime, were labelled 'good-time girls' and became associated within official discourses with venereal disease, thus becoming a threat to the nation's health. But women who openly expressed their sexual selves and sexual desires in encounters with black servicemen were particularly vilified and seen as a threat to the nation's future.

The minutes of an August 1942 Bolero Committee meeting, held to discuss the stationing of black GIs, reveal that participants were speculating about whether 'an open statement on the danger of venereal disease would deter British women from associating with the blacks'. Someone suggested initiating a 'whispering campaign' along those lines. Despite objections from others at the meeting, historian Graham Smith thinks it 'likely that a programme of rumour-spreading' about black GIs and VD '*was* started' and that it was facilitated through the vehicles of the Women's Voluntary Service (WVS) and, possibly, the BBC.

Both black male and white female bodies were designated vectors of disease, carriers of a threat which could literally and metaphorically infect the nation. The greatest fear, however, was reserved for what the future population of the nation would look like. If white women became the bearers of half-caste children, the postwar era of peace and stability hoped for by so many would be irrevocably disrupted.

Contagion

Iris and Carl assumed that after the war their offspring would belong to, and be an integral part of, British culture, but their intimate coexistence at the centre of the empire created a series of problems, problems that originated with their marriage and multiplied with the birth of a child. How was their association, ceremonially sanctioned by church and state, a threat? What was the nature and manner of their contagion?

Their duality, their coupling, did not contribute to the reproduction of white manhood, guardian and conduit of imperial, patriarchal power, the raison d'être of colonial life. Imperial patriarchy was an absent presence, a metaphysical element in a relationship that was an explicit challenge to the social and political relations of colonialism. The marriage of Iris and Carl in the metropole was a provocation, their domesticity conspicuous, a distasteful reminder of proscribed but commonplace interracial

Who, that has any sense or decency, can help being shocked at the familiar intercourse, which has gradually been gaining ground, and which has, at last, got a complete footing between the Negroes and the women of England? No black swain need, in this loving country, hang himself in despair. No inquiry is made whether he be a Pagan or a Christian; if he be not a downright cripple, he will, if he be so disposed, always find a woman, not merely to yield to his filthy embraces, that, among the notoriously polluted and abandoned part of the sex, would be less shocking, but to accompany him to the altar, to become his wife, to breed English mulattoes, to stamp the mark of Cain upon her family and her country! Amongst white women, this disregard of decency, this defiance of the dictates of nature, this foul, this beastly propensity, is, I say it with sorrow and with shame, peculiar to the English.

William Cobbett, 1804

sex in the peripheries, sex regarded not only as evidence of colonial degeneracy but also as a threat to the regulation and governance of empire. Their 'half-caste' daughter was an offence against nature and society because she was a public statement of closeted colonial sexual desire.

To tell this story, I need to begin again, for to say that this girl was born and grew up in a post-Second World War Britain is insufficient. In order to grasp the relocation and dislocation, the complex calculations of nationality and racial logic, which surrounded her birth, I need to be specific, particular. She was born not just in Britain but in England, in the village of Folly Gate on the edge of Dartmoor in Devon. Iris had to resign from the Civil Service when she married because, in 1944, the government would not employ married women. Iris repeated the same story over and over again to the girl, of the day she found a major accounting error, thus saving the Air Ministry not only unnecessary expenditure but also the embarrassment that would have ensued had the error ever been made public. For this discovery she received expressions of gratitude and high praise from her supervisors for her skills and tenacity. They told her she showed great promise, predicted a stellar future, and promoted her. These same supervisors were horrified when Iris told them she wanted to marry, and tried to dissuade her from what they considered to be a major error of judgement. Did she not understand that she was throwing away not only a prestigious career but a rare opportunity for a woman to have a successful and fulfilling life?

When, unwillingly, Iris left the Civil Service, she exchanged being part of a close and supportive community of young women, a community she was never able to reconstruct, for a social isolation and ostracism so profound it would mark her forever. She developed an account of her self-fashioning through a script of sacrifice and resentment, of what she had lost, of what she had given up for her husband and her child. Life with my father and me was a bitter disappointment in comparison to the career she envisioned for herself as a civil servant. My mother lived for her dreams of what might have been.

I have saved letters sent to Iris during the war from a cousin serving in Burma and India. Even though I have only one side of this lengthy correspondence, it is obvious that their relationship was very close. Reading these letters makes me wonder if Iris was in love with her cousin, if they had an affair before the war, for he protests too much in his insistence that he is in love with his wife, that he regards Iris only as a 'little sister' and that she must look upon him only as a 'big brother'.

One letter, dated 1 October 1944, suggests that Iris had doubts about marrying Carl and sought her cousin's advice. In response to what must have been negative remarks Iris wrote about 'Yanks', her cousin makes disparaging remarks about the behaviour of English women and negroes. At the end of the same month in which these words were written, Iris married a West Indian, to the shock and dismay of all her relatives.

> I was surprised to hear your opinion of the Yanks, we see a lot of them up here, and found most of them alright, but very childlike in their habits, not the tough guys they kid us they are, and the Negroes I admit they have had a better education than the average Indian, but on the whole are no more intelligent, how the English girls can allow themselves to be mauled about by them like we read of in the papers beats me.
>
> Letter to Iris from a cousin,
> 1 October 1944

Three years later, about to become the mother of a black child, Iris did not go to her dismayed relatives in Wales. Instead, in the winter of 1947 she left London, on her own, and went southwest to Devon to give birth to her brown baby in the house of a distant relative, Ivy Smale, a district nurse and midwife.

In June 2006, accompanied by my partner, I park our rental car at the fifteenth-century Crossways Inn, Folly Gate, and set off down the lane to locate the house where I was born. On my birth certificate the name of the house is Roselands. We spend the morning in pleasant conversation with helpful residents who direct us to different cottages and search their memories of people and place. Discussions range: we hear about, though do not meet, a contemporary Smale, a butcher who slaughters the local animals; we discuss the illness and death of spring lambs, and hear of vets who charge more for shots than a lamb is worth; one resident who leads a New Orleans Jazz band knew the musician who taught our son. We drink cups of tea in the beautiful gardens of friendly, interesting and generous villagers, two of whom still describe themselves as 'newcomers', having lived in their house for only twenty years. I am a stranger but everyone I meet considers it of paramount importance to assist in locating the house where I was born. I came to the village following the stories of my mother and wanting to imagine what it was like for her here. But having arrived I realize that I have no idea what, if anything, my having been born here signifies to me, or what it should mean to return to the place of one's birth, but everyone else seems to think it should be important to me.

As we walk down lanes between tall hedgerows, pass farms and cross streams, we are unaware that a series of telephone calls are being made within the village and to adjacent villages. Eventually, a collective memory is assembled of the village in January 1948, of the house and of Nurse Smale. Official history is corrected by villagers, the information entered on the birth certificate is wrong, the name of the house was Roselyn not Roselands, though it no longer bears that name. The cottage where Nurse Smale once lived has been identified, and one of the villagers volunteers to escort us there and introduce us to the current owner. Grateful and impressed, we make our way back to the centre of Folly Gate and down Chapel Lane. The bricks and mortar of what was Roselyn Cottage mean nothing to me: I have not come to find a house, or an affiliation to a place; my journey is the journey of a daughter trying to comprehend the enormity of her mother's transgression, but there are no clues in this charming and welcoming village.

What can help me as a writer, as a daughter, to understand the presence of Iris and her child in the close-knit community of a small English village on the edge of the moors? The presence of a pregnant woman lacking a visible husband was likely to become the subject of scurrilous gossip, but under the stresses and strains of wartime and its aftermath it could have been rationalized by more sympathetic strangers as an impetuous mistake. In the winter of 1947–8, however, this particular cultural narrative was the romantic stuff of movies yet to be made. Excusing the temporary absence of a husband, how did

Iris weigh her options; how did she imagine she was being classified and categorized?

The presence of Iris's black husband would have – in fact already had – unleashed outrage upon her head, bitter condemnations which always threatened violence with no room for rationalization. The coming into the world of her brown child meant mother and child were both to be ostracized. Did the mother whisper her fears into my ears?

I try, and fail, to recreate the scene when my black father finally appeared, coming down from London by train to register the birth at the local registry office in Okehampton. All I can do is conjure a question: What did Carl see, or what did he not want to acknowledge he had seen, in the eyes of the official Registrar of Births and Deaths?

Their child – the girl – became an obsessive reader of fiction, through which she came to think of Dartmoor and Exmoor as enticing sites of mystery and tragedy: dramatic powerful landscapes that haunt me still. During the summers spent with relatives in Wales the girl read late into the long evenings; she learnt that the moors were inhabited by a passionate and volatile populace deeply suspicious of outsiders and surrounded by dark, unnameable forces. She imagined Iris walking along the paths that Lorna Doone rode in daylight and the Hound of the Baskervilles padded in the depths of the night. When the girl's white Welsh cousins gently picked at, pulled and rubbed her skin in their futile but frequent attempts to rub her 'clean', she sat patiently, wondering if her skin was evidence of the dark forces and powers of the moors. Ivy Smale recommended daily walks and Iris walked constantly, restlessly, three times a day to escape Ivy's disapproval, registered in raised eyebrows, sighs, tuts and sneers. Were the baby's black hair, dark eyes and brown skin successfully hidden under the layers of clothes and blankets tightly wrapped around her as protection from the bitter January winds? Her presence in public became a humiliation.

I have to speculate about the changes in Iris's sense of self once she became the mother of a brown girl, because she refused to speak of my birth at any level of particularity no matter how many times I asked her. If she became conscious of her whiteness in her encounter with Carl, did the bloody, brown emergence of an infant reconfigure that whiteness in relation to motherhood? There are many historical and feminist approaches to these questions but they do not help me understand how and why Iris constantly refused to acknowledge that I was regarded as black. 'You are not coloured!' she emphatically declared, when the girl came home with stories about racist bullying at her primary school; so the stories ceased. In later years Iris was utterly bewildered by a daughter deeply immersed in the world of black British activism.

Mother and child did not remain in Devon; they returned to the greater anonymity and cosmopolitanism of South London after several weeks. I am a Londoner to this day except in the space on my passport in which I am required to insert my place of birth, a place to which it is difficult but necessary to return. I feel I should take my son and daughter-in-law to Devon, that I should try to find the words to explain what it must have meant to have been born there, but this would be a burden of pastness they do not need to carry. Writing is a partial substitute for return.

Living in the metropolitan heart of the empire did not enable Carl, Iris or their child to escape the consequences of their racialization. On the contrary, their being together jeopardized any sense of cultural belonging. The history my parents refused to acknowledge, and of which I gradually became aware, was the absolute nature of our outcast status. No family members or friends attended their wedding, but perhaps no one was invited. The witnesses were passing strangers.

Iris and Carl were unable to find anyone willing to rent accommodation to a black and white couple with a brown child. They had to live separately in South London until they could afford the deposit for a house. The city that I would come to claim as the source for my liberated, worldly identity was ground Iris and Carl had to tread with caution. They had very little money: Iris had a small amount of savings, Carl had to support his mother and siblings in Jamaica from his student allowance. They found a house selling cheaply because it had suffered extensive bomb damage, and the three of us lived in one room, the only one habitable, until the council made repairs. Then we lived on the ground floor and rented the first floor rooms to students from Africa and the West Indies studying in Britain. Thus, other parts of the empire came home.

From being responsible, loyal, young people serving their country, Iris and Carl were now derided as irresponsible adults whose actions threatened the stability of its racial order and culture: first, for their act of miscegenation, and, second, for bringing into the world a 'half-caste' girl who, by definition, could not be incorporated into definitions of Britishness because she contaminated them. The story of her becoming, of my becoming, is a political not a personal history.

The girl was born as British politicians were facing two discomforting postwar realities: the first was that the United States and the Soviet Union had emerged from the war as the pre-eminent powers on the global stage; the second was that British subjects abroad, in India, Pakistan, Canada, Australia and New Zealand, were seeking to exercise rights of national autonomy. The result of their deliberations was the British Nationality Act, 'an opening ploy in the game of citizenship politics in postwar Britain', which was passed by Parliament in 1948.

The aim of the Act was to secure Britain at the centre of empire in the face of American and Soviet hegemony, as a great power among great powers. The Act responded to the right of the self-governing Dominions to grant citizenship to their populations while seeking to maintain Britain's place as an international power and influence in the world. If it was emigration from Britain that established its international presence, it was the ties of those emigrants to Britain that maintained it.

Part I.
British Nationality.

1. – (1) Every person who under this Act is a citizen of the United Kingdom and Colonies or who under any enactment for the time being in force in any country mentioned in subsection (3) of this section is a citizen of that country shall by virtue of that citizenship have the status of a British subject.

* * * * * * * * * * * * * * * * * * *

(3) The following are the countries hereinbefore referred to, that is to say, Canada, Australia, New Zealand, The Union of South Africa, Newfoundland, India, Pakistan, Southern Rhodesia and Ceylon.

British Nationality Act, 1948

In practice, the British Nationality Act created a multiplicity of definitions of Britishness, while extending what appeared to be a universal definition of the status of British subject to all members of the empire. The white settlers in Canada, Australia, New Zealand, The Union of South Africa and Southern Rhodesia were regarded as 'British stock'. As Kathleen Paul describes this distinction: 'British stock' were British subjects, but the political elites of the UK and the 'old' Dominions did not consider all British subjects to be British stock. Policy-makers conceived of separate spheres of nationality: residents of the empire with a white skin and European cultural descent were British stock; residents of the empire with a skin of colour and African or Asian heritage were British subjects only. 'British stock' described 'a familial community defined by blood and culture', by breeding. 'Stock' was a restrictive term that contradicted the universal language of the Act. The word summons associations with breeding animals and resources for future replenishment. Embedded within the notion of imperial subjecthood were incompatible ideas of belonging, the minefield of 'Where are you from?' that the girl had to negotiate. In schemes for emigration, the multiple meanings of Britishness on the imperial stage became irreconcilable: Iris's dreams of building a new life for all of us in Australia were destroyed when she discovered that its postwar migration programme was for white immigrants only. In 1962 the Commonwealth Immigrants Act was passed, eradicating any remnant of equality, policing the borders of the nation against black migrants, and scarring the child in profound ways.

Throughout the 1950s different branches of government debated ways to limit the migration of black British subjects while not threatening the stability or unity of the Commonwealth upon which Britain's 'greatness' depended. The racial hostility toward black citizens on the national stage had its counterpart in the girl's local universe. While totally unaware of the machinations of Anthony Eden and Harold Macmillan in Cabinet-level discussions of the 'immigrant problem', the girl felt keenly that her belonging was in question.

Postwar histories of race in Britain are dominated by the narrative of migration. From the girl's kindergarten, through to her adult life as a secondary school teacher of English in the East End of London, national history could be characterized as a simple equation: the beneficence of the English had been betrayed. British political, social and economic generosity was understood to have been embodied first in the abolition of the slave trade and, second, in the unstinting imperial labour to bring civilization and enlightenment to a third of the globe. This selfless mission was undermined when the empire came home. Boatloads of coloured immigrants, who had the nerve to think they were British, betrayed the spirit and practices of English liberalism. Having landed on the shores of a kind-hearted and generous-spirited island, *they* just didn't know how to behave like decent English people. 'This generosity just had to stop' was the mantra which accompanied the girl's self-fashioning. Immigration was 'getting out of hand', 'they' were everywhere, 'they' loved crowding together, and 'they' were so noisy and smelly. As the girl became a young black woman she insisted that she was homegrown, but no hyphenated identity existed that she could adopt, wear or proclaim. When asked 'Where are you from?', she braced herself to be seen as an ungrateful black immigrant, an eternal outsider. When officials asked where she was born and she replied Devon, England, they demanded to know where she had come from before that. School friends would ask, 'But how did you get here?' Being black British was incomprehensible, an impossibility between two mutually exclusive terms. Insisting that she was both placed her at the nexus of a domestic ambiguity that made her white classmates and teachers uncomfortable, so she learnt to live with being an unresolvable contradiction, an historical impossibility. Being black, there was no flexibility or malleability to her unbelonging.

Brown Babies

Among the sequelæ of the war are many social problems which will tax the genius of statesmen, doctors, educationists, psychiatrists and social workers for many years to come. Few are more baffling than one which has arisen in Great Britain, and possibly in other countries – the problem of the illegitimate child born of a 'white' mother and a 'coloured' serviceman.

Harold Moody, March 1946

I was wrong to assume that being born a British 'brown baby' in the tiny village of Folly Gate in 1948 meant being born into a homogeneously white social and cultural world. I had read Equiano's account of his landing in Plymouth in 1777, and could find no historical trace of him there, but renewed interest in local history has revealed a black presence in the Devon landscape which stretches back for centuries. Folly Gate borders the Mariners' Way, a linking of numerous field paths between Bideford on the north coast and Dartmouth on the south. Dartmoor tradition has it that this ancient footpath was walked by seamen who were transferring from a ship in one port to a ship in the other. Black seaman, like Equiano, were recruited into the Royal Navy and the merchant fleets, so they would have trodden these pathways. The enslaved, servants, labourers, soldiers and mariners have passed through, lived and died in Devon; bodies of the enslaved were buried after a shipwreck had washed them ashore on Devon's coast. During the Second

World War upwards of 30,000 black American troops were based in the southwest counties of England. Reckoning with the birth of brown babies in Britain produced a complex series of calculations that contested their right to belong and estimated that their existence devalued the currency of British nationality and diminished the worth of those around them. In the aftermath of two world wars, brown babies were too young to account for themselves.

During the 1920s white, middle-class teachers, public officials, churchmen and social workers in the port cities, particularly Liverpool, Cardiff and London, expressed alarm at what they regarded as a moral problem: sexual relations between black men and white women in communities where 'coloured' seamen had settled. These respectable, god-fearing white citizens regarded 'coloured' seaman as immoral, and urged that those in residence in the country be deported, and future immigration banned. The 'mixed-blood' progeny of the black seaman and white woman was the stuff of respectable nightmares.

In 1927, Rachel Fleming, from the University College of Wales, embarked on an anthropometric study that reproduced the despicable logics of scientific racism. Fleming's subjects were black British children in Liverpool schools. Fleming imagined that she could capture and classify some essential difference in 'half-caste' children, so she busily set about assessing, measuring and weighing their bodies in an attempt to correlate their physical, psychological and 'racial' traits. Her practices are uncomfortably similar to the ways in which the bodies of the enslaved and formerly enslaved in North America were measured in the nineteenth century and their proportions calculated as 'demonstrable proof' of their inferiority.

In the course of her 'research' Fleming shared her findings and her concerns about 'the unhappy condition of their life and the dismal character of their prospects' with colleagues at the University of Liverpool, who subsequently instigated a series of meetings with various institutions and organizations in the city, each of which was addressed by her. The meetings led to the formation of the Liverpool Association for the Welfare of

Half-Caste Children. Members of the Association decided that a more detailed survey was required to determine the nature and extent of 'the problem' and to formulate 'possible solutions'. The result was the *Report on an Investigation into the Colour Problem in Liverpool and Other Ports*, produced for the Association by Muriel E. Fletcher, who placed particular emphasis on 'the prevalence of prostitution and venereal disease', the 'low moral character of white women

a) The problem of the half-caste child is a serious one, and it appears to be growing in most of our seaport towns.

b) It is practically impossible for half-caste children to be absorbed into our industrial life and this leads to grave moral results.

c) The white women themselves mostly regret their marriage with a coloured man and their general standard of life is usually permanently lowered.

Muriel E. Fletcher, 1930

who live with Negroes, and the difficulty of finding employment for "half-castes" – particularly girls'. Fletcher recommended that 'coloured men be eliminated from the merchant navy'.

Reaction from black communities to the Fletcher Report was immediate and hostile. They condemned its prurient obsessions and reliance on second-hand data and the opinions of the police. In 1931, two organizations were established in opposition to the practices of the Liverpool Association and like-minded groups, and to the conclusions of the Fletcher Report. A predominantly white, Quaker-led organization, the Joint Council to Promote Understanding Between White and Coloured People in Great Britain, elected a nationally prominent black man, Dr Harold A. Moody, as their vice-chairman. The Joint Council was committed to opposing the colour-bar using strategies of quiet opposition including boycotts and publicity. Within a month, however, Moody, with the help of Charles Wesley, an African American Professor, had formed the League of Coloured Peoples (LCP), an international organization led and run by black people: the membership of their inaugural executive committee was West Indian and African. The LCP described itself as 'An organization for bringing together Africans and West Indians in Britain; for helping them in their needs and giving advice as occasion arises; for breaking down barriers and educating English people and others about

Coloured peoples . . . which holds a watching brief in the interests of the present and future good of our peoples everywhere.' In spite of such opposition groups, the fictional racial logics in the work of Fleming and Fletcher remained intact, and cast their calculations over what became known as the 'Brown Babies' debates of the 1940s.

As early as 1944, George Padmore, London correspondent for *The Chicago Defender*, reported that: 'Among the post-war social problems which will soon have to be tackled by the British and American military and civilian rehabilitation authorities . . . is the future of large numbers of colored children born of American Negro soldiers and English women.' Anxieties about the legacy of black troops in Britain, about what 'the procreation of half-caste children' would mean for the future of the country, were expressed on the other side of the Atlantic too, particularly in the African American press. Their perspective on 'the problem' was not always as distinct from that of the British government as one might have hoped. In 1947, the headline of a four-page exposé in *Ebony*, a magazine published in Chicago, read: 'Britain's Brown Babies: Illegitimate Tots a Tough Problem for England'.

In the pages of *Ebony* these babies were represented as 'fatherless children', whose coming into the world tested the British reputation for 'racial liberalism' because Britons refused to adopt them. The black American writer did not question whether the British were, in fact, racially liberal before the babies arrived. Rather, *Ebony* assumed that it was the appearance of the small brown bodies in the world that provoked a racist reaction: the babies were the agents who put the liberalism of the British to the 'test'. With the stroke of a pen the *longue durée* of British imperial and racial thought and practice vanished from view, absorbed into the bloodstreams of infants.

On both sides of the Atlantic there was acute anxiety about how many 'brown babies' had been born to British mothers. A calculus of unreasoning dominated both antagonistic and sympathetic responses to the presence of these new black citizens, who were reduced to numerical threats. In 1947, under the headline 'Brown Tiny Tims', an article in *Newsweek* cited figures circulating in the UK of 1,000 Negro GI babies according to the Home Office', 5,000 according to the Negro Welfare Society and 10,000 according to the Anti-Slavery Society. In the US, the *Ebony* article contained an unattributed guess of 'not less than 2,000 to not more than 5,000', and a figure of '20,000 Little Brown Bastards' was cited in a pamphlet sent to all members of Congress by Larry Ashman, Michigan director of a group called Christian Veterans of America.

Not a few GI's were startled, when they arrived in England during the war, to discover that many English girls thought nothing of dating Negro soldiers. Some of the girls even preferred the Negro soldiers to whites.

Last week, the Reuters news agency reported from London that an organization calling itself the Negro Welfare Society had applied to Home Secretary James Chuter Ede for permission to ship to America 5,000 mulatto babies, the illegitimate children of Negro GI's and white girls who had dated them. Another organization, the Anti-Slavery Society, was quoted as estimating that in all there were 10,000 such children in Britain, 'whose mothers', Reuters declared, 'cannot fit them into English family or community life.'

'Brown Tiny Tims', *Newsweek*, 29 December 1947

In 1945, the LCP sent the results of their own survey, 'Illegitimate Children Born in Britain of English Mothers and of Fathers who are Mostly American Coloured Service-men', by Sylvia McNeill, to the Minister of Health, Aneurin Bevan. Acknowledging that their figures were incomplete, the LCP estimate of 550 was nevertheless rather more conservative and sober than the scare-mongering numbers quoted in the press. By the last quarter of 1948 the Children's Welfare Committee were reporting in the LCP Newsletter that in addition to the 750 cases they had in their files, twenty-five new cases had come before them in the course of that year, and they noted an increase in cases involving West Indian servicemen and British mothers. Harold Moody wanted the children to be 'treated as "war casualties" for whom provision should be made jointly by the British and United States governments'.

The general consensus was that numbers mattered, that an accurate count would identify and define the true extent of the 'problem' which, once calculated, could be more easily contained and managed. St. Clair Drake, best known as a sociologist and as co-author of a rich historical and sociological account of life on the South Side of Chicago, also wrote a dissertation on black Britain for his PhD in Anthropology from the University of Chicago. After the war, Drake travelled to the UK to study black communities in British seaports. This work is rarely mentioned in appraisals of Drake's scholarship and, where it is, is summarized as an analysis of Tiger Bay, Cardiff, even though in the title, 'Race Relations in the British Isles', we can see a broader and more ambitious project. Drake scoured the records of the LCP in an attempt to determine a verifiable final magic number of brown babies, a figure impossible to establish.

Beneath the moral outcries about illegitimacy and 'fatherlessness', beneath the surface of the investigative journalism and the exposés of 'tragic' and 'pitiful' children in the care of local councils and the African Churches Mission in Liverpool, lie many layers of disguised racist logic. White women were counselled by families, friends and authorities against marriage with black men; black American soldiers who wished to marry white British women carrying their children were refused permission to do so by their Commanding Officers and were quickly transferred. Black journalist Ormus Davenport, 'himself a wartime GI, claimed that there had been a "gentleman's agreement" to prevent mixed marriages', but 'in the 8th Air Force Service Command where most of the American Air Force blacks were concentrated, a total ban on such marriages was quite explicit'. The result was disastrous for their children.

The LCP insisted that the children were British and be recognized as such, but a number of local authorities disagreed. In 1945, when Sylvia McNeill attended a meeting of the County Welfare Committee for South Devon, which had submitted forty-five of their 'cases' to the LCP, she had to confront officials who were thinking in terms of segregation and removal. McNeill was asked to provide information not only about the aims of the LCP survey, but also about the possibility of establishing homes 'strictly reserved for coloured children' and of 'getting children sent to the United States in such cases where the fathers were anxious to have them'.

Stories about sending black British children to the USA circulated in the press from 1947. Under the front-page banner headline, 'Ship Tan-Yank Babies to US', *The Chicago Defender*, a black newspaper, published an article written in a tone of nationalistic pique: 'England will literally drop *another* problem in America's lap when 5,000 children of British mothers and Negro GIs leave for the US sometime this year.' A week later the paper printed a retraction, acknowledging that UK adoption laws were stringent and would probably prevent such a transfer. Nevertheless, there were those who advocated for a change in the adoption laws so that the children could be sent out of the country, among them Somerset County Council, who wanted all their 'coloured children' removed.

Towards the end of the war, the county of Somerset had made the decision to take all 'brown babies' known to county authorities into care, irrespective of whether the mothers were single or married ... The decisive force behind the policies across the whole county, and particularly with regard to Holnicote House, was Celia Bangham, Superintendent Health visitor responsible for the county's children. Her efforts, not only visible in her supervision of Holnicote House, but more importantly evident in her attempts to work towards a transatlantic adoption of the mixed-race children of Somerset, received significant feedback in the United States.

Sabine Lee, 'A Forgotten Legacy of the Second World War'

In August 1948, under the headline, 'The Babies They Left Behind Them', *Life* published a photograph of and an article about seven children who were among the black British wards of Somerset County Council. The council tried to hide the fact that it was running Holnicote House as an 'orphanage' even though the children were not orphans. *Life* referred to the children as the offspring of black US soldiers and white English women: 'Their fathers have returned to the US. Their mothers have given them up, in most cases reluctantly, because of ostracism by village neighbours.' These British children were not being imagined as citizens but as 'problems' that should be exported. The British government, the article continues, 'are now considering offers of adoption received from US negro families'.

The Superintendent Health Visitor for Somerset County Council was Celia Bangham: she set the policies for the county, was responsible for its children and supervised Holnicote House. Calling the children housed in Holnicote orphans concealed the council's decision to take into care *all* the 'brown babies' in the county, 'irrespective of whether the mothers were single or married'. Bangham worked tirelessly to achieve her aim of shipping these children out of Somerset and across the Atlantic for adoption; she sought allies among Members of Parliament in a campaign to persuade the Home Secretary of the postwar Labour government, Chuter Ede, to amend the Children's Act of 1948.

Somerset County Council broadened its campaign to the national level with the intention of ridding not only the county but also the country of brown babies. The council sent a letter to each of the sixty-five other county councils seeking their support to put pressure on the Home Office for a change in the law which prevented British children being sent abroad for adoption by those unrelated to them. The letter described how being confronted with 'the problem of coloured children', the county council sought to amend the law and proposed their emigration to America 'for ultimate adoption by coloured families there'. Because Somerset does not allow access to the records of Holnicote House during this period I could find only one response to their letter as reported in the African American press: Derbyshire

The case for permitting the emigration of the children, whose fathers were colored American soldiers stationed in Somerset during the war, was submitted to the Home Secretary [by] five Somerset members of Parliament, says the Somerset County Gazette.

Replying on behalf of the Labour Government, Kenneth Younger, Undersecretary of the State for Home Affairs, let it be known that Chuter Ede, after full consideration [of] the arguments advanced on behalf of the County Council's plan had reached the conclusion that he would not be justified in supporting legislation designed to modify the existing statutory of restrictions ... Any implication there was no place in Britain for the coloured children who had not a normal home life would cause controversy and give offence in some quarters.

George Padmore, *Chicago Defender*, April 23, 1949

Children's Committee supported Somerset's proposal.

George Padmore was vehement in his condemnation of 'the plans of the Children's Committee of the Somerset County Council to get rid of the 31 coloured kids – whom they call 'Pickannies' (sic) – now living in County Council nurseries'. The LCP and the Pan African Federation in Manchester launched protests against their expulsion and Padmore gives them credit for the defeat of the scheme. Instead, the council dispersed its children to orphanages and homes in other parts of the country, a few ending up in the African Churches Mission in Liverpool.

After requisitioning by the Ministry of Health, the Land Agent of The National Trust, the owners of [Holnicote House] reported that members of the Somerset County Council were visiting the property 'aiming at occupation ... in March 1944 ... with the prospect of 40 children and 15 others.' Figures about the numbers of occupants varied, but it appears that between 1944 and 1951, when what was commonly believed and reported as being an orphanage was closed, between fifty-five and ninety children and adult carers resided at Holnicote House, the children being mostly mixed-race children of GIs who had been stationed at Taunton.

Sabine Lee, 'A Forgotten Legacy of the Second World War'

My mother grew up in Somerset and we regularly travelled from London to the village of Huish Episcopi, to visit my grandfather. We would wander after him while he worked in the fields or walk down the lane with him as he held my hand and carried my brother on his shoulders, descending a steep hill into the village. What did the people of Somerset think when they saw us together? Did they think that the brown brother and sister were pickaninnies left behind by mistake, a pair of aberrations the county council had somehow missed?

One person in Somerset wanted brown children and volunteered to foster them. On 31 March 1949, Kathleen Tacchi-Morris, Principal of the International School in the village of North Curry, sat at her desk and composed a letter to Somerset County Council in which she offered to take into her school for 'boarding and a general education', twelve of 'the coloured children' resident in Holnicote House. The day after the Home Office decided not to amend the provisions of the Children's Act of 1948, and announced that the children would not be sent to foster homes in the US, the *Daily Mirror* published a brief article about Tacchi-Morris under the headline 'Let Me Give a Home to 12 Children, She Asks'.

The life of Kathleen Tacchi-Morris is little known outside of certain artistic and radical circles. When she has been written about, details of her own life have been side-lined to give prominence to her associations with the rich and famous. The portrait Tacchi-Morris draws of herself in her autobiographical manuscript is that of a child rebel incensed by the tyranny of compulsive religious instruction and corporal punishment in her school in Acton, London. The socialist and free-thinking world of her father, Percy George Tacchi, one of the early members of the Secular Society, exerted a profound and lasting influence on Tacchi-Morris. Her grandmother financed her life in the dance world of Paris where she trained with Margaret Morris and Emilé Jaques-Dalcroze. After suffering a leg injury, Tacchi-Morris became a dance educator in eurhythmics, a method of experiencing and learning music through movement, and opened her first school in London in the 1930s. She eventually settled in North Curry, Somerset, where she remained for the rest of her life, converting her house and outbuildings into an International School eventually known as Taccomo.

In 2006, I made a journey hoping to discover why this woman offered to adopt twelve of the brown wards of Somerset County Council. I began in the Kathleen Tacchi-Morris Collection, housed in the old Somerset Record Office in Taunton. Now that heritage has become an industry in Britain, the Record Office has been absorbed into the huge steel and glass Somerset Heritage Centre that opened in 2010. I sat at an old desk, on an old chair, both of which smelled of years of attentive care through regular applications of wood oil. The process of uncovering the many layers of racism and inhumanity aimed at the black British babies born in Somerset after the war had left me disgruntled and jaded. As I sat sun streamed through windows and coastal walks beckoned. I wondered why I was persisting searching the archives for material that distressed me. What I had learnt about Tacchi-Morris before I visited the archives led me to expect that her offer to adopt the brown babies was a shallow gesture of British upper-class paternalism. She was a woman who had lived among a European elite, rubbing shoulders in Antibes with the Duke and Duchess of Windsor, notorious Nazi sympathizers, after the abdication in 1936.

Reluctantly, I opened the first of many folders and had to dramatically revise my assessment. The first item in the folder was a pamphlet by the black American stage and film actor, concert artist and left-wing activist, Paul Robeson, entitled 'The Negro People and the Soviet Union', published in 1950. Not at all what I expected to find, and the first indication of the direction of Kathleen Tacchi-Morris's political sympathies. Behind the Robeson pamphlet was a copy of Sylvia McNeill's 'Illegitimate Children Born in Britain of English Mothers and Coloured Americans', the survey she completed for the LCP in 1945. The next document was an application form to apply for membership in the LCP. Brochures and a prospectus for her school, 'What is Taccomo?', were followed by extensive correspondence with M. Joseph-Mitchell, General and Travelling Secretary for the LCP. The letters revealed Tacchi-Morris's many attempts to arrange for Joseph-Mitchell to address various organizations and clubs in the area. He lectured in Taunton in May 1949, on the subject of world unity, and subsequently in October at the school, where he talked about 'coloured youth'. Tacchi-Morris's commitment to education was evidently not limited to the children in her care but extended to the anti-racist education of her Somerset neighbours.

Tacchi-Morris sought Joseph-Mitchell's support in her campaign to care for and educate twelve of the black children in Holnicote, support he was eager to provide, though Somerset County Council rejected his recommendation of Tacchi-Morris. The council members only wanted to ask him if he knew of potential homes outside of the county. It was heart-breaking to read the exchange of letters between Tacchi-Morris and the council. She was clearly unaware of the council's real intentions, nor did she realize that its members would not give any serious consideration to her plans to offer the children a general education free of charge, 'including piano, music and riding', languages, and opportunities to stay in Italy and France in the summers, if the council would just agree to pay for their board, costs they already expended on the care of the children in Holnicote.

The rejection took two months and two brief bureaucratic letters. The first response was from Harold King, Clerk of the County Council, who stated that the Children's Committee would consider her offer with the proviso that it was 'unlikely to arrive at any early decision'. For this reason, King felt it would be premature to act on her suggestion that they inspect the school. Tacchi-Morris offered to go to the council offices to meet the committee but no inspection or meeting was pursued by members of the council. The second letter stated, 'the Children's Committee have decided that as the Council were not successful in obtaining amending legislation to enable the children to go to private families in America to be adopted . . . they will be admitted to Children's Home under the control of the Children's Committee'. In other words, the children were to remain within the unwelcoming embrace and under the control of Celia Bangham.

Joseph-Mitchell summarized the rejection in a letter to Tacchi-Morris, finding it 'both surprising and strange to read the Council's letter because, while regret has been expressed at their inability to allow you to have the children, they have written to me to question the bona fides of another applicant. It is therefore clear that the intention is to have Coloured "Trotters" out of Somerset altogether.' Tacchi-Morris then applied to become a foster parent but this was also denied.

Despite her failures with Somerset County Council, black children found their way to a place at the International School through referrals from the LCP and from women who wrote to her directly, and the LCP made continued efforts to support them. In her unpublished autobiography, Tacchi-Morris talks about 'children of white mothers and black British soldiers from African and other colonies', evacuees who were being housed in a camp in Dorset, 'very small children, up to about four years old', the youngest being 'Johnnie, the seven month child of an Indian mother'. She described how she housed thirty-four of these children during the war, in addition to 'blitz victims' and many refugees. I found no records of black children being kept in a Dorset camp but there is an undated, handwritten note in the Tacchi-Morris files, 'heard from Negro child, ck Dorset Camp, Miss P. Blackwell'. There is also a letter dated 3 June 1949, from Tacchi-Morris to The Health Officer, County Hall Taunton, which states, 'Dear Sir, A little half Jamaican boy aged 4 1/2 name "Tony Blackwell", joined the school this week. The mother's address is 17B Mormal Road Bovington Camp Dorset.' Bovington Camp is a British Army base which, together with Lulworth Camp forms the Bovington Garrison, a centre for training in armoured warfare. T. E. Lawrence, imperialist adventurer and officer in Military Intelligence, trained there in the 1920s and died there in 1935. Though Mormal Road no longer exists it is clearly marked on the map of 1930 as being part of the Bovington Camp.

Rachel Fleming and Muriel E. Fletcher wielded the differential calculus of racial thought to capture and calculate an essential difference that made black children into aberrations in the national landscape. Tacchi-Morris was an internationalist who regarded *all* children as future world citizens. The educational philosophy of Taccomo was internationalism, the bringing together of 'children and students from all countries ... to develop a world outlook'. 'Intercommunication and co-operation', she believed, 'develops tolerance and international understanding.' Taccomo's pedagogy built upon an intellectual foundation free from religious dogma and punishment, integrating body and mind and enabling expression through the arts, drama, music and ballet.

In a letter to Joseph-Mitchell in November 1949, after thanking him for recommending her and the school, Tacchi-Morris reported that three more black children were arriving, the parent of one of whom, a singer, was able to pay the full fees. I had to smile when I read the conclusion to her letter: 'in the Kindergarten House, the colour will be fifty-fifty now – enough to frighten off everybody in Taunton'.

Half-Caste

I went to Holnicote House in the village of Seaworthy, Somerset, to where the seven children sat on the lawn to be photographed by *Life* magazine. The Holnicote Estate belongs to the National Trust, who lease the house to HF Holidays to run as a hotel. The estate extends across 12,000 acres of Exmoor National Park. I thought that if I pretended to be a holidaymaker perhaps I would blend in, but Holnicote House so unsettled me that I was pacing to and fro and muttering. No one took any notice of my behaviour but I questioned my motives for the visit. Did I want to pay homage or was I simply curious?

I am intimately tied to the seven children through the girl that I was. We are joined by what our bodies represented to the British public and the state in 1948; that intimate connection has been cemented at each moment when our right to belong was contested. On the lawn of Holnicote House, I felt the folding of space and time as I became both an adult and a small brown child. When I stared at a photograph of the two-year-old girl that bore my name I also saw the girl in the polka-dot dress, with a neat white collar, sandals on her feet, clutching tightly to her books. I not only recognized but also felt her tight grip on to her books and the worlds within them.

The contradictions that arose in the encounter between black and white appeared resolved when the transgressive bodies of their offspring, categorized as 'half-caste', were rejected. Narratives of racialized subjects in the 1940s and '50s wove complex sets of beliefs about gender, class, race and sex into an apparently coherent story. The British counterpart of *Life* magazine, *Picture Post*, is a particularly rich source of these images as it translated the global into the local frame of Britishness, depicting what belonging meant. In the immediate postwar years, when it was evident to the world that the United States was the dominant political and economic force, there was deep anxiety in Britain about empire, about what would constitute Britishness within the terms of empire, about what values it did, or could, or should embody. The *Picture Post* revealed the cracks, fissures and contradictions of this project.

Images of Britain's post-war 'coloured' citizens appeared in this context. Black Britons appeared as outsiders, colonial subjects and migrants, but never as belonging to the nation. Next to the girl in the polka-dot dress I place the family photograph of the two-year-old girl. I am still trying to measure the sway of affiliation and estrangement.

The girl is two years old, a young black British subject standing in the back garden of the bomb-damaged house in Streatham in South London. There is nothing unusual about this photograph, a typical family photo in a typical London back yard – small, with a fence, flowers, weeds and a stone path. Her dress was made by her mother and has the smocking and gathered sleeves fashionable in 1950; her socks and shoes are clean and bright. She was obviously dressed for the camera, not for play; she is looking at her father. The photograph was taken for others to view, to be sent to Jamaica, to be mailed to Wales, to be seen and admired by relatives who spoke the girl's name. I too speak the girl's name as I sit at my desk in North America and wonder about her expression – do I see a frown? I place the family snapshot between the girl in the polka-dot dress and the *Picture Post*'s 1948 image of 'The Lonely Piccaninny', with the caption 'so small and defenceless, so waiting to be comforted'.

The young girl in the *Picture Post* image was located nowhere, a blank white space emphasizing her lack of affiliation and dislocating her from time and place and from the community looking at her. She is merely 'the body which is not ours'. There is no possibility of imaginative attachment. Erwin Blumenfeld, the photographer, delighted in contrivance. His 'photographic

setups were composed with infinite care . . . In
the arrangements and then again in the dark-
room, he went to such lengths that it can be
almost impossible to tell how the picture was
made, and the contrivance occasionally overshadows the subject.'

Looking at 'The Lonely Piccaninny', I asked
myself what caused that girl such distress and
made her look so miserable. Was the photograph taken against a blank studio wall, or in a
location that that was subsequently erased?
Was the misery caused by the photographer?
What meanings did the photograph carry for the editors of
Picture Post in the context of Britain in April 1948, and the raging
controversy over 'Brown Babies?' Why did they publish it?

Absent from the pages of *Ebony*, *Life*, *The Chicago Defender*,
The Pittsburgh Courier, *Newsweek*, *The Daily Mirror*, *The
Picture Post*, the newsletters and reports of the League of
Coloured Peoples, the surveys of McNeill, Fleming and Fletcher
– absent from the thousands of words written about black
British children who were the subjects of the 'Brown Babies'
moral panic – were the local and particular details of their past
and present which would have granted these children autonomy. These children were not cases, they were not an aggrega-
tion of numbers to be calculated, they were not problems to be
surmounted, they were not impediments to the growth of a
harmonious community. They were children.

Between 1947 and 1948, St. Clair Drake undertook an
impressive amount of meticulous research, conducted interviews, made lasting contacts with Pan-Africanists, and dove into
the files of the League of Coloured Peoples, although he did not
use all the material he found there. If film directors bemoan how
much of their creative work is left on the cutting-room floor, I
wonder if Drake felt a pang of regret over the stories of the children that he did not incorporate into his dissertation.

In Drake's papers, my research assistant, Zach, found a brown
envelope. Carefully tucked away inside were a series of index

cards stapled together. These cards are transcriptions of the LCP case files of the 'brown babies' referred to them, except, of course, they are not anonymous 'brown babies'. They are Dennis, Mary Anne, Marguerite, Keith, Alex, Janet, Raymond and Wendy. In the cards are accounts of their mothers' struggles to find employment – 'I find no one seems to want to employ a girl who has a coloured baby [with] her' – and of insults they faced in the workplace: 'The news that ******* has a coloured child has spread, and this girl is constantly taunted, and has, on occasion, had to leave her employment because of the unpleasant remarks that have been spoken and because of writing on coatroom walls.' There are also accounts of women facing not only job discrimination but also housing discrimination and eviction because of their black child.

The cards hold the precious records of women battling the hostility of their families: a daughter devoted to her son, 'but parents say don't bring him home to Cambridge. Both must leave home'; or whose partners will not tolerate a black child. 'I am sorry that I do not want the child because I am getting married soon and the Boy that I am marrying would not like the child to live with us – not only that but we would not be able to get lodgings with it.' 'I know Dorothy loves Wendy and it will be more than difficult for her to part with the child. On the other hand she realizes that she cannot expect that the man she marries will take this little girl.' 'Raymond is breaking up family . . . letter is from sister who says she has got a very nice boyfriend with whom been going out for 18 mos. He wants to get married but will not have Raymond which is natural.' Some face the hostility of the social services: the mother 'wanted to marry Negro but was talked out of it by social worker'.

There are also statements from women seeking assistance but who 'have no intention of letting baby go' and who 'adore' their child. There are histories of the fathers in the United States who paid for their children to join them and of women with children whose fathers were lost or killed in action but who found loving men willing to care for them and the children: 'now there is no need for a home for Terry as I married a Jamaican airman last

October and he thinks the world of both my kiddies. In fact we are only waiting for a passage to Jamaica to join him.'

The women in these records came from everywhere; there were nurses, factory workers and domestics, and one was a BBC announcer. They range from the well-educated to the poorly educated; from being 'well off' to having so few resources they cannot afford to send a photograph of the child. They came from counties all over Britain, from small villages and from large towns and cities: Bournemouth, Bristol, Bury St Edmunds, Burton-on-Trent, Cornwall, Devon, Dorset, Cambridge, Fife in Scotland, Kent, London, Lancashire, Leicester, Reading, Southampton and Yorkshire.

... it appears to my committee that Mr. and Mrs. ***** are prompted by the highest possible motives in offering to adopt Sandra, they, the Committee, are nevertheless of the opinion that the general circumstances and environment of the home are not such as would ensure that a coloured child could be placed there with safety and in the best interests for her happiness. My Committee feel that they would only be able to consider the adoption of the coloured children in their care by coloured people in reasonably good circumstances, although they appreciate the considerable difficulty which may be encountered in finding such people. You will appreciate I am sure that in taking this attitude my Committee are prompted only by their desire to ensure the happiness and security of the child.

Director of Public Assistance,
Leicester County Council to LCP

When Zach sent me these cards he warned me that the information they contained was 'intense, amazing, and frustrating'. Despite his warning, I was not prepared for reading them and not for the first time in this project I cried.

I remember being the girl who located herself with photographs. Her parents took them out of a red shoe box stored on the top shelf of the wardrobe and used them to tell her stories, ensuring that she would not be huddled against a blank wall. There were pictures of her Jamaican father in his RAF uniform; pictures of her parents with and without her; pictures of her Jamaican relatives, over for a visit; pictures of her Welsh relatives and English grandparents; and pictures of her alone or, later, with her baby brother.

That girl longed for transformation. When she went to ballet school she fell in love with dance and dreamt of becoming an ethereal being floating across a stage in a blue tutu. For reasons forgotten long ago, it had to be the palest of blue, ice blue. I rummaged around in the tattered boxes to find photographs of the dancing girl and encountered her costumed. Costuming made it possible to inhabit multiple racialized bodies, yet exposed the tension that maintained the space between black and white.

When the girl was selected for a solo performance in her ballet school's first public concert at a London theatre, her parents seemed very proud of her. They had a photograph taken by a professional photographer, an extravagance they could ill afford. The girl was blissfully unaware of what I came to realize many years later: the solo performance ensured that her dark presence did not interrupt the homogeneity of the corps de ballet. There wasn't anywhere for her *to be* in the ballet company. Did the girl's parents understand that?

In the photograph the girl is dressed for her first solo not in a blue tutu but in a gypsy costume, unruly black curls pushing out from under a head wrap, gold bangle earrings, rows and rows of beads cascading down the bodice and wide flowing skirt that she is holding with her left hand to show-off its rows of multi-coloured ribbons to their best advantage. The girl's right hand clutches a tambourine that she shook in rhythmic accord with the movements that her dance teachers had taught her to perform with just the right element of abandon.

How odd and yet how appropriate to cast that girl as the gypsy: an ethnicity that referenced a rootlessness in contrast to the rootedness of Englishness. This rootlessness meant that she could be an oddity while explainable, a temporary aberration. Travellers, who were referred to as 'gypsies', used to pass regu-larly through their district in South London and were dispar-aged by neighbours as an exotic, mysterious, irritating and potentially dangerous presence; a presence here today but, they hoped, gone tomorrow. How appropriate that the same gypsy costume could be recycled as the child's entrée to the street party held in celebration of the coronation of Queen Elizabeth II. This child could be in England but not of it.

For her next solo the girl's dreams of a blue tutu dissolved into a grass skirt, a garland of papier-mâché flowers around her neck and one wrist, a flower tucked behind one ear. The child was a 'hula, hula girl', sensuously weaving her way across the stage with the voices of her teachers urging her to 'shake those hips, shake those hips', ringing in her ears.

As Anne Anlin Cheng has argued, 'racial signification has always come into its fullest play precisely at the intersection between materiality and fantasy, between history and memory. At these intersections', she continues, 'the racial body acquires its most prominent outlines – and requires its greatest camou-flage.' The girl's many camouflages, which reproduced the instructions supplied by the dance teachers, were created by her mother in the time between working two jobs, one by day and another at night.

Perhaps as she sewed Iris imagined that costumes would provide armour against the constant taunts of 'nigger'. Though Iris denied that her daughter was black, when she measured, tucked and pulled these costumes into the shape of the girl's body I think she was trying through her dressmaking to make the girl fit into the society in which they lived. One bitter winter's day mother and daughter drove all the way to Brighton, about sixty miles each way, to collect a custom-made pale blue tutu.

At ballet school the girl's closest friends came up with a plan to fit this aberration into British history, their way. Why did she have to insist on being West Indian, they asked? Giggling with satisfied delight, they concluded she could say she was Persian. While not one of them was Persian, or of Persian ancestry, or even knew where on the classroom globe Persia could be found, Persian was somehow conjured up from the little they knew of Britain's imperial history. Persian gave their friend a useable past, the right balance of rationality, a satisfactory re-reading of her otherwise objectionable features. It was offered as a gift that could counteract an unacceptable racial narrative that her colour threatened to betray.

Part Three

Dead Reckoning

dead reckoning, n.
The estimation of a ship's position from the distance run by the
log and the courses steered by the compass, with corrections for
current, leeway, etc., but without astronomical observations.

OED

The human mind when it sails by dead reckoning . . . will some-
times bring up in very strange latitudes.

J. R. Lowell, *Witchcraft*

He felt invaded by a dread of home.

Peter Matthiessen, *Shadow Country*

HOME

The Moth

On the stage the girl delighted in the variety of costumes she wore because they allowed her to dance multiple personas. She would slip one over her head, perform her part, then discard it in favour of another; she was circumspect when her friends urged that she renounce ambiguity in favour of fixing her genealogy to an alternative imperial dynasty. At home she refused the racial narrative Iris tried to impose to bring her body into alignment with her middle name, Veronica.

Iris was first captivated by moving pictures when she was a teenager in Somerset, playing the piano accompaniment to silent films in a village theatre. Sitting in the dark of the Gaumont Cinema in Worcester after the newsreels and propaganda shorts finished, Iris and her girlfriends from the Air Ministry could put aside the brutality and anxiety of war for ninety minutes and be drawn into the romance and mystery offered by Hollywood. Of all the female stars she saw on the screen it was the American actress Veronica Lake that held Iris spellbound.

The girl's first name, Hazel, was shared with Iris's best friend during the war. The girl did not know what this other Hazel looked like, but her mother kept copies of film magazines from the 1940s and showed her photographs of Veronica Lake. The girl scrutinized the images because her mother thought Veronica Lake was the epitome of female beauty. It was obvious how Iris tried to model herself on her.

The girl saw the exact shape of

Memoirs are stories of redemption.
Zia Haider Rahman

III

her mother's plucked and pencilled eyebrows on the face of Veronica Lake and she understood why her mother glued long lashes to her eyelids each morning. At night Iris used black hair grips to create waves or slept with a variety of metal clamps or rollers on her head so that in the morning tresses would ripple down the side of her face and caress her cheek. The only difference in hair style that the girl could see was that her mother parted her brown hair on the opposite side. I remember how intently the girl stared at these pictures and can feel her heart contract, for while the girl understood that her mother wished to be seen as a sultry beauty ready for a life of romance, it was she who carried the name Veronica and yet could not recognize any part of herself in this blonde, blue-eyed movie star.

Hair was the cause of just one of the many struggles between mother and daughter. Iris sought to corral her daughter's hair into a form it resisted. She insisted the girl cultivate very long hair and would hover by the elbow of the local hairdresser to make sure no more was cut off than was necessary to eliminate dead ends. The mother's hair was fine and could be moulded to any shape; the daughter's hair was curly and thick and became frizzy in damp air. It was always damp in London it seemed. The girl's hair deliberately thwarted her mother's ambitions; the longer it grew the more uncontrollable it became. An aunt was recruited to tame it, shaping it into long corkscrew locks called ringlets, and the girl had to sit for hours while warm oil was applied and rags wound to hold each lock in place. The aunt despaired when the girl's hair unwound and returned to its undisciplined self. The school asked Iris to make her daughter's wild hair neater in appearance, so it was braided into two tight plaits out of which unruly strands would coil by mid-morning.

Romance eluded Iris on every front. Disappointment replaced possibility and eventually became despair. A large part of what it meant to be a child of empire was being a spectator as her parents' marriage was destroyed by the stomach-churning, acidic tides of racism. Perhaps, if Iris and

Memory ... often strikes me as a kind of dumbness. It makes one's head heavy and giddy, as if one were not looking back down the receding perspectives of time but rather down on the earth from a great height, from one of those towers whose tops are lost to view in the clouds.

W. G. Sebald, *The Emigrants*

Carl had been middle class and wealthy, the corrosion of ignorance and prejudice would have affected them less. Perhaps. In
South London, amid the racial tensions and anxieties of a postwar Britain, an acid rain fell on their interracial parade, replac-
ing affection with bitter resentment.

The relationship between Iris and Carl was not a romantic
union but a step into purgatory. The result of crossing the line of
acceptable British conduct and breaking racial and sexual
taboos was not a process of magnetic fusion but a violent repul-
sion by which they became bound in mutual emotional isolation. The force of public antagonism turned their domestic
realm into a zone of intolerable pressure, constant nagging,
intimidation and harassment. They met as strangers, and the
practices and prejudices of the British social order ensured they
remained estranged throughout the years of marriage and
parenting.

The two children, brother and sister, navigated their way
around, through and over the currents of extreme violence that
hardened into a core of alienation between their parents. They
feared the night when one or the other of them tumbled, or was
pulled, into the vortex of their parents' wrath. When their
parents were spent, the children were left to drag themselves out
of the ashes alone. At first, I try to locate them with an academic
compass attracted by the lure of revelation, the hope of harvesting knowledge from the bleak years of the British postwar
world. But it is impossible to create reason out of unreason in
such intemperate latitudes.

Finding my way into and through the lives of Iris and Carl is
less like the work of academic detection, assembling details into
a recognizable pattern of events with discernible causes and
effects, and more like the instinct of a moth flying toward the
open flame of their resentments. Virginia Woolf, watching a
moth fluttering from side to side across a square of window
pane, mistakenly imagined that 'it was as if someone had taken
a tiny bead of pure life and decking it as lightly as possible with
down and feathers, had set it dancing and zig-zagging to show
us the true nature of life'. When the moth fell on its back she

reached out a pencil to help it right itself but laid it down when she recognized the approach of death. Like Woolf I have to confront the fear that the fluttering of this 'frail and diminutive body' to find its way beyond the glass is futile and doomed to fail.

All moths are convinced of their invulnerability; they do not deviate when they feel heat, they do not hesitate as they head into the flame. I have to reckon with the dead.

The Bathroom

The mother held the girl at arm's length, using her, as usual, as body armour to protect herself. A fist punched through the glass in the bathroom door. Time stuttered and stalled. Sound muted. Struggling to free herself the girl found she could not escape her mother's iron grip. While the storm of voices raging over her head became an incoherent and distant babel, the fury contorting her mother's face intensified, sharpened, imprinting what she did not want to remember into the back of her mind. The girl stared at a mouth, lips teeth tongue working rapidly to shape sounds she could no longer distinguish as words.

The air over the girl's head glistened white and pink, crystals caught in the bleak light of the small bathroom, crystals became flakes, flakes turned into slivers, slivers transformed into shards and the shards pierced her, not the shards she could see falling either side of her onto the floor but the ones she could not see, the ones she could only imagine were shards as they drove through layers of skin on her back, their acceleration slowing as they met resistance from muscle, gristle and, ultimately, bone.

Then there was blood. Then sound returned and there was screaming.

The Kitchen

It was in Iris's kitchen that the girl first encountered the dead and felt the longing of the living to be among them. She had not known anyone who had died, had not stared into clouded eyes, nor touched cooling and stiffening limbs, but being born in the aftermath of the Second World War meant that the presence of death permeated the girl's childhood. The landscape was pockmarked with the residue of aerial bombardment, the minds of the adults around this girl were scarred by knowledge of death by war

In this place, archaeology was not a science, nor a search for the actual, nor a painstaking catalogue of parts and bone fragments, but an art of memory and this, I thought, is how legends have been, and will always be, edited – not by saying them, but by unsettling one layer of meaning from another and another ...

Eavan Boland, *Domestic Violence*

and its social and emotional geography was mapped in their stories. And yet, the event that had wounded Iris most deeply, the death of her mother, Beatrice, preceded the war. Beatrice was resurrected in her kitchen. Iris reserved the story of Beatrice's protracted death for the girl because the story delineated the intimate contours of a model mother and daughter relationship. Beatrice's dying established the expectations for the sort of daughter for which Iris yearned.

I exhume descriptions of Beatrice's dying from beneath my own witnessing of a long, protracted dying which was not yet death. My mother suffered from Parkinson's disease. When her dopamine-producing brain cells progressively disintegrated, her body curled into itself and assumed the symptomatic posture of the affliction: then she crept rather than walked into her kitchen. Iris haunts my kitchen still.

I unsettled sedimented memories as Iris forgot. Her memories faded and the pain associated with them diminished, while I reached to capture both in a net of words. Iris would not have wished her memories preserved in this kind of literary taxidermy, stuffing the immutable into a skin of text. She held firmly to a fixed, perhaps rigid, set of ideas that gave her life meaning. What I create no more resembles those ideas than a moth sees itself as a specimen pinned to a tray in the drawer of a museum cabinet, stainless steel piercing its thorax.

The girl was the sole audience for her mother's stories but she felt as if Iris was talking to a different daughter in the kitchen, the daughter who fulfilled her ideal of the perfect daughter. Iris became animated plucking strands from her blanket of the past and worrying its torn threads with a longing rooted in melancholia. She measured and weighed the value of her postwar life with her husband and offspring, comparing it to the possibilities that life had promised when she was single, before she met Carl and bore children. Her calculations always resolved into the same unforgiving equation: she would be better off dead. The girl was reared in a kitchen haunted by ghosts of a still-born future.

I deliberately associate the kitchen with my mother's malaise to avoid remembering my father lying unconscious on its linoleum floor. The rectangular blue and white room had a counter running down the left wall which ended at the pantry. Tucked underneath were cupboards and a twin-tub Hoover washing machine. Three or four steps took you from the front hall, past the refrigerator, stove and cupboards on the right, to the kitchen sink and the back door. Because each item occupied an allotted space it qualified as modern for a working-class terraced home in late 1950s Britain.

When the estate agent showed my mother the house, sensing a potential buyer, he would have used the word 'compact' to describe the kitchen. He would have deftly stood aside and ushered her in through the doorway to stand alone, while he kept her two children at bay in the hall. The estate agent would not have wanted to demonstrate, by his or the children's presence, that two people could not walk, or work, in the kitchen without getting in each other's way. In my mother's kitchen the arc of a cupboard door ended in the back of a knee, an elbow thrust into a spine when a dish was pulled from a shelf, an unanticipated turn toward the sink with a saucepan full of hot liquid threatened disaster. It was not a place to linger for leisure or pleasure; if you entered the kitchen for any reason other than to work in it, you were 'a hindrance', 'in the way', 'underfoot'. I remember the kitchen as a space of tension and antagonism, a cage, a site of struggle.

My father enjoyed cooking. When the girl was young enough to be lifted up to perch on a stool, he took pleasure in preparing Jamaican dishes and sharing them with his daughter. This food they ate together in the kitchen, not in the dining room where meals were usually served. Iris disapproved of Carl's cooking and wouldn't eat Jamaican food herself, but the girl devoured her father's curries, fried rice or banana fritters and drank his homemade ginger beer, flavours, spices and textures more tantalizing than boiled vegetables and the mush that was served at school. I am sure the girl found a certain pleasure in the intrusion into the kitchen, eating so eagerly from her father's hand precisely because it had the allure of defiance.

Eventually the kitchen became a domain ruled by Iris. She created a 'home' in which Carl was an unwelcome presence. Consequently, he did all he could to make himself disappear. Later in life, Carl was found in the kitchen stretched out with his head in the gas oven and the gas taps turned full on. Subsequently, he obediently entered the kitchen only when told to assist in the preparation of traditionally English meals and to do the washing up. Jamaican food disappeared from both our lives.

The choice of the kitchen as the location for my father's attempted suicide does not appear to me to be spontaneous or arbitrary but a concession at the site of his defeat. I was away at college but I can imagine how my father laid himself down on the floor gently, crying, and served himself up as a sacrifice on the altar of my mother's oven: a sacrifice for a woman for whom sacrifice was a way of being in the world. Sacrifice was Iris's shield and her most effective weapon.

The girl tried to be a well-behaved daughter but she was often described as having her head in the clouds. It must have been frustrating to have to raise a girl who preferred to live in her own imaginary world rather than the world of her parents. Her mother accused her daughter of not listening to her, which was partly true, and of being thoughtless, which was inaccurate: the girl was thinking all the time, just not about what she was supposed to be paying attention to. A reprimand from Iris for an act of childish neglect like forgetting to remove every item of school uniform before climbing a tree, or messing around on the common collecting tadpoles from a pond, or hiding a hedgehog in her bed, rapidly deviated from the circumstances of the actual offence and became a tirade about her having to sacrifice her career in order to marry and sacrifice her life working at jobs she hated in order to raise children.

When Iris worked in the local Smith Meters factory she, like all the other women on the assembly line, was bullied and harassed by male foremen. When she went to evening classes to learn shorthand and typing she imagined that work in offices would improve not only her income but also her quality of life. The various secretarial positions she held disabused her of this hope. When her male bosses realized how smart Iris was they extended the hours they spent in the pub or on the golf course while she ran their department or business for no increase in pay or respect. Iris found that the personal in personal secretary meant that she was expected to manage many aspects of the domestic life of her boss, purchasing birthday and holiday gifts for his children and sexual partners while also arranging travel and hotel arrangements to enable extramarital affairs. She could run an office efficiently as long as she was willing to be humiliated – male gratitude for her work was expressed through suggestive compliments on her legs as she took dictation, or unwelcome touching of her body as she passed her boss in the hall or when he stood over her at her desk.

If Iris had no control over her life at work she tried to control all aspects of life within the walls of her house. Like other working women of her generation, when she returned home from the factory or office the demands of child care and domestic labour were waiting for her. Iris was tired and angry about being exploited even before she opened the door to a home she felt was occupied by a neglectful husband and ungrateful children. The slightest dispute over what had or had not been done led Iris onto a pathway of escalating recriminations that always culminated in a litany of the sacrifices she had made in her life, sacrifices from which only they benefited. Iris believed her husband and her children grew strong from her suffering.

In my academic life as a black feminist I have taken great pleasure in reading and teaching Paule Marshall's essay, 'Poets in the Kitchen', and Alice Childress's novel, *Like One of the Family*, texts which represent kitchens as places of nurturance, strength and creative inspiration as well as sites of resistance. For many African American women novelists and poets, kitchens generate shared memories and intimate exchanges between and among women and their daughters. I salute when walls of convention, circumscribing how women's lives can be represented, are breached by these talented black female wordsmiths. I support and admire projects to reclaim, reconstruct and rehabilitate spaces of domesticity as sites of female power. But I find kitchens to be troubled and troubling spaces.

Looking backwards to see myself as a young girl, rather than as the teacher I became, I am unable to describe kitchens as sources for creativity and inspiration. Paule Marshall is able to situate her childhood kitchen as a 'wordshop' and trace a line directly from the kitchen to the neighbourhood library. She graduates from the spoken to the written word, from being a listener to becoming a reader and, eventually, a creative writer who can claim that women-talk in her childhood kitchen was her first lesson in narration.

The girl also found her way to the library, from the spoken to the written word, from absorbing stories to writing them, but her route was an escape: she was a fugitive. This girl was desperate to leave behind what she heard and eager to forget what she saw: she hungered for alternative worlds. Her mother's words were a weight, in her presence the girl became inarticulate, which makes it impossible for me to recover kitchens as a source of creative friction.

I fold two separate kitchens into one memory – they were indistinguishable for the girl. The first house was in Streatham, London, the second just a mile or so away across the county line in Mitcham, Surrey. Both houses were terraced and belonged to housing stock built between 1938 and 1939. The war immediately halted any further building, other than the rapid construction of the air-raid shelters which sat outside of both kitchen doors. Both houses were of similar design – the front door and hall led straight to the kitchen – front and rear doors were directly opposite each other. In wintry weather a powerful cold draft swept through the house. In the summer, opening one of these doors when the other was already open, even just a crack, caused either or both to slam shut suddenly, with a crash that shook the house and vibrated in our bones. Doors were always slamming, though the cause was not always the wind. Each kitchen, in Streatham and in Mitcham, was cramped, suffocating, oppressive. When the girl had to work in the kitchen her mother would declare that kitchens (and houses) were (badly) designed by men and that women, who had to work in these spaces, would have designed them very differently. As I remember these kitchens as one kitchen, I also conflate myriad kitchen tasks into one task – washing laundry.

Iris hated working in the factory; having been a civil servant she felt ashamed, as diminished in status as being a domestic servant. So she found a baby sitter because Carl was always out, and enrolled in evening classes to 'better' herself. There she learnt Pitman's shorthand and typing, the postwar skills necessary for women to enter the white-collar world of offices, as secretaries since the managerial ranks were reserved for men. As a modern mother, working night and day, Iris needed labour-saving machines because being a 'modern' woman meant holding multiple jobs inside and outside of the household. As a modern mother she also required a daughter to labour alongside her.

Strict controls on hire purchase, instituted in the years immediately after the war, were temporarily lifted for seven months in 1954 and sales of washing machines rose dramatically. I cannot remember a time without one and believe we must have been among the 20 per cent of households in the UK in 1956 that had a washing machine in the kitchen. I hesitate to say that Iris owned it, because she saved up for the deposit and then grasped the opportunity of easy credit. In anticipation Iris waltzed her infant son and the girl to the store in Croydon to purchase her first washing machine and then had to drag them home after she was told that hire purchase forms required her husband's signature: all women needed a man's signature on application forms to be granted credit. In the 1950s and early '60s Iris bought many 'labour-saving' appliances on hire purchase. She became so mired in debt that she was eventually arrested and detained in jail. It fell to her teenage daughter to bail her out.

Premier among these appliances was the washing machine. In 1948, the American company Hoover opened a manufacturing plant in Pentrebach, Merthyr Tydfil, South Wales which was declared 'A triumph of vision, enterprise, faith, courage and work.' Two years later the factory received royal blessing with a visit from Princess Margaret. The washing machine promised to take care of the soiled clothes, bed linen and nappies produced by two young children in the privacy of the domestic realm. In dour, postwar Britain, washing machines were promoted not only as modern labour-saving devices, promising women that 'wash-day drudgery was gone forever', but were presented as sources of mutual joy for mothers and daughters.

Standing on each side of the washing machine in spacious kitchens, a mother and daughter beamed at each other from the pages of newspapers and magazines: in one advert, the daughter plays contentedly on the floor with her dolls; in another, a girl smiles beatifically at her spotlessly clean sweater. These images promoted a vision of North America as the epitome of a utopian modernity to British purchasers. Iris worshiped the USA because she was convinced that it was the Americans who had saved Britain from Hitler. I think she also imagined that along with her modern American Hoover washing machine, assembled in Wales, she would acquire a modern, contented, admiring daughter.

The girl was not in the kitchen to play, nor was there any room on the kitchen floor for her to sit with dolls. Mother and daughter would stand on either side of the machine: the girl's place was between the washer and the kitchen sink. While her mother sorted laundry and placed items in the tub it was the girl's task to attach the rubber pipes to the hot and cold taps in order to fill the machine with water. After items had been washed, she pushed and pulled them through the rollers of the wringer, being careful to compress laundry rather than crush fingers, and to avoid spilling water onto

the linoleum floor. The wet laundry was very heavy and had to be lifted in copious armfuls up to the wringer and pushed and pulled through multiple times. Then the procedure was repeated after rinsing. Finally, each load had to be picked up and placed into a laundry basket. The girl had to push the machine aside with her hip, so she could negotiate her way around it and have room to open the back door. As she carried the laundry outside and hung it on the washing line she prayed it wouldn't rain. When the girl returned to the kitchen her mother had another load washing and the cycle began again. At no stage of the process did this feel like a labour-saving device.

Washing machine technology evolved and Iris acquired a twin-tub Hoover. Gleaming white and blue, this washing machine was lower, longer and narrower than its predecessor and had a spin-dryer next to the washing compartment. Accommodating this larger machine in a small, narrow kitchen caused much aggravation: cupboards had to be removed so that the twin-tub could nestle under the counter. The washer and spinner had to be accessed from the top, so the girl still had to pull it out from under the counter and drag it across the kitchen to attach its pipes to the sink.

The girl despised the washing machine. It was a barrier: it denied access to the back door; to the gooseberry bushes and the earwigs that lived between the roots; to the pear tree in blossom at the bottom of the garden next to the gate; to an exit from suffocating domesticity. The back alley passed between the tall fences and garages at the rear of all the houses so the girl was well hidden from view as she ran down her avenue to the outside world, to the pathways across Mitcham Common, to the ponds and the library. I despise doing laundry to this day, even though I no longer have to drag, pull and push machines out of and back into spaces too tight for them to fit with ease.

The girl did not live up to the advertised promise of the contented daughter. When doing laundry, she knew that men always had something much more interesting to do: her father was probably playing cricket and her brother was either in his playpen with his toys, with the next door neighbours or, when he was older, out with his friends on his bicycle. She figured that if men didn't do laundry why should she? Her truculence about washing prompted Iris to describe what laundry days were like before the war. These were stories of the women in her family.

Through my mother's stories I learnt of how arduous laundry was for my grandmother in the 1920s and early '30s in Somerset, and then of laundry days in the house where Iris lived with her aunts and unmarried female cousins in South Wales after she left domestic service. Upon reflection, I think the girl was supposed to feel grateful that doing the laundry was so much easier for her than for the generations of women who preceded her. I have never felt the least bit grateful.

Being modern also meant that the girl and her mother washed laundry whenever they could; on Saturdays, after the morning shopping expedition if the weather was fine, or on Sundays, or on a weekday evening. Dirty laundry threatened to disrupt all other plans; it crouched in wardrobes and baskets ready to spoil any fine weather. In Iris's youth, Monday was traditionally laundry day, which the girl thought was a good idea: a designated day meant it didn't sneak up, surprise anyone and ruin plans. Of course, living modern lives meant that on Mondays, modern mothers were out of the house earning wages. In contrast, in South Wales before the war, Monday laundry was a communal affair, involving labour but laughter too: women sweating over tubs full of soaking dungarees worn by the men of the family who worked on the Great Western Railroad. Wives and daughters bent their backs, rubbing stains from the tough fabric, turning and gently swirling the more delicate materials of their dresses and petticoats in large tubs.

In Somerset, in the 1920s and early '30s when Iris was a girl, it was her mother, Beatrice, who washed away the sweat, soil and shit of agricultural labour from her husband's work clothes. Iris described, in vivid detail, what Beatrice had to do at each stage of laundering the clothes and household linens for a family of three: the hauling of water in buckets to fill large cauldrons; the lighting of fires underneath to heat the water to a boiling point; the endless scrubbing on a washboard; the searing pain of cracked hands; the steamy, unhealthy atmosphere in their small cottage when laundry had to dry inside on rainy days. The girl pictured her mother in a cottage helping Beatrice with the Monday laundry during school vacations. Then she had to correct this image because her grandmother's slow death from tuberculosis over two years would have meant that the laundry was entirely her mother's responsibility. When Iris should have been sitting at her desk in her high school, she was ministering to a dying mother and running a household.

The girl always wanted to hear more about the characters who populated her mother's stories. She would interrupt and pepper Iris with questions about who they were, what they did, and whether they should carry the label of great uncle or aunt or, as her mother was an only child, whether they were a 'cousin' once, twice, thrice removed. But the girl's relatives appeared only to stage the life of her mother; they had no script, no substance of their own. Iris's real purpose in telling these stories was not to explain family relations but to talk about herself.

In her eighties, my mother was physically weak and frail, but her will to dominate everyone around her had strengthened. Iris clung tenaciously to her image of herself as a woman who had suffered through life and deserved reparation. I shuttled to and fro across the Atlantic to be greeted by the same stories she had told the girl throughout childhood and teenage years. Some passages were reproduced word for word, but the adaptations, the new versions of what was being said, carried new conclusions which seared as intensely as when the girl first heard them.

The daughter had failed her mother; she never came close to her exacting ideal. I did not bow to my mother's demands that I resign from my job, leave my husband and son, and return to my mother's kitchen and devote myself to her care. My brother stayed in England and doggedly and devotedly daughtered in my place, flanked by a team of professional 'carers'. Iris refused to acknowledge his, or anyone else's, attentive care as she was wrapped tightly in so many layers of seething resentment that her son's daughterly labours were invisible to her.

I came to disbelieve my mother's stories and considered them self-serving. I orphaned myself to cling to my desk and books. My final act of defiance as my mother's errant daughter is to rewrite her stories to retrieve a different kind of sense from the remains. This begins by reconstructing the life of Iris's mother, Beatrice.

The Hamlet

Beatrice Leaworthy (born Beatrice Williams) had married into the Leaworthy family with roots in the West Country stretching back through the eighteenth century. Generations of Leaworthy men were agricultural labourers in villages in Devon and Somerset, the borders between the two counties being irrelevant to their search for a place, a place being both work on an estate and the shelter that was tied to it. Once the men secured employment and a dwelling, the women shouldered all responsibility for the labour of the household, raising children and providing food. Inside Beatrice did all the cooking, cleaning and repairing of clothes; outside she did the laundry, maintained a garden, grew vegetables, raised chickens and a goat for milk. If and when they could afford it, families would acquire a sow to breed as an investment toward the future. Women supplemented the poverty wages of agricultural labourers by sewing long into the night and, by all accounts, Beatrice was an accomplished seamstress. Over the decades, this life did not change much for the Leaworthys who stayed on, or returned to, working the land; it was the life of Iris's childhood and the life that I came to understand when I stayed with my grandfather in Somerset. Settlement was often temporary: the making of a home was contingent on seasonal employment, on the demands of a fluctuating agricultural market, and on the needs and whims of the local squire.

According to family legend, Beatrice's sister-in-law, my great aunt Mabel, attached wallpaper to walls with drawing pins.

This was a story that caused the girl and her brother to laugh in scorn. They were regularly conscripted into a domestic decorating brigade, so were well-trained in the proper application of wallpaper paste. On Christmas Day, they untied the string and removed the wrapping paper from a pair of hand-knitted woollen socks sent to each of them by great aunt Mabel. They giggled, reminded themselves of the wallpaper story and, to their shame, mocked her, and her socks. I am sure we were admonished to appreciate Mabel's care and concern, but the girl and her brother were already captive to concepts of modernity they barely comprehended, and manufactured items, purchased and gift-wrapped in a store, were of greater value than handmade goods. They were profoundly ignorant of conditions of rural insecurity, conditions to which Mabel not only adapted but also worked to control.

In their own sphere of existence, the girl and her brother constantly battled the forces of racism but were also citizens of the metropole, ideologically inscribed into believing in the superiority of a metropolitan modernity which romanticized the rural past while relegating the rural present to the margins. It was many years before I came to recognize the imperial nature of these ideologies, before I understood the relation between the marginalization of areas dismissed as rural backwaters, and the marginalization of colonies, their inhabitants and their ways of life.

> Stories are dangerous . . . the form itself is dangerous, not the content. You know what a metaphor is? A story sent through the super distillation of imagination. You know what a story is? An extended metaphor. We live in them.
>
> Zia Haider Rahman, *In the Light of What We Know*

Beatrice died of tuberculosis in 1938 at the age of fifty, in the tied cottage she shared with her daughter Iris and her husband Charles Leaworthy in the hamlet of Huntworth, Somerset. Tied meant that their dwelling belonged to the estate on which Charles worked as an agricultural labourer; they were only entitled to rent it for as long as Charles was employed by the owner. The tied cottage system was rife with exploitation; it kept wages low, discouraged dissent, and made farm workers easily disposable.

A cluster of dwellings clinging to the banks of the River Parrett, Huntworth lay on the Somerset Levels, a low-lying region of fields and moorland between the Quantock and Mendip Hills. A few miles to the north lay the market town of Bridgwater where Iris attended high school. Huntworth was the place my mother remembered most vividly from her adolescence and teenage years. She rode her bicycle to and from The Bridgwater School for Girls, following the course of the Parrett which drains the Levels, flows through Bridgwater and, eventually, empties into the Bristol Channel. For its first nineteen miles the River Parrett has a tidal bore which builds up gradually in the wide stretches of the estuary, growing in strength and volume as the water is forced into the increasingly narrow channel until it rolls and roars through Bridgwater.

The Leaworthys had lived and worked in other villages in the Levels when Iris was younger, but seem to have found a more settled existence in Huntworth, in the centre of a richly biodiverse region now designated as 'natural character area No. 142' by the British government. Daily life was too arduous for Beatrice to take much time to appreciate or draw comfort from the rural beauty of the landscape, but Charles, labouring in fields, was attuned to minute details of the flora and fauna of the Levels. He told the girl to listen out for the riot of birdsong which announced the arrival of Spring. But when I stand in the centre of Huntworth listening for echoes of the past, all I hear is the constant drone of combustion engines from the M5 motorway.

Huntworth was not isolated from the British colonial world even though it was classified as a hamlet, a collection of houses without a church, the smallest unit of rural dwelling in England. Between 1929 and 1940, soaring 80 metres above Huntworth was a line of five lattice masts, each of which was 800 metres in length. Spaced 200 metres apart, vertical wires hung between them forming a curtain antenna. This technology of empire, 'one of the most extraordinary milestones in the history of global telecommunications', consisted of a pair of 'beam stations' in Somerset, the receiving station in Huntworth and the transmitting station in Bodmin. Each was an essential component of the shortwave Imperial Wireless Chain, an international wireless telegraphy communications network that linked the distant parts of the British Empire. The purpose of this beam station connecting Britain to Canada and South Africa would have been a subject of gossip and speculation among locals. Electromagnetic low frequency waves cannot be heard by the human ear, but when Beatrice, Charles and Iris continually passed underneath the antenna did they try to connect their daily lives with a wider existence?

It is easy to ignore English rural life, its villages and hamlets, in writing histories of the imperial world. Although invisible in its landscape, buried deep in the historical records is Huntworth's much longer relation to colonial ventures. Originally an ancient lordship, Huntworth entered British legal and cartographic history when it was first surveyed during the reign of William the Conqueror, 1066–87. 'Hunteworde. Alwi [a Saxon thane] held it in the time of King Edward, and gelded for one hide. The arable is two carucates, and with it are two servants, and seven cottagers. There are four acres of meadow, and ten acres of moor.' A hide was a unit of land for tax assessment, the geld. The carucate is a measure of land which can be tilled with one plough and a team of eight oxen in a year; but it was not only a unit of size, approximate to an area of 120 acres, it also served as a measurement of soil quality and fertility, an assessment of productivity.

Nine centuries after the first survey, Charles Leaworthy stood next to his young granddaughter still a 'cottager', a tenant beholden to the ancient rights of large landowners. My grandfather farmed this land and tried to teach the girl about its soil quality. He towered over her as they stood, side by side, in their Wellington boots, in the furrows of a recently ploughed field. He would compare the soil of the many Somerset villages where he worked, villages with names that rolled around in the mouth and challenged my London tongue, like Huish Episcopi and Westernzoyland. The girl held her arms outstretched, small hands cupped to catch the earth her grandfather pressed between his thumb and forefinger and then let trickle from his large calloused hands into hers. In a deep, resonant voice, he would intone words used for centuries but which were unfamiliar to her, a litany of words she received as poetry, rather than science, a vocabulary she acquired and I remember: 'loamy-rich', 'clayey', 'peaty', 'sandy', 'lime-rich', 'acid', 'freely draining', 'slowly permeable', 'bog'.

Generations of agricultural labourers, 'cottagers' as they were described in the first survey, had worked the same land as my grandfather. Each generation utilized their knowledge of the soil to enrich the lords who owned it. Huntworth had been owned by knights of the realm who advanced their prospects through marriage to female heirs to the property until Sibilla, widow of Kentisbury, Knight of Huntworth, married Sir Hugh Popham in 1285. The hamlet was, subsequently, the seat of generations of Pophams. Hamlets like Huntworth are imagined as places isolated from the mercantile world of building and maintaining colonies, but no region in England was isolated from the web of empire. Huntworth is tied, through the adventures of the Popham 'family gang', to colonial ventures in Trinidad, Guiana and Maine. John, born in Huntworth in 1531, became the most famous and influential figure of the Popham family, and his elder brother, Edward, inherited the Huntworth Manor.

After attending Balliol College, Oxford, John Popham entered the Middle Temple of the Inns of Court, became Member of Parliament for Bristol in 1571, and rapidly rose to power under Queen Elizabeth I and her successor James I. He prosecuted Catholics accused of treason as Attorney General, received a knighthood, and as Lord Chief Justice persecuted non-conformists. Sir John was an acquisitive man, and each stage of his meteoric rise was accompanied by the acquisition of property, sometimes through nefarious means: his immense wealth came not only from amassing profits in property but also from legal piracy. He berthed a caravel in Bridgwater and financed the colonial ventures of the family led by his nephew, Edward's son George Popham, who was appointed captain of the vessel.

George Popham may have grown up in a hamlet but he dreamt of finding El Dorado. In 1594, on one of his pirate adventures, he captured a Spanish vessel carrying letters from Domingo Martines of Jamaica, which made mention of the famed 'Nuevo Dorado' and its extraordinary riches. George kept the contents of these letters secret from all but the patron and promoter of his career as a privateer, his uncle John, because he was determined to find El Dorado before Sir Walter Raleigh launched his own expedition to Guiana and Trinidad. George and his partner, Robert Dudley, son of the Earl of Leicester, became the first Englishmen to invade the interior of the Orinoco: they searched for but failed to locate a mine either on the mainland or, subsequently, in Trinidad. Raleigh followed quickly on their heels, sacking and burning San José de Oruña and slaughtering its residents before leading his own expedition up the Orinoco. In the title of his book, Raleigh pronounced himself the discoverer of the *Large, Rich, and Beautiful Empire of Guiana*.

The culmination of Sir John Popham's colonial ambitions, after an aborted attempt to establish a plantation in Ireland, was to obtain a Royal Charter from the King in 1606 to establish colonies in 'Virginia'. 'Virginia' was, until 1616, the name given to the coast of America stretching from what is now South Carolina to Nova Scotia. George Popham was appointed leader of the northern expedition which also included Sir John's son, Francis, and two grandsons. In 1607, they sailed to colonize the west side of the Kennebec River in what is now Maine. Despite the brief history of the settlement – it lasted only from August until the following spring, and George Popham died there – it stands in history as the first English colony in New England and is memorialized in Maine as Popham State Park. More than a wireless antenna connected Huntworth to the empire.

The Sacrifice

Beatrice was not a descendant of the English aristocracy or gentry, and she inherited neither land nor wealth. Poverty and labour granted her a legacy of tuberculosis, a disease that was the scourge of the Williams family and their generation of the British working class. In 1936, Iris left school to care for Beatrice for two years through her painful illness and slow deterioration.

When the girl was seven years old the local GP told Iris that her daughter's life was in her hands, that she was gravely ill and far too weak to be transported to hospital by ambulance. Iris lived in constant fear that the tuberculosis that had haunted her mother's family for generations would be visited on her own daughter. I believe Iris pictured herself at Beatrice's bedside during the many sleepless nights she spent administering hot poultices and penicillin to a daughter close to death with pneumonia. She watched and waited while the girl's lungs slowly responded to the treatment and the infection began to clear. It was months before she was well enough to return to school. Iris was afraid she would have to bury a daughter as she had buried her mother. The girl grew into her adolescence convinced that the disease was lying in wait inside of her, ready to strike at any moment if not carefully monitored. She constantly trekked by bus to and from the local hospital for tests and check-ups.

I believe the stress of willing her daughter to live, as she had willed Beatrice to live, never completely left my mother. Iris was like a coiled spring, the tension inside her winding tighter and tighter until something snapped and she was broken beyond repair. The dead cast their shadows over Iris who grieved the loss of Beatrice every day, summoning her presence and casting her shadow over her daughter's life through incessant storytelling which the girl came to dread.

Beatrice was a powerful, intimidating, unsettling, brooding presence, and the girl forced her grandmother into the recesses of her mind. Iris's interminable accounts of her life with Beatrice were impossible to absorb and generated conflicting emotions, so these memories beaded on the surface of the girl's skin to be sucked down the drain with the soapsuds. She refused to relate to her dead grandmother because her slow, painful dying damaged the mother who, in turn, tried to pass this damage onto the girl.

Iris's stories always ended with the same melancholy lament. Weeping copious tears through half-closed eyes she would sob, 'they had to stop me from throwing myself into my mother's grave'. Raising her head and lifting her arms toward the spectre of her mother, Iris would gasp for air as if drawing her last breath, and proclaim that her life had ended the day Beatrice died.

But the worst was yet to come. Calming, Iris would then turn her head toward the girl, her eyes focused on a distant past, and whisper her ardent wish that she lay buried, at peace, clinging to the remains of her mother. At these moments Iris was so consumed that she couldn't see her own child in front of her. She retreated back through time, reliving the moment when her father and cousins reached for her as she leapt into the grave and dreamt of escaping their clutches.

And Pity, like a naked new-born babe
Striding the blast, or heaven's Cherubins, hors'd
Upon the sightless couriers of the air,
 Shall blow the horrid deed in every eye,
 That tears shall drown the wind. – I have no spur
 To prick the sides of my intent, but only
 Vaulting ambition, which o'erleaps itself
And falls on th' other
Macbeth, Act I, Scene 7

Time and space shifted; the walls of the house collapsed. The girl stands at the side of a bottomless pit in Arnos Grove cemetery in Bristol, watching while her mother is drawn closer and closer to the precipitous edge. The girl steps slowly away. If she so much as takes a single breath Iris will fall. Though her mother's tears

LEAR
Tell me, my daughters –
Since now we will divest us both of rule,
Interest of territory, cares of state –
Which of you shall we say doth love us most,
That we our largest bounty may extend
Where nature doth with merit challenge.
King Lear, Act I, Scene 1

CORDELIA
Unhappy that I am, I cannot heave
My heart into my mouth. I love your majesty
According to my bond, no more nor less.

LEAR
How, how, Cordelia? Mend your speech a little,
Lest you may mar your fortunes.

CORDELIA
Good my lord,
You have begot me, bred me, loved me. I
Return those duties back as are right fit,
Obey you, love you and most honour you.
Why have my sisters' husbands, if they say
They love you all? Haply when I shall wed,
That lord whose hand must take my plight shall carry
Half my love with him, half my care and duty.
Sure I shall never marry like my sisters
To love my father all.
King Lear, Act I, Scene 1

caused her heart to swell until the girl thought it would burst, her words drowned any pity at birth. The girl was helpless in the face of her mother's despair, her wish for death, her yearning to be alongside her mother. Iris's desires always rendered her children irrelevant appendages, excess baggage, burdens.

As the girl grew older she convinced herself that Iris's constant iteration of her desire to 'be with her mother' was pedagogical. She did not, at first, grasp the lesson she was supposed to learn. At the heart of these stories lay a model of daughterly affection and devotion she could not aspire to equal. She imagined her grandfather, great aunts and cousins dragging Iris back from the brink of Beatrice's grave knowing that she could never be such a daughter.

I see Iris as staging her model of daughterly devotion as a dictum, a demand to be loved, if not worshiped above and beyond all others, as did King Lear. Like Cordelia, I now know I never had such merit; I was unwilling to make such a promise. I reject my mother's memories and version of the past but, in spite of my determination to forget her lamentations, I can reproduce every single one of them verbatim, against my wishes that they remain buried, with the dead. If I am to write my way through this melancholia a reckoning with Iris's version of the past is necessary.

Upon returning from school one afternoon Iris found Beatrice crying in the arms of a close friend. Iris understood the diagnosis was a death sentence and decided, at once, to leave school to become her mother's full-time nurse. Did the tuberculosis take Iris by surprise, or had her suspicions already been aroused when she found reddish mist on a mirror, when she worried that her mother was becoming more remote, seeming to turn inward upon herself, when she closed her eyes to her mother's increasingly translucent skin and wasting body? When Iris reached for Beatrice's hands she must have noticed how they seemed to float toward her from thin blue-veined wrists. 'The white death', as TB was known, 'took its victims slowly, racking their bodies and exhausting their minds.'

Wealthy Europeans chose to be admitted to exclusive private sanatoria which offered an open-air treatment regime 'in the bracing air of mountains, pine forests or coastal islands', one of the most famous of which was the Nordrach clinic in the Black Forest. Twenty-five miles from Huntworth, in the Mendip Hills, two sanatoria were established which modelled themselves on this form of open-air treatment at moderate elevations and also seemed to be promoting themselves to a wealthy clientele.

> Nordrach-upon-Mendip, Blagdon, Bristol. Accommodation for 40 patients. Terms 4 to 6 guineas. Resident Physician and Proprietor, Rowland Thurnam, M.D.; Assistant Physician, Charles Wheeler, M.D.

In my mother's narrative of her sacrifice she had to leave school to become a full-time nurse because the family was too poor to afford any other form of treatment. But this does not take account of a variety of state interventions which established a network of medical institutions for the free

> Mendip Hills Sanatorium, Hill Grove, Wells, Somerset. Accommodation for 25 patients; 2½ to 4 guineas. Chief Physician, Dr. C. Muthu.

treatment of tuberculosis. The National Insurance Act of 1911 made provision for a sanatorium benefit for tuberculosis, the only disease specified in the Act for which free treatment was offered. From 1921, local authorities were required to provide free sanatorium treatment to all patients in their area, and Beatrice's doctor was obligated to make a referral. Iris could easily have remained in her school but this was not the route she followed and I wonder why. Beatrice must have been appalled but perhaps she was too tired and weak to resist her daughter's determination to stay at home.

It is true that sanatoria for the poor were often regarded as little better than prisons. Women were more reluctant than men to enter these institutions for fear of what would happen to their families while they were away; this was particularly true of women who did not employ servants and had no one, including their husbands, they could call upon to take over their domestic tasks. Many patients derided the state of sanatoria, complained of poor food, and discharged themselves. These complaints were reported in the newspapers. Iris and Beatrice would have heard from Welsh relatives of the dreadful conditions in sanatoria there, and perhaps were unaware that institutions in the West Country had better reputations. It is also true that sanatoria were more likely to accept as patients those who were young and in the early stages of the disease rather than people like Beatrice, adults whose tuberculosis was more advanced and chronic.

The *South Wales Argus* reported in 1937 that all the patients in the South Wales Sanatorium were complaining of the cold and that a visitor who was wearing an overcoat also felt cold.

Iris left school to care for her mother at home. The Beatrice of my imagination, of Iris's stories, would have been utterly dismayed if not horrified at the prospect of her daughter leaving school. The Beatrice that I have assembled desperately wanted her daughter to be able to earn her own income, to establish her own career, to avoid being dependent upon anyone, particularly men. My mother acknowledged with pride that Beatrice saved every penny from her earnings as a dressmaker to pay the fees for her school, confident that an excellent education would secure her future.

Iris's descriptions of her independent school, the Bridgwater County School for Girls, made it appear more progressive and more enlightened toward the education of women in the 1920s and '30s than the schools I experienced, as both a student and a teacher, in the 1960s and '70s. Beatrice sent her daughter to a school which had a strong academic curriculum and embodied female achievement. It was staffed entirely by women, many of them single, and all of them university graduates committed to the serious project of preparing their charges for careers. Many had attended Oxford and Cambridge and swished into and out of classrooms in their academic robes. Iris was in awe of them and thrived in the atmosphere of intellectual rigour and female aspiration.

I found photographs of the school's staff and pupils in the Somerset Records Office. It was the daughters of doctors, independent farmers and large landowners who remained in school long enough to sit for their final examinations; Iris promised to be the exception. In the admissions register Beatrice finessed the class position of the Leaworthys by listing her husband's occupation as 'Farmer', not 'agricultural labourer', presumably to raise expectations about her daughter's possible future. In the headmistress's reports I discovered what Iris did not say about her decision.

Beatrice, weak and exhausted, was unable to counter the determination of her daughter by herself, so she made an appointment with the headmistress in the vain hope that together they could persuade Iris to stay in school for the winter and spring terms and sit for her final examinations. The teachers predicted she would pass with high grades. Iris was not persuaded by the headmistress's reasoning and remained deaf to her mother's pleas. Beatrice had dreams that her daughter could rise above her station and perhaps even attend college if she finished school, but these dreams were no match for her daughter's stubborn determination.

This was the point at which, for Iris, sacrifice became the model for how a daughter demonstrated love. Isn't this dilemma a perfect example of the political nature of personal limitation in women's lives? Iris did not characterize leaving school to take care of her mother as a decision. On the contrary, she claimed that there was no decision to be made, that she had no choice in the matter, that as a daughter she had no other option but to do what she did. In other words, Iris came to believe that she sacrificed her own best interests out of necessity.

This sacrificial practice of daughtering became my legacy. I know that Iris was shaped by the material and historical conditions of her world, that what appeared to be a personal decision was actually political, and that it seemed to her as if sacrifice was the only option. The myriad sacrifices of poor women have always disguised gender and class inequalities and plastered over the gaps in social care, substitutes for the inadequacies and oppressions of an economic, social and political order. Beatrice had not intended to die in poverty as the wife of an agricultural labourer, a dependant of the local landowners. On the contrary, she was a very ambitious woman, ambitious initially for herself, then for herself and her husband. When those ambitions were thwarted she focused all her energy upon securing a quality education for her daughter. Iris had watched Beatrice work extremely hard to secure her future and must have felt culpable. The residual effect of burying guilt under sacrifice was a resentment.

The long days of dying at home were interrupted when the local lady of one of the manor houses granted Beatrice and her daughter the favour of her attention. Perhaps in gratitude for Beatrice's skill as a dressmaker, perhaps in recognition of the contribution that Beatrice had made to the gown that her daughter wore when presented at the court of King

> ... the Edwardian countryside was economically and socially moribund ...
>
> As Lady Bountifuls, distributors of winter blankets, coal and soup, landowners' wives claimed a natural right to interfere with the lives of village families, and took any challenge to that right as ungrateful insolence.
>
> Paul R. Thompson, *The Edwardians*

George V, her ladyship descended from her manor house at regular intervals during Beatrice's illness.

Bearing calf's foot jelly, jelly made no doubt by her cook but carried in her own fair hand, her ladyship would flutter and poke about inside the small, cramped peasant cottage, doing her duty while never removing her gloves, and registering her disdain for their poverty. Because their home was a cottage tied to an estate, these unwelcome, deeply resented intrusions could not be refused. Iris retained vivid, bitter memories of this condescension and spoke frequently of her humiliation.

Paternalistic visits from the lady of Huntworth House served as particularly unwelcome reminders that Beatrice had not been allowed to share in the promises of modernity. She had cultivated dreams of an independent life for herself and for her daughter; being female in addition to being poor, those dreams were anchored in the desire for education as a route to social advancement. Instead of watching her daughter leave their cottage and mount her bicycle to ride to school, Beatrice saw her daughter tied to her bedside and to household labour, a galling daily reminder of how completely those dreams had collapsed.

Iris had one option that offered her a temporary respite from nursing and provided a modest income, if not sufficient to replace the loss of income from Beatrice's dressmaking: she was a pianist. Beatrice had ensured that Iris had piano lessons as a child and, in subsequent years, she had passed Royal Society of Music examinations in classical piano to an advanced level. Iris rode her bike to play a variety of venues: she accompanied silent films at the local cinema; she played with a dance band for local events; she played the organ in the local church.

Iris's talent offered a measure of peace in the turbulent relationship with her daughter. She played nursery rhymes and taught the girl to read music and play the piano. They would sit side by side on the piano stool, the girl turning the pages of Iris's favourite Chopin Preludes or Beethoven Sonatas. Those moments were the only times that mother and daughter were in complete harmony, sharing a love of music and a bond with each other. As Iris aged, becoming increasingly tired and careworn, she played less and less until the piano fell silent. Her daughter had abandoned her to live on the other side of the Atlantic Ocean.

I imagine Iris playing for Beatrice, offering solace and love. In the days, weeks and months of encroaching death, Beatrice turned her head toward the wall, directed her mind away from her present and returned through memory to days when the future held promise. In fevered dreams, through the violent fits of coughing that wracked her body, that had wracked the body of her siblings and her mother, Beatrice remembered and spoke to Iris of Bristol.

Bristol was where Beatrice's ambition took root and flourished, the city that nurtured and nourished her dreaming; as Beatrice walked and rode through its streets, as she passed its libraries, schools, museums and theatres, the city's architecture appeared to confirm her ambition. I am convinced that Bristol offered my grandmother a sense of entitlement, the right to participate in a rich civic life; that it led her to imagine that she could become a modern, educated British citizen, even though she was a young woman without means learning to be a dressmaker.

In 1938, Iris returned Beatrice's body to Bristol where she was buried in Arnos Grove cemetery near her mother, Rose Williams. Beatrice lived in dread that if her daughter did not complete her education she would remain in a position of dependency; her worst fears were realized, for without her high school certificates and despite her fierce intelligence, after burying Beatrice Iris went into domestic service.

Beatrice will always remain in the shadows of stories told to her granddaughter, but from her figure radiate lines of force that continue to exert their power. I am aware that my narrative is suspect, that it projects my own desires back onto the figure of a grandmother I would have wanted to know. I resurrect Beatrice from the darkness of my mother's rage to unravel and find different meanings in her stories. If I can re-weave the warp and weft of her ambition, an ambition Beatrice nurtured in furious resentment of the orthodox customs and conventions of class and gender that ruled the place and time in which she lived, she can become the 'poet who never wrote a word'. I cannot interrogate this imagined grandmother; I can only measure and weigh the lives, hopes, dreams and silences in the family stories passed on, in the context of a world shaped by colonial expansion, the Great Western Railway, and the cities of Bath, Bristol and Cardiff.

FAMILY REGISTERS

If metaphors increase our understanding, they do so only because they take us back to a familiar vantage, which is to say that a metaphor cannot bring anything nearer. Everything new is on the rim of our view, in the darkness, below the horizon, so that nothing new is visible but in the light of what we know.

Zia Haider Rahman

Arrival

Each summer, beginning in the late 1950s, the girl and her younger brother were sent to stay with one of Beatrice's nieces in South Wales for the entire length of the school holidays. Their absence from home enabled Iris to work at night as well as by day, thus earning sufficient money to pay school fees due in the autumn. The first of these annual journeys began very early in the morning

To do your first works over means to reexamine everything. Go back to where you started, or as far back as you can, examine all of it, travel your road again and tell the truth about it. Sing or shout or testify or keep it to yourself: but know whence you came.

James Baldwin, *The Price of the Ticket*

when they left home to travel to Paddington Station where they would board a steam train bound for Cardiff. They quietly followed their mother to the ticket office and then to be registered as unaccompanied minors travelling under the care of the passenger guard. Resigned to these formalities they were impatient for the fulfilment of Iris's promise to take them up to the front of the train, to inspect the engine and its tender piled high with coal. Crowds of people rushed about and a cacophony of station announcements filled their ears, but they stood silent, awed by the immensity of a locomotive, 'throbbing in anticipation ... an admixture of steel, iron, copper, brass and white metal ready to tackle moor or mountain, valley or viaduct'.

A number of different locomotives were used to haul the trains to and from their destination but I remember only one, a glossy green and black monster with two gleaming chimneys, one brass, one copper, and on the front of the engine, *The Red Dragon*, embossed on a headboard. Boy and girl were steeped in dragon mythology and craned their necks to evaluate what they saw. In relief, between *Red* and *Dragon*, there was a cast iron rendition of a creature, covered in scales. The dragon reared up on its back legs, spread its bared claws, wings and tail as if prepared to take flight, but to our disappointment it did not breathe flames. Beneath the dragon and below the boiler sat two lanterns, one on each side, eyes peering out over a bright red buffer beam. If the carved and painted image did not measure up to the dragons of their imagination, when the giant locomotive snorted, hissed and expelled a vast cloud of steam, they were astonished and enthralled but also thought it prudent to step backwards.

In control of this mighty machine was the driver, a person of heroic stature who under no circumstances was to be disturbed by the likes of children. They stood in silent adoration and were rewarded for good behaviour when, with the hint of a smile and wink of an eye, the driver bestowed upon them a slight imperious nod. Or did they just imagine such an acknowledgement?

When he leant out of the cab, the driver's eyes surveilled the entire train and platform: engine men checking couplings, mail being loaded, and guards directing and assisting the passengers climbing aboard with luggage.

Behind the driver they could see up into the engine cab, a complex whorl of levers with red and black handles, brass pipes, copper dials, throttles and valves. In the heart of this world a crimson and orange glow reflected on the skin of a fireman in constant motion, feeding the monster, shovelling coal into the maw of the firebox, rising briefly to check the meter registering pressure before bending again to his task. Once satisfied with the meter reading, the fireman would clamber down from the cab to crouch and peer underneath. Walking sideways like a crab he examined pipes, brake blocks, couplings and connecting rods between the tender and coach before leaping back onto the footplate to shovel again. Firemen were agitation, anxiety and bent backs, while drivers exuded power, control and superiority through stillness. A driver supervised others through facial expressions, conferring or withholding approval with a glance: a tightening of jaw muscles, lift of chin and eyebrow, or a narrowing of eyes and turning down the corners of his mouth. We learnt to read the face of our great uncle, who had been an engine driver.

Because the train was already waiting when its passengers arrived, the children were unaware that four hours before beginning a journey, staff in the engine shed had lit the fire to build pressure in the locomotive boiler, and a fireman had supervised the loading of coal and water into the tender, inspected the firebox for any damage, and regulated the boiler pressure and water level. The driver, who was responsible for the overall condition of the locomotive, had checked that there was sufficient oil in the reservoir to reach the bearings and ensure that the engine would run smoothly.

Once the children had examined the train, Iris placed them in the care of a passenger guard who helped them clamber aboard a cream and maroon-brown coach. He found seats, clipped tickets, and carefully inspected the large labels the boy and girl wore, inscribed with their names and their destination, 'CARDIFF'. The previous evening Iris had attached the labels to school blazers with string threaded through buttonholes. The next morning when the children put them on the girl thought they looked like Second World War evacuees, but neither brother nor sister would have dared to remove the labels. Being prominently identified and smartly dressed (school uniforms were our best clothes) we felt as if were embarking on an adventure of consequence.

We were on our best behaviour for this annual journey, travelling by ourselves on a steam train with a restaurant car. Any nervousness the girl felt was tempered by the serious responsibility of being in charge of her younger brother, and by the burden of remembering and following each one of her mother's numerous instructions. Occupying reserved seats, with a table between them, girl and boy sat up straight and looked out of the window. Her brother blinked away tears as the coach lurched, their mother waved, and Paddington Station gradually disappeared. It was replaced by the backs of houses, streets and neighbourhoods of West London and then villages, small market towns, flowering hedgerows, open fields full of cows, and hillsides dotted with sheep. The children settled into their seats, books lying unopened in front of them for there was too much to see, hear and feel.

The movement of the train produced distinct rhythms, rhythms that pulsed through the coaches, passed from coal fire to steam, from piston to wheel and track, rhythms that vibrated through their seats and into muscle and bone with increasing speed and intensity. They were attuned to the peculiar amalgam of sounds: the squeaking of springs in the cushioned seats; the creaking and groaning from coaches as they slowed, hauled around bends, then tugged and pulled straight; the ringing of steel as couplings between the carriages clashed when the brakes were applied. The engine announced its presence in the landscape in a variety of registers, huffing a steam song and blowing its whistle before navigating railway crossings, bridges and junctions, or descending into the bowels of the Severn tunnel.

Many hours later, *The Red Dragon* arrived in Cardiff. The guard who had escorted girl and boy to the dining car for lunch, and closed their windows before entering the Severn tunnel so they wouldn't be dusted with smut and cinders, now delivered his charges to their relatives and touched the peak of his cap in farewell. Another guard scanned the length of the train to make sure all the doors were closed, signalled to the driver that all was well, and climbed aboard as *The Red Dragon* vented clouds of steam, and with a loud snort and much chuffing and puffing slowly pulled out of the station on its way to complete its journey at Carmarthen.

Caerdydd Canolog Railway Station, Cardiff General to the children, was not as vast as Paddington, but when they arrived they still felt small and vulnerable. Paddington was always crowded but it was part of London, which they knew how to negotiate. Cardiff unsettled the girl. Their uncle carried suitcases, their aunt walked beside him, she held her brother's hand and followed in their wake, weaving her way through throngs of people as they left the platform and entered the concourse.

GWR had rebuilt Cardiff General in the 1930s. The girl did not yet know how to name what she saw, but the 'Art Deco' architecture caught her attention and she slowed to gaze at the vaulted ceiling with hanging lights and walls with marble columns. Her lingering forced her uncle to turn back and usher his charges across the concourse, through an archway under the words *The Great Western Railway* carved into the Portland stone, and out onto the Square, where he nervously scanned a sea of automobiles to see where he had parked his Ford Anglia. The girl and her brother stood next to the gleaming, newly waxed car, waiting with their aunt while their uncle arranged the luggage in a spotlessly clean boot. When he lifted the front seat, they clambered into the spotlessly clean rear seat. The interior had been vacuumed and polished, it had a smell the girl could taste in the back of her throat; it was sharp, like sucking lemons. One of the first lessons the children would learn from their aunt and uncle was that dirt had been banished from their lives, that cleanliness, along with being neat and tidy, was essential to Methodist godliness: dust must never be allowed to accumulate. This made the children extremely self-conscious and they sat unnaturally still, peering out of sparklingly clean windows with hands clasped tightly in their laps so they did not stray and sully the polished surfaces with fingerprints.

Their uncle was a methodical and sedate driver, which allowed the children time to adjust to the unfamiliar accents of uncle and aunt, and to the sights, sounds and smells of Wales. Leaving the train station behind they passed railway lines on the left and crossed over the River Taff. Did either uncle or aunt mention that they we were driving past the street where their grandmother was born? I forget. Instead, the car headed northwest in the direction of Llantrisant, the village where the children knew their mother had been born.

The girl adored the small Welsh village nestling at the foot of the Rhondda Valley. To avoid being summarily dismissed as aloof Londoners by cousins and village residents, she and her brother learnt quickly to stop comparing Wales to London and England, but they remained oddities because of their brown skin that cousins thought could be washed off. One teenage cousin who pinched their arms whispered that they must know that they were sent to Wales because their parents despised them. This fear haunted the girl's brother who would wake crying in the night. Despised was a word the girl added to her vocabulary. When thinking about these summers I realize that being recognized as kin did not suffice to give an account of their selves.

In Somerset, Beatrice and Charles Leaworthy were the parents of only one child, Iris, but Beatrice's elder sister Maud and her husband Walter Leaworthy had raised five children, all of whom married and had children themselves. Iris, as an only child, grew up thinking of her Welsh first cousins as the brothers and sisters she longed for, so she passed on explanations of familial relations that left her son and daughter befuddled. They simplified the issue by referring to all elder relatives as uncle or aunt. All younger people were cousins – the degree of relation seemed irrelevant – what mattered was that in the summers they were absorbed into a large extended family that tried to mould Iris's children in their own image. The children's self-making was largely determined by their stubborn resistance to the mores they attempted to instil.

The girl gradually came to understand the significance of the Great Western Railway in the history of this branch of her mother's family. Generations of Leaworthy men, with the exception of her grandfather, had spent their working lives as engine cleaners, firemen, guards, porters and shunters, and one great uncle even drove an express train. She thought she knew all there was to know about the complex world of railways just because she and her brother rode on steam trains. She was mistaken. When aunts and uncles exchanged stories, nuances escaped her. She could not begin to imagine the labour necessary to maintain and run the trains or what it was like to be a member of the family of a GWR employee.

From late June to September the girl and her brother lived in South Wales among the descendants of great uncle Walter and great aunt Maud. Walter lived until 1965, but they never knew Maud, who had died in 1943, five years after our grandmother Beatrice. Walter was a lifetime employee of the company that was always referred to in reverent tones as 'the GWR'. What the girl was told during those summers about the joining of two Leaworthy brothers, Charles and Walter, with two Williams sisters, Beatrice and Maud, was spoken of in the same weighty tone and resonant with pedagogical and moral injunctions.

The young live in and for the present, so it was difficult for the children to locate themselves in tales of ancestors. And yet there was an insistence in the telling that they mattered for their future. Two distinctly different philosophies of life and work were their legacy. The girl and her brother were meant to heed and follow the path of their industrious grandmother Beatrice, and their great aunt and uncle, Maud and Walter. On no account were they to follow in the footsteps of Charles Leaworthy. Their grandfather, they were warned, was stubbornly fixed in his ways; to his cost he remained unmotivated by their grandmother's ambition, drive and vision. Charles, the story went, failed to achieve upward mobility and was thus peremptorily dismissed by the rest of the family as irresponsible, unfaithful, a ne'er-do-well.

The sons of Walter and Maud followed their father into the GWR and some ascended to working in shirts with collars and ties, instead of in overalls. Older generations set expectations for Iris's children and their cousins. Above all, they were instructed, they must be responsible citizens if they were to attain security in life. If they worked diligently at school they could attend a teaching college, or even a university, but they must aim for a job which offered a lifetime of stability, security and steady advancement. Achievement was the result of self-discipline: learning to persevere in the face of any difficulty or obstacle; being diligent in work habits; and paying attention to detail. They were not to be unrealistic and challenge the barrier of class that prevented them from becoming lawyers or politicians; they should be careful not to overreach, daring to imagine that they could join the Establishment, but they could aim to work in a bank, become a nurse, or a teacher in a state school.

We were admonished to be respectable. Respectability was defined as keeping up appearances, cleanliness of body and mind, having respect for the self, and for the hierarchies of class. It was important to obey those with greater social standing for, without a ladder of ascension, how could we climb and gain the respect of those below us? Elders inserted themselves into a narrative of progress like pieces into a national jigsaw puzzle, and its principles were instilled through this litany to the young.

The children were led to understand that respectability in the Leaworthy and Williams families had been conferred by the GWR and the long-term security it offered, but this was misleading because the company did not confer respectability but required it. In order to be considered for employment, the GWR demanded that all potential employees provide written testimony regarding prior conduct and standing in their community, testimony that they were upright, honest and trustworthy. A prospective employee had to provide multiple written assurances, in the form of references from clergymen, doctors or teachers, that he was already regarded as a respectable, upright and responsible citizen.

The growth of the railways appeared to herald a new modern order and era of industry, but it was, in many ways, just as authoritarian as the feudal order of the village. Railway companies encouraged recruits from rural villages and believed that 'docile countrymen made an ideal employee'. The GWR wanted obedient employees in their service and at their command. From their earliest days the railway companies realized that their housing policies were a way to foster company loyalty and control their labour force. Three decades prior, Charles Leaworthy recognized this contradiction and concluded that if he remained a GWR employee he was exchanging one feudal order for another, bending the knee to a squirearchy or industrial employer. It was a bargain he refused and this refusal made him an outlier in the family.

Railway companies had a distinct advantage over agricultural and seasonal labour: they offered stability in terms of steady employment. This must have been attractive to anyone who grew up in the precarious conditions of households dependent on casual labour. In return, railway companies required that their workers move where and when they were told to move and be content to work the long shifts they were allocated without question. They resisted all attempts to improve working conditions and rigorously opposed demands for the regulation of work hours in a shift. Records of employees show a workforce resistant to GWR paternalism, authoritarianism and the ideal of malleable, 'docile countrymen'.

Beginning in 1837, the GWR administered a literacy test. All prospective employees had to write the following: 'Zealously try to excel. Industry is commendable. Perseverance deserves success. Quietude of mind is a treasure.' Writing these words recalled the counsel of Welsh aunts and uncles. The stories of individual achievement passed on during those long summers in Wales were actually verbatim accounts of the work discipline advocated by the GWR, internalized and adopted as an individual work ethic. The girl understood that, like their Welsh cousins, she and her brother should abide by this work ethic and by this conception of one's place in the grand narrative of British modernization and class formation. But, just as deeply embedded in her memory are the casual references to black children in Cardiff as 'pickaninnies'.

It was never just class that was at issue, for one's *place* was also determined by a taken for granted, not fully articulated story about white supremacy. As offspring of Iris and Carl the children were awkwardly shaped, multifariously coloured pieces of a puzzle, and who knew how, or where, they would eventually fit into the nation. Yet it was not just the girl and her brother who represented potential conflict within the familial contours of the national narrative. Digging beneath its surface reveals fissures in the continuity of stories of successful striving and upward mobility, for there were other misfits, pieces gone AWOL, lost, escaped, fallen by the wayside. A few were lying hidden and ignored having been deliberately kicked under the carpet.

Sunday dinners were solemn and formal occasions which followed long hours at the local Methodist Chapel, most of which the girl spent in sullen resentment because she was not allowed to read. One Sunday, she shocked everyone at the table with an announcement that she intended to become a dancer. She might as well have stated that her ambition was to practise sex work. I remember the collective intake of breath, the stunned silence from a tableau of frozen attitudes, mouths gaping, forks and napkins half way to mouths.

When my mother and my Welsh relatives composed family history they defined progress as a decisive, deliberate turn away from an itinerant, rural existence toward settlement and security, from demeaning labour in fields owned by a squire to the acquisition of artisanal skills and, eventually, white-collar work. They took for granted that this also meant being rulers of an empire. Progress and modernization were measured across generations from the precarious, unstable conditions of farm labour to a future of stability and predictability achieved through and evaluated by the attainment of self-discipline.

There was to be no looking backward toward the past; deviation was censured and dismissed as retrograde. This commitment to a steady, incremental rise upward, to job security, was the fruition of hard work and obedience and became the cornerstone of the Welsh and Bristol family lore.

Upon each arrival in South Wales, the girl and her brother had to learn, or relearn, how to belong: to adjust to expectations of what sort of children they should be; to reimagine how to inhabit the pathways of sociality, landscape and architecture; and to find their place in its design. As they grew older, the annual journeys no longer left them feeling bereft and needing to cling to one another in despair. To the girl Cardiff was a bewildering, complex network of neighbourhoods, roads, railways, bridges, a river and a castle. When I visit those villages now, the M4 motorway skirts the city. Driving at 70 miles an hour, I cannot see the circuitous route through busy urban streets, open fields and small villages the girl travelled with her brother in the back of their uncle's car.

Rebecca

I combed city archives, stared at fire insurance plans and ordnance survey maps, and navigated the political arithmetic of census records, knowing that the everyday details of the lives I looked for could not be visualized on a map and fell through the net of questions asked or not asked on a census form. My grandmother, Beatrice, was at my side nudging me into places bypassed by contemporary life, but I was unable to tell whether I was being taunted or tempted by the slivers of information I gleaned. In the midst of my dissatisfaction I glimpsed Beatrice's mother, Rose. Curious, I followed Rose until I found her mother, Rebecca. I have travelled further than family stories could guide me and it was a relief to move beyond memory to history.

> The rastaman thinks, draw me a map of what you see
> then I will draw a map of what you never see
> and guess me whose map will be bigger than whose?
> Guess me whose map will tell the larger truth?
>
> Kei Miller, *The Cartographer Tries to Map a Way to Zion*

The connections between the Leaworthy and Williams families traced a triangle of settlement and movement between the West Country, Bath and South Wales, with Bristol as the fulcrum. At first, I believed that this conformed to conventional British internal migration patterns: the availability of work on the railways brought security and upward social mobility for the Bristol/South Wales side of the family, while the precarious conditions of English agriculture between two world wars led to a life of insecurity in Somerset and Devon for my grandparents and mother.

Mapping the lives of the dead with the historian's tools alone is insufficient. Buried with the bodies of the women who preceded Maud and Beatrice were family histories which confound linear narratives of progress. I was not told what those lives were like in Bath, Bristol and Cardiff, and I was not told about the depths of poverty, of struggles to survive squalor and filth, to breathe air free of pollution. I also inherited a limited and flawed cartography because maternal family stories failed to account for empire.

From the depths of her melancholia my mother would summon Beatrice into her kitchen as if recruiting an ally in her battle to forge a perfect daughter. But the daughter Iris yearned for was not meant to become a writer who strayed beyond the tales she received: I was not meant to be curious; I was not meant to burrow beneath their plots; and I was not meant to undermine their narrative foundations, disrupting their silences, excavating what had been so assiduously hidden.

I began with a mother's memories but I had become a writer and researcher and I uncovered stories that were not meant to be passed on. As a scholar I was familiar with the egregious calculations of imperialism which reduced the curved surface of the earth to 'a geometrical grid with squared off empty seas and unexplored regions in measured boxes', filled in 'by explorers, surveyors, and military forces . . . on the march to put space under the same surveillance which the census-makers were trying to impose on persons'. In my search for Rebecca, Rose and Beatrice in the cities of the imperial metropole the districts inhabited by the poor were the equivalent of those 'unexplored' regions of the globe, spaces that needed to be known and placed under the gaze of not only politicians and the state but also 'Clergymen, teachers, doctors, employers and charity workers . . . who gave evidence to official and unofficial investigations of working class life and labour'. I have tried to restore the density, tumult and miasma of lives in poverty.

Rebecca Williams (née Tuggay) was born in 1843, and gave birth to Rose in Bath, Somerset, in 1867. In the eyes of UNESCO, the city of Bath is of 'Outstanding Universal Value', first, for its Roman remains, particularly the Temple of Sulis Minerva and the hot springs baths complex, and second, for its Georgian architecture. UNESCO recognizes these characteristics as making Bath 'one of the most beautiful cities in Europe, with architecture and landscape combined harmoniously for the enjoyment of the spa town's cure takers'. Bath symbolizes English cultural elegance and civility. Buildings constructed with honey-coloured Bath Stone glint gold in the sun, pleasing the eye; curved residential terraces like the Royal Crescent, and the urban design of the squares, are emblematic of the city's measured, capacious, grace.

One of Bath's most prominent residents in the first half of the nineteenth century was William Thomas Beckford, who moved there in 1822, purchasing adjacent properties on Lansdown Crescent and Lansdown Place, which he connected into one residence. A connoisseur and collector of art, Beckford owned several sugar plantations in Jamaica. Blood money from these plantations, which was not honey-coloured, financed his acquisition of objects, gave him the leisure to cultivate his refined aesthetic tastes, and supported his elegant manner of living. William Thomas had inherited these plantations, and the immense wealth produced from the enslaved who laboured on them, from his father William Beckford, granting him fame as 'England's wealthiest son'. He spent his fortune recklessly but, in 1835, the British Treasury boosted William Thomas's finances at a time when they were dwindling: he was awarded more than £12,800 in compensation for the loss of his 'property'. The property in question was 660 enslaved human beings emancipated in 1834, from three estates in Clarendon and one in St Dorothy parish, Jamaica. This compensation enabled the purchase of two more gracious houses on Lansdown Crescent in Bath.

The Grand Pump Room and the Assembly Rooms, in the heart of the city, were meeting and recreational spaces for the eighteenth-century fashionable elite who were drawn to the city, not only to take the waters, but also to participate in 'the Season', a period which ran from October to June, during which they launched their daughters into the turbulent stream of high society through a series of balls which functioned as a marriage market. The ostentation, superficiality and grotesque attributes of this social life were recreated in the novels of Jane Austen, a resident of Bath from 1801 to 1806.

In the nineteenth century, Bath remained a city of stark class divisions, health disparities and wealth inequality. Though many writers probed such inequities in literary representations of London, the area where Rebecca lived, and where Rose was born, is inscribed in only one novel, and dismissed in a brief wry remark in the city's archive of photographs as one of 'the less glamorous locations in Bath'.

> Properly to estimate the health and average age of the inhabitants of Bath, it should be borne in mind that it is a place of much resort for persons in affluent and easy conditions of life ... who reside in good houses, and for the most part in well-ventilated streets, or crescents and ranges of building well exposed to the sun and winds, especially to the mild and prevalent southerly and westerly breezes.
>
> Report of the Commissioners of the State of Large Towns and Populous Districts, 1844

In the 1860s and '70s, Rebecca lived south of the city centre, only a half a mile from the Roman Baths, and the hotels which housed tourists, and a mile from the celebrated gracious architecture, elegant manner of living, and green spaces occupied by the city's wealthy residents and visitors. Rebecca, her husband James, and their three children dwelt in Back Street Place, where there was no fresh air and where light was absorbed by the stones of a dark, grim, narrow, dead-end alley.

I bend over an ordnance survey map from this period; its ordered and orderly view of the city offers certainty and assurance in its accuracy and meticulous partition of space. I see a measured scale of a physical

> Maps ... make birds of us all.
> *Rob Cowen*

environment which eliminates the organisms that exist within it. There is no room for the messy, dangerous, uncertainties of life that characterized the 'planless, knotted chaos of houses' in urban areas reserved for the poor and which the bourgeoisie wished out of their sight.

Rebecca worked as a laundress in the city centre. When she walked home in the gas-lit nights, after a long day, every muscle in her body must have ached, making her drag her feet, though she was a young woman. She had to turn her back on the warmth, bright lights and music emanating from a concert at the Assembly Rooms and walk away from the harmonious landscapes of Roman and Georgian architecture. Not until Rebecca crossed St James Rampire and Lower Borough Walls, part of the medieval city boundary, would she have entered the lower and older section of Bath, heading for the Avon Street rookery where there were no spacious streets.

> Signs scratched on walls and daubed on rough boards – Lockyer's Court, Back Street, Bull Paunch Alley, Lambs Yard, each of them more squalid than the last – all part of the Avon Street rookery, a labyrinth of back to back slums, boarding houses, paupers' hovels, stables and pigsties.
>
> Paul Emanuelli, *Avon Street*

In the 'labyrinths of narrow lanes' that constituted the Back Street neighbourhood, residents and businesses were squashed into a congested area between the city centre and the River Avon. Rebecca would immediately have been assailed by the stench as she picked her way through the rubbish-strewn cobbled streets, trying to avoid the effluent from the gutters, and must have sighed as the streets became narrower, lanes became meaner, dirtier and increasingly cramped, until they became alleys. Back Street Place, the narrowest, meanest and most cramped dead-end alley of them all, was just north of New Quay. The area lacked adequate drainage and sewer systems, and flooded when the river rose.

It was a neglected urban universe of windowless hovels and 'tumbling tenements . . . a swarm of misery' where the unsightly poor were out of sight of the Bath's wealthy residents and visitors, though as charwomen and laundresses they performed the most intimate of services for them.

The neighbourhood was primarily a commercial space interspersed with dwellings and lodging houses: Rebecca passed a large timber yard, a pipe factory, a pottery and Chandlers &

Mawers Malthouse. There were numerous stables and stock-yards, lofts for animal feed, carpenters shops, sheds for carts, chandlers, a timber store and two slaughterhouses with animals penned in their courtyards. Rebecca and Rose lived among the scenes, sounds and stink of death, of slaughter and butchery: the screaming and howling of distressed cattle, sheep and pigs who evacuated their bowels in terror; the pungent smells of blood, of offal and excrement that always hung in the air, tainting hair, skin and clothes, entering through nostrils, forcing bile to rise in the back of the throat.

The seven buildings of Back Street Place were terraced but not graciously so. They were lined up like sardines in a tin on the west side of the alley, facing a damp, grimy wall: five were very narrow but the first two were larger and could have accommodated workspaces. One neighbour was a mason, the other thirty-three were charwomen, costermongers, labourers, laundresses, hawkers, servants, weavers and children living cheek by jowl in dank, dark, poorly ventilated buildings. There was a Common Lodging House around the corner on Little Corn Street where, if they could afford it, itinerants could obtain a portion of a bed, shared by two or more, for a few pence a night. Maps and census records fail to render the cold and dampness of the dwelling that Rebecca returned to at night, the anxiety and helplessness she would have felt hearing a child cough throughout the night, looking at flushed sweating skin, hearing cries of pain and hunger when she had no means of relief.

Several private water companies served Bath but they did not serve the city's poorest residents. Rebecca and her family had no direct water supply and there were only a few standing pipes in poor neighbourhoods. Even though the Romans had built an innovative water, sewer and sanitation system in Bath, it fell into disrepair and was destroyed by flooding after their withdrawal from Britain in the fifth century. In the 1880s, there was only one drainage system that ran from the city centre south along the edge of this neighbourhood: waste emptied into the River Avon.

Disposal of animal and human waste, and the pollution of the river, were major sanitation and ecological issues for the city in the nineteenth century. In Back Street Place, there might have been space behind four of the buildings for outdoor privies, but more likely they were located at the end of the dead-end street in the space next to the last house where Rebecca and her family lived. Privies emptied into cesspools that polluted basements, seeped into wells and were breeding grounds for insect infestation and disease. To bathe and to wash clothes they had to walk down past the lodging houses on Little Corn Street, to New Quay and along the river to a public bath house with laundries at the bottom of Milk Street.

The Bath City Council took an active role in city planning beginning in the latter half of the eighteenth century, but only on properties that it owned in the city centre. In the middle of the nineteenth century, Parliament passed a series of Acts addressing public health and increasing the powers of local councils to control housing conditions. Bath City Council passed its first building regulation bylaws in 1866 and 1868 but they affected only new construction. While politicians were debating the need for local councils to purchase, clear and rebuild slums, Rebecca and her husband, James, found ways to survive and raise children.

To the east of Bath the River Avon was navigable to Bristol, to the west the Kennet and Avon canal continued to the River Thames and thus connected Bath to London. In 1840, the city was also linked to Bristol and London by the GWR, and ten years later the company purchased the canal, a competing form of transportation of goods. James Williams had migrated to Bath from the Somerset village of Frome, where the main sources of employment were the Wallbridge Woollen Mills or agriculture, where illness and deaths from consumption and other lung diseases were far higher than average, and where many children died before the age of five. At sixteen, James was apprenticed to a blacksmith, his younger sisters were working as general servants, and all three were living with their widowed mother. Three years later James married Rebecca in Bath.

Like many young men from rural areas at the time, James probably had dreams of finding a secure job on the railways, but he is not to be found in the employment records of the GWR. He followed the River Frome and washed up on the shores of the Avon working as a mason's labourer. Renting rooms on Back Street Place meant that he was close to opportunities for work, but is also a sign of the precarious nature of their situation, an indication that he and Rebecca were living on the edge among the poorest in the city. Perhaps James had met his future neighbour, the mason, on a construction site and was told about cheap rooms available on Back Street Place, a location from which he could seek work on a variety of sites. There was an abundance of stone in local quarries and two stone yards close by, one on either side of the river, where labourers unloaded stone brought into the city on barges then loaded it onto carts for delivery to construction sites around the city. Masons were working on the ongoing restoration and repair of the Roman Baths and would have needed labourers to fetch and carry for them.

Poor widows and female partners of unskilled or semi-skilled labourers in casual employment subject to seasonal fluctuations became laundresses to sustain their working-class lives. The growth in the size and number of institutions like hospitals, hotels and restaurants created a surge in demand for laundresses and they were often concentrated in communities with significant numbers of tourists and temporary residents, like spa towns. In the Regency and Victorian periods Bath's population, both wealthy and poor, continued to grow and visitors could travel to take the waters by train rather than carriage.

The Royal United Hospital was then located in the centre of the city on Beau Street, opposite the Royal Private Baths and just around the corner from the Grand Pump Room. Its infirmary was established at the end of the eighteenth century to provide medical treatment for the destitute and working poor of the city. Looking out of the windows, the ailing poor could peer at the ailing rich wrapped in blankets and wheeled by servants in bath chairs between their lodgings and the Baths. Did they compare their own starved frames to the well-fed bodies of the rich? Did they jeer, or was scorn replaced by empathy?

The hospital, the Baths, and guests at the Grand Pump Room and other hotels in the city would have generated enormous amounts of soiled linen and garments. Some women could take laundry into their homes, making it easier to care for children, but where Rebecca lived it was too small and lacked the necessary facilities, like running water. Instead, in the early hours of every morning she walked to York Street to a commercial laundry that shared the water supply of the Queens and Turkish Baths and could service the clients of all the institutions, collecting their soiled linens and returning them free of dirt and obnoxious smells. When not employed by a commercial laundry, Rebecca, like other professional laundry women, would have become itinerant, seeking work in the houses of the affluent; either way she would have worked for twelve hours or more a day, six days a week. The seventh day would have been spent labouring for her own household.

For Rebecca the laundering of garments, sheets, towels and blankets was accomplished by unassisted muscle power. It was as arduous and demanding as the work of a mason's labourer: laundresses were 'hired as much for their brute strength as for their expertise'. Laundry had to be sorted and heavy loads lifted, carried to and from and in and out of tubs to be soaked or boiled, scrubbed, blued, starched and rinsed. Agitating water in tubs for heavily soiled items, or for blankets, quilts and sheets, was backbreaking work. Laundry was rotated by hand using a wooden dolly, which resembled a milking stool at the end of a long stick with two handles mounted cross-wise at the top, or dolly pegs resembling a toilet plunger with perforated metal at the base. The wet linen, even heavier than the dry, had to be wrung out before rinsing and again before ironing. This was accomplished by passing it through a heavy box mangle with levers and a wheel that had to be pushed, pulled and turned by hand – steam mangles were not installed by commercial laundries until the end of the century. Every item had to be hung until it was damp, dry enough to be carried to an ironer who used red-hot flat irons which had to be constantly reheated. Finally, everything had to be folded and packed for delivery. In a commercial laundry, Rebecca would have specialized either in the cleaning or the ironing process. Working in a private residence she would have done it all, and have hauled tubs of water on and off sources of heat. In both situations the pattern of the week was the same: the collection, labelling, sorting and cleaning of the wash began at dawn on Mondays, the work of ironing started toward the middle of the week and continued into the weekend. Rebecca would have been constantly exhausted.

When employment was available, Rebecca and James worked long hours. The Education Act of 1870 created publicly funded compulsory schooling for children from the age of five to thirteen: Rose, her elder brother James and the baby, Emily, were the first generation to benefit from the Act. James would have been old enough to attend school in 1871, but Rose and the baby would have been cared for either by adult relatives, or neighbours who had to be paid from the meagre earnings of their parents. At some point in the 1870s, life in Bath became untenable for the Williams family; perhaps in 1875 when Rebecca realized she was carrying another child, or the following year when she gave birth to another daughter, Sarah.

Seeking to improve their lives, Rebecca and James moved the family to Bristol, to a street on the edge of the floating harbour, where the River Frome flows into the River Avon. They lived near the docks, close to the slate and marble works, a saw mill, a timber yard and a rope manufactory on Canon's Marsh, all potential sites of employment. There James appears as a 'labourer' in the census, and at sixteen the younger James was employed as an errand boy. Emily attended school but Sarah, now aged four, was too young to go.

Rebecca imagined a future for Rose beyond the laundries, which meant she had to acquire other skills. In Bath, Rebecca had a close friend, Ann, who moved to Grangetown, Cardiff when she married a tailor. Ann and her husband were a childless couple and Rose was sent to live with them in a house shared with another family on Kent Street, close to the River Taff. The needle trades, throughout the nineteenth century, were notorious for utilizing child labour, and Rose, though attending school as required by law, seemed to be working as an apprentice to the tailor. These are skills she would pass on to Beatrice, as Beatrice taught Iris and Iris tried, fruitlessly, to pass on to me.

By 1902, the dwellings on Back Street Place in Bath had vanished and were incorporated into the business of J. Foster, Carpenter and Builder. The district, unpleasing to the eye, was ultimately eradicated, wiped from view and from memory, and replaced by the Avon Street Car Park. To the modern mind it is as if people had never lived there.

Rose

In 1886, my great grandmother, Rose, aged nineteen, married thirty-seven-year-old Henry Williams in Bristol, where her parents lived, a month before the birth of their first daughter. Rose, Henry and infant Maud then settled in the rapidly growing city of Cardiff and Rose returned to tailoring work. They moved into a newly built house in Canton where my grandmother, Beatrice, was born, followed two years later by the birth of her sister Lillian Estella. If it was possible to stop time, at this particular moment in Rose and Henry's lives, it must have seemed as if the future promised greater financial security than either had previously known.

Canton, bordered by the River Taff, was a thriving agricultural community until it was transformed from 1850 onwards by the GWR and the expansion of Cardiff which followed. Railway lines were laid across Canton commons and a maintenance depot erected which became the engineering base for the GWR in Wales, and Canton's biggest employer. In 1883, there were no houses or streets between the railroad tracks and the Cowbridge Road, but within five years fields were transformed into a dense cluster of working-class terraced Victorian houses, many of which were built by the GWR. Rose and Henry's immediate neighbours included a number of railway porters but also a carpenter, shopkeeper, grocer, boilermaker, upholsterer, shoemaker, general labourer and ship steward. Henry had been an upholsterer for twenty years, so probably contracted with the GWR to use his skills working on their carriages.

Rebecca's granddaughter, Beatrice Williams, was born in this house in 1888. As an infant she lived and breathed in an environment and soundscape dominated by the maintenance depot: her small body was assailed by smoke from burning coal, fumes from hot oil, the pungent sweat of men covered in grease, grit and grime, the thunderous sounds of steel clashing against steel, the sonorous huffing and chuffing and high-pitched screeches, squeals and whistles of steam locomotives. Stink, sounds and soot produced inside and outside the gigantic sheds were expelled through funnels, flew from the tenders of steam trains and filled the air and the nostrils of every living thing in Canton. Cardiff was the 'coal metropolis'.

Beatrice spent the first eight years of life in a house next to the vast GWR junction and not far from the docks to which the coal mined in the Rhonda Valley was transported for export. Her mother Rose, Rebecca's daughter, fought a constant battle against soot coming to land on clothes, curtains, furniture and flesh. Soot coated the

Air pollutants produced by coal combustion act on the respiratory system, contributing to serious health effects including asthma, lung disease and lung cancer, and adversely affect normal lung development in children.

Physicians for Social Responsibility

surface of things, but also burrowed into seams, penetrated the weave of fabric, and gathered in every corner and crevice. Its removal demanded constant vigilance. Rose spent many hours of labour washing, scrubbing, dusting and sweeping to banish it, only to see it seep back through windows and doorways. Coal dust colonized air. She waged war against the filth visible on surfaces, on what she could see, but the particulate matter and toxic chemicals which were invisible to her were inhaled and lay in wait in the lungs of her family to ambush them later.

Is this where the family history of consumption began, with specks of coal dust and pieces of grit, with the inhalation of air polluted with particles? Is this where it began for all of them, for Beatrice, for her mother Rose, and for her sister, Lillian

The combustion phase of coal's lifecycle exacts the greatest toll on human health. Coal combustion releases a combination of toxic chemicals into the environment sulfur dioxide, particulate matter, nitrogen oxides, mercury, and dozens of other substances known to be hazardous to human health.

'Particulate Air Pollution'

Estella? Born two years after Beatrice, Lillian Estella was referred to as Stella by members of the family but was listed as Lillian in census records. Iris described her as a tragic figure; sickly through-out her life, she died in puberty. Pulmonary tuberculosis is caused by a bacterium, an airborne infection which is contagious, but scientists now believe that susceptibility to the disease is increased by ambient air pollution and, in particular, by exposure to particu-late matter. The constant presence of irritants and residue in the respiratory systems of Beatrice, Rose and Stella would have increased their susceptibility to TB. Unlike the effects of pollution, which can be calculated, it is difficult to measure the consequences of generations of poverty on the health and well-being of Rebecca, Rose and Beatrice.

Modernity and imperialism were celebrated and commemo-rated in the naming of streets. Some bore the name of British civil engineers and inventors: Thomas Telford, who designed roads and bridges, and Isambard Kingdom Brunel, Thomas Craddock, John Smeaton, George Stephenson and Richard Trevethick, all of whom were associated with steam locomo-tion. The street on which Beatrice lived celebrated an arch conservative, Lord Eldon, a Tory politician who twice held the position of Lord Chancellor, and whose reactionary politics and policies included fierce opposition to the 1807 bill to end the slave trade.

Eldon Street abutted and ran parallel to what had become a huge, complex network of rail tracks and junctions. The house Rose and Henry rented from the GWR was directly opposite the gigantic engine shed which serviced Cardiff's massive railway industry. To the west the street ended at the electricity works. Nearby, there were non-conformist chapels of every denomina-tion, primary schools, a large cattle market, and the Union Workhouse with over 400 residents. Vaughn's Steam Dyeing and Laundry works employed many of the women and girls in the area but, because Rebecca had sent her daughter to Cardiff as a child to live with her friend and apprentice with a tailor, Rose did not have to follow her mother into laundry work. Likewise, Rose brought her youngest sister Sarah to live with them. After leaving school at fourteen, Sarah took care of her nieces, cleaned and cooked, while Henry and Rose were working. The history of women's work was not passed down to me by family memories, which focused on men's employment and the singular significance of acquiring respectability. In the stories of the rise from poverty the key was securing a foothold on a ladder to job security via the GWR, but even as a child I sensed that this was an incomplete version of pastness.

Rose was a tailoress, probably employed by a tailor to finish garments to be sold in his store. If she finished trousers and waistcoats in her home she would have had to rent a sewing machine, which risked accruing debt when work was scarce. I thought Rose might have returned to employment with the tailor to whom she had been apprenticed, but Rebecca's friend Ann and her husband left Cardiff after a high tide combined with gale-force winds caused a sea dyke to burst in October 1883, flooding their street with 7 feet of water, which badly damaged houses. The loss of furniture, provisions and clothes rendered residents destitute.

If Rose did not work at home she would have gone out to work in a garment workshop finishing men's clothes, or making women's skirts or bodices, or trimming them. In a small factory, Rose would have inserted button holes or linings into coats. Conditions in tailoring workshops and factories varied and could be dreadful: some workers suffered from the extreme heat from the presses, and in ill-ventilated rooms fumes from gas irons were overwhelming. The pay was notoriously low, and there were plenty of middle-men taking their share of the income before the garments were sold either directly to individual clients or in the shops.

In choosing to name herself a 'tailoress' on the census, Rose was making a claim to be acknowledged as a skilled worker in a needle trade that was rapidly becoming a deskilled garment industry. The term 'tailoress' was analogous to the term artisan, equivalent to the 'journeyman' recorded for her husband. However, 'tailoress' also registered the ongoing struggle of women for recognition and representation within the Amalgamated Society of Tailors. A female section was established in 1900, and the name changed to the Amalgamated Society of Tailors and Tailoresses.

Women in the needle trade had long been associated with sweated labour, 'linked to dirt, disease, and prostitution', and the home workshop was considered the most degraded of all conditions of work. Historians describe how needlewomen were regarded 'not as self-sufficient', but as 'parasitic on the community', because their labour often had to be 'supplemented through poor relief or charity'. In the late 1890s, the socialist reformers Beatrice and Sidney Webb, while advocating for greater supervision of home work and the implementation of a minimum wage, also characterized women in the needle trades as 'breeders of a degenerate race that posed a very real threat to Britain's imperial future'.

Within a decade of the birth of her first child Rose, not yet thirty, had five children. When I found the registration of the birth of the fifth child in 1896 in Bristol I realized that the story of Henry and Rose's steady ascent upward in Cardiff had ended. Henry seemed to have disappeared. From the census I could see that Rose had moved to the poorest section of Bedminster in a tiny cul-de-sac of seven cottages abutting the railway just west of the Pyle Hill depot. By 1901 she had seven children and the first five I could identify as Henry's: Maud 15, Beatrice 13, Lillian (Stella) 10, Henry George 6, and Herbert 5. The two other children were William 1, and Winifred, just 2 months old. The problem was that the male head of the household was listed as a Henry Williams but was a much younger man. I did not solve this apparent discrepancy for a long time.

In the meantime, I concentrated on what I knew of Rose's daughters and what I could discover about where they were living. The Railway Cottages were very small and must have been cramped for Rose, who needed workspace. Maud was employed as a general domestic servant so Beatrice must have shouldered a significant amount of responsibility for childcare and household labour. Lillian would have required intensive care for she was, by then, ill with tuberculosis and would live only fifteen more months.

When I first found Rose living in Railway Cottages, the street name triggered a childhood memory of meeting a man who, from the perspective of the girl, appeared ancient. Usually, when she was taken to meet one of her elderly relatives in South Wales, the visit was accompanied by an account of how each person was related to her. On this occasion the girl was driven to Bristol. She was squashed in between an aunt and cousins in the back seat of a car for what seemed like hours. The journey ended when they arrived in a dead-end street of cramped, shabby houses. Later that summer or the next the girl was told that the man she visited that day had died. The words 'great uncle' and 'Bertie' echo in memory, but whose great uncle? I do not think the girl was at all curious about him. Now, however, I struggle to recover his story, or even his name.

I know this man had spent his life working for the GWR, but am unable to place him in my extensive family register. I think he was probably Herbert Williams, son of Henry and Rose, Beatrice's younger brother who joined the GWR as a Lad Clerk when he was fourteen. I wish I could go back and ask him about my grandmother and great-grandmother.

The girl was guided into a room in which this old man sat in an armchair, wearing baggy trousers held up with braces and a collarless shirt with stripes. He talked animatedly in a wheezing voice, stopping frequently to cough into a large handkerchief. The girl was not listening to what he said, her attention, as usual, being focused outside. Through the window behind him she could see trains pass. The back of the house abutted the railway lines: when a huge steam locomotive hauling a long train of wagons filled with hundreds of tons of coal passed, the windows rattled in their frames, the glass threatened to shatter, the house shook to its foundations and all conversation was drowned in a cacophony of sound and vibration. The girl was the only one in the room who seemed to notice. Perched on the edge of her seat, she was convinced that the house was about to collapse. She had never been in a building that felt so fragile. The name, Railway Cottages, would have perfectly described the brick houses on that dead-end street. I set out to find where Beatrice had lived in order to confirm this childhood memory.

Researchers can appear odd. I wandered the district of Bedminster with a map to locate King Street, my only means of access into the Railway Cottages cul-de-sac. Walking around, holding open the paper map, and stopping at street corners to consult it, attracted the attention of local residents who interpreted this behaviour as a silent plea for assistance. I bewildered each of the good Samaritans who glanced over my shoulder and delivered the bad news that my map was completely inaccurate. I tried to offer assurances that I was not lost, and that I knew my map was dated 1902. My explanation caused even greater puzzlement. Those who had smiled warmly at me when they approached became suspicious. One by one, men and women stepped away from me thinking that anyone who walked around contemporary Bristol with an out-of-date map, instead of using the GPS on her cell phone, was beyond their help.

The Railway Cottages had gone and so had King Street. I walked via the only remaining entry into the area, New Queen Street, which must have been named for the young Victoria soon after she became Queen in 1838, when the population of Bedminster was rapidly, and traumatically, expanding. The first wave of migrants from the depressed county of Somerset sought work in the collieries and smelting works. The subsequent growth of the industrial base included engineering workshops, tanneries, glue works, paint factories and glass works which employed even larger numbers of migrants. Industrial development expanded much faster than the infrastructure and workers were housed in high-density, poorly constructed, terraced slums and alleys: two major cholera epidemics were the result. By the time Rose and Beatrice moved to Bedminster two other major businesses, E. S. & A. Robinson's paper bag company and W. D. & H. O. Wills tobacco, had opened large factories.

When I raised my eyes from my map, I saw that I was unable to go any further: the past was inaccessible. A mossy cobblestone path underneath my feet ran along the bottom of a decaying grey stone wall about 2 metres high. The cobblestones and wall dated from 1841, when the first section of the Bristol and Exeter Railway opened to Bridgwater, which meant that Beatrice could not have seen the railway lines from the back of her house, just the wall. Above it rose a wild tangle of overgrown shrubs and trees that climbed up to another wall bordering the railway, about 10 metres above ground level. The map in my hand, and the information on the census, flattened planes of existence and squeezed the life and the dying out of it. The vibrant, fleshy, chaotic, morbid materiality of the district and its residents disappeared when marshalled into columns and grids in ledgers by the state.

I was clutching a map which could not lead me to Beatrice. A trading estate has replaced Railway Cottages and its adjacent streets. The mossy cobblestones and stone wall on my right continued past Unit 1, so I took a leap of imagination toward the place where my grandmother became a young woman. Without blinking, I stared at the map to create an afterimage on my retina of the area in 1902. My mind leapt over the parked cars, trucks and vans, passed through a gate and railings, crossed a factory floor, and penetrated the rear brick wall. I stopped only when my imagination reached mossy cobblestones outside of the first of seven Railway Cottages huddled against the stone wall.

Fault lines emerge from the archives. Rose and her children were dwelling in an alley of slums in a congested area 'notorious for its poverty', the worst housing area in Bristol. There was a branch line directly behind and above the dwellings; between the spur and the main line were cattle pens, into which terrified cattle were herded after they were unloaded from trains. Every day, Rose must have been reminded of Back Street Place in Bath, an alley that she hoped she had escaped forever. Instead, she was living in another back alley from which she could hear the cattle bellowing and smell their fear as they were driven down the ramp to be slaughtered. In one of the five tanneries that dominated the area, their hides were stripped from still quivering bodies, scraped clean of gore, and processed into leather; their bones were boiled down in the local glue factory.

The middle classes and wealthy who suffered from pulmonary tuberculosis sought the fresh air of the sea and mountains, but Beatrice, Lillian Estella and Rose were housed next to industries that produced nauseating smells: the smelting works, the killing pens, the processing and dyeing of the skins of dead animals for luxurious leathers, and the reduction of their bones and other waste for glue. There was no fresh air to breathe, just the putrid stench of the glue factory and the strong fumes from the tanneries, one of which was only two streets away.

> They had consumed the most evil smell in history, they were consuming it now, flesh death, which lies in the vacuum between flesh and skin, and even if they never stepped into this pit again – a year from now they would burp up that odour. That they would die of consumption and at present they did not know it.
> Michael Ondaatje, *In the Skin of a Lion*

Underneath the district ran the contaminated, foul-smelling Malago River. These noxious odours were inhaled and tasted, they lingered in saliva, at the back of the throat, so pungent it was impossible to remove them from the bodies, hair or clothing of tannery and glue factory workers.

In 1882, Robert Koch, a German microbiologist, identified the tubercle as an infectious microorganism. The tubercle is the lesion in the lungs, bones or glands of those who suffer from consumption, and from this point on, the disease became known as tuberculosis, or TB, after the Tubercle Bacillus. Because it was infectious it became identified as a public health problem and the middle-class organization, the National Association for the Prevention of Tuberculosis (NAPT), was founded. Rather than attacking the economic, environmental and social conditions of poverty, members of the NAPT decided that the disease was 'maintained through ignorance and folly'. Blame was placed on the behaviour of the poor. Charles Booth, a social researcher and reformer, undertook a survey of London between 1889 and 1903, which demonstrated that 30 per cent of the population survived on an income far less than was required to maintain an adequate level of nutrition. Booth's response to this information was that the poor should be placed in labour camps and educated.

Karl Marx condemned sanitary officers, industrial commissioners and factory inspectors who agreed that workers required

500 cubic feet of breathing space while acceding to the impossibility of wringing such a concession from their bosses. Their acquiescence, Marx concluded, was a declaration that 'consumption and other lung diseases among the workpeople are necessary conditions to the existence of capital'. In areas where manufacturing continued to expand, incidents of TB increased, and this was as equally true of Bath, when Rose was a child, as it was of Bedminster, when she was trying to support her own children. There was no breathing space in her cramped railway cottage; there was no breathing space in the district.

When life became precarious, as it had for Rose and her family, there were two ways to save money: on rent and on food, which resulted in women and children going hungry in order to divert food to the primary breadwinner, usually a man. Being malnourished, and living in unsanitary, overcrowded conditions, increased the risk of TB, and children who suffered from pulmonary tuberculosis tended to develop more severe forms of the disease. Lilian Estella died in 1903, the year Rose gave birth to her ninth child, Elsie. The smell of death would not have been confined to the outside air; a body with rotting lungs emanates a sweetish smell of decay.

Census records cannot reveal or account for the physical deterioration of a woman's body caused by the struggle to survive in conditions of dire poverty, from years of bearing and caring for nine children, and from the never-ending demands of domestic labour and piece work. The little money Rose earned was spent on food for the children and medicine for Lillian Estella. No matter how tired she must have been she made time to teach Beatrice the craft of tailoring. In 1907 in Jamaica, my great-grandmother Marie struggled to feed and clothe her children and keep her family together after her husband died and with him their main source of income. In Bristol, in the same decade, my great-grandmother Rose faced a similar crisis, but I did not understand the cause, and everyone I could have asked was dead.

My first mistake was trusting the census taken at the turn of the century, which had brought me to Bedminster. Henry was listed as the head of the family even though his age and place of birth were wrong and instead of being a skilled journeyman he was described as a labourer in a warehouse. I did not know how to account for the discrepancy because there was a space of silence in family memory about this decade of Rose's life, other than an acknowledgement of her death. I doubted that Henry Williams had abandoned her and the children, but I was sure that the Henry Williams listed on the census was not the same man. Why should Rose, why should anyone, living in dire poverty because of state and local council neglect give those same authorities details of her life that could be used to blame her and her children for their condition?

Many fragments of the stories from my mother's kitchen remain unassembled after years of trying to piece them together. Iris said that she knew she had cousins in Canada, but had never met them. At the time this snippet of information was delivered in such an offhand way that I took little notice of it, but there were so many threads I could not untangle in Bristol's records that I turned to the extensive immigration records that the Canadian government makes available online. My search triggered a response from Ontario from a descendant of Rose's youngest child Elsie and I began to assemble a surprising and tragic story that my maternal relatives did not pass on.

I scoured the notes I had made on my visits to my mother during the years of her illness. Upstairs in my room I would sit and write all night: the windows were wide open because Iris always felt cold and set the thermostat as high as the tropical Palm House at Kew Gardens. She slept in a chair downstairs, like many who suffer from Parkinson's disease, with the BBC 24-hour news channel on at full volume, and loud and clear in my bedroom. In the days of my mother's illness I heard stories of her childhood I did not remember hearing before. In my notes from March 2003 was another reference to Canadian cousins. In the early 1930s, when eleven or twelve, Beatrice took Iris to Teignmouth in Devon where she met people who had 'something to do with the second marriage of her grandmother Rose'. I did not remember hearing these words or writing them down, my only excuse for forgetting being that I scribbled to the soundtrack of the 'Shock and Awe' campaign, the US bombing and invasion of Iraq, over which was layered the voice of a journalist reporting from the theatre of war.

Beatrice must have told my mother the story of a second marriage for Rose which was pure invention. Perhaps there was a pact among the women in the family to keep what happened to Rose a secret. Were they ashamed? Henry Williams had died in Cardiff leaving Rose a widow with four children and about to give birth to a fifth. She had no means of support other than her needle, and returning to Bristol meant she was closer to her family: her mother Rebecca, sisters Emily and Sarah and her brother James. But all her siblings had large families of their own; they could not house Rose and her children and had no money to spare. The man Rose lived with I only know as George. He adopted the name Williams and gave Henry's name to the census enumerators. Rose had four more children with George – William, Winnifred, Elsie and Annie – all of whom grew up thinking that Maud and Beatrice were their aunts, not their half-sisters. George was not interested in parenting or supporting a family and was frequently unemployed, so he too was dependent upon Rose. The person Beatrice took Iris to meet in the 1930s was Annie, the tenth child of Rose.

The conclusion to Rose's life is a story of falling as far as it was possible to fall. She tried to stitch the family together with her needle though she was increasingly careworn from so many pregnancies and births and battles with poverty, illness and death. In the last years of her life Rose could no longer pay rent or feed her young children and George was no help. They separated. Rose entered the Stapleton Workhouse, Fishponds, run by the Bristol Board of Guardians who administered the Poor Law. She took two of her children, Winifred and the infant Annie, with her into the workhouse, where she continued to sew. William and Elsie went to live with their father. Conditions inside workhouses were deliberately harsh to discourage any but the utterly destitute from applying for entry. Stapleton was built by the Admiralty in the late eighteenth century to hold prisoners from the wars with the American colonies. French prisoners were incarcerated there during the Revolutionary and Napoleonic Wars after which the Bristol Corporation of the Poor took it over and expanded the workhouse throughout the nineteenth-century.

A year after Rose's death, Winifred, now ten, and Annie, four, were still inmates in one of the children's homes of the workhouse. Life inside these homes was harsh and mirrored the Victorian discipline of the workhouse with uniforms and strict routines; female children were trained for domestic service. For a while William and Elsie remained with George and lived in the shadow of his neglect until being separated and taken into care. Each of Rose's older siblings had five or six children of their own and did not offer to adopt any of her young children. William was fostered by a family, Elsie was removed to a sheltering home for women and girls run by the Bristol Female Mission.

Maud had married four years before her mother's death and she and Walter took Herbert to live with them. When he left school, Herbert worked as a printer's labourer but, with encouragement from Walter, ended up working for the GWR. From this point on Maud and Walter became the lynchpins in the family narrative of ascent. Beatrice went to work as a live-in domestic servant cleaning and caring for six adults before finding another position as a sewing maid. Whatever ambitions she may have had for her own education or advancement were never realized, but she kept in touch with her half-sister Annie.

Once she gave birth to Iris, Beatrice decided to have no more children. Instead, she excised her thwarted desires and the failed dreams of her mother, Rose, and grandmother, Rebecca, in an effort to ensure that her own daughter was not confined to domestic drudgery. Beatrice was strong-willed and determined that her daughter have a chance to gain independence through education. The descendants of Maud and Walter inducted the girl into the lore of male ascent from farm labourer, to railway worker, to white-collar employee. They were silent about the desperate struggles of women in the family to sustain life through domestic service, laundry, needlework and the workhouse.

Bristol

When Henry and Rose left Bristol for Cardiff in 1887, they left a city of horse-drawn vehicles. Eight years later, Rose returned with her children to a rapidly modernizing, bustling metropolitan hub with one of the first electric tramcar systems in the country. All the stories I was told anchor my maternal family's identity in Bristol, the West Country and Wales, but I know Beatrice must have felt she also belonged to the larger world of the British Empire. How was her sense of self shaped by her environment and what did she know of the city's past? Bristol had been intimately entangled with the colonial world for centuries, so how did Beatrice come to understand herself as a British subject who was part of an empire that ruled over a third of the globe?

I lean in through time and space to tap my grandmother on the shoulder and speak to her. As she turns toward me, I ask Beatrice if she is like her granddaughter, if the streets of a city are her avenue of escape as they were to the girl. I make Beatrice explore every inch of her city as her granddaughter explored hers. The girl was only seven years old the first time she ran away from home; how old was Beatrice when she first closed the door behind her and walked away?

When my grandmother had the time to leave Bedminster, cross the River Avon and explore the city centre, she would have walked up East Street, crossing the New Cut on the Bedminster bridge. On her way to the Prince Street bridge, an iron swing bridge that crosses the floating harbour, she would have passed

Guinea Street near the docks. Was Beatrice aware of the derivation of the name Guinea? Once the site of the homes of men
who traded in human flesh, the street's name resonates with
associations, not only to the West African coast but to the coin
of exchange used by the Royal African Company.

The built environment of the centre of Bristol still exudes self-
satisfied achievement in character and appearance. The architectural grandeur and grace of public institutions and residential
squares is ample evidence of centuries of accumulated wealth.
When Beatrice was a young woman the city appeared to wear
history on its surfaces, but for centuries Bristol's public face hid
the ignominious origins of its wealth. Without exception, my
maternal relatives revered Bristol; they lived and worked in its
poorest districts but emulated the stolid respectability of its
wealthy citizens. My grandmother's desire to achieve, a driving

ambition she instilled in her daughter, has its roots in Bristol, a city that nurtured and nourished the dreaming of strivers.

Bristol had an exceptionally robust civic culture embedded in libraries, schools, museums and theatres, which encouraged and confirmed ambition and proffered a sense of entitlement to its citizens. Even if Beatrice was unable to afford tickets to attend the theatre, the library was free, as were lectures, lantern slide shows, and many other public events. For a young woman whose working life was confined to domestic labour, the wealth of civic life offered scope for her imagination. However unattainable, the city held promise for a future: becoming modern and becoming educated. I believe that Beatrice's fierce determination to send her own daughter to a fine high school for girls was stimulated by the flourishing educational institutions she saw around her, including the University College of Bristol, which became Bristol University in 1909.

Colston's Girls' School had opened in 1891 for the daughters of the city's elite. Although Beatrice was excluded by her class and lack of money from attending, it was a model for female education. Perhaps it was memories of walking past, rather than through, the gates of Colston's Girls' School that Beatrice recalled in the 1930s, when the profits of her needlework ensured her daughter's passage into another model institution for the education of women, Bridgwater School for Girls.

Did being excluded from such institutions and then working in domestic service breed desires for radical change in Beatrice? The activism of the Women's Social and Political Union (WSPU) exploded into popular consciousness when Beatrice was a young woman. Sitting in a library reading about suffragettes in the city, I thought about my grandmother and wondered. Annie Kenney arrived in Bristol in 1907 to organize a local branch of the WSPU, and the streets soon rang with the cries of 'Votes for Women!' Did Beatrice attend any of their open-air public meetings where speakers were 'pelted with rocks, fruit and rotten bananas?' Would she have ducked as the missiles flew over her head or would she have turned and yelled at the men who threw them? As Beatrice walked the streets did she see the pavement chalking, or the wagonette of banners driven around Bristol, announcing a rally on 18 September 1908? Was she drawn to stand among the crowd of over 6,000 on Durdham Down and listen to Emmeline and Christabel Pankhurst? Or, after work, did she attend the evening meetings in Colston Hall? What did Beatrice think when suffragettes burned down the University Athletic building, threw bricks through windows and attacked Winston Churchill when he arrived in Temple Meads? Was Beatrice the feminist rebel I want her to be, or was Iris the version of a Beatrice I do not want to see?

It was the city's wealthy merchants, philanthropists and large, stable bourgeoisie that had endowed Bristol with its libraries, schools and university, and with the eighteenth-century Georgian architecture of its monumental civic buildings, broad avenues and substantial houses. Nourished by its civic pride, Bristol made strivers of my maternal ancestors, all of whom clung to the ethics and values of bourgeoise aspiration. They felt an allegiance to the British bourgeoisie even though they could never achieve its level of financial wealth. The city was alive in the girl's imagination long before she ever saw it. Generations of relatives had lived in Bristol, loved it and felt intimately tied to the city. The girl heard a deep sense of longing in the voices of her mother, aunts, uncles and cousins as they wove tales drawn from their own memories and those handed down to them by their parents, tales passed on with the intention of linking her to the city. Iris dreamed that her daughter would be admitted to Bristol University and was bitterly disappointed when her application was rejected.

Only when I became an adult was I able to distinguish between the subtleties and variations of allegiance, the

Bristolians had extensive interests in the plantations of the Caribbean and Virginia in the late seventeenth century. As early as 1679, Bristol was already the centre of an internationally based sugar-refining industry. In that same decade, a coffee house, that symbol of the brave new regime of colonial consumption, opened its doors in the city's High Street. By this time too, tobacco had become an increasingly important trade commodity ... Formally barred from participating in the slave trade until the 1690s, some Bristol traders ... supplied plantations with slaves from at least the 1680s ... In addition to slaves, the slave plantations of the Caribbean, Virginia and Maryland also needed commodities and manufactured goods which Bristol was happy to supply.

Madge Dresser, *Slavery Obscured*

multiple meanings of Bristol in the particular lives and individual pasts of my relatives. Bristol exerted symbolic power for them in its promise for the future. The possibility of progress was the realization and fulfilment of a peculiar form of British dreaming. Gradually I learnt to question the foundation upon which British dreams of futurity and belonging were built. Promise flourished because it was grounded in, and generated by, the wealth and stability visible in the bricks and mortar of everyday Bristol life, constructed by the city's merchants. The architecture was testimony to the British success in trade, to the ethics of hard work, the value of profit, and imperial power. Concealed was the source of that profit: the enslaved labour that financed the city's economy in the eighteenth century and which paved the way for Bristol's modernity; the enslaved labour that enabled its Georgian grace, founded its civic culture and made possible its philanthropic works.

Sugar, tobacco and cocoa were integral to Bristol's economy and culture. The city was noted for its chocolate, and confectionary works, alongside tobacco factories, employed large numbers

of its residents. The structures that were emblems of the city's modernity, however, physically disguised the roots of its wealth in enslavement and colonial oppression.

One of these structures, a five-story baroque building, looms over its surroundings and sits on the edge of Bristol harbour at St Phillips Bridge like a temple to modernity. Converted into luxury

apartments it is increas-
ingly difficult to unearth its
many-layered   history.
While it has been desig-
nated a Legacy building by
Historic England what
counts as a legacy is only
bricks and mortar not the
previous use of the site.
The designation makes no
mention of the previous
sugar refinery which stood
there. Yet, some signs
remain, if we wish to recognize them.

The Society of Merchant Venturers, an exclusive business and commercial society, has been intimately tied to the fortunes of the city since it was granted a monopoly over all seaborne trade to and from Bristol by Edward VI in 1552. In 1832, the Society helped found the Great Western Railway that would eventually employ my great uncles, uncles, cousins and, for a short period of time, my grandfather. The Merchant Venturers also established and managed hospitals and almshouses, and founded the colleges which were incorporated into Bristol University, as well as schools including Colston's Girls' School. The University was able to apply for a Royal Charter in 1909 because of the financial support of two Bristol families: the Wills family who made their fortune from tobacco plantations worked by the enslaved, and the Fry family whose wealth came from chocolate.

Centuries of brutal exploitation of African peoples enabled the philanthropy that brought enormous benefit and civic grace to this English city and its citizens. The Wills family became abolitionists, yet donated the profits of enslavement to Bristol, not to the enslaved who had laboured to grow and harvest the tobacco they sold. The city's abolitionist hero, Edward Colston, considered Bristol's 'great benefactor', built schools, almshouses, hospitals and churches with money that he had accrued from the trade in enslaved human beings while a member of the Royal African Company and the Society of Merchant Venturers.

Bristol was deeply bound to the enslavement and transportation of Africans in the Atlantic trade, but it is misleading to reduce this history to the economic activities of a few wealthy individuals or traders, some of whom eventually became abolitionists. The contemporary Society of Merchant Venturers, for example, did not publicly recognize their role in the slave trade until 2006. It did not admit women to its membership until 2003, and, at the time of writing, there were seven women out of seventy-three members listed on its website. From its public visual presence its membership appears whiter than that of the Augusta National Golf Club.

On 5 December 2006, the Master of the Merchant Venturers joined the Lord Mayor of Bristol in the signing of a statement 'regretting Britain's role in the slave trade'. In 2007, expressions of regret became pro forma during the 200-year commemoration of the abolition of the North Atlantic slave trade. Regret, however, is distinct from an apology: the expression of regret is a legal loophole which avoids liability, particularly any responsibility for debts owed, or other financial obligations. In Bristol, the Merchant Venturers made no mention of the enormous profits gleaned from the enslavement of human beings. The Lord Mayor made no mention of the contributions of slave labour to the building of the city, or of the £158,000 (equal to almost £20,000,000 today) that was sent to the city by Parliament as compensation for the loss of property: the property being the people her ship owners and merchants held enslaved at the time the trade was declared illegal.

From the beginning of the 16th century until the early 19th century, the Society managed Bristol's harbour. During the 18th century, Bristol's trade with Africa increased substantially, in particular through the 'triangular trade' whereby manufactured goods were shipped from Bristol to West Africa, where they were exchanged for slaves, who were shipped to the West Indies and exchanged for sugar, molasses and rum, which was brought back to Britain.
Merchant Venturers House, www.mapyourbristol.org.uk

Beatrice and her family passed by and went in and out of Bristol's schools, libraries and churches, but nothing enabled them to 'see' the connection between trading in human beings and Bristol's history, wealth and civic culture. Impressed by the grand Georgian houses of Queens Square, Royal York Crescent and Clifton, they would have regarded the buildings as a confirmation of achievement, the realization of ambition, and success in business.

If Beatrice was aware that these houses were built for West India Merchants, nothing in the public space through which she moved, or in the history that was taught in schools, acknowledged the source of the profits that accrued to those merchants or to the city. Would Beatrice have even cared, if she had known?

Profits to Bristol and its citizens were enormous, both from the export of their goods to the African coast for the purchase of human beings and from the resale of human chattel in the Caribbean.

How to See Bristol in 1906 carried a disinterested, stark economic assessment which described how a financial outlay by merchants of £660 could reap a profit of 1,000 per cent minus the cost of transportation. A plantation owner, for an outlay of £31, was purchasing an enormous amount of labour power.

Investment in the trade was only one source of profits that accrued to Bristol. Residents of the city could reap financial gain from participation in the

In 1727–8 a cargo of 270 slaves could be obtained at a cost of £2.15s. per head, paid in the shape of iron and copper rods, cotton fabrics, spirits etc., and could be sold in Jamaica for nearly £31 per head, making a gross profit of £7,600, or vastly more than the value of the small vessel engaged in the transit.

How to See Bristol, 1906

The city also grew because the increasing wealth from trade, including the slave trade, meant that there was money to invest in new buildings. Many new houses were built in streets and squares. Men enriched by slave or sugar trading could build themselves comfortable town houses or grand country houses. Some of the houses in Bristol's grand Queen Square (built between 1700 and 1718) were built by people linked to the slave trade. For example, James Woodes Rogers who lived in the square invested money in slaving voyages. The Elton family, also of Queens Square, supplied brassware for the trading cargoes which were used to buy slaves in Africa. They also invested in slaving voyages. John and Nathaniel Day were involved in slave and sugar trading. Others with links to the slave trade living in Queen Square at various times included John Anderson, Isaac Hobhouse, Joseph Jefferis, Henry Bright, Thomas Freke, James Laroche, John Becher, Lewis Casamajor, Joseph Earle, Abel Gant, John Gresley, Nathanial Foy, Thomas Harris, Noblett Ruddock, Elias Vanderhorst and Thomas Quirke.

'The Growth of the City', PortCities Bristol

myriad trades related to transatlantic slavery: through investment or employment; producing goods for export to Africa and the American slave colonies; servicing and manning the ships that left Bristol on transatlantic voyages; refining in Bristol the products of slave labour; and handling sugar and tobacco cargoes from plantation colonies. The trade in enslaved people was closely interwoven with the wider commercial and economic fabric of the city: 'In the late eighteenth century at least 40 per cent of the income of Bristolians derived from slavery-related activities.' It was not only the merchants trading in enslaved human beings who profited but barrel-makers, brothel-keepers, chandlers, candle-makers, carpenters, dockworkers, inn-keepers, laundresses, sailors, sailmakers and shoemakers. Everyone benefited.

Bristol was a city produced in circuits of exchange with Jamaica. If the history of Bristol's financial dreams has been intimately tied to the enslavement of others it is also true that at the centre of this intimacy was the island of Jamaica. In 1655, Oliver Cromwell seized Jamaica from the Spanish, initiating British imperial rule of a nation that would become one of the world's leading sugar-exporting, slave-driven countries, and establishing the close economic relationship between Bristol and Jamaica for sugar, tobacco and the trade in enslaved humans. This relationship would transform and enrich both Bristol and Jamaica planters. Jamaica was the largest sugar island in the British Caribbean and, traditionally, the best market for slaves transported in Bristol ships.

The total number of Africans who were forcibly dragged aboard British ships in chains will never be known, and exact numbers are not available for the 2,106 ships that left Bristol for the African coast and from there sailed with their human cargo to the Caribbean. 901 of these ships sailed to Jamaica. Although final inventories are not available for Bristol ships, historians estimate that 587,000 Africans were enslaved and that '486,000 (or 82.8 per cent) landed alive in the Americas. From the 1,591 voyages to the Caribbean 445,487 enslaved humans were embarked onto Bristol ships and 371,306 disembarked, 217,263 of them were landed in Jamaica.'

I seek a reckoning with these inventories. I have to find a way to decipher the apparently unfathomable oceanic computation in which my ancestors remain shackled. Among these anonymous hundreds of thousands penned in blank ink on graph paper are girls and women who survive the Middle Passage and are sold in Port Antonio, Jamaica, where they will become the property of a man called Carby. But just as Beatrice is unable to recognize the past in her present, neither can she imagine a future in which her daughter will marry a descendant of this man and one of these women.

I imagine Beatrice charting a route for herself through the hustle and bustle of rapidly modernizing Bristol, walking, running and hopping on and off the city's omnibuses, negotiating its busy streets with confidence. Attendance at school had been compulsory since 1880, elementary education was provided free from 1891, and the school leaving age was raised to twelve in 1899. In 1901, Beatrice turned thirteen. Tuberculosis at home meant she was needed to nurse Lillian Estella and help her mother with tailoring. Beatrice was used to responsibility, but the grandmother of my imagination is also savvy and streetwise, a young woman dressed modestly but neatly, in an outfit that has been passed down from Maud and which she has carefully repaired: lace-up boots a little thin but clean, a gored ankle-length skirt, high-collar blouse, and a jacket mended at the elbows.

When she first opened her front door to leave the Railway Cottage, Beatrice would have been downcast, her shoulders slumped, as if bearing a tremendous weight. For a brief moment, she stood still, slowed her racing heart, then lifted her chin, until she was ready step into the outside world. Once she crossed the threshold and closed the door of her crowded home behind her, Beatrice felt an enormous sense of relief at escaping the claustrophobic atmosphere of sickness and slow dying and the endless domestic demands of the household. Leaving to buy food or medicine, pay the rent, or just stealing time for herself, I think she would have walked away with a determined stride, alert and eager for whatever the city had to offer.

As Beatrice grew from child to adult the most pervasive ideology of modernity was the New Imperialism of late Victorian and Edwardian Britain. This was a period of massive and rapid territorial expansion for the industrial countries of western Europe who, in competition with each other, sought new colonial acquisitions and the consolidation of their control over indigenous peoples in Africa, Asia and the Pacific. Through image and spectacle Beatrice would not only have become conscious of the vast reach of the British Empire but would also have been introduced into the racial logics of whiteness. Did she become convinced of the superiority of imperial power and did she believe, despite her poverty, that she was a member of a superior race destined to rule over a third of the globe?

One of the most popular forms of entertainment was the 'magic lantern', but lantern slide shows were also quickly recognized for their educational potential in schools, where they were used for teaching geography, history and science. The head teacher of Bath Road Board School in Bristol, for example, built a collection of over 2,000 slides for use in the classroom.

Lantern shows infinitely expanded the spatial and geographical horizons of everyday life. In 1902 a Visual Instruction Committee was set up by the Secretary of State for the Colonies to produce lantern slides on the UK for use in the territories of its empire, and five years later the committee embarked on a scheme to provide lecture materials for use in British schools. But imperialism and the racism which was its primary characteristic existed in many forms of lantern slides. A comic slide produced for children by the Wesleyan Methodist Sunday School Association in the 1880s depicted racist stereotypes of scantily clad 'African tribesmen' in the form of a 'joke' which depended on their supposed ignorance and terror when threated by smartly suited British businessmen

portrayed as cannons about to fire out of their top hats. In school classrooms, in town and village halls, the magic lantern shows projected the racism and imperialism of the age, justifying the need for, and rightness of, British rule in their portrayal of the peoples of the empire and of military exploits in colonial wars in Egypt and the Sudan, South Africa and India. In 1897, hand-tinted lantern slides of Queen Victoria's Diamond Jubilee were shown all over the country. These shows were visual enactments and affective realizations of imperialism. Watching the jingoistic spectacle of colonial genuflection to the mother of empire generated patriotic emotion and desire. The sequences of ceremonial procession were manifestations of colonial possession and scenes 'of general joy and unbounded loyalty', of the visceral pleasure of dwelling in and belonging to a Greater Britain.

Local stores not only evoked colonialism in their names, like the British and Colonial Meat Company, but also signalled a shift away from dependence on domestic agriculture toward the increasing importation of food. The Home & Colonial Tea Stores began as a trading association in 1885, and by 1903 had over 400 retail outlets in Britain, including a branch on East Street, in Bedminster. In addition to tea they sold a narrow range of products – sugar, bacon, ham, margarine and butter – but increased their profit margin through ownership of their producers and processors overseas as well as in the UK. Their shop counters had rows of compartments filled with different varieties of tea from plantations developed in India and Sri Lanka (then the Crown Colony of Ceylon).

Retail stores with multiple outlets competed for urban shoppers through competitive pricing and long opening hours. Although they aimed to attract the working class, Beatrice would not have entered these stores: she could only stare through their windows, for they protected their profits by refusing to issue credit on which the poor depended. There was much to see even from outside, since window displays formed a rich street culture of colonial information and advertising. The companies that adopted innovative advertising techniques were those whose goods were at the heart of the imperial economy: tea, chocolate, soaps and oils, tobacco, and meat extracts. Biscuit tins, chocolate wrappings, mugs and tea cloths commemorated coronations and the Jubilee, reproduced colonial flags, and used celebratory images of British royalty and military might. Though the family could not afford to purchase them commemorative mugs and biscuit and chocolate tins would have brightened the shelves of 1 Railway Cottages because they were distributed free to school children, being 'one of the prime means by which school boards encourage patriotism in children'.

The windows of newsagents were festooned with visual representations of the empire on which the sun never sets, including picture postcards and juvenile papers with images of colonial adventurers, which were widely circulated through the practice of swapping individual issues. Young people were also avid collectors of cigarette cards. On East Street sat the large factory of W. D. & H. O. Wills, the largest manufacture of tobacco products, which incorporated twelve other companies to form the Imperial Tobacco Company in 1901. The ciga-

rette cards they produced were, perhaps, the most influential form of collectable imperial propaganda, combing visual and textual information with clear pedagogic intent. They were issued in series and blank albums were sold to mount and display the cards. In addition to subjects like coronations, aviation, flora and fauna, insects, fish, dogs, sports figures, stately homes, lighthouses, artworks, authors and English period costumes, there were a number of card series devoted to all aspects of empire, including Arms, Flags, Builders of Empire, Britain's Defenders, Children of all Nations, Indian Regiments and Governor-Generals, Engineering Wonders, Army Life and the Royal Navy.

For Beatrice as for her generation, a prerequisite of being a modern British citizen was being an imperial subject; visual spectacle generated and confirmed their patriotism, their loyalty not only to nation but to empire. The aggressive expansion and maintenance of territorial dominance necessitated war in far flung regions, the significance

of which was brought home through public celebrations of military might. The return of units of the British Army from the Boer War in 1902 were occasions for patriotic spectacle as they paraded through the streets of cities and towns all over the country. Mitchell and Kenyon, a Lancashire-based film company who were pioneers in the production of British motion pictures, travelled south to produce a film of the crowds gathered in Bristol to greet the return of war hero Lord Methuen, despite his failures on the battlefield. For Beatrice, like many others, this would have been her first experience of witnessing the making of a moving picture. Death also occasioned spectacles of patriotic sentiment aimed at cementing local ties to soldiers killed thousands of miles away. In Bristol large groups of spectators were drawn to the pomp and ceremony surrounding the 1905 unveiling of the Boer War memorial in honour of the Gloucester Regiment garrisoned in the city.

Beginning in 1902, Empire Day was celebrated annually on 24 May, and the British Empire League furnished schools with flags. This was Beatrice's last year in school and she would have been among the students who performed in the patriotic plays and processions which were supported by local councils, who contributed refreshments and commemorative mugs. These were also lucrative occasions for lantern slide makers, who would photograph the children and their activities and then sell the shows to the schools. Pageants celebrating empire were held in Bristol throughout the decade and one of the most spectacular is recorded on a postcard.

Ten months after burying Rose, Beatrice was working as a live-in domestic servant for a household less than five minutes away from where her half-brother and sister, William and Elsie, lived with their father. I think Beatrice took this position so she could visit them and keep an eye on their welfare. In 1911 shops closed for half a day on Wednesdays, so perhaps she was able to negotiate a couple of hours away from her duties to attend the Empire Day celebrations. Did she stop and collect William and Elsie to take them with her to the park? They would have passed Colston Hall, then crossed Queen Square and headed to the bridge over the River Avon, walking toward their old neighbourhood of Bedminster. As Beatrice passed the street leading to Railway Cottages she must have felt a deep sorrow for the loss of Lillian Estella and her mother, while breathing a sigh of relief that she no longer lived there. But she could not afford to focus on the past. As she looked at William, now 11, striding beside her, and held Elsie's hand, she knew she had a responsibility toward them now, for they were ill-clad and seemed to be always hungry.

As Beatrice approached the tunnel under the railway tracks did she increase her pace in anticipation of seeing her sister Maud and younger brother Bertie standing waiting for her on the other side? I see them all together, joining the throng gathered to see hundreds of children forming a living Union Jack in Victoria Park.

Soon after this event, I think Beatrice must have decided that William and Elsie were in danger and had to be removed from George. William was successfully fostered with a family, but only temporary sheltering care could be found for Elsie at Bristol Female Mission's Elm House. Beatrice's uncle James signed his niece, Elsie, into a Dr Barnardo's home.

Dreaming Empire

Dr Barnardo's Homes was among the philanthropic and church organizations, including the Bristol Emigration Society, that became notorious for sending young children from Britain to Canada to become a cheap source of farm labour and domestic help. Over 100,000 orphaned, abandoned and pauper juvenile migrants were sent to Canada between 1869 and 1932, many of whom were badly treated or abused. On 29 March 1915, Rose's ninth child, Elsie Annie Williams, twelve years old, landed in Saint John, New Brunswick, Canada, having been sent there by the Dr Barnardo's Home in Bristol. Elsie became a domestic servant for a family in Ontario. She lived in the province for the rest of her life and raised her family there. Apparently, she

always remembered her 'aunts' Maud and Beatrice. She died in 1989.

If the child emigration movement was the unsavoury underside of Canadian immigration programmes, the public face of promoting settlement was very different. From the late nineteenth century until the 1920s, overseas agents of the Canadian Department of the Interior travelled throughout the United States and Europe promoting migration to the dominion with a missionary zeal, bombarding their populations with billboards and posters publicizing free land grants, distributing literature, and giving lectures in cities and towns. No village was too small, no hamlet too remote for their reach. Emigration from Britain to the white settler societies of the British Empire was promoted as 'merely a redistribution of the population within Greater Britain'.

In 1905, under the direction of Frank Oliver, Minister of the Interior and Superintendent-General of Indian Affairs, Canadian immigration policy became more racially and culturally restrictive, favouring 'Anglo-Saxon' immigrants who were deemed 'most able to assimilate'. How many members of the Williams and Leaworthy families were tempted by the promise of owning land and leading a healthy life? How many dreamed of escaping their hardscrabble poverty while standing in front of a poster or watching a lantern slide show? How many realized that their whiteness opened up opportunities they thought their poverty had foreclosed? How many came to believe that they were, justifiably, rulers of the earth even if they didn't have enough to eat?

CANADA
Healthy Climate! Free Schools!
160-Acre Farms in Western Canada
– Free!
'Cinematograph and Stereopticon Views
of . . . Canada and its resources:
a Field for British settlers.'

The presentations of the recruiters attracted large crowds of 800 to 1,200 people, and were a form of free mass entertainment. Audiences sat spellbound by the promise of futurity realized in light: visions of prosperity and high yield; scenes of bountiful harvests and healthy domestic livestock; portraits of sturdy, smiling white men, women and children standing in fields of grain. Lantern slides portrayed summer and autumn, but the accompanying lectures also emphasized that winters were easily managed as they were dry and sunny and healthier than the foggy dampness of Britain. Surviving the winter was merely a matter of wearing the right clothes. How difficult was it to leave these glowing visions behind and return through foul, polluted air to houses full of coughing, contagion and rotting lungs?

Racism was peddled as bait. Climate was a popular reference point from which lecturers launched explicitly racist appeals to their listeners. One additional benefit attributed to Canadian winters was that they did 'an enormous good in keeping out the Negro races and those less athletic races of southern Europe'. Other racist practices were concealed. The missionary agents of migration made no reference to the fact that they were trading in stolen lands. What was being given away for 'free' in 160-acre parcels, under the Dominion Lands Act of 1872, was not empty land but forcibly emptied land. As the lantern slides rolled in England, First Nations peoples and the Métis were dispossessed in Canada, confined to reservations and 'hobbled like horses'. Oliver increased the powers of coercion and amended previous agreements and treaties in order to remove peoples from reservations and redistribute their lands to Euro-Canadians and immigrants. First Nations peoples and the Métis were forbidden from applying for homesteads, nor were they allowed to own any land in the prairies.

If the public face of Canada was one source of colonial assurance of white superiority, what did Beatrice or Rose know about Jamaica and Jamaicans, other than what could be found on the back of a Wills cigarette card? My maternal relatives were vehemently, implacably, opposed to the relationship between my mother and the Jamaican airman who would become my father. Their understanding of their allegiance to empire, their belonging as white, imperial, racially superior British subjects, was formed, maintained and reinforced in the mundane details of daily life – in shopping, storing biscuits and drinking tea. What could have exposed the history of violence and exploitation that bound Bristol and Jamaica?

Beatrice may have noticed a poster advertising 'Jamaica: The New Riviera' on a museum notice board, or in the window of the Dunscombe Optical Lantern and Photographic Store on St Augustine Parade. If she had it would have been the subtitle, 'A Veritable Mecca for the Invalid', that caught her attention and enticed her to attend. I imagine her carefully noting the place, date and time of the lantern show, which promised vibrant images of 'a beautiful island of luxurious vegetation and lovely scenery, refreshed by invigorating sea breezes', then hurrying home with a quicker, lighter step, eager to announce this promise of 'restored health' and glimpse of paradise. These unexpected and unfamiliar words would have tumbled out of Beatrice's mouth at home, but was there enough force and conviction in her voice to persuade Rose to accompany her to hear James Johnston, from Brown's Town, Jamaica, give a lecture on the island colony? The Beatrice of my imagination would have attended 'Jamaica: The New Riviera' on her own if no one wanted to go with her; as a teenager she already demonstrated the fierce determination that was a dominant trait of the woman she became, and of the daughter she would raise.

James Johnston's lecturing tours in the UK between 1901 and 1903 were part of a larger capitalist project of colonial modernization, and heralded the opening of a new shipping service between Bristol and Jamaica under contract with the Imperial Direct Line. Joseph Chamberlain, Secretary of State for the Colonies from 1895 to 1903, was the leader of those advocating for a New Imperialism and the architect of programmes for its implementation. He was convinced that Britain had to ensure its economic future and military dominance through closer links with the colonies and the expansion of empire. Chamberlain organized the celebration of Britain's first Diamond Jubilee, in 1897, as an imperial spectacle because he understood how empire could be visualized and enacted, harnessed for its ideological potential to secure the affiliation and allegiance of British citizens. Chamberlain financed a coterie of imperialist men in a plan to increase trade and open Jamaica to tourism. Bristol was the fulcrum of this plan intended to impel Jamaica to become modern, by which was meant becoming a more profitable colony.

To this end the British government awarded Alfred Lewis Jones, Managing Director of the Liverpool-based Elder Dempster shipping company, a contract to take over all steamships running between the West Indies and the UK. Jones was to form a new shipping line – the Imperial Direct West India Mail Company, to run between Bristol and Kingston – and open a transatlantic market introducing bananas to the British and the wealthy British to Jamaica. Chamberlain promised to subsidize the venture if Jones would take the leading role in promoting a 'New Jamaica' and building a market in the UK. In the 1750s, luxury items like chocolate and coffee were available in the shops of Bristol; during the early years of the twentieth century, the British public were to be persuaded to consume bananas and dream of Jamaica.

" Bananas two for 1½d."

I wonder if Beatrice, or Maud, purchased bananas from a cart being wheeled down a Bristol street by a black man selling the fruit at two for a penny-halfpenny? Would the sisters have stood stock still at such a sight? Would they have been taken aback? Were the black residents of Bristol a familiar sight to them, so common that they took their presence for granted? An African banana skin, dated to approximately 1460, was discovered during excavations at the Museum of London in 1999, and a bunch from Bermuda was displayed in the window of a London herbalist in 1663, but bananas were not regularly imported into the UK until 1884, and were not widely available until the early twentieth century. The closely woven political, economic, social and cultural ties between Jamaica and England formed an imperial intimacy that had been rendered historically invisible by the turn of the twentieth century, but bananas were the tangible evidence of a connection. Or perhaps not. My grandmother's generation would have taken for granted the presence of sugar in their tea, and chocolate and tobacco in their shops, just as they took for granted the tea itself. But bananas, all imported through Bristol, appeared throughout the nation during Beatrice's teenage years and their presence needed to be explained. The banana must have seemed such an exotic fruit at

first sight. If Beatrice knew what bananas were, did she have an image of Jamaica in her mind as she unpeeled one and tasted it? Was a black banana seller a commonplace sight? What would Beatrice have known about Kingston, the city from which Imperial Direct ships exported bananas to Bristol 'at a rate of thirty thousand bunches a fortnight?'

Minstrel shows and troupes of Jubilee singers from the United States regularly toured the UK, and they performed in Bristol in the latter half of the nineteenth century. In 1886,

'The Great American Slave Troupe and Brass Band', with '16 REAL NEGROES', mounted parades through the streets the day they arrived, and performed free serenades outside the Old Theatre Royal each day before their show. Black performers were to be found all over the UK in the Victorian and Edwardian periods, at carnivals and on the stage in vaudevilles and theatres.

Alfred Jones arranged for the Kingston Choral Union to make three tours of the UK between 1906 and 1908. They travelled to and from Jamaica on his ships, which docked in Avonmouth. From there, the KCU travelled by train to tour cities and towns all over the country; in 1908 they performed in Wales and the West Country. Even if Beatrice and Maud did not go to the theatre, they would have seen posters and postcards announcing their performances.

The only photograph I ever saw of my grandmother showed a prim young woman. A studio image lost long ago, I believe it was taken in Bristol at about the same time as the photograph of the banana seller. I remember Beatrice's hair was tied back tightly with ribbon, and that she wore a belted dress with long sleeves, a series of small buttons running up each of the long cuffs. The broad pleats of the skirt ended in ruffles falling over tightly laced ankle boots. To me my grandmother looked every inch a proper Edwardian miss. Confronted by a banana seller did Beatrice hesitate and furrow her brow in concentration, trying to imagine where such fruit, or such people, had come from? Would her curiosity have impelled her into a lantern slide show about Jamaica? My mother learnt to dream of Jamaica in her own way, but perhaps Beatrice also instilled in her daughter a particular form of English colonial dreaming. My grandfather would not have encouraged her to dream of far off places; he was too grounded, and placed his faith in hedgerows.

Chamberlain and Jones employed James Johnston, a Jamaican missionary, and Alfred Leader, an amateur photographer from Bristol, to photograph the landscape of Jamaica as a space of desire in the British imagination. The camera was a technology essential to colonial projects of modernization but in this project they imitated a photographic campaign by US businesses. In 1875, the English photographer, Eadweard Muybridge, had been employed by the American Pacific Mail Steamship Company to make a photographic tour of Central America. The shipping company wanted images to 'stimulate Central and South American commerce' with the aim of generating the interest of tourists and investors. Muybridge was instructed to photograph coffee plantations in Guatemala so that his images could be used to attract capital investment.

James Johnston was perfectly suited for this work. As a young boy growing up in Scotland in the 1860s, Johnston became enthralled by the writings of explorers like Robert Moffat and David Livingstone, and he dreamed of going to the 'Dark Continent' himself. He wished, he wrote, 'to see for myself the actual condition of the African, that I might be better qualified to plead his cause among English-speaking people, who have ... proven themselves above all other nations the pioneers of civilization, Christianity, and humane government'. These desires were thwarted by his ill health. In 1874, Johnston was told he had contracted tuberculosis and needed to move to 'a more genial climate': such a climate he found 'in Jamaica, West Indies'. Scottish migration to Jamaica over several generations had established plenty of connections for him there, particularly in the parish of St Ann, which was where Johnston resided for forty-seven years.

Although migrating to the British West Indies was not following in the footsteps of Dr Livingstone, Johnston did not stifle his dreams: Jamaica was a colonial space in which he could imagine himself as one among 'the pioneers of civilization, Christianity, and humane government'. He also consoled himself with the thought that 'the bulk of the population, though not African, are at least of African descent'.

For fifteen years Johnston practised medicine in his Evangelical mission in Brown's Town. By 1890, 'his lungs were healed, the mission was on a sound footing, [and] his aides were trustworthy', so Johnston turned his thoughts, once again, to David Livingstone and masculine colonial adventures in Central Africa. He wanted to alleviate the 'privations, hardships, and sufferings', as well as the high death rate, of white African missionaries, 'those who were endeavouring to lead the van of light and knowledge into the dark interior', while receiving 'little or no aid or sympathy from the natives'. Johnston concluded from his experience with Jamaican men and women – the trustworthy aides who established and maintained his mission in Brown's Town – that, as white men were not capable of undertaking the physical labour necessary for missions to survive in the tropics, he should take 'young men of Jamaica' to the African continent to be the 'mechanics, builders, and planters', relieving 'the white man of manual toil'.

For eighteen months, from May 1891 to October 1892, Johnston travelled from mission to mission, town to town, across spheres of French, Portuguese and British colonial influence, from the West African coast, across Central Africa to the Indian Ocean. Initially, he had six 'young Jamaican men' in tow, four of whom remained to 'assist' the Rev. W. T. Currie, a missionary in Cisamba, while the other two, referred to in the account as "Frater and Jonathan" were 'entrusted' by Johnston to a Rev. Elliott in Bechuanaland. There is no account of this journey from the Jamaicans themselves, but all six eventually made their own way back to Jamaica. I assume these young men reached a point where they had seen enough of the future Johnston was shaping for them, and had enough of being his colonial beasts of burden, that they abandoned him and his venture. Johnston returned alone to Jamaica where he wrote an account of his journey and his disappointment at its failure. How did he end up in Bristol?

In the decade after his return from Central Africa, Johnston became a member of the Jamaican Legislative Council and determined that his evangelical talents could be most effectively deployed by promoting the 'New Jamaica', converting his listeners not into souls for God but into investors and tourists. In 1898, Johnston, referred to by the American press as 'the well-known African explorer', was lecturing in the United States and Canada. He sought to persuade American businessmen to invest capital in the Jamaican fruit industry, rather than in African countries, as he could assure them from his own experience that 'there's no money there – in crops, or gold or anything else'. Johnston also guaranteed the high standard of tourist facilities in Jamaica and told his audiences that 'a great deal of [their] pulmonary suffering could be easily relieved by a visit'. By 1901, Johnston was lecturing for Sir Alfred Jones and his Imperial Direct West India Mail Service – a sign of modernity (and age), perhaps, that the intrepid explorer had become a well-paid creator of tourist dreams.

Lantern slide shows inducted crowds into a particularly modern form of individual and collective subjectivity, forever changing the ways in which the world was known. The metropolitan subject learnt to become a tourist even without the means to travel; they learnt to observe others as objects susceptible to their mastery. Knowledge of the limitations of their existence, the misery of their daily realities, melted into "fascinated absorption" and longing in the evanescent light of modern-day colonies and foreign landscapes.

The first hurdle to be overcome in representing Jamaica as a 'New Riviera' was the entrenched belief that the island was a site of disease, tormenting insects, parasites and a recalcitrant black population. In order to see for myself what verbal strategies Johnston employed to accomplish this transformation, I had to visit the library at the University of Cambridge. Sitting reading his script my mind travelled back in time to Bristol in 1903, where I sat with my grandmother in a darkened auditorium.

Johnston advised all amateur lecturers to tell their stories in a 'natural, conversational, free and easy style', which would put them 'in touch with [their] listeners, fixing the attention and carrying them along with you'. In the dark, we are captivated by Johnston's words, mesmerized by the glow of image after image passing in front of our eyes and hypnotized by the soothing voice which moulds how we see. The audience boards the SS *Port Antonio*, one of the 'palatial yachts' of the Imperial Direct West India Mail Service, and are transported from the grey skies, cold and damp climate of Bristol to the port of Kingston, 'the most important city in the West Indies', set against the backdrop of 'the magnificent range of the Blue Mountains'. We arrive on a 'beautiful island of luxurious vegetation and lovely scenery, refreshed by invigorating sea breezes', where it is possible to enjoy 'a degree of health and life' such as is found nowhere else. We experience a reality so intense it renders our lives mundane.

We travel from the harbour to the Constant Spring Hotel on the tramway of the Canadian owned West India Electric Company. Once there we look across the Liguanea Plains to 'a sea view of unrivaled beauty, the Caribbean in glorious tints of emerald and blue' and collectively hold our breath. Moonlight brings 'enchantment': we are lulled to sleep breathing air 'laden with the perfume of flowers' and listening to 'the murmuring fronds of the graceful palm tree'.

The next morning, we travel along Half Way Tree Road where 'the fields and foliage assume a deeper green, the glare is less, and the air freshens as [we] ascend the hill' toward Castleton Gardens. On the journey we are enticed ... crowds of women and children ... walking briskly along with their baskets on their heads, carrying yams, plantains, potatoes, breadfruit, limes, lemons, oranges, pineapples, cocoanuts, mangoes, shaddock, grapefruits, papaws, melons, custardapples ... sweetsops, soursops, roseapples, sapodillas, cherrymoya, granadillas, cashews, chochos, tamarinds, avocado pears, poultry and eggs etc., destined for market in Kingston.

by the synchronicity of language and sight. Words tumble upon words in Johnston's recitation, overwhelming us with a sense of abundance. We take pleasure in the quality of their strangeness, of the alien and unexplored; the weight and wealth of their accumulation, the resonance of sound and image, produce an erotic delight. What does it matter if we do not understand what we see and hear? What matters is what we feel: the sensuality of excess.

We find ourselves perched above the lush vegetation of Castleton Gardens, Jamaica's famous botanical garden, looking down upon a public footpath. There is a mountain in the distance. The perspective exaggerates the size of the foliage and vegetation while dwarfing the human and the social. Our eyes follow a path of light from our high vantage point to a man and a woman, standing apart where the paths converge surrounded by palms, pines and banana trees that diminish them. Behind the man in a white shirt a tree casts a solid shadow diagonally across the path; as our eyes follow the shadow we are startled to find another person almost, but not quite, hidden in dappled shade. A shadow delineates the folds of the woman's skirt and runs into the ground. We have the impression that these people are as rooted in place as the enormous trunks of the trees which tower over them. We experience Castleton Gardens both as a study of detail and as a curious absence of detail: we are unable to distinguish any of the features of a human face, but the palm fronds are sharply defined, etched in sharp contrasts of light and dark.

We then find ourselves at a 'Lily Pond' where to northern eyes the abundance and productivity of the natural world verges on the alien, chaotic and out of control, like the sinister landscape of H. G. Wells' scientific romance, *The Island of Dr Moreau*. Johnston becomes aware of our discomfort and fearfulness ripples through the auditorium as we shift in our seats, lower our eyes, and lose concentration. Beatrice does not know what to make of what she sees and feels. It is all too overwhelming.

I leave the auditorium, and my grandmother, and force myself back to the University library and the script in front of me. Johnston reasserted control at the point where the unknown seemed too strange, too wild for his audience. His lecture belonged to a larger modernist project to teach the British to view Jamaica as a well ordered, domesticated landscape brimming with picturesque places, so he countered their unease by sitting his audience down by the Cave River for a picnic. The lecture struck a canny balance between thrilling his listeners and offering comfort and reassurance, regularly reminding them that Jamaica was a benign and healthful paradise, 'one of the fairest countries in the habitable earth . . . a land of picturesque views . . . [and] unrivaled beauty'. In his lecture the phrase 'In what other country could you find . . .' was repeated many times. Jamaica, the audience were constantly assured, was a 'dreamland'.

'Jamaica: The New Riviera' was designed to ease any latent anxieties about the perils of the island and to erase fears of Jamaican belligerence, whether that was thought to reside in nature or emerge from its people. Johnston's images titillated and soothed at the same time, eradicating any worry that the dreamer would awake to find him or herself among resentful, restive and rebellious colonial subjects.

On the contrary, Jamaicans are revealed to be gardeners, purveyors of abundance, bearers of the island's agricultural riches for the dreamer's consumption. Presented in the neat, clean attire that everyone in Edwardian Britain would recognize as the uniform of servants, these Jamaicans are posed with yams, bananas and unhusked coconuts. As they hold, balance and lift into view gigantic examples of produce, viewers are reassured that Jamaicans successfully handle nature that otherwise could appear to be out of control. Offering up to the viewer the fruits of their labour and their island, Jamaicans become people who, like the landscape against which they are posed, are managed, tamed and domesticated. The population of the 'New Jamaica' is safe, willing and eager to serve their island's bounty to future tourists.

Johnston and his flickering images held his audience spell-bound: 'this picture exhibits not only fair types of the ordinary domestic servant', he intoned, 'but also good specimens of the Jamaican staff of life, the ubiquitous yam', weaving Jamaicans and Jamaican produce seamlessly together. Johnston's voice rose while his head swept the room and his eyes sought to make direct contact with each member of his audience, pausing for effect before declaring Jamaica to be 'the brightest jewel in the British Crown'.

If Beatrice, Maud and Rose were among Johnston's audience, they would have learnt that, poor and female though they were, they owned Jamaica: land, people and produce.

Maud, Walter and Charles

Beatrice's eldest sister Maud began work as a domestic servant when she was fourteen, and married Walter when she was twenty and he twenty-three. Walter was the first of the Leaworthys to turn his back on agricultural labour. His migration from Uffculme, Devon to Bristol at the age of seventeen made him part of what historians refer to as a great wave of rural migration to towns and cities in the Edwardian era. Walter was drawn not merely by the magnetism of an urban environment, but by the particular promise of steady work on the Great Western Railway. He obtained the necessary letters of reference and found lodgings in a boarding house in Bristol. The stories I heard as a child, the lives I was supposed to emulate, were less abstract when I found Walter's rise through the ranks recorded in pen and ink and could trace it, with my finger, across the columns of a GWR register for 'drivers, firemen and cleaners'. Each entry marked a stage on a ladder of promotion and an increase in wage. This was the defining characteristic of the internal labour market of the railway companies: workers were hired at the entry level, higher levels were filled from within, and wages were determined by administrative procedures not by external market pressure.

In August 1900, Walter began a forty-five-year career with the GWR at the entry level position of engine cleaner, paid on the piece-work system. When steam engines stood waiting for passengers in train stations they shone; they glistened in railway posters, and twinkled in the pages of children's story books. By the end of the day they were encrusted in filth. Before the First World War, the GWR at Bristol employed cleaners in two different wage schemes, piece work or day work. As a piece worker, Walter would have worked in a gang of four on one engine at a time, being paid 'four hours for top of boiler, four hours for the tender, four hours for the side and four hours for gears and motions'. The cleaning process was demanding, systematic and meticulous.

The hundreds of thousands of young men who flocked to work on the railways may have dreamed of becoming engine drivers, but engine men had to start as cleaners and firemen. Steam engines accrued layers of smoke, ash and grease as they travelled. Cleaning the exterior was gruelling work, but cleaning the entrails of an engine, crawling around inside the smoke box and chimney, or climbing down underneath the engine in the ash pits, was dangerously hot and filthy labour which had deleterious effects on the body: overalls would become encrusted with dirt; lungs filled with sooty deposits from inhaling sulphurous smoke, ash, coal dust and fumes from cleaning and lubricating oils; eyes and throats were constantly irritated.

Side and connecting rods were polished bright and covered with a film of petroleum jelly for protection against the weather. The brass work was scoured and then rubbed over with dry soot from a smoke box to give a high finish. Boilers, tenders and tanks were all washed with cleaning oil, and then wavy patterns were made in the oil by applying tallow fat. On completion, the leading cleaner would 'pass' the engine as cleaned by rubbing his hand between the axle spokes or under the foot plate.

Walter was a piece worker for only one year, after which he was appointed a shunting fireman with a regular wage of 3 shillings a day. He proceeded on his steady rise through the ranks of railway employees and down the columns of the GWR employment records from cleaning to shunting to goods, to fireman 3rd, 2nd and 1st class. He was earning 3 shillings and sixpence a day, 21 shillings for a six-day week, when his first son was born in August 1906. This was more than he would have earned as an agricultural labourer and, he would have argued, the GWR offered better future prospects.

Walter would have worked night shifts, but there is no register recording Maud's daily life. If she worked as a domestic servant in someone else's house before she wed, as a married woman
she cleaned her own home. In addition to running their household, Maud would have had the task of laundering encrusted
coal, ash and oil residue from Walter's overalls. Over a period of
six years, she gave birth to four children; each of her three sons
eventually became employees of GWR.

In 1912, Maud and Walter left Bristol and did not return.
Walter was transferred to Bridport in Dorset where their youngest son was born, and on the eve of the Great War they settled
in Llantrisant, South Wales. Their family will stay in this district
of small villages for generations. Walter's wages crept up to 5
shillings and sixpence as the war approached, and more than
doubled after the war when he finally became an engine driver.

The bottom half of the page recording Walter's employment
is headed *Record of Fines, &c.* At first glance Walter Leaworthy
has a clean record. Included in a plethora of annual tests for
colour vision and examinations for general health are notes
from a medical officer regarding the cardiac disease that will,
many years later, kill him, but there is also a brief notation that
makes me stop. Dated 12 June 1912, it states: 'notice handed to
Leaworthy in consequence of the transport workers strike'. This
strike had taken place the previous July and August 1911, during
which 500 railway workers had blockaded two level crossings
in Llanelli, on the line through Carmarthenshire which the
government used to transport troops to Ireland in order to quell
Irish protests in favour of Home Rule. Because of the military
value of the line the government did not hesitate to deploy the
army against the strikers. In the process of dispersing the protesters, soldiers from the Worcester Regiment shot and killed two of
the strikers. I search to see if all employees were served with
such a notice, but they were not. Walter must have had something to do with the strike and, perhaps, the blockade. The
notice was probably a warning. I remember the place name,
Llanelli, because as a child I was told stories about it by my
great uncle 'Walt'.

Of course, these memories are partial, embedded in other stories I heard from Walter and his sons, men who spent their lives working for the railways starting at age sixteen. In the swirl of memories I carry are tales of the unionization of railway workers, stories of labour activism, and of Walter as a union man. There were limits to Walter's company loyalty. When I came to know Walter Leaworthy he was an elderly man who wove tales for me as he pottered in his greenhouse. These stories and strikes and battles are spectral, they haunt me in the archive but can't quite become more than brief notations. Those who could make them substantial are dead.

Walter and Maud lived in South Wales for the rest of their lives. Charles, Walter's younger brother, my grandfather, left Somerset to join the army in 1914, and spent most of the First World War in Turkey. Beatrice left Bristol and went to live with her sister and brother-in-law in Llantrisant, where she worked as a milliner. Upon his discharge in 1918, Charles went to stay with them, courted Beatrice and married her in Pontypridd in 1919. Their child, Iris, was born in Llantrisant in 1920.

Walter fulfilled his ambitions, being promoted to the position of train driver on the Great Western Railway, an excellent job I was always told. Thinking that Charles shared his aspirations to middle-class status, Walter secured a job for his brother as a railway porter. But Charles had other ideas.

Charles Leaworthy ignored the advice of his elder brother and Beatrice. His deviation from the family script led to an endless battle of wills between Maud, Walter and Beatrice on one side, and Charles on the other. Listening to my mother's tangled reasonings of the dissension between her parents, I was aware of being recruited to the cause of my grandmother, as Beatrice had recruited Iris. Looking backwards at their lives, it is evident that the constant friction between my grandparents was rooted not only in their differing attitudes toward social mobility but also in their contrasting beliefs about modernity, modernization and war. Their domestic conflict was inflamed by the development of distinct moral codes and spiritual values which eventually generated a firestorm of opposing desires for, and definitions of, an honourable and respectable manner of living.

It seems as if my grandfather disappointed everyone in his family, including his own daughter, with his lack of ambition. My mother criticized her father for being content working the land, accusing him of being backwards, of refusing to be a part of modern life. She could or would not see his need for intro- spection and his lifetime search for peace. Private Charles Leaworthy served with the Welsh Regiment during the Great War, and I found his record in the First World War Medal Rolls Index. He was sent to Gallipoli where casualties in 1915 were catastrophic not only from combat but also from disease and cold. He rarely spoke about it to his granddaughter though she heard him rail about officers and generals on many occasions. The girl overheard bits and pieces about what happened to her grandfather from whispered conversations between her rela- tives, scraps of information I wish she had never known, images so vivid that they cannot be forgotten: soldiers drown- ing in flooded trenches; weeks spent surrounded by unburied corpses; someone returning at dawn and tossing the severed head of a Turkish soldier at his feet; the slaughter of hundreds of horses and mules when they were evacuated. I think my grandfather deliberately turned his back on the human social and political order that practised this brutality, his trauma producing an alternative set of ethics. He taught me to under- stand and value the natural world, for which I am ever grateful.

My grandfather tried working as a porter after the war but, to the dismay of his wife Beatrice and his brother Walter, turned his back on the GWR and returned to life as an agricultural labourer. Beatrice, Charles and their daughter Iris went to live in a tied cottage on the Penllyn Castle Estate, then owned by the Homfray family. My mother's earliest memories were of grow- ing up on this estate and living in a tied cottage. When she was four or five years old they heard of smallholding for sale in Ash Thomas, Devon. Beatrice resented being dependent on the largesse of the local lords, so she financed the venture from her savings and she and Charles set out to see if they could make a life as independent farmers.

The disaster that followed was transmitted to me in fragments that I assembled into a montage of my mother's despair: Iris as a child finding Beatrice leaning over a gate crying that Charles was a 'philanderer'; Iris as a mother telling me that Charles lost all of Beatrice's money; anxious weeks waiting for the birth of the sow's litter so debts could be repaid; anxiety dissolving into despair when the sow was found dead, caught up in a wire fence. At the start of the Great Depression in 1929, dispossession and eviction followed the death of the sow: all they owned – house, furniture, land and animals – was sold at auction. Iris said that she watched as even her doll went under the hammer.

Beatrice walked away from Charles and Iris and returned to Bristol. Charles returned to the life of an agricultural labourer and my mother was sent to live with her father's elder sister, her aunt Florrie. I do not know how long this separation lasted but my mother never forgot that her aunt and uncle made it clear that they did not want a child in their house and that Iris was to spend most of her time outside. Beatrice eventually returned and the family reassembled but they would never own their own land again.

My grandmother Beatrice and grandfather Charles had very different desires in the rapidly transforming world of Edwardian Britain. By the turn of the century, 'Britain was the most urbanized country in the world', with less than 25 per cent of its population living in rural areas and only 7 per cent working in agriculture. While those who wanted to rise from rural poverty left Devon and Somerset and migrated to Bristol, Beatrice's husband had led her in the opposite direction. In response she rebelled.

Charles was a large, warm, ebullient figure who taught the girl, a city child, not to be afraid of the cows that loomed over her, or of the pigs that ran around her in unpredictable directions. When the girl bravely declared that she was not afraid of the sheep, he explained that sheep were too stupid to be scary.

Sheep were the only animals she ever heard him disparage. Her grandfather's weathered face creased with smile wrinkles and his eyes twinkled mischievously when he was faced with the challenge of the girl's lack of knowledge or fear of the natural world. Though she always had the feeling that her mother did not quite trust Charles to take care of her daughter properly, the girl felt secure. He would take her by the hand and march her across fields and ditches and down lanes, teaching her how to negotiate turnstiles and cattle crossings. As she plodded along beside him in her Wellington boots into and out of woods, her grandfather opened her eyes to the world of living things flying, buzzing, crawling or growing around her. One drizzly day, he pried his reluctant granddaughter out of her comfortable chair, away from her book, and into her mackintosh, coaxing her out of his cottage into the woods. I expect she was dragging her feet and looking at the ground when they stopped in a copse. She looked up and fell in love, as he knew she would, with the magical sight of bluebells in full bloom, a carpet of pure indigo in the woods.

In London, where the girl was the guide, Charles Leaworthy was a different person. Riding on the top of a double-decker bus or walking around the centre of the city he held tightly to her hand, transmitting through his grip how insecure and fearful he felt. In London he did not laugh. In the city he depended upon his granddaughter, whose head barely reached to his waist, to navigate their way through what he regarded as urban chaos. It was not only the noise and crowds of the city that terrified him but also its unpredictability. In the country he knew where he was, and could trust the land and its animals. Only now can I begin to comprehend how deeply wounded he had been by Great War when he just was twenty-one years old.

Part Four:

Accounting

*There is a story always ahead of you. Barely existing. Only grad-
ually do you attach yourself to it and feed it. You discover the
carapace that will contain and test your character.*
Michael Ondaatje, The Cat's Table

Writing by Hand

My father has, or more accurately used to have, beautiful hand-writing. The headmistress at my secondary school, a Miss Pym, prized the art of penmanship and would have considered his handwriting exemplary.

Before dementia began its relentless encroachment through his mind, before an autoimmune disease wrought havoc on his muscular system, my father wrote lengthy, thoughtful and care-fully composed letters to me and mailed them across the Atlantic. He was a man who was reserved yet quick to anger. When he wanted to express emotion, affection, or explain a deeply held belief, my father wrote it down, for over time he had become fearful of mis-speaking. The act of putting pen to paper, of shap-ing individual letters into words in solitude, of making many drafts of a letter before being satisfied with it, allowed my father to say exactly what he meant.

Every day Miss Pym wore a tightly buttoned suit jacket and pencil skirt and secured her steely grey hair in a knot at the nape of her neck. She had a ramrod straight back, and a stern demean-our. Miss Pym was a woman of convictions, one of them being that the content of my character did not reside in the colour of my skin or my 'mongrel' background, another that one's future was not determined by the social status of one's parents. I loved Miss Pym without reservation, even though she could be very aloof and her grave frown of disapproval made me a little afraid of her. She took her responsibilities as headmistress very seriously. For some reason she believed that I – one of the few day pupils on a scholarship, a gangly almost-teenager who ran when she should have walked and who was accused of 'having her head in the clouds' – had the potential to become, in her opinion, an accomplished woman.

Among the accomplishments that Miss Pym was determined I should acquire was the art of the English round hand. 'Penmanship', Miss Pym declared, 'reveals qualities of character'. I considered her dictum: recipients of correspondence in an elegant hand judged the writer as a person of confidence and worth; I concluded this was true. My mind was not so much in the clouds as saturated with the fictions of the nineteenth-century English novel. I was a young woman possessed by Jane Austen, Anthony Trollope and George Eliot. From these fictional worlds of country houses and estates I gathered that, after breakfast, gracious and elegant women retired to a 'morning room' to deal with their 'correspondence'. Correspondence was among the words I savoured, rolling it around in my mouth, tasting it.

Miss Pym also proffered advice on dress. Clothes made of quality British cloth were a statement that signalled good taste and judgement. Her own severely tailored dark blue suits were made of the finest serge, her feet were encased in tightly laced, brown English leather Oxford brogues, her legs wrapped in thick grey woollen stockings in winter and white cotton stockings in spring and summer. I imagined rows and rows of identical blue suits hanging above rows and rows of identical brown shoes in an imposing wardrobe in Miss Pym's bedroom in a large Victorian house. Being a pupil in a private school surrounded by girls from wealthy families, I assumed that everyone but me was rich. It only occurred to me years later that Miss Pym may have only possessed one or two suits and that the sharp tailoring may not have been a sign of wealth but disguised the lack of it.

My mother made all my clothes, except for certain items of my school uniform: a rust-coloured school blazer and beret, a grey gabardine raincoat and indoor (red) and outdoor (brown) lace-up Oxfords. My scholarship to this private ballet school did not include an allowance for the compulsory uniform but the 'College Handbook' declared that these items must be purchased from Burberry, an exclusive London department store, at a price my mother could ill-afford. It was fortuitous that she was a talented dressmaker, like her mother before her. Although my mother worked full-time in the city she would spend her winter evenings sewing for me, creating elegantly tailored grey skirts, cream shirts and blue and white polka-dot shirt-dresses from beautiful wools and soft cottons. Consequently, I never had reason to feel dowdy or envious among the girls I saw as glamorous: girls with confidence and composure, young women who possessed an unselfconscious equanimity about their place in the world, a self-assurance that I gradually came to associate with words like 'good breeding' and 'family'. These girls never ran; they sauntered.

When we day-pupils arrived each morning by bus we arrived as outsiders, unfamiliar with the alliances and discords of dorms and bathrooms, confidences whispered and secrets spilled at night. After hanging up our coats and tying the laces tightly on our red shoes, we hurried toward the assembly hall only to hesitate at its threshold before entering a world already in the full flow of conversations that our arrival now interrupted. We were not unwelcome, but we returned to our own separate houses and families, each with its own particular stresses and strains, while the boarders remained a community without us, a separate world of intimacies.

I longed to be best friends with a girl whose surname was Bathurst, and I was a constant presence on the margins of her circle. Her parents would not allow their daughter to visit the house of a Jamaican. Even from my distant orbit I learnt that the name Bathurst was a name to be found in '*Burke's*', along with the names of a few other girls at the school. I thought I was hearing 'Berks', the abbreviated term for the county of Berkshire. The word was spoken with such reverence that I imagined the Bathursts must be connected in some way to the Royal Family and Windsor Castle. The significance (and correct spelling) of

'*Burke's*' was revealed in one of Miss Pym's history lessons on '*Peerage*'.

What was not to be found in my school history books or in Burke's was that Bathurst is also the surname of descendants of enslaved persons in Barbados, Grenada, Trinidad and Jamaica. This discarded, forgotten family I unearthed for myself many years later sitting in one of the leather and oak chairs of the old British Library Reading Room.

While researching the lives of black Britons in the eighteenth century, I was startled to come across the name Bathurst in a biographical sketch of Frances Barber, who was born in Jamaica and became well-known as the black servant of Dr Samuel Johnson, English author and lexicographer. Now a confident academic, rather than a teenager intimidated by Britain's arcane class system, I set out to discover the ancestry of my old classmates. Consulting *Burke's Genealogical and Heraldic* histories of the *Peerage, Baronetage and Knightage* and of the *Landed Gentry*, what I had considered a historical detour returned me to my main concern with colonialism, plantation slavery and, my particular interest, Jamaica.

Weaving my way through a bewildering array of Bathurst 'issues' was a process akin to being in a Scripture class at school, poring over the endless repetition of 'begat' in the books of the Old Testament in the King James Bible. Arriving with the Saxons in the part of Britain that would become known as England, the Bathurst estate and castle were established near Battle in Sussex. During the Wars of the Roses, a Laurence Bathurst supported the Lancastrians and was summarily executed in 1463 by Edward IV, after his defeat of Henry VI; the Bathurst lands were forfeited and the castle destroyed. A Lancelot Bathurst was Alderman of London during the reign of Queen Elizabeth I, and a Dr Ralph Bathurst a Latin Poet, and President of Trinity College, Oxford. In 1712, the family advanced to the Peerage. I was most interested in the moment at which Bathurst activity entered the colonial arena: Sir Benjamin Bathurst, MP, 'was elected in the reign of Charles II, Governor of the Royal African Company, and, under James II, Governor of the East India

Company; the 2nd Earl Bathurst became Lord High Chancellor of Great Britain in 1771; and Henry, 3rd Earl Bathurst, was Secretary of State for War and the Colonies from 1812–27'. In a less illustrious branch of the family tree in Jamaica, a John Bathurst acquired land in 1674. His grandson, Colonel Richard Bathurst, who inherited the 4,000-acre Orange River estate, brought Frances Barber to England with him shortly before his death. The colonel's son, also a Richard Bathurst, was born on the estate but left to study medicine in England, where he became a great friend of Dr Johnson. According to James Boswell, Johnson's biographer, it was Colonel Bathurst who 'bequeathed' Barber to Johnson in his will.

It was listening to the conversations of girls at school that made me aware of a set of associations for the word 'family' beyond my immediate horizon of parents, sibling, aunts, uncles and cousins, Jamaican and Welsh. To distinguish new knowledge from old I imagined their definition of 'Family' began with a capital 'F'. Family, I learnt, referenced a history echoing across generations and resonating through surnames; Family was a form of belonging given substance by a long association with particular English counties, with legacies, inheritances and, sometimes, even titles. Family meant lineage, Ancestors with a capital 'A'. When they spoke of Family it was a flood of information about possible pedigrees and lineage tinged with elements of swagger. I was intimidated and silenced by these exchanges. Now I see that they must have been anxious performances of class insecurity, presumably second-hand versions of conversations overheard at home. In the 1960s, these young women appeared incredibly wealthy and 'well connected' to me, but their fathers were professionals rather than aristocrats: solicitors, chartered accountants or government bureaucrats, whose wives did not work outside the home. Perhaps one or the other parent came from a minor branch of the British elite. True, untrue, or exaggerated, boasting about lineage and social position was my first introduction to how ideologies of Englishness and of national and colonial belonging were inherited possessions.

At school, the accounts of ancestors that captivated me came from Miss Pym, for they were not just about Family. I learnt little about her personal history, except that she was a Quaker descendent of the Pym family of Ireland, that she was not married and that she refused the word spinster. Miss Pym created a world of stories in the classroom, prompted by an historical incident or an event recounted in a novel. Miss Pym introduced me to History, not Family, and I was hooked.

She described the Puritans, the English Civil War and the period of republican rule by Oliver Cromwell, not only because she claimed that John Pym, one of the leading Parliamentarians, was a distant ancestor but also because Cromwell's ambition to seize Spanish colonies in the Caribbean led directly to the British invasion of Jamaica in May 1655. I do not know if she was trying to make historical connections between her ancestors and mine via British and Jamaican history, but I created analogies.

The most famous of Miss Pym's ancestors, John Pym, was born in Somerset. This was the county where my mother grew up in a series of tied cottages, and the place where I used to walk in bluebell woods grasping my grandfather's hand. Pym, born in 1584, became famous for his financial abilities, which I could appreciate as my father, born in 1921, was clever with figures though never famous for it. Whereas my father's ancestors were listed among the property of an estate in Portland, Jamaica, John Pym was landed gentry and held a post as a tax collector for the King, receiving his revenue from the counties of Hampshire, Wiltshire and Gloucestershire. My father was treasurer of the local cricket club in Mitcham; Pym became treasurer for the Providence Island Company, founded by a group of Puritans who wanted to establish a colony on Providence Island in the West Indies. In 1625, Pym was elected to Parliament, eventually becoming the leader of the Puritan opposition to Charles I. I sided with Oliver Cromwell and the Parliamentarians, not the Royalists, when we learnt about the English Civil War. In 1642, John Pym became 'the architect of Parliament's victory', raising sufficient money from City financiers' loans, taxes on land and the seizure of Royalist estates to allow Cromwell to raise an army to defeat a King. John Pym organized the committee structure that would administer the nation during the war and throughout the existence of the Commonwealth and Protectorate. I knew that my father was a magician with figures who had saved more than one local club from bankruptcy, but we couldn't lay claim to illustrious predecessors whose expertise in accountancy had financed a war. Miss Pym solicited information about my background but, it seemed to me, the more I revealed the greater was her conviction that my handwriting was paramount in announcing my worth to the world.

Hunched over my school desk or dining room table, fantasizing that I was sitting gracefully at a desk in a morning room, I raised my treasured silver and turquoise Parker pen over the page of my exercise book, bottle of ink and blotting paper in close proximity. I took a deep breath, determined to wield the pen to my advantage. Yet endless hours of patient practice produced unruly results, evidence, I suppose, that a beautiful hand is not an inherited trait. I disappointed Miss Pym, my father and myself, eventually settling for a readable, functional, inelegant scrawl.

More than fifty years later I still have my pen but it lies, ignored, in the velvet confines of its original box, usurped by a laptop computer. Sitting at my table in the National Archives at Kew, I remember what Miss Pym used to say about handwriting and British character. I am scrutinizing a document, hoping it will reveal the character of the man who wrote it.

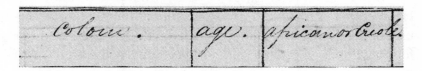

My finger slowly traces the fluid but faint lines of ink originally penned 200 years ago in Jamaica: broad, flowing, upward and downward strokes that, with the slightest movement of the wrist, become whisper-thin, curve, then end in a graceful, controlled flourish. As I work my way down each column on the copy of a copy of a page numbered 37, the act of tracing triggers body memory: wrist, hand and fingers anticipating the changing angle of the pen nib as it captures letters and words and phrases in measured, elliptical black shapes, evenly spaced and inclined at an angle of 55 degrees. I recognize the English round hand I tried to make my own.

My father's writing always appeared controlled and deliberate; I never knew him to make a careless stroke. His letters left the impression of precision, constancy, careful consideration and exactitude of meaning. Is this what is meant by character? My aging hand with its wrinkles, bulging veins and encroaching rheumatism, abruptly stops moving down the page. I can feel my child's hand grasping the barrel of a pen tighter and tighter in a fruitless attempt to prevent its wayward ramblings, random deposits of blots, nib skittering off the page, gouges in its wake.

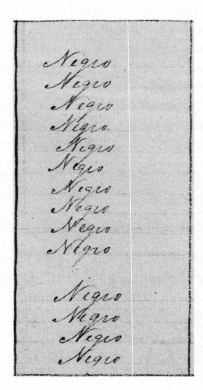

When my father raised his pen as an adult and began to write, did he remember learning how to form his letters in a Jamaican classroom between 1925 and 1927? In a letter, he once told me the story of how he learnt to write. My grandmother, Rose, paid for my father to attend a local nursery school between the ages of four and six years old. It was very small, just eight to ten pupils, and run by two English sisters referred to as the Misses Lopez. My father's natural inclination was to pick up a pen with his left hand, but the Misses Lopez not only believed in the early inculcation of the values of the British Empire, they considered left-handedness an intolerable and un-English perversity: a sin deserving a sound whipping. 'They insisted', his letter read, 'that I wrote with my right hand, so when I was caught using my left to write – I had to place my hand on the desk only to be lashed with a 12 inch ruler or cane. I had to go home with my left hand swollen and in pain – I could not complain to anyone.' Is each en dash an act of extraction or exclusion? In the spaces between words lies the memory of punishment: in the first a conflicted hesitation, an anticipation of pain, a reluctance to place the hand, which had been rapidly hidden between thighs when footsteps approached, back on the desk. In the second, a young black child's agony and anxiety, slow steps on the path toward a home without a sympathetic ear, with each attempt to suppress a sob, a swallowing of the bitter taste of injustice.

I do not know how often my father must have picked up his pen with his left hand, despite instructions to the contrary, but it must have been many, many times. Assiduously, deliberately, systematically, the Misses Lopez instilled character into this black male child, teaching him to conform to their wishes, to conform to the order of the classroom, to conform to the British order of things by beating his left hand with a cane. Daily beatings crushed and broke the knuckles of each and every finger of his hand, as they lay spread-eagled on the blood-soaked desk.

Negro	10	Creole
Negro	6	Creole
Negro	5	Creole
Negro	1	Creole

It was when my father picked up a pen with his right hand as an adult that he glanced at the deformed knuckles of his left hand and told me this story for the first time. Did his hand ache with memory? Is this why he made such circumspect, studied and deliberate movements when he wrote? My dad learnt his lesson; his English round was perfect.

The art of English round hand is a conduit through which multiple histories and geographies flow – it was taught to my father in Jamaica and to me in England more than thirty years later. In the same hand accounts of empire were produced in meticulous detail by its ambassadors: clerks, bookkeepers, lawyers, merchants, planters and traders in enslaved human beings.

As academics we sit in archives and stare at these records and registers, ledgers and lists, each carefully rendered in measured and elegant script. But the terror and the violence camouflaged by this cosmetic beauty can be exposed through a starkly different aesthetic practice. John Hearne, in the opening pages of his novel, *The Sure Salvation*, recreated such a moment when Hogarth, the English captain of a ship becalmed in the Atlantic, sought pleasure in the task of the daily entry in his ship's log:

> For a little while, etching with such precision, Hogarth had been happy. It was not often at sea that he could experience the dutiful pleasure of fashioning letters as he had been taught. Too often the shudder of the barque as it lunged into a wave would mar the smooth hook that should have completed an *a*, or the bows would toss briskly, forcing the table up against his hand and squashing the perfect curve at the top of the 9. Now, in this calm, the deck steady as the floor of a room, his fist returned effortlessly to its first lessons . . . he closed his log on the lines that read
>   *Noon, May 17, 1860 – Lat 1° 14' S, Long 32° 16' W. No distance. Calm continues. Full sails set. Cargo in prime condition because of our special care.*

Hogarth's 'Cargo' lay in the dark beneath the desk at which he sat, which held 'a desk set of heavy silver; two inkwells, one covered, sunk into a broad slab', and his pens. His 'Cargo' consisted of 'four hundred and seventy-five bodies he had discriminately culled along the coast from the Congo to Angola . . .'. In the 1790s, women who were in the future to be called *Nancy*, *Penny*, *Betsy* and *Bridget* were items among the 'Cargo' of such a ship on their way to be sold in Jamaica.

All the Hogarths who compiled accounts for empire lived and breathed within the carapace of their own (un)reasoning; each and every carefully controlled mark of a pen was intended to inscribe British character, the truth of civility, discrimination and taste, testament to the enlightened values of the civilization that bred them. Hogarth's pleasure in his accomplished hand denied the hand that traded in human flesh, revealing the depths of its inhumanity with each letter of *'Cargo in prime condition because of our special care.'*

Acts of gracious writing that account for empire are evidence of the bottomless depths of unacknowledged violence and brutality embodied in British character and values across the colonial and imperial landscape. As I held my father's letters I could feel the imprint of his deformed fingers steadying the paper as he lifted his pen to write to me.

Correspondence

I should not have been surprised when I encountered my father's English round hand in the National Archives of the UK, but I felt disconcerted. I came across Carl Carby following a tenuous lead in eighteenth-century Lincolnshire looking for a different Carby, a person who was the owner of a Jamaican plantation and its enslaved men, women and children. I added a substantial file of correspondence headed 'Colonial Office: Welfare and Students: Selected Personal Files. Carby CC. 01 January 1946 – 31 December 1969', to unbound, folded and tied eighteenth-century militia records from the county of Lincolnshire, massive books of Regimental records for the Revolutionary and Napoleonic Wars, bound in leather with marbled endpapers, and the heavy, disintegrating registers of the enslaved in Jamaica from 1817–34.

These ledgers were accumulations of the minutiae of imperial knowledge and administration; each one documented a particular aspect of the routine workings of empire that contributed to my tale. The raising of militias to defend the East Coast of England from a French invasion was accomplished by ballot. Almost 90,000 young men in the British Army were transported in converted merchant ships to the West Indies just before the French Revolutionary and Napoleonic wars to aid in the suppression of slave rebellions and to protect those profitable islands from invasion by competing colonial powers. Almost half died of disease. The registration of each and every enslaved human being in the British Empire began in 1817; 130 years later, in the aftermath of the Second World War, the Colonial Office supervised the lives of students.

The *Discovery* catalogue is the public entry into the archives. Holdings are organized chronologically into categories, divisions and subdivisions which offer an orderly and apparently well-reasoned passage into knowledge of the past. What is less easy to see is that this organization is itself a product of colonial rationality; not a pathway to enlightenment but a form of containment. To find what I wanted to know required thinking in a disorderly manner. I burrowed into the archives of the Colonial Office, Her Majesty's Treasury and the War Office, questioning the logic of classification and gathering a disparate variety of materials unrelated by time or place, or the number allocated to them in the catalogue. The materiality of black life, of colonized life, of enslaved life, does not correspond to the archival codification of knowledge and I was searching for ways of knowing and being disregarded, silenced or unimagined.

Carl remained in the RAF until 1950 but in 1947 was seconded to attend further education courses in accountancy. Like many other recruits, his education had been disrupted when he volunteered to serve in the armed forces. The Colonial Office kept detailed records of the 'welfare, education and training' of people from British colonies who were in the country to study. The series of 'personal files of colonial students' contained a 'selection' of 139 records without explanation of the basis for selection. A number belonged to prominent people, including scions of Royal Families of African countries and men who subsequently became leaders of independent nations, like Julius Kambarage Nyerere, who was awarded a scholarship from the Tanganyika government to attend the University of Edinburgh. An outspoken anti-colonialist with a radical socialist vision for the future of the African continent, he became President of Tanzania in 1964, and one of my political heroes. I was more interested in reading his file than Carl Carby's. All files were closed for at least thirty years and many for seventy-five years or longer. Julius Nyerere's was closed.

The file on Carl Carby had been opened to the public in January of 2000. I had to consider if I wanted to know what was inside. Libraries had always been places of sanctuary for me but I felt insecure. I did not want to confront official documentation of the years I had worked diligently to forget: the bitter disintegration of a marriage; the venomous recriminations of a contentious divorce; copies of police records containing details of the violent incidents they were called upon to subdue; and a description of an attempted suicide. I stared at the number of the file on the computer screen while I hesitated, torn between intellectual curiosity and misgiving. I could have run away, gathered up my pencils and notes, pushed back my chair, stood up and pretended I had never come across the file. Instead I pressed enter, submitting a request.

In 1946 Carl applied to the Welfare Department of the Colonial Office for an award for further education and training in economics, mercantile law, company law, practical accountancy and statistics, income tax law and practice, auditing and general commercial knowledge – courses appropriate in preparation for the final examination of the Association of Certified and Corporate Accountants.

Wartime austerity was tangible in the flimsiness of each yellowing page tied to its neighbour with a length of fading, worn, green string through a hole punched in the top left-hand corner. Unable to loosen a fifty-year-old knot, it was difficult to read into the corners of the pages.

I imagined the young Carl almost twenty-four years old, married for two of them, completing his application. He was stationed at RAF Waddington in Lincolnshire; Iris was living in rented accommodation close by in the city of Lincoln. The war was over and their future was uncertain. Iris could not continue in the Civil Service as a married woman and Carl did not know where his next posting would be. At a table in the Sergeant's Mess he entered information in black ink. In lined rows under 'Particulars (with date) of school or other higher education, with certification . . .' he inserted the information in the accompanying photograph:

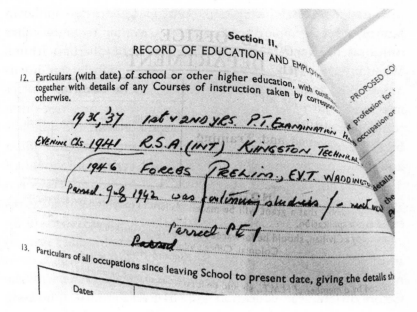

Section II.
RECORD OF EDUCATION AND EMPLOY...

12. Particulars (with date) of school or other higher education, with certific... together with details of any Courses of instruction taken by correspon... otherwise.

1936, 37   1st & 2nd YRS. P.T. Examination H...
Evening Cls. 1941   R.S.A. (INT) Kingston Technical...
1946   Forces Prelim., E.V.T. Waddingto...
Passed. 9-8 1942 was continuing studies for next w...
Passed P.E.
Passed

13. Particulars of all occupations since leaving School to present date, giving the details sh...

Dates

Carl offered extra assurance of his level of achievement (passed) when it wasn't necessary. He also wanted to establish that he was ambitious. The form did not ask for this information. Inserting 'passed July 1942 was continuing studies for next examination' turned the 'particulars' he considered incomplete into a narrative important to him. The lines he drew connected past to future. Taking advantage of the Forces Preliminary Exam, which was offered to military personnel to provide prima facie evidence of a candidate's eligibility to be considered for admission to university, was confirmation of the continuity of his desire to pursue further education. Where Carl's future lay, however, was not in question for the Colonial Office, for as far as they were concerned it would be in Jamaica not in the UK. All applicants were advised 'to consider carefully' whether the further education or training for which they were applying 'will further the welfare of the Colony'.

Colonized lives do not correspond to the realities imagined in colonial accounting; their presence has to be prised out of the cracks between rows and columns and sentences. There was no room in the application or anywhere in the file for an account of the circumstances which caused Carl to leave Franklin Town School and seek employment, no place to explain the significance of his taking evening classes at Kingston Technical High School. When my father talked to me about his education he said it was 'interrupted' because he needed to earn money to keep his siblings in school. Carl never forgave his own father for deserting them, for plunging the family into destitution and placing the responsibility of caring for an alcoholic mother, four younger brothers and sisters, and his grandmother on his fifteen-year-old shoulders. The education system in the British West Indies did not correspond to the education system of the metropole, but this cannot be seen in Carl's correspondence with the Colonial Office.

Franklin Town School, in Kingston, like all primary schools in the British West Indies in the 1930s, educated children for nine years, from ages five to fourteen. However, the hierarchical nature of Jamaican education had changed little since the institution of Crown Colony Government in 1865, in the wake of the Morant Bay Rebellion. The wealthiest Jamaicans, the plantation elite, traditionally sent their children to be educated in England. The children of the Jamaican middle class, aspiring to fill the colonial bureaucracy, obtained a secondary education in Jamaica in schools that offered Cambridge examinations and scholarships to British universities: pathways to the professions. The most prestigious of these schools, Jamaica College, Munro College or Wolmers, could boast Rhodes Scholars, but the average secondary school life was short: very few actually sat for these examinations and scholarships; even fewer were chosen. For working-class and poor Jamaicans, even elementary education was not universally available. In most Caribbean colonies under British control there were never more than 50 per cent of children of elementary school age actually enrolled, and seldom were more than 60 per cent of those enrolled in attendance. Commissioners who led an investigation into secondary and primary education in the West Indies between 1931 and 1932 found that the proportion of the population in secondary school for the islands as a whole was 0.34 and that in no island was it more than 1 per cent.

I didn't know that 'P. T.' in the entry for Franklin Town School denoted Pupil Teacher examination, awarded only to the highest-ranking elementary pupils. The commissioners complained that elementary schools suffered from 'a shortage of trained' and 'lack of certified teachers', and placed the blame for their poor standards on an excessive dependence upon pupil teachers. This is what was absent from Carl's Colonial Office file. He was among the 1 per cent who received secondary education and was certified as being among the best of them.

Patronage was a way of life in Jamaica. A recommendation from his employer N. A. Taylor paved the way for Carl to enter Kingston Technical High School, and therein lies another story. Taylor contacted Dr John Harris, Principal of the Kingston Technical High School from 1930 to 1943, on Carl's behalf. It was Harris who instituted many reforms to the school, among them an expanded programme of evening classes and the introduction of the Royal Society of Arts examinations. Instead of languishing in the back room of a hardware store, nursing dreams of self-improvement, my father became one of only 300 West Indians who qualified as aircrew out of the almost 6,000 men and women who volunteered for the RAF and Royal Canadian Air Force during the Second World War.

I made an appearance in Carl's Colonial Office file in 1947, in utero, when reference was made to a 'wife expecting a child'. Application was made, and subsequently granted, for an allowance for it. The educational award, which included maintenance for a 'wife' once the appropriate forms were completed, was granted in September of that year to run until July 1949. But there was a condition. Carl had to make 'a solemn declaration affirming [his] intention to return to [his] Colony by the first available ship after completion of [his] course of training'. The requirement of this declaration echoes the anxiety expressed in the Foreign Office memo of 1942: that the consequences of recruiting 'Coloured British subjects' into the United Kingdom would lead to an undesirable outcome, their permanent settlement. Carl was put on notice that he was under surveillance, assured that his career would be 'watched with interest in the Colonial Office'.

The welcome mat for colonial troops during the war was only temporary; it was always intended to be immediately swept from under their feet when they were no longer needed on the battlefields of Europe, North Africa and the Pacific. A thick curtain of amnesia was drawn over all the dark-skinned British bodies who rallied to the cause of saving Britain even if they were unwilling to save its empire.

Carl's plans for his future went seriously awry. I try to create a portrait of his life with Iris from the fragments in the Colonial Office documents. They left Lincolnshire for South London, where Carl attended college. In their search for accommodation as a black and white couple with a brown baby, Carl and Iris confronted racist aggression: hatred for what they represented was spat at them from angry, cruel mouths. The file reveals that three months after their child was born Carl was dejected. His request for accommodation at the Colonial Centre on Hallam Street, submitted out of pain and despair, was granted. Possibly he imagined that Iris would stand a better chance of finding somewhere decent to live on her own, but she was not on her own, and the colour of her baby's skin led to her ostracization too. Racism must have placed a terrible strain on their relationship and made them contemplate a separation. A month later Iris applied to the Colonial Office asking if the allowance for herself and her four-month-old daughter could be paid directly to her, instead of being included in the amount allotted to my father. Money, or rather the lack of it, was a constant source of tension between them. Iris always resented the fact that Carl sent part of his allowance to Jamaica to support his family there.

It takes a few hours to read through a file that covers twenty-three years, years it is excruciating to relive. I never fully understood the dreams of the young RAF flight sergeant photographed in his uniform in 1945. This formerly ambitious, educationally successful, hard-working young man failed one of the subjects in his Intermediate Examination in 1949. His award was terminated. On appeal, and with the supportive intervention of the principal of the college, Carl's award was reinstated to allow him to retake the exam. He failed again. Carl would never realize his ambition to become a Chartered Accountant. He was recalled to the RAF in September 1949, 'for early repatriation and demobilization'. A liaison officer for West Indian students offered him assistance finding employment in Jamaica.

I am unable to explain why the woman it is difficult to acknowledge as myself kept reading that file. She could have pushed it aside at any point and returned it to the main desk. She ached for the lives of Iris and Carl that seeped from its pages, lives locked in mutual misery. She ached for the lost girl who fled to Mitcham Common, the sound of violence, of screaming, echoing in her ears, for the girl who hid in libraries to lick her wounds and heal. Yet here she was in another library remembering, all grown up but the girl once more. I left the file on a table and walked away, down to the cafeteria in search of strong coffee. This schizophrenic experience in the archive left me exhausted. If I smoked I would have walked outside to the terrace and joined the small group subversively puffing away. Instead, I headed for a table far from anyone, sank into a moulded plastic chair which offered no comfort and sipped from a cup of lukewarm, insipid brown liquid which did not even have enough body to be bitter. I was facing the windows, looking out onto a courtyard and the lake beyond. The shape and size of the murmuration of smokers constantly changed. I envied them their addiction and their solidarity in nonconformity – I swallow, hard. The cup I was gripping tightly in my hand grew cold. Water began to dribble down the window and became a steady flow. I expected the circle of people to disappear to seek shelter from the rain but it remained, dissolving gradually into an assemblage of shadows. No umbrellas were raised. My cheeks were wet, tears for a lost girl.

If I was not to waste a transatlantic research trip I had to regain historical perspective, remind myself that I was a scholar, that my project was not about that girl (but of course it was about her, cowering while her parents fought each other). The girl and her nightmares must be reburied, forced down the throat with cold coffee, swallowed like distasteful medicine. Feeling nauseous and dragging my feet, I resisted the impulse to collect my belongings from the locker room and leave. Instead, I returned upstairs, carrying the girl on my back.

I turned to the next page and read a typed letter from a squadron leader in the Record Office of the Royal Air Force in Ruislip, Middlesex. The letter was addressed to the Under Secretary of State for the Air Ministry and referred to a request from Carl that he be discharged in the United Kingdom not in Jamaica where he was recruited. The RAF granted consent explicitly because the Welfare Department of the Colonial Office recommended that it be approved. Under paragraph '652(1) of the King's Regulations' this airman was discharged conditional upon his signing of a 'Waiver of Repatriation Rights', which meant, I think, that he would have to pay his own way back to Jamaica if he changed his mind about living in the UK (I realize that I may be wrong and that there were probably other 'rights' attached.)

I paid particular attention to the last paragraph of the letter because of the squadron leader's admonition that 'In no circumstances [are the contents] to be communicated to the airman or his Unit.' Writing 'in the strictest confidence', he stated that the 'Welfare Department at the Colonial Office has intimated that, in the event of this airman becoming destitute in this country, the Department is prepared to give advice to the airman.' This suggestion of possible future assistance from the Colonial Office is written eleven months after the *Empire Windrush* docked at Tilbury in the spirit, manner and tone of fearing to be *seen* to be encouraging black people to stay in the UK. The injunction of secrecy implicitly acknowledged the climate of increasingly open hostility toward British black migrants, so recently comrades-in-arms. Urging the necessity for secrecy not only assumed that 'the airman' would take unfair advantage of such support if he knew it existed but also sought to avoid public criticism of, and possible political repercussions against, the Colonial Office.

The climate of virulent and violent British racism in the postwar period was what governed Carl's daily existence. Black ex-servicemen confronted racist exclusions in the job market as well as the housing market, and the Colonial Office knew it. The next letter was written by an I. G. Cummings, one of the civil servants in the Welfare Department, to an A. H. King in the British Council. From the informal nature of the address, I gathered King was an acquaintance of his, perhaps even a friend. This letter acknowledged the climate of open racism, couched in a reference to the 'usual difficulty' men like Carl faced trying to find 'a suitable job', and described how Cummings had tried to intervene on my father's behalf with the British Transport Commission. This letter constituted another intervention, seeking to mobilize the assistance and support of this friend or former colleague in a position to influence events.

Cummings received a reply from the office of the Director of the Personnel Department of the British Council which, in its circumspection and cautious phrasing, revealed its own hesitant negotiation of the British racial formation. It stated: 'The only post available at present for which a man would be suitable is in the Despatch Department, which involves a certain amount of portering, and we do not think it would be desirable to offer such a post to a coloured man with good clerical qualifications.' The director concluded by saying that he will keep 'Mr. Carby's name on the waiting list' for a more suitable post.

The decision not to offer a job fetching and carrying to 'a coloured man with good clerical qualifications' reveals that the British Council did not want to be accused of practising workplace discrimination but, at the same time, refused to condemn the racism that ex-servicemen suffered. Reading the text and subtext of this correspondence between the RAF, the Welfare Department of the Colonial Office and the British Council was an exercise in political futility. There was no principled, ethical stance to confront and counter the postwar racist social formation. Instead racism was neatly side-stepped. The correspondence was a polite dance around the shit on the pavement in which others were mired. Unspoken rules did not allow officials of the Colonial Office and the British Council to adopt a language that corresponded to the reality of black life: there could be no open acknowledgement that they could do anything to help. Prevarication and dissimulation governed all written responses. These letters were the deployment of a rear-guard action, moves to protect the flanks of the British Civil Service and the British state. Nowhere, nowhere, in this entire correspondence was it acknowledged that the 'airman'/'ex-service-man'/'pleasant young man' in question was a British citizen.

Bookkeeping

Carl did not walk away from his family as his father had done, and he and Iris found a house in which to live. The girl was their only child until one day she wasn't. She was roused by her father's voice early one midsummer morning and swept up in a whirlwind of blankets and clothes. Anxiety propelled him as he ushered his daughter down the stairs, out of the house and into the first glimmer of the light of dawn. I only recall the pulsating rhythm of our movement, the currents of air swirling around us. Time stopped. I stood in the open doorway of the house of a friend and watched as my father hurried away through a triangle of light, down a narrow path and through a gate. He turned, eyes down to secure the latch, then disappeared.

A button that should have been behind the girl's neck pressed sharply into her throat. Her socks bunched around her ankles and formed uncomfortable folds under the soles of her feet. The metal clasp on a sandal strap dug into an ankle. She complained. Her clothes were rearranged and she was seated at a table to eat. At the end of a day she was taken home. Her dolls had been removed from their pram and replaced by an item called, 'your baby brother'.

Carl and Iris entered the second Elizabethan Age as poor as the proverbial church mice, but Iris never allowed her children to refer to themselves as poor. 'The poor' were other people in the neighbourhood. The poor were an undifferentiated, undeserving mass of people, 'they' did not work hard enough, lived in council houses and took handouts from the state. Carl and Iris constantly bickered about the lack of money. They had married in the late autumn of 1944 and in accord with the marriage bar in the civil service, Iris had lost her position in the Air Ministry the following year. In 1948, she used the last of her savings as a deposit on the bomb-damaged house in Streatham, and worked the night shift at a local factory assembling electric meters.

If the civil servants in the Welfare Department of the Colonial Office and the British Council refused to take a public stance against racism, a local businessman, Alfred H. Giles, had no such qualms. He offered Carl the position of an accounts clerk in his engraving firm in Croydon, a respectable position but with small remuneration. Perhaps Giles was a person of principles. Perhaps he wanted a clerk who was cheap. Perhaps he admired Carl's gentlemanly deportment and style despite his impoverishment. Carl worked for Mr Giles for fifteen years during which he was promoted to being a bookkeeper, a position he retained until Giles retired and the firm closed down in 1967. Carl seemed settled, if poorly paid, though both he and the girl complained about the provincial and frequently small-minded nature of Croydon, where she attended school from the age of eleven onwards. Carl and his daughter wished that they could commute from the hateful suburbs to the cosmopolitan atmosphere of central London.

The girl and her brother were inured to being 'only ones': the only black children at their respective schools; the only black children in their immediate neighbourhood; and the only black people on the bus, until the bus arrived in Brixton. The girl was convinced that her father led a life of being 'an only' too. She imagined that he was the lone black employee at the firm, just as she and her brother were the only black children in their schools, but in photographs taken at the retirement dinner for Alfred H. Giles it is evident that three out of the ten employees were black, two out of the seven men and one out of the three women – an exceptional ratio for British white suburban life. After the closure of the firm Carl found work in central London and quickly improved his salary. He must have remained with Giles for so long out of loyalty.

For the next thirty years Carl was employed by the Westminster City Council, in a position of responsibility in their accounts department. Again, he experienced being 'the first' but, eventually, not the only black person in the department. Looking back, I understand why he was proud of this position, because it fulfilled his original ambition to be a government employee. When the British Transport Commission refused to employ him in their offices he did not succumb to their low expectations of him – fetching and carrying for British Rail, or mopping the floors in a National Health Service hospital. Westminster City Council would employ him, and he was happy there; he had never compromised. My father took pride in the fact that he wore a suit, a starched shirt with a collar, and a tie, every day. Each time my scuffed and dull footwear catches my eye I feel ashamed that I failed to follow the standards my father set: every night he shined his shoes, 'until you could see your face in them', I can still hear him say. He was dignified – a black man offended but unbowed by colonial rule and metropolitan racism.

In school the girl found arithmetic difficult and I still struggle with maths. Carl believed that there were truths in numbers and that if the girl ceased distributing the elements of a sum randomly across the page of her maths book then she would come to understand the principles of mathematics. On accounting paper, he demonstrated the relations between numbers and made her enter them in regular, orderly columns. After working for years at the dining room table with her father she still failed to understand mathematical logic. But what she gained was an aesthetic appreciation for accounting practices.

There were always accounting ledgers and cricket scorebooks in our house because my father was the treasurer of several local cricket and bowls clubs. He passed on his definition of what it took to be a sportsman when he instructed younger players, teaching them the history of the sport as well as technique. In Carl's opinion, dedication to both was the foundation on which to build character. He told all his students to model themselves on Learie Constantine, whom he regarded as a man of ability, determination and moral fibre. Constantine was not only an outstanding Trinidadian cricketer but a lawyer, a politician and the first black peer in the UK. Carl despaired when he encountered the haphazard bookkeeping of local clubs. He was of the opinion that sloppy bookkeeping equated with a profound disrespect for the sport and a lack of regard for the security of its future. Unsatisfactory bookkeeping indicated a weakness of will, and as a club treasurer he took pride in correcting it.

My father was a colonial subject but I think his ability to execute accounts provided him with a measure of control over his existence in postwar Britain, a world which otherwise could be unpredictable, capricious and volatile. His sober suits, starched shirts and perfectly knotted ties, his dark English overcoats and immaculately polished dress shoes, his restraint in dress and manner, each and all bespoke British imperial education and accountancy.

The girl visited one of the bowls clubs with her father once. It was a world made by men for male leisure, which women entered only to make tea and serve sandwiches. When watching her father play she was asked to go inside and help in the kitchen, which she refused to do. Cricket matches were much more interesting: large gatherings in open green spaces and a blanket to lie on while she read. The girl was never part of her father's world of accounting. She was oblivious to, and uninterested in, the practical application of scorebooks and ledgers, but the visual aesthetics of bookkeeping and of performances measured and noted was fascinating: tallies of batsmen and bowlers; calculations of runs scored, balls bowled and wickets won or lost; all tabulated in columns between green lines. How mathematics produced this order was irrelevant to her then.

There is harmony and design in imperial ledgers: proportion in the relation between headings and subheadings, elegance in the curvature and spatial distribution of lettering, solidity in the diligent detailing of assets and expenditure straining toward equivalence, a finely calibrated balancing act in the listing of credits and debits coming to a resolution.

As early as the ninth century, Muḥammed ibn Mūsā al-Khwārizmī, a mathematician, astronomer and geographer in Baghdad, referred to this resolution as 'completion and balancing' in the title of his treatise, *A-Kitāb al-mukhtaṣar fī ḥisāb al-jabr wa-l-muqābala*. Resolving all discrepancies and closing in balance was central to what became known as the system of double entry accounting, where it was elevated to the status of a moral imperative. The first printed synthesis of the method of double entry was published by Luca Paciola in 1494; it spread throughout Europe and forms the basis of all modern accounting systems. It was a crucial technique in the governance practices of the British Empire and in rationalized colonial modernity. Establishing the 'foundation of equallizing and ballancing of values' structured the writings of the seventeenth-century English economist, scientist and philosopher, Sir William Petty. Petty left his position at Oxford University in 1652 to travel with Cromwell's army on its campaign to invade and subdue Ireland; his Survey of Ireland published in 1656 was the first English imperial surveying and mapping of a conquered nation. Petty was a polymath and his subsequent work made him an important figure in the institution of natural philosophy and the creation of social science. The theoretical issues he addressed in his *Several Essays in Political Arithmetick* were influential in the formation of the field of modern economics. Colonial subjugation, the surveying and mapping of bodies and space, and accounting systems for measuring and estimating their value, all emerge simultaneously.

> Sadly and again typically, those who write about Petty's place in the development of economics and statistics are not usually interested in his significance as an early theorist of racial hierarchy, while those who address his innovative contribution to the history of racial thought tend not to be engaged with his contribution to the seventeenth-century transformation of the arts of government.
>
> Paul Gilroy

Petty described his method in *Political Arithmetick* as being expressed 'in Terms of *Number, Weight,* or *Measure*', using only 'Arguments of Sense', and considering 'only such causes, as have visible Foundations in Nature'. Paul Gilroy has argued that we must also take account of how Petty adds the concept of 'scale' to this method when he develops a discourse of creatures. International and national scales of value were applied to Petty's numbering, weighing and measuring of people (the poor, the rich and children) against the cost of their sustenance, and in his calculations of land, trade and taxes as potential sources of revenue for the raising and equipping of armies of soldiers and horses. The balancing and completion to produce value, evident in *Political Arithmetick*, proved advantageous to practices of colonial accounting that weighed and measured people as commodities.

Petty was not only the first to produce an English imperial survey but also made, as Paul Gilroy has shown,

> the first English statement of what will become the fundamental principle of racialised order. He repudiates the Christian theology of mankind's unity and connects natural difference – [phenotypical variation] – to a colour-coded hierarchy specified with precision in the open space between the notion of race and that of species. The novel relationship he proposes between observable differences, cognitive capacity and natural constitution of humans is part of the gradual shift from race as static taxonomy to race as a matter of historical lineage.

Three decades later, John Mair followed William Petty's methods and declared 'Book-keeping is an Art.' One of the many benefits to be derived from the adoption of the double entry system, he continued, is discipline of the mind: 'The Theory of this Art or Science is beautiful and curious, very fit for improving the Minds of Youth, exercising their Wit and Invention and disposing them to a close and accurate way of thinking.' Double entry became 'good' bookkeeping practice and good bookkeeping practice conferred moral legitimacy. There is an enduring historical association between rectitude and accurate accounting practices.

John Mair's *Book-keeping Methodised*, was the standard accounting text in Britain and North America for over fifty years and the most popular bookkeeping text of the eighteenth century. It offered instruction for all aspects of commercial transactions in Britain and its empire. The sections on bookkeeping in the colonial territories was organized according to the dominant produce of a region, and tailored its instructions to each area: 'Jamaica, Barbadoes, and the Leeward Islands' were designated 'The Sugar Trading Colonies', and Jamaica predominated in the examples. Mair was assiduous in the precision with which he defined terms and selected appropriate words. Precision was crucial to the process

That of man it selfe there seems to be severall species, To say nothing of Gyants and Pigmies or of that sort of small men who have little speech and feed chiefly upon fish ... for of these sorts of men, I venture to say nothing, but that 'tis very possible there may be Races and generations of such since we know that there are men of 7 foot high and others but 4 foot ... I say there may be races and Generations of such men whereof we know the Individualls ... there be others (differences) more considerable, that is, between the Guiny Negroes & the Middle Europeans; & of Negroes between those of Guiny and those who live about the Cape of Good Hope, which last are the Most beastlike of all the Souls (?Sorts) of Men whith whom our Travellers arre well acquainted. I say that the Europeans do not only differ from the aforementioned Africans in Collour ... but also ... in Naturall Manners, & in the internall Qualities of their Minds.

William Petty

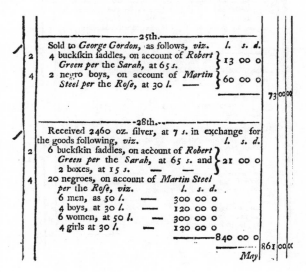

of attaining balance and completion and the seamless integra-
tion of science with art. This scrupulous attention to language
was a prerequisite of resolution which could not be achieved by
numerical balance alone. The process of logging entries of trade
in produce and commodities into ledgers and sales books was
far from seamless in the colonies. It took linguistic gymnastics
to leap over the entries of the traffic in human beings that was
the foundation of the sugar trade.

In the 'Sugar Colonies', Mair began: by people, 'I mean whites,
or white people all originally natives of Great Britain.' No
'people', then, would appear in the accounts – only commodities
without distinction. 'Negroes', he advised, should be listed in
the books like any other form of goods.

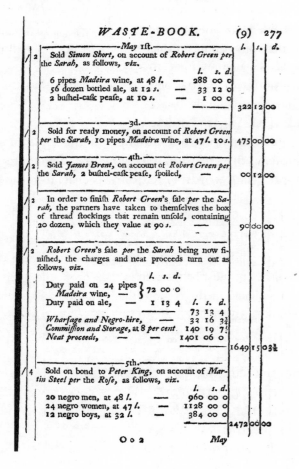

Mair's accounting pages were presented as a simple matter of transcription and calculation. Transcribing 'negroes' as goods confirmed their dehumanization while the precision and detail of the formal design and manner of the bookkeeping entry proclaimed accuracy and asserted the right to trade in flesh. The listing of '20 negro men, at 48*l*.', '24 negro women at 47*l*.', and '12 negro boys at 32*l*.' measured their value and confirmed their commodification as 'fact'.

Nevertheless, the horror of enslavement could not be successfully erased from imperial accounting, for bookkeeping was not only a numerical practice. It was necessary for Mair to provide instruction in the use of language to negotiate its ideological fiction that human beings were merchandise:

> when any parcel of goods is sold at a low rate, or under the current value, on account of their being damaged by bad package, long keeping, or any such other cause, some word expressive of this is inserted in the column of price, such as *Spoiled, Tainted, Soured, Dry, &c.* And with respect to negroes, the words *Sick, Meagre, &c.* Are used for the like purpose.
>
> When the goods belonging to any sale are all disposed of . . . you are then to add up the several columns that contain the parcels of goods sold, compare their total with the heading, and see if they agree: or if there be any defect, which often happens for some goods are apt to lose in weight, others again . . . may be so far [diminished], as to be quite useless and unfit for sale, and negroes may die while under the factor's charge; in all which cases the quantities deficient must be inserted in their proper columns, and the reason assigned in the column that contains the purchasers names, by some expression or word suitable to the purpose; such as *Lost in weight*, [Usage], *Broke, Stinking, Dead, &c.*

Calculating the depreciation of value in decrepit, decaying bodies or corpses is particularly tricky when defects affect sale price, because the same words cannot be used to describe 'damage' in 'negroes' as 'damage' in other types of goods. Against all the intentions of colonial bookkeeping, 'negroes' were revealed to be mortal: their dying proved that they were living commodities, human beings, and their 'damage' established their suffering.

The techniques and technologies of imperial governance – the gracious script, the silencing of colonized existence, the dissimulation of language and the duplicity of financial transactions – coalesce in the imperial ledgers of enslavement on my desk in various states of decay. As the daughter of a bookkeeper I was familiar with the contours of these accounting pages; as a descendant of the enslaved I am simultaneously estranged from them. My hands and fingers barely touched fragile paper or bindings, but with each turn of a page the detritus of history and geography rose as motes through the bands of sunlight that streamed over my shoulder. I inhaled, smelt and tasted the past.

In 1816, the British government instituted a process to register all of the enslaved in every territory of its empire. Human beings who lived and breathed were confined within the straightjackets of columns and bound within ledgers: 'REGISTRATION'; 'SLAVE REGISTERS'. By 1817, the first year of registration was complete, and henceforth, until emancipation, records of 'increase' and 'decrease' were updated every three years. 'Increase' covered birth and purchase, 'decrease' covered sale, escape, being sent to the workhouse, and death, but did not distinguish between death from torture, punishment, disease or a broken heart. The language of these registers of bodies confirms that the only interest in keeping them was as accounts of profit and/or loss.

Horizontal and vertical lines segmented each page, securing and containing, dividing and subdividing, creating intimacy through proximity. Unforgiving lines contrasted with the generous flow of letters and words which were meant to be imprisoned within separate tabular cells but often spilled over edges. Cells accumulated in columns headed by categories above lists; columns were used for the input and extraction of data.

Detailed instructions regarding the correct insertion of information into the registers, instructions published in every Jamaican newspaper in 1817, read:

Every such list or return ... shall specify in distinct columns, according to the form in the schedule marked A, hereunto annexed, the following particulars: beginning with the list of males, and distinguishing them from the list of females; that is to say, in the first of the said columns, and which shall be entitled, 'Names', shall be inserted the name of such slave by which he or she has been usually called or known.

Such meticulous instructions left no room for deviation. The data, in this instance, were people represented by lists of assigned names, approximated dates of birth and the colour coding of their bodies.

Above and below the columns, in rectangular spaces, were attestations from those who owned and controlled the bodies and affirmed the authenticity of the accounts with their signatures. There was the name for which I searched but did not wish to find: *Carby*. Here was an apotheosis, if not a resolution. I whispered the names my fingers traced.

There are similarities between this slave register and my father's ledgers: both pronounced their ability to list, order and represent truths through the detailed transcription and accounting of property, of assets, of procurement. Those among the enslaved who refused to be accountable to their owners, those who refused to accept their authority to hold them in servitude, those who not only imagined the overthrow of the plantation system but actually had the temerity to damage or destroy property in Jamaica in 1817, were executed, promptly and efficiently. They were wiped from the books without hesitation.

Political Arithmetic

Although a national census was not established in the United Kingdom until 1801, as a form of governing by measurement it was anticipated by the practice of counting people and surveying the estates of large landowners to establish property boundaries beginning in the seventeenth century. Landlords collected increasing amounts of information about those who lived on their estates and these records of property and residents became integral to the micropolitics of exclusion. The political arithmetic of surveys were the form of accounting used to justify the social violence of enclosure, expropriation of customary rights and dispossession. The British Parliament sanctioned this systematic land grab by wealthy landowners, whereby open fields, woods and common lands, on which local villagers had grown food, grazed livestock and hunted for generations, became private parks on large estates, ground on which only the landowners and their guests were allowed to tread.

In eighteenth-century Jamaica, surveys were used to settle boundary disputes but did not require the inclusion of buildings that housed the enslaved. Surveyors frequently eliminated these dwellings, or hid them behind another element in the landscape. Increasing patterns of absentee ownership meant that surveillance of the enslaved became the prime responsibility of the overseer; as William Beckford observed of his sugar plantation in 1790, 'The negro houses are, in general, at some distance from the works, but not so far removed as to be beyond the sight of the overseer.' The few surveys in the eighteenth century that represented the houses of enslaved human beings showed them huddled together in layouts often ordered by the enslaved themselves. Patterns of surveillance and representation began to change late in the eighteenth century as the laws governing the daily lives of the enslaved proliferated, a change marked in the landscape of the plantation itself. By the early nineteenth century, surveys increasingly showed slave houses in exposed regimented rows that were easier to surveil. But containment in the apparently impermeable boundaries of maps could not account for the fluid crossing and re-crossing of these lines after dark.

Rebellions in Jamaica and other Caribbean colonies, particularly the Haitian Revolution from 1791 to 1803, increased the fear among British slave owners that they would lose control over their property. Colonial laws were instituted and renewed, amended and revised, abandoned and replaced in attempts to govern the ungovernable, to control absolutely that which could not be totally controlled: the thoughts, behaviour, acts and movements of the enslaved and the formerly enslaved. The Governor and the Jamaica Assembly passed laws which the militia tried to enforce. Lawmakers, soldiers, plantation owners and colonial officials were perpetually anxious, afraid of what the enslaved were doing when they were out of sight or in the dark of night. 'It has been found by

34th. And whereas it is absolutely necessary that the slaves in this Island should be kept in due obedience to their owners, and in due subordination to the white people in general ... all means and opportunities of slaves being concerned in rebellious conspiracies, and committing other crimes, to the ruin and destruction of the white people and others in this Island, prevented, and that proper punishments should be appointed for all crimes to be by them committed; Be it further enacted ... if any slave or slaves shall, after the commencement of this Act, enter into or be concerned in any rebellion or rebellious conspiracy, or commit any murder, felony, burglary, robbery, or set fire to any houses, out-houses, negro-houses, cane-pieces, grass or corn-pieces, or break into such houses, out-houses, or negro-houses, in the day time, no person being therein, and steal thereout, or compass or imagine the death of any white person, and declare the same by some overt act, or commit any other crime which would subject white persons, or persons of free condition, to be, indicted for felony, such slave or slaves shall, for every such offence or offences, upon trial and conviction thereof in manner hereinafter mentioned, suffer death, transportation, or such other punishment as the court shall think proper to direct ...

Colonial Laws Respecting Slaves, House of Commons Parliamentary Papers, 1816.

experience, that a large concourse of slaves belonging to different plantations is dangerous, and that nightly meetings tend much to injure the health of negroes.' The enslaved were never out of the minds of their owners.

Jane Austen's novel, *Mansfield Park*, is symptomatic of a similar bifurcation and anxiety on the other side of the Atlantic. While Austen linked the past and future fates of English estates to Caribbean plantations, she kept any detail of plantation life and labour well out of the reader's sight. If the land for estates and parks was acquired through dispossession, the bricks and mortar of great houses like Mansfield Park were bonded by the wealth produced from enslaved labour. The character of Sir Thomas Bertram is a model of the iconic absent planter, finally summoned to attend to a crisis on his plantation in Antigua which threatened the stability and financial well-being of all who lived at Mansfield Park: disturbance on the plantation disturbed life on the estate. The cause of the crisis is kept obscure – reference is made to 'poor returns' and to a large part of Mansfield Park's income being 'unsettled' – and when Sir Thomas is asked to talk about the slave trade he and his entire family respond with dead silence. Despite such silence, and the distance from Northamptonshire to Antigua, it is clear that the plantation and those who work there are at the forefront of Sir Thomas's mind.

> ... no master ever was allowed here to take a slave by force to be sold abroad because he had deserted from his service, or for any other reason whatever; we cannot say the cause set forth by this return is allowed or approved of by the laws of this kingdom, therefore the black must be discharged.
>
> Lord Mansfield, 1772

However sympathetic Austen may have been to the movement for the abolition of the slave trade, *Mansfield Park* is characteristic of the profound ambivalence in Britain about the ontological and material status of the black subject, and future conditions for black existence. The title of novel echoes the name of Lord Chief Justice Mansfield who, in 1771, reluctantly found himself having to deliberate on the case of an enslaved man, James Somerset. Somerset, while in England, rejected the ownership of his master, Charles Stewart, ran away and declared himself a freed person. Stewart directed Somerset's capture and imprisonment on a ship bound for Jamaica, intending to sell him to a plantation.

In a series of prior juridical cases, Mansfield had expressed sympathy with the owners of enslaved persons who asserted their right to sell their 'property' as they wished, though he avoided making any final determination of the status of the enslaved in the UK. Mansfield's 1772 ruling in the Somerset case was equally ambivalent. While some took his judgement to mean that all enslaved persons brought into the country were free, the question of the status of the enslaved in England actually remained unresolved.

In *Mansfield Park*, the constraints which order the daily life of its female protagonist, Fanny, resonate with James Somerset's assertion of the right to individual freedom and with the ambivalence of Justice Mansfield's final judgement. The geographical boundaries of the novel remain stubbornly local because Austen cannot account for the ways in which the domestic space was an integral part of a colonial world of exploitation and dispossession. Out of sight, the instabilities of plantation economies merely haunt the novel, as they haunted the historical moment of its writing and publication in 1814. Equivocation and indeterminacy characterize and threaten to undermine character and daily life. The struggles of enslaved people to exercise their will and claim their own liberty as subjects within and without the boundaries of the UK is reduced to an 'imaginary surface'; it is a struggle displaced by a literary meditation on the limits and possibilities of freedom for an unmarried white woman. The ending in 1807 of the transatlantic trade in human beings in British ships left unresolved the question of black emancipation, and in 1815 the government in Westminster decided that it required a complete accounting of all its slaves in all its colonies.

My father told me, 'We come from Portland, from Skibo, near the Swift River. In the summers I would leave Kingston with my grandmother and go to Portland and nearly everyone in that place had the name Carby.' I followed my father's voice to the

1817 register of the enslaved on the Carby plantation in the parish of Portland, Jamaica, stored in the records of Her Majesty's Treasury. It seemed replete with information, lists of assigned names, allocations of colour-codes and ages approximated. But I knew it could not tell me where we came from.

Executors of Empire

After 1807, dead, diseased, injured, incarcerated or fugitive enslaved humans could no longer simply be replaced by a new shipment transported in chains from the West African coastal trading forts. The end of the trade and the ever-present fear of uprising meant that plantation owners had an investment in accounting for and documenting their human chattel. But it was Westminster and the influential absentee West India planters that determined how and when the enslaved would be counted. Early in the nineteenth century new forms of management and governance of a restive black population were introduced and changes made to the spatial layout of the plantation. Jamaican surveys mapped boundaries and people, and practices of containment were enacted through law in combination with threat, force and violence. As with the practice of enclosure in Britain, when gradual emancipation eventually came in 1834–38, planters tried to severely limit the independence of 'free' black Jamaicans by grabbing their land, ending their customary rights over provision grounds, and instituting the payment of rent for dwellings and the right to grow food. But colonial practices of governance also have their own distinct characteristics.

Empire is accounting: continuous and rigorous accounting. The technologies and techniques of imperial governance were wielded by its bureaucrats in myriad colonial offices and in the metropole. Scriveners created order from disorder with pen and ink, purging the subterfuge and insurgency of the enslaved from their account books. Clerks concealed horror within the gracious lettering of English calligraphy. Bookkeepers invented and maintained an imperial fiction of order when they rendered the turmoil and violence of plantation existence into regimented rows and columns with headings and subheadings. Accountants transposed people into profits and losses in their ledgers as they whipped them into shape as numbers. Colonial officers erased black life from their correspondence.

Slave registers produce a particular way of seeing, presenting a regime of truth that governs visibility. The politics of this arithmetic is not only about rendering invisible the humanity of those listed but also about rendering what is visible within particular frames. Writing within the confines of these registers and plantation records is an act intended to submit the enslaved to the *use* of those who wield the pen: pen and ink and paper, hands copying and re-inscribing relations of domination and subordination. The orderly columns and headings and lists belie the disorder of field, plantation, estate, house and bedroom. Slave registers purport to be a rational measured form of accounting, but in the face of the unreasoning and arbitrary violence that governed the plantation they are a symptom of imperial insanity.

The Act for the More Particular Return of Slaves, passed by the Jamaican House of Assembly in December of 1816 in response to the demands of Westminster, required these returns. The Assembly had reluctantly bowed to pressure from abolitionists, as well as the West India interest in Parliament, to provide an account of all enslaved persons even though such a demand was considered an abrogation of their rights. The Act stipulated in exacting detail how truths were to be defined and how the lists were to be rendered. Following the name or names of the possessor or possessors, and the character and capacity of possession, 'Schedule A' had to list 'in distinct columns the following particulars':

> beginning with the list of males, and distinguishing them from the list of females; that is to say, in the first of the said columns,

and which shall be entitled, 'Names', shall be inserted the name of such slave by which he or she has been usually called or known; in the second of the said columns, and which shall be entitled, 'Colour', the colour of such slave, that is, whether Negro, Sambo, Mulato, Quadroon, or Mustee; in the third of the said columns, and which shall be entitled 'Age', the age, or reputed age of such slave ... in the fourth of the said columns, and which shall be entitled, 'African, or Creole', it shall be shown whether such slave is an African or Creole ... and in the fifth of the said columns and which shall be entitled, 'Remarks', it shall be shown opposite the name of each and every slave, the name of the mother of such slave, if the mother be returned in the same list or return.

The return had also to list the name and description of each and every slave absent for three months or more as 'Runaway'. Schedule B was for the entry of increases and decreases since the last return. The meticulous instructions contained in these clauses of the Act were published in newspapers along with forms of the schedules to be used. Those who were designated as owners had to provide the information and submit it to the clerk of the Parish Vestry, before whom he or she had to swear in writing 'that the above list and return consisting of my sheet is a true, perfect and complete list and return to the best of my belief in every particular'.

I William Dormer, do swear that the above list and return consisting of one sheet is a true and perfect and complete list and return to the best of my knowledge and belief, in every particular therein mentioned of all and every Slave and Slaves possessed by me as Executor to Lilly Carby. Considered as most permanently settled, worked or employed in the parish of Portland, on the twenty eighth day of June one thousand and eight hundred and seventeen without fraud deceit or evasion. So help me God.

If the register for Lilly Carby could not tell me about those he enslaved I could use it to track the people who wrote, signed and attested to its authenticity. Lilly Carby himself was deceased so his signature did not appear on the return. He is listed as the owner of the enslaved and the plantation in the register, but both were 'in the possession of William Dormer', who completed the declaration 'as executor to Lilly Carby'. Lilly must have died not long before the register was recorded, and his will not yet proved, otherwise ownership of the plantation would have passed to his heir rather than be in the hands of an attorney. Jamaica had a Vestry system of local and ecclesiastical government modelled after that of England. Vestries have been characterized as the 'obedient instruments' of the planters who ruled the Jamaica Assembly. On 14 July, two weeks after the inventory date, Dormer took his record to the Portland Parish Vestry Office in Port Antonio and attested to its truth before William Thomas Downer, a Vestryman and the other signatory on the register.

The register I located in the National Archives was not the single sheet stipulated in the instructions issued by Westminster and the Jamaica Assembly. It takes up only half a page and is combined with an inventory from another plantation. It is a copy of the copy that William T. Downer made sometime between November 1817 and February 1818, which was transcribed into a record book that was sent to the Secretary of the Island in Kingston, and from there was shipped to Britain and incorporated into the records of Her Majesty's Treasury in the metropole. I gently brushed the surface of the slave register with my finger, as if I could wipe clear the accretion of time and reveal the character and historical presence of the writer as I traced his hand.

The source of the status, power and influence of a man like William Thomas Downer lay in his multiple occupations and offices. He was not only a bureaucrat with a gracious hand but also a planter with substantial property, a Magistrate and an Assistant Judge. He owned the Snow Hill estate which, in 1809, had 137 slaves and twenty-seven livestock, although by the time he signed his own register in 1817 he had reduced the number of slaves to forty-nine, through sale or a transfer of ownership to his children as he was getting older. Downer was also a Colonel in the Portland Regiment of the Jamaica Militia. In Jamaica the scribes were also land and slave owners, administrators of the law and members of the military: they wielded the pens, the guns and the whips.

Colonels in the militia were criticized for their corrupt system of patronage where commissions were partially and indiscriminately distributed 'to whoever had favour, interest, or influence with the colonels of the different regiments'. Downer would have paid £21 for his commission but reaped far greater returns in the distribution of favours. Major General Sir George Nugent, Governor of Jamaica from 1801 to 1806, was acknowledged to have improved 'the *esprit du corps* of the militia martinets [drills], by giving them a handsome uniform (scarlet with blue and gold), and a hat (*chapeau bras*) and a feather quite *a la militaire*'. In London, however, Jamaican martial law was the object of derision.

A seventeen-panel print, Martial Law in Jamaica, published in London in 1801, satirized members of the militia, shown preening in their elaborate uniforms, or as inept, drunk and debauched. The second panel, 'The Generals preparing for the defence of their respective districts', targeted the issue of corruption in the dual roles of planter and soldier. Unrepresented are the insurgent black bodies which made military defence a necessity. The three figures in the panel are wearing uniforms that evoke the dress uniforms worn by officers in the regular British Army during the Revolutionary Wars: scarlet long-tailed or short-tailed jackets with blue lapels and cuffs, gilt epaulettes, scarlet sashes, white breeches, black boots and bicorn cocked hats. The conflicts and contradictions between their multiple positions, allegiances and divided responsibilities as planter soldiers are visualized as unresolvable, the disparities conveying the metropolitan critique of the colonial condition.

... every clerk of the vestry, under the penalty of five hundred pounds, and incapacity from holding his office, shall, by the first day of February one thousand eight hundred and eighteen, cause the said first returns required by this Act, and by the first day of February in each year next, after the triennial returns are required to be made into his office, cause all and every such triennial returns received into his office, to be fairly and faithfully copied in a neat manner, and as closely as convenient; at the end of which, he shall annex an affidavit, to be taken and sworn before any judge of the supreme court, or of either of the assize courts, or of any justice of the peace for the parish in which such return is made, who are respectively hereby authorized and required to administer an oath in that respect, that such copy has been carefully copied, examined with the original returns, and is a faithful and true copy thereof, to the best of deponent's endeavour, knowledge and belief ...

Act for the More
Particular Return of Slaves

The Generals preparing for the defence of their respective Districts.

The first satirical figure kneels, weighed down by a gigantic hat in the shape of the entire east of the island. The second figure is standing but divided between soldier on his left half and planter on his right: half dress uniform, sword and pistol vs a planter carrying a sack in his hand and a large hoe on his back, wearing half a green planter jacket, white cravat, tan breeches and one black shoe beneath head gear segmented into military bicorn and tan planter hat with brim. The vision of the third figure is impaired by the largest bicorn cocked hat of all. Poking out of the pockets of his dress uniform on the left are papers representing the financial transactions of commissions and favours, while on the right are musket and sword.

This is one way to imagine William Thomas Downer, as a person satiated with the power he could wield over others, lowering his aging and no doubt overweight body slowly into his chair, over-dressed in the breeches, waistcoat and jacket that signified his station, and tugging to loosen his cravat before lifting his pen. All over the empire its military and civil servants clothed their bodies not in response to the climate where they lived but as a sartorial demonstration of their right to rule. Civil and military dress signified cultural and political superiority and advancement. The multiple roles that William Downer played in the life of Portland epitomized how Jamaican planters had consolidated every aspect of power – civic, economic, legal and military – into their own hands.

Portland, on Jamaica's northeast coast, is wetter than most of the island. In November of 1817 it was probably warm and humid when William Downer sat again at his desk to begin the task of making a faithful copy of each return submitted to him by everyone in possession of enslaved persons who were 'permanently settled, worked or employed' in the parish on the 28th day of the previous June, whether they held them 'as owner, mortgagee, trustee, guardian, executor, administrator, sequestrator, committee, receiver, assignee, lessee, attorney, agent, or otherwise'. The hand that could caress, whip, beat, torture and rape human beings carefully rendered 'a faithful and true copy' of the register, of all the registers submitted to him as a member of the Vestry. Did William Downer take as much pleasure in shaping each and every letter and number as Hogarth, John Hearne's fictional captain of a slave ship? Downer had until the following February of 1818 to submit his copy to the Secretary of the Island, so he could take his time.

William Dormer, the executor for Lilly Carby, was an attorney and a planter who owned the Content estate with sixty-two slaves and six livestock: the entry on his own register declared ownership of *thirty-six males* and *twenty-six females*. By 1823, he had an even larger estate called Industry, on which he owned 112 slaves and fifty-two livestock. Though neither William Dormer nor William Downer were 'Sugar Barons', the archetypal figures that have dominated histories of planters and plantations in Jamaica, each are an example of what Kamau Brathwaite called the 'old guard' of the island, the conservative group of 'middle-range creole planters, attorneys and traders making a reasonable living locally'. This old guard administered and lubricated the constituent parts of the plantation system of enslavement, maintained it in working order, kept it running smoothly.

I carried fragments of my father's memories along with half-remembered stories that I heard from various relatives, many of which I didn't believe at the time. My academic career began in the Reading Room in the Great Court of the British Museum reading narratives written by enslaved women, so I thought I understood the arithmetic of slavery in the Atlantic world and the politics of its libidinal economy. One of my aunts told me stories that focused exclusively on ancestors who were planters. I think she found more comfort in thinking about them than about those who were enslaved or laboured in fields. My father would talk often of a female ancestor that he referred to demurely as the 'housekeeper' for a planter. Father and aunt, each in their own way, domesticated the sexual economy and politics of enslavement in Jamaica.

The distant echo of these stories and the politics they denied provided a path through a daunting and bewildering array of historical sources. I was looking for a brute who owned and raped the black women whose offspring carried the name of their owner, Carby. In 1817, Lilly was dead but his estate was not yet settled: the human beings who constituted his 'property' had not been sold or transferred to anyone else. William Dormer, as attorney, was still acting on Lilly's behalf and the latter's wishes concerning the 'disposal' of those who were enslaved to him had yet to be fulfilled. But who was this Lilly Carby, where had he come from and how could I find him?

In the histories of the transfer of 'property' in the eighteenth and early years of the nineteenth century, there are many examples of young white men, born and living in England, inheriting estates in Jamaica, particularly among the wealthiest of the Jamaican planter elite. Inheritance leaves an abundant paper trail in Britain, easy to locate and follow, but there were no equivalent records for a Carby. My father told me that the name suggested that the people who determined the names of our enslaved ancestors were probably German rather than English or Scots, but he didn't seem convinced. It was an explanation he offered whenever he saw that I was struggling to provide others with a reason for my being. It also explained his first name, Carl. He offered it to me as something to try on, but I knew that he didn't *know*.

My search for Lilly Carby led me to the parish records of Coleby, seven miles south of the English city of Lincoln. Coleby is an ancient village which had been settled by successive waves of Romans, Saxons and Danes long before the Norman Conquest of 1066; its name is derived from *kollr*, an Old Norse word which means summit or high place. The Viking Way runs right through the centre of Coleby village. Assumptions about the name 'Carby' not sounding 'English' were predicated on the deeply flawed notions of Englishness that had been drilled into my father and his daughter throughout their school years. I was well aware that 'Englishness' has been produced from successive waves of migrations and migrants. What I had not examined was how this history was embedded in my name. In English Carby has two habitational associations: one from Careby in Lincolnshire, 'which is named with the Old English personal name *Kári* + *býr* "farmstead", "village"'; and the other, deeply embedded in the first, is from 'places in Sweden and Denmark named Karby, from *karl* "(free)man" + *býr* "village"'. How ironic that after all those generations my father, a descendant of the distinctly (un)free, would be given the name Carl – 'freeman' – in Kingston, Jamaica, in 1921. The name Carby in all its derivations resonates not only with a sense of place and settlement but also with the movement and migration of peoples.

Preserved in the Lincolnshire Archives I found the original record book of baptisms for Coleby Parish Church in which was inscribed in English round hand, '1771 October 20 Baptized Lily the son of Wm. Carby and Bridgit his wife'.

Part Five:

Legacies

History is the fruit of power, but power itself is never so transparent that its analysis becomes superfluous. The ultimate mark of power may be its invisibility; the ultimate challenge the exposition of its roots.

Michel-Rolph Trouillot, *Silencing the Past*

There are times when she needs to hide in a stranger's landscape, so that she can look back at the tumult of her youth.

Michael Ondaatje, *Divisadero*

What's in a Name?

When I was a newly minted assistant professor of English, I asked Professor Michael Thelwell, author of *The Harder They Come*, if he would be willing to come and talk to my students about his novel, which I was teaching in my course on Caribbean literature. I had composed and mailed a letter of invitation which covered all of the basic information and said that I would follow it with a phone call. I practised what I was going to say and also imagined various questions he might raise about the course, the students and the novel. I had these notes in front of me, on my office desk, when I picked up the phone. I felt nervous at the prospect of talking to such a prominent Jamaican author, academic and activist.

I was totally unprepared for what Professor Thelwell wanted to discuss – my surname. He had clearly been mulling it over because as soon as I introduced myself he asked:

'Now how come a young lady with the Jamaican name of Carby speaks with an English accent?'

'I was born in England', I stammered.

'And your father is?'

I gave my father's name and a brief account of how he grew up in Kingston, volunteered for the RAF in 1942, and ended up marrying and settling in England. But it was clear from the deep sigh that issued from the other end of the line that what I said was a woefully insufficient response to 'And your father *is*?'

The actual question was a question I didn't even realize I was being asked. Exercising patience with this obviously slow-witted young British woman, the Professor eventually had to spell it out:

'Are you from the black Carbys or the white Carbys?'

I didn't hesitate to reply with utter conviction, 'The black Carbys.'

I would repeat that response if I was asked the same question again more than three decades later. However, I would now add:

'In Jamaica, it is never quite as simple as that.'

Lincoln Settlement, Jamaica

In the latter part of the eighteenth and early years of the nine-teenth century, the parish of Portland had the fewest settlements in the island. Those that had been established either hugged the north coast or clustered near the border with the parish of St George. Parish boundaries, though clear and sharp on a map, were less significant in the lives of those who lived and died there than the four watersheds dominated by the Rio Grande, the Swift River, the Spanish River and the Buff Bay River, which established the character of the environment. As a consequence of Lilly Carby's acts and decisions, some of the inhabitants of the steep slopes and deep valleys of the region who bore his Lincolnshire name were enslaved, while others held humans as property. Looking for descendants of both branches, I travelled to Hope Bay, where I turned my back on the Caribbean Sea and headed south, inland, up toward the northern flank of the Blue Mountains.

Because Portland, in northeast Jamaica, is the coolest and wettest part of the island, the vegetation is thick and lush. Before Columbus, the Tainos ruled; after Columbus they fled the Spanish to hide in the mountains. They were joined by fugitives from Spanish enslavement, forming communities known as Cimarron. Following their successful invasion in 1655, the British imported forced labour from Africa to the island, some of whom escaped from plantations and swelled the size of these fugitive communities in the eastern and western mountains. The

Maroons, as they came to be known, were formidable guerrilla fighters and pursued almost continuous warfare for the first eighty years of British colonial rule. In addition to offering sanctuary to fugitives, Maroons also joined rebellions of the enslaved. In the early eighteenth century, British governors yearned to acquire Maroon agricultural land and install white settlers in their stead. To this end, the parish of Portland was formed in 1723. But even surveyors were fearful of working in the area around Port Antonio, in Portland, without armed security. The British failed to defeat the Maroons and hostilities did not cease until 1739–40, when the Maroons were granted tenure over their lands and limited self-government; in return they agreed to cease harbouring runaways and to assist the British in the protection of the island, which meant assisting in the suppression of black rebellion. War broke out again in 1795, resulting in the forcible deportation to Nova Scotia of most of the Maroons from Trelawny Town in the west. In the east, descendants still live in the Maroon settlements of Moore Town and Charles Town, Portland, in existence since the mid-eighteenth century. When my father mentioned the Maroons, he spoke of them with respect.

Several Parliamentary Acts were passed in the eighteenth century that encouraged white people to become settlers: a series of Royal land grants enabled elite planters to accumulate wealth, acquire credit and purchase people. Some of them, the Cosens, Downers, Manns and Shirleys, received multiple grants and their names became intertwined in the story of Lilly Carby, those he owned and their descendants. The British Parliament defrayed money for white 'artificers' – skilled men and women – and their families to settle in the island, and the Jamaica Assembly offered them inducements to settle in Portland, though without much success. A report in 1702 claimed that the enslaved outnumbered white servants by nearly thirty to one. Colonial rulers, who feared the stark imbalance in the population because of the prospect of black rebellion, became obsessed with racial thinking and constantly calculated the ratio of black to white bodies in a series of Deficiency Acts. Planters were eager to take on white men like Lilly Carby, not only for their useful skills, but also because these laws required planters to employ white people to meet the required mathematical ratio or pay a fine: most paid the fine. Lilly was a white body that could be counted to alleviate the tax.

Lilly did not receive a Royal grant of land, or arrive from Britain as a government-supported artificer: he and two of his cousins, Bryon and Aminadab Carby, washed up on Jamaica's shores in 1788–9 as soldiers with the 1st Battalion, 10th Foot Lincolnshire Regiment of the British Army. In order to transport an army with all its baggage, stores, ordnance, provisions, medical resources and horses for the cavalry regiments to the West Indies, the British government had to charter sufficient vessels from privately owned merchant shipping companies to form a convoy. These merchant ships had served a variety of other purposes, from shipping coal to trading in the Atlantic, the Mediterranean, the West Indies and the Baltic. Embarking and disembarking soldiers and their equipment was a hazardous and expensive undertaking. Keeping soldiers and horses at sea for prolonged periods of time presented the army with major problems. Bouts of sea-sickness, especially if caused by heavy swells just prior to or during deployment, could render an entire battalion temporarily unfit for duty. Horses needed weeks to recover from a journey at sea.

Lilly landed in Kingston ill and disoriented from a six-week transatlantic voyage. Much has been written about the Edenic scenes and scents of tropical ecology that overpowered new arrivals as they tottered ashore in Jamaica, but Lilly's senses were first assailed by the pestilential stench of death and decay that emanated from the Guinea ships in the harbour. Soldiers disembarked weak from vomiting and diarrhoea caused by spoilt food and beer, as well as being unsteady on their feet from the incessant churning of the ocean. In intense heat they assembled in columns wearing flannel shirts and wool-lined uniforms before being marched either to the crowded, filthy conditions of the fort at Port Royal, on the aptly named Mosquito Point, or to other coastal or hill barracks on the island. The 10th Foot, first stationed on the island in 1786, remained for nine years, during which the regiment sustained such a serious loss of men to disease that it was ordered to return to Lincoln in 1795 to recruit more soldiers. Bryon and Aminadab left Jamaica with their unit when it was redeployed to Europe, and served through the Revolutionary and Napoleonic Wars. But Lilly remained.

As soon as he disembarked in Port Royal, Lilly would have encountered *Aedes agypti*, the mosquito carrying malaria and yellow fever, diseases to which newly arrived troops were particularly vulnerable. When he fell ill with a fever Lilly would have been told by the more experienced soldiers to seek care from Jamaican women of colour, whose nursing skills were considered far superior to those of the military doctors, whose treatment was usually fatal.

The British Army was garrisoned in Jamaica, as in other islands of the West Indies, to protect trade, prevent invasion and suppress rebellions of the enslaved on the plantations. Soldiers were barracked in different kinds of military installations around the coasts and in the hills. The West Indies was regarded as the death trap of the British Army. The scale of fatalities from dysentery and dropsy, in addition to fevers, terrified the medical personnel as well as the ordinary soldier: a garrison had to be replaced every six years. Between 1793 and 1801, 89,000 soldiers served in the West Indies and half of them died there. If discharges and desertions are included, the loss rises to 70 per cent. Confinement in the pestilential, infested, overcrowded conditions of the West Indian barracks amid such a high rate of mortality had a profound effect on soldiers, and desertion was an option that hundreds chose even though it was a serious offence punishable by death. Few deserters were found. It is possible that Lilly was discharged because of disability, but I found no record of it. Everyone knew that the higher the elevation the healthier the climate, so when Lilly found himself barracked at Fort George in Port Antonio, I believe he deserted into the mountains. Either through discharge or desertion, Lilly was one of the 20 per cent of the army that stayed in the island. He was rapidly absorbed into Jamaica's plantation order.

The road I travelled climbed gradually, then steeply, toward the junction of the Swift River and its tributary, the Back River, where, in the nineteenth century, Lily Carby, his 'heir and assigns', held fourteen people enslaved on a coffee settlement in Portland until the emancipation of 1834–38 (after which the supposedly emancipated found they were still not free). The road had been hewn from pathways trodden for centuries; it traced the contours of the landscape, doggedly clinging to slopes when the land dropped away into a gully. At times it followed the older pathways of the Maroons and the enslaved, at others it crossed and deviated from them: bordered by John Crow bushes, paths vanished into the forest only to return to sight at a higher elevation. I travelled in a car; Lilly Carby, like other planters and overseers, would have ridden horses up these paths. Whatever could not be transported by river, donkeys carried between the coast and the plantations; the enslaved, also beasts of burden, climbed up and down on foot. I thought about the people who had carved these tracks into the hillsides with their feet, those who brushed thick carpets of ferns as they shambled, shackled together, in a coffle driven from port to plantation. I wondered what they had carried, in their arms, in their memories, in their souls.

How little and how much the landscape had changed since then. Colonizers wrought drastic transformations in the biogeography of Jamaica at all elevations, harnessing the bodies, energies and skills of enslaved and indentured labour to clear and cut, plant and harvest. Sugar and coffee plantations were designed so the enslaved would be under constant surveillance while they laboured, but within the 'moss forest' of the Blue Mountains, among Tree Ferns, Yucca, Jamaican Bamboo, Soapwood, under bromeliads and other epiphytes, the colonized maintained and preserved routes where they were out of sight: paths that led to and from their provision grounds; tracks trodden quietly at night to attack the Spanish and British settlers; trails between estates used to visit kin, or gather at secret meeting places; routes of escape on which to run.

In the 1730s, the Jamaican plantocracy considered the cultivation of coffee 'well suited to the poorer sort of people, whose stocks and plantations are small': coffee, they thought, might prove to be the means to bring that sort of people into areas 'very thinly inhabited by white people'. The overthrow of the slave regime on the island of Saint-Domingue disrupted coffee production, and from the 1790s, coffee production in Jamaica expanded exponentially, entering a boom period of exports that peaked in 1814. Coffee cultivators were still regarded as 'whites of lesser social standing', and many of them, like Lilly, 'derived income from serving the sugar complex'. Lilly was exactly the type of smallholder the Jamaican government had been encouraging to settle the interior of Portland. The relatively low set-up costs of a coffee settlement was an opportunity for a white man of modest means, and Lilly seized the moment

When he was garrisoned in Port Antonio, Lilly would have met overseers or bookkeepers working on the estates of George Harrison Cosens, who owned two sugar and rum plantations above the army barracks on the coast and in the hills. White men who worked on plantations for the first time were employed as 'bookkeepers': their job was not keeping the accounts but roaming the fields and works managing and disciplining black bodies under the direction of an overseer, the man who managed the estates and reported directly to the owner. While the Revolutionary War raged, the Elysium and Shrewsbury estates belonging to George Cosens were the sites of Lilly's 'seasoning', his period of adjustment and acculturation among hundreds of the enslaved. Here he learnt to become a white man in a British colony; here he came to realize that as a white man he could exercise power with impunity; here he raped and punished and tormented.

This power was granted to Lilly because of the colour of his skin, despite his modest background as an ex-foot soldier and the son of a Lincolnshire village carpenter. His skills as a mason would have been very useful on an estate, but Lilly's military experience would also have been of value to the island's militia. Lilly subsequently became an overseer himself, on Elysium, on the St George side of the border, before he set himself up as a coffee planter in Portland where white people were being encouraged to settle with gifts of land.

Lilly lived in Jamaica for almost twenty years, in a climate and ecology of economic, racial, political and social entanglement as thick and inextricable as the aerial roots of a strangler fig smothering its host tree. White slave owners and their white managers, overseers, bookkeepers, lawyers and administrators exercised control over the natural and social world, attempting to manipulate and police how space was inhabited and traversed. A population of free people of colour, 'natural' offspring of these same white men, struggled to secure the conditions of their own existence, to gain economic, political and social rights, and to attain positions if not equal to their fathers, then certainly superior to the small free, or huge enslaved, black populations. The enslaved were subject to arbitrary violence from white and free coloured alike; they survived, reproduced and died in conditions of extreme deprivation and hostility. Nevertheless, they carried knowledge of an Atlantic world the extent of which their oppressors could not begin to imagine, knowledge gleaned and exchanged through whisper and gesture in ports, on board ships, from produce markets, in fields and sugar houses, kitchens and bedrooms. This knowledge and cultural memory perpetuated in African practices was transmitted, reproduced and transformed in conspiratorial spaces.

Writing, thinking about, and being in Jamaica requires plumb-
ing the depths of the cruelly paradoxical and confronting the
callous incongruities of the application of the English language
by the British. Sugar plantations were the most dangerous places
to be enslaved because the labour regimes were most intense
and labourers were literally worked to death. Planting and
processing sugar had the highest annual death rates of any agricultural labour. Digging holes and trenches in the fields was the
heaviest work, followed by cutting canes and feeding them to
the mills, chopping firewood and boiling sugar. Workers received
few provisions and were allowed little sleep when the mill was
working; if exhaustion slowed their pace they were lashed.

There were three sugar and rum estates on the border between
the parishes of Portland and St George, in close proximity to
Lilly's plantation, all of which used the Swift River and its tributary, the Back River, to power water mills: 171 people were held
in bondage in Eden, 210 in Paradise, and 335 in Elysium. How
such sites of purgatory could be given names that evoked ideals
of perfect happiness, and locations of bliss and joy, beggars
belief. Naming practices were a performance, an enactment of
political power and control. They were also a sick joke which
registered the depth of contempt for the enslaved inhabitants.

Lacking an education in the classics, Lilly followed more
prosaic naming practices. He registered his coffee plantation
'Lincoln', after the city close the village where he was born. I do
not know what names his enslaved people used to address each
other because they were not recorded: the Jamaica Assembly
and the colonial government had no interest in recording African
names, only in aggregating the number of bodies, so all I know
is what was listed in the registers beginning in 1817. There are
no family memories of African naming practices because Carbys
found it difficult to admit to, or claim, enslaved ancestry.

Whether Lilly purchased people he knew from George
Cosens, or from strangers at one of the slave markets, or from a
merchant who purchased people at a port and drove them
inland for resale, he renamed some of them. A cluster of the
names of the people Lilly could torture and rape, the people

who had no rights to question the regimes of discipline and punishment that ruled Lincoln, reverberate with associations from his past in England. Lilly was a small proprietor and he could not build a plantation house in the manner of English architecture, like the large landholders, or model his grounds upon the English landscapes adopted by the Sugar Barons. But he could imitate them in smaller ways, evoking his English past through the naming of his enslaved: he named one adult male Lincoln, and others were allocated the names of members of the family he left behind: John, George, Dick, James and Bridget.

Following common practice, all the enslaved listed on this page of the register as belonging to the Lincoln estate have been given a single name, with the exception of one of Nancy's sons who was given two, John Carby. John was the name of the first-born son of Lilly's parents. Lilly did not claim John Carby as his offspring though he may well have been the result of Lilly's rape of Nancy. I think this enslaved child was given Lilly's surname primarily because he was the first child to be born as Lilly's property. Carby was a stamp of ownership, a form of branding. Nancy would have had her own names for her sons but we will never know what she called them out of Lilly's hearing. The names of Lilly's other brothers also appear on this list: George, Dick (the diminutive version of Richard), and James twice, given to an adult and a child, the son of Penny. Bridget, an enslaved woman, carried the name of Lilly's mother. Lilly acknowledged that he had an enslaved 'brown child' on Elysium who bore the name of his younger brother, Matthew. In the 1817 register for the Elysium estate he was listed as 'A mulatto Matty, 10, Creole, son of Big Fanny.' At ten years old Matthew was old enough to work in the cane fields.

Lilly would not have selected this cluster of family names from Lincolnshire out of sentiment but to reinforce his position as a patriarch, a man with absolute power: a man who tried to rule interior and exterior landscapes of labour and leisure; who controlled how bodies existed in space and time; who attempted to penetrate the most intimate, interior, affective spaces of the psyche; whose judgement and authority was not open to question; a man who was a tyrannical monarch on a Jamaican plantation.

The name Nancy did not exist in Lilly's Lincolnshire family, although it could have been the name of someone he knew who was significant to him, or a name from her previous owner. Nancy might have been named after the slave ship *Nancy* that delivered 2,519 captives to Jamaican ports from the Bight of Biafra and Gulf of Guinea Islands, the Bight of Benin and West Central Africa and St Helena. The *Nancy* made seven voyages between 1792 and 1801, voyages on which 118 people died.

The Trans-Atlantic Slave Trade Database – Voyages of the ship *Nancy*

Years	Montego Bay	Kingston	port unspecified	disembarked
1792	0	0	310	310
1793	462	0	0	462
1794	0	330	0	330
1795	0	330	0	330
1796	0	495	330	825
1801	0	0	380	380
Totals	462	1155	1020	2637

If Nancy, who was born around 1787, arrived in the first of the two voyages of the *Nancy* in 1796, she would have survived the Middle Passage when she was only eleven. If Lilly purchased her himself I think it would have been from the shipment that arrived in 1801, when she was fourteen. Nancy is the oldest woman on the register in 1817, and her son, John Carby, the eldest child. Perhaps they were both firsts for Lilly: the first enslaved person he acquired and her son the first born into his ownership. Perhaps, when he looked at Nancy, or touched her, or beat her, or raped her, Lilly wanted to remember the first day he had gone shopping for flesh and congratulate himself on what a successful purchase she was. Though his first visit to a slave market was probably a shock, a horror from which he might have initially recoiled, Lilly would have quickly rational-ized the condition of the enslaved as providential, part of the natural ordering of the world in which these beings were divinely ordained for his use. Nancy's worth was evidence of his own worth. She proved that he was a planter of discernment, of good judgement, who could continue to successfully breed from African captives after the abolition of the Atlantic trade in 1807, the year in which John Carby was born. The experience of purchasing and owning slaves was integral to Lilly's self-regard, to his aspirations for raising his status in the plantocracy: slave owners were gentlemen, after all.

Nancy, Betsy, Penny and Bridget did not leave a record of their responses to Lilly's rule over them, but I think they would have agreed with Mary Prince, enslaved on Bermuda, who wrote: 'I have often wondered how English people ... when they go to the West Indies, they forget God and all feeling of shame ... They tie up slaves like hogs – moor them up like cattle, and they lick them, so as hogs, or cattle, or horses never were flogged ... they put a cloak about the truth.' Names were not the only signs of the subordination of the enslaved to those who owned them, their bodies also bore the visible signs of punishment in their flesh, scars from whippings and, for some, the initials of their owners.

But perhaps the English had no shame. When Lilly was growing up, public executions for burglary and sheep, cattle or horse stealing were frequent in Lincoln; the Lincoln Assizes passed down sentences of floggings, burning of hands, and forced transportation to the colonies. As the prices of wheat in England rose dramatically and people starved, stealing became more frequent and so did executions. In March 1785, twelve prisoners received a sentence of death, the largest ever at the county assizes, and nine were executed on the Lincoln gallows watched by 20,000 spectators. Lilly, his brothers George and Mathew, and his cousins Bryon and Aminadab, probably walked from Coleby to stand among this enormous crowd.

While Lilly was enacting his fantasy of unlimited domination by day, his sleep must have been disturbed by nightmares of uprisings in Jamaica, acts of revenge and hatred undertaken by the enslaved. Tacky's War in 1760, for example, had been a major shock to the entire imperial system. It began with the takeover of four plantations, the killing of fifteen overseers and a raid on the armoury at Fort Haldane at Port Maria, St Mary's parish, before it spread to other plantations. It lasted for seven months, involved over a thousand enslaved, and remained engraved in the historical memories of all white residents of Jamaica. Such a threat was always present. Daily resistances and refusals were feared for what they might herald, and rumours of conspiracies were common. In 1807, a conspiracy was uncovered at Orange Vale, a coffee plantation on the Buff River, a few miles from Lincoln: this must have made Lilly and his neighbours permanently anxious.

The Lincoln plantation bordered the Shrewsbury estate and the Swift River tributary that gave easy access to water needed to power its mill and grinder and to wash the skins from the coffee beans. The land rises rapidly and steeply away from the river, and Lincoln began at an elevation of about 1,700 feet. Lilly's house and that of his overseer or bookkeeper would have occupied the highest part of the ground so that they could monitor every movement as George, Lincoln, Dick, James, Smart, Neptune, Nancy, Betsy, Penny and Bridget built and maintained his coffee settlement and produced his profits.

The leading contemporary handbook on growing coffee insisted that all an enslaved labourer required at the outset was 'a hoe, a scraper, [and] an axe'. With these tools and the strength of their muscles in backs, arms and legs, George, Lincoln, Dick, James, Smart and Neptune, joined by a 'gang' of enslaved labourers leased from the Shrewsbury estate, would have established the settlement. First, the heavy bush had to be cleared and a series of terraces and pathways would have been carved into the side of the hill for fields in which coffee trees would be planted. Nancy, Betsy, Penny and Bridget would also have swung hoes, scrapers and axes and been called upon for planting and the harvesting of the first crop four years later. Among other tasks, the children would have been responsible for the endless task of weeding.

The enslaved had to build access roads and an aqueduct system, erect buildings for the pulping mill where beans were extracted from berries, platforms for rinsing and drying coffee beans called barbecues, a dwelling with store rooms for Lilly, Mary Ivey Mann, his housekeeper, and their children, dwellings for themselves, for the overseer, and shelter for the horses and mules. As it was a small settlement they might not have had a pulping mill but instead washed the beans and removed their casings by hand in buckets. Lilly would have provided his human property with meagre provisions for their first year at Lincoln, so they also had to establish and maintain their own provision grounds.

The process of pulping required a vast amount of water, not only to power the machinery, but also because the processor separating the beans from pulp required suspending the pulp in water and then separating the beans from the solution. Coffee works thus required holding tanks or vats and an aqueduct system to divert water from a river, stream, or spring to the coffee works.

P. J. Laborie, *The Coffee Planter of Saint Domingo*

There are no remains of Lincoln, but the accompanying site plan for the Chesterfield estate in Portland, owed by James Bradshaw, is an example of the design of a small

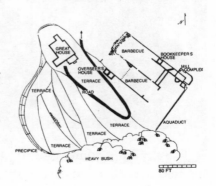

286

coffee plantation of comparable size run by seventeen slaves in 1817. It shows the houses of the planter, overseer and book-keeper, but there is no surviving textual or archaeological evidence of dwellings for the enslaved, which would have been made of perishable materials. Survey records for larger coffee plantations reveal densely occupied structures, housing from eight to fourteen persons in each. At that ratio Lincoln would have had only one, or at most two, structures to house the enslaved.

In addition to whatever duties they had in field and bedroom, Nancy, Betsy, Penny and Bridget would have also undertaken all the domestic tasks for the entire estate: they cooked and cleaned, planted, weeded and harvested their master's gardens; they took care of goats and chickens and laboured with the men on provision grounds. They would also have done all the estate's laundry in the Swift River.

Lilly may have taken advantage of a boom in coffee production in Jamaica to establish his settlement, but he had to face a number of problems. The first was the falling price of coffee because of oversupply: by 1805, Jamaica was producing more coffee than Britain could import. Coffee consumption within Britain was restricted in order to protect the tea trade, so once Jamaica's coffee arrived most of it was re-exported to Europe, where there was an increased demand for it from the Dutch and North German cities and towns through which it reached the continent. However, the Napoleonic blockade that began in 1807 and lasted until the conclusion of the war in 1815, devastated the coffee industry in Jamaica. By midsummer 1811, Lilly was in the midst of this crisis. Did he fear that the economic situation may deteriorate? Was he worried about his health? Whatever his concerns he decided to put his affairs in order and make a will.

I imagine Lilly tossing and turning in his bed, aching, sweating and shivering so hard he was unable to sleep, fearing that he was beginning another of his regular bouts of fever. The fear of fever would have been ever present even though Lilly had moved to the higher, healthier elevations of the island. Each time it returned I expect he wondered if this was the bout that would kill him. His fevers made Mary, the woman he and everyone else referred to as his housekeeper, who had borne him two children, extremely anxious. I think Lilly would have been uncertain whether Mary was worried about him or anxious for herself. She would have asked him to consider what would happen to her if he died as she had no legal connection to him or to his property. Of course, it would never have occurred to Lilly to marry Mary, because white men didn't marry women of colour even if, like Mary, they were free. Lilly would have reasoned that Mary would find some way to survive and I am sure other planters would have said the same.

Only yesterday Mary was telling him that it was time to put his affairs in order and this time she brought up the children, asking him to consider their future for they could not inherit Lincoln if they were not named in a will. That pricked his conscience. As Lilly turned over on his side, pain rolled through his abdomen and bile rose in his throat. He needed comfort but he was alone. Mary must already be with the children. Or, wait, he reconsidered, was Mary not there because he had dragged Bridget into his bed last night? It was impossible for Lilly to penetrate the fog that too much rum had left behind, so he lay still and tried to gather his thoughts. The harsh call of the jabbering crow would have startled him, an announcement that it was dawn already and time to be about. The leaves of the broad thatch also chided, signalling that a wind was rising even if he wasn't. He wondered if Nancy would have chocolate tea and arrowroot porridge ready to settle the gnawing in his stomach and clear his head. As he sat up and reached for his breeches Lilly would have barked Nancy's name. Then he shook again, more violently this time. He decided. If he could find Neptune, who was never around when you wanted him, he would tell him to saddle the horse Beaumaster. After breakfast he would ride over to the Shrewsbury estate and find his friend, the overseer Francis Shelton. Perhaps Francis could offer advice about making the will that Mary had been nagging him about.

If these were Lilly's concerns, the women who had to deal with him thought differently.

Who Inherits?

Lilly may have been the original source of the name Carby in Jamaica but what evolved was a tangled web of Carbys, from the enslaved, the manumitted and the free. The people they married or set up house with, and the children they gave birth to, had various gradations of skin tone, from parchment to the warm earth browns. All grew and aged in the hills and valleys of Portland and St George but their condition varied dramatically. For some the names they carried were signs of affinity; for others a severance. For a few their names could flaunt lines of descent or, more modestly, announce a chosen affiliation. For many, the names they carried had been imposed on them, a sign that they did not belong to themselves but were the property of another.

While a single name was usually recorded in the registers of the enslaved, like Nancy, Betsy or Bridget, it was rare that two names were written down, like John Carby. However, the free women of colour in this story, like Mary Ivey Mann, bore three names, and they gave their children three names which were recorded in the parish registers of baptism. Unmarried, and therefore outside of secular and religious determinations of legitimate familial relations, free women of colour declared their relation to the white men who fathered them and to the fathers of their children. By establishing a nomenclature of descent, free women of colour made a claim to respectability in defiance of those white men who refused to legitimate their lineage or publicly acknowledge an affiliation. Perhaps free women of colour imagined that three names in the records of the parish could be a genealogical anchor for their precarious lives. Baptism in the Anglican Church was one important measure of respectability within the free community of colour in Jamaica. Three names distinguished them from the unfree, as different to and distant from the enslaved even if they shared the same father and lighter skin tone. Free women of colour did not establish bonds of sisterhood with their enslaved kin and their three names only thinly disguised the fact that they were also caught in a form of sexual servitude as a means of survival. A sign that one is adjacent to power is distinct from holding and wielding power oneself but, perhaps, for these free women of colour it was a measure of their class aspiration.

Mary Ivey Mann must have been the woman my father and my aunt Joyce referred to as a 'housekeeper', to avoid any acknowledgement of sexual impropriety. Mary had two children with Lilly, and when she took her daughter and son to be baptized in January 1811, as her mother and grandmother had done before her, she ensured that three names were entered into the parish record for each child. Lilly was not present. The eldest, William, born in 1806, was given the first name of Lilly's father in Lincolnshire; the girl, born in 1810, was called Bridget, after Lilly's mother. To these names Mary Ivey Mann added her middle name Ivey. Because their mother was free, William Ivey Carby and Bridget Ivey Carby were also free.

In the naming of her children Mary Ivey would have been under pressure from her family, and from the free black community to which she and now her children belonged, to mark how William and Bridget were linked to antecedents. Because Lilly was one of 'the poorer sort' with only a small estate I expect the women in Mary Ivey's family thought Lilly didn't amount to much and that he could offer little in the way of status or financial security. Even though Lilly was white, because he was only the poor son of a Lincolnshire carpenter, an ex-foot soldier and ex-plantation bookkeeper, his name would have carried no weight with the elite members of the free black community upon whom William Ivey Carby and Bridget Ivey Carby would depend for their future social standing. As they could not look to the white community of planters for support, it was important in the racialized class formation of Jamaica that William and Bridget carry names of consequence.

The name Ivey linked them to a wealthy scion of Jamaica, William Ivey, planter, born in 1707, who purchased 1,000 acres of land in St George to add to the 3,500 acres he already held in three other parishes. I expect Mary Ivey's mother and aunts ensured that she carried the memories of the black and mulatto women who had birthed William Ivey's children and given them his surname. They must have passed down stories of the early history of the small free population of colour in Portland and St George in the mid-eighteenth century, of the Mann family who owned a plantation on the Swift River and of the children, born out of wedlock to white male planters and black and brown women, who bore various combinations of the names Mann, Ivey and Valette. In the first decade of the nineteenth century, the names Carby and Lilly would be linked to these other weightier names and the association became more refined for those who were light skinned. William Ivey Carby and his sister Bridget Ivey Carby gradually ascended into the lower echelons of the plantocracy as brown-skinned owners of land and people.

The community of free people of colour in Jamaica was not homogeneous: some were the 'natural offspring' of wealthy and influential men who had never been enslaved and who were able to mobilize their social connections for concessions to the laws that limited their rights; a few had been manumitted but lacked the support of a white patron and had meagre resources to sustain themselves. Racial designations in the island deviated from the 'one drop rule' that determined racial classification in other British colonies and which came to dominate conceptions of racial descent and classification in the United States. The term 'mulatto' had become so complex in Jamaica by 1733 that a law was passed determining that a free person four generations removed from African ancestry could be legally white. At the time the law was instituted no one was more than three generations away from their African roots.

In the middle of the eighteenth century, the numbers of people of colour began to increase exponentially, while the white population declined. By 1774, there were said to be approximately 23,000 people designated 'mulattoes' in Jamaica, 4,000 of them free. To counter this threat to the maintenance of white supremacy, numerous restrictions were placed on the rights of free people of colour to inherit land and accumulate wealth. The wealthy and those who had connections to elite members of the plantocracy evaded these laws by petitioning the Jamaica Assembly for exceptions for their children. Most free people of colour, however, remained without resources or rights. Internal rebellions and conspiracies, the loss of the thirteen colonies of North America, the mass insurgency of the enslaved in Saint-Domingue – which led, with support from mulatto communities, to the founding of Haiti as an independent black republic – all stimulated debate about possible threats to white hegemony in Jamaica.

By 1797, when Lilly was establishing his plantation, the colony consisted, in the words of the Jamaica Assembly, of four classes: 'whites, free people of colour having special privileges, free people of colour not possessing such privileges and slaves'. In the face of the constant threat of black uprising, voices were raised within the Assembly both for and against a restriction on the rights and power of the free population of colour. Those opposed argued that repression would lead to alliances with the enslaved and foment rebellion. The Assembly ceased approving privilege bills after 1802, and as private elite networks lost their effectiveness as a means to attain and retain rights, free people of colour shifted their political sights away from individual petitioning and sought to improve their situation by lobbying as a group.

Racial and class positions in Jamaica were determined not only by wealth and access to power. Free people of colour collaborated with efforts to maintain white supremacy; subtle differences in the shades of skin tone marked social standing: the lighter the skin the greater the value in the marriage market, and those who were dark skinned were barely tolerated. The emergence of free people of colour as a class in Jamaica is not just a story of a shift from the individual petitions of the wealthy to the rise of a community able to mobilize political pressure as a group. The consolidation of their position was also the story of individuals making and cementing alliances at local levels, often through marriage, so that they too would benefit from increased proximity to whiteness, become incorporated into the plantocracy and reap profit from the emancipation of the enslaved population.

This was the context of race and class and colour in which Mary Ivey Mann sought to secure her future and that of her children. I often wonder how Lilly and Mary Ivey came to meet in Port Antonio. Perhaps the women in her family had medicinal knowledge of local herbs and cared for this discharged or deserted soldier when he was ill. If she had such knowledge, perhaps Mary Ivey was a nursing assistant to Edmund Shirley, who practised medicine in Portland and who she would marry after Lilly died.

I try to imagine the relationship between Mary Ivey and Lilly on the Lincoln plantation and speculate that for Mary Ivey it must have been a life of careful negotiation. I expect she asked herself what Lilly was thinking when he stared at her with his grey eyes, as if he was assessing and questioning her motives without saying a word. Could Lilly ever fully trust any of the black and brown people around him? Even if he wanted to comfort himself with the thought that he was obeyed because he was respected, if not loved, at other times he must have recognized fear, hatred and a desire for revenge in the eyes that looked at him, even those of Mary Ivey, who must have felt resentment at Lilly's lack of regard for her precarious legal standing. If Mary Ivey gazed steadily back at Lilly was he the first to turn away because he did not want to know what she was thinking, did not want to acknowledge that she might have a mind of her own, did not want to see that she was afraid of him?

Mary Ivey Mann lived and worked in Lilly's house, but I wonder if she thought of it as hers, if she cared for Lilly or only for her children. When she was a girl, perhaps Mary Ivey watched her mother wring a series of small concessions out of the man who fathered her and her sister, Lovinia Ivey Mann, while suppressing the urge to wring his neck. For generations, this was the only way free women of colour could survive. From the moment her children were born Mary Ivey would have utilized all her powers of persuasion in urging Lilly to make a will. And Lilly possibly enjoyed watching Mary Ivey plead with him because it would have confirmed that he had power over her.

A will, however, would not have alleviated all of Mary Ivey's anxiety because as a single woman of colour there were so many restrictions on her rights she would have been unsure if she could make a successful claim. There was a limit of £2,000 on the amount that free people of colour could inherit imposed by a law of 1761, and a law of 1775 severely restricted women's inheritance rights. I am sure Mary Ivey and her family would have been among those in the free community of colour who believed that it was time to band together to lobby the Assembly for protections for their children to prevent them from becoming destitute.

In the meantime, Mary Ivey was not paralyzed by her fears of Lilly's mortality and the precariousness of her situation. In January 1811 she took her son William, five years old, and daughter Bridget, fifteen months, to be baptized, in spite of the fact that Lilly refused to go with her and enter his name into the parish records of Portland alongside the names of his children. She was following the example of her sister, Lovinia Ivey Mann, and cousin, Mary Valette Mann, both of whom had their children baptized without the presence or acknowledgement of their fathers.

Six months later, in the midst of the coffee crisis, Lilly made his will. When he was in the British Army he would have consumed liberal amounts of rum like all soldiers stationed in the West Indies, who were issued generous daily rations. As a planter I imagine he continued this drinking along with his friends Francis Shelton, George Norman and Sam Pugh, who witnessed his will. Mary Ivey would have been nervous when they were in the house. Francis, George and Sam were bookkeepers on the Shrewsbury and Elysium estates; they had reputations for being brutal in the cane fields and all of them, like Lilly, forced themselves on enslaved women and fathered children. When they came to Lincoln I can imagine them scanning Mary Ivey's, Nancy's, Bridget's, Eve's and Betsy's bodies as if stripping away each layer of clothing with their eyes, and following their appraisals with crude remarks to Lilly. Their laughter would have trailed Mary Ivey as she left the room. She would have avoided them as much as possible, but on the occasions when Lilly had consumed so much rum that he passed out, every woman at Lincoln would have been Francis, George and Sam's prey. I can imagine nights when, as they were leaving, Mary Ivey was slammed up against a wall and groped while the stink of rum on their breath filled her nostrils.

When Lilly announced that he had made the will Mary Ivey was relieved, but she took note that in it he had ignored the second names she had given the children. William was the primary beneficiary, in accord with the practices of primogeniture, and an annual allowance was made for Bridget when she came of age. This must have pleased Mary Ivey because an allowance plus her light shade of skin enhanced Bridget's chances of making a desirable marriage within the free community of colour. Mary Ivey was to receive, for her lifetime, twenty acres of land that bordered the Shrewsbury estate on which Lilly instructed his executors to erect a house for her from the net proceeds of the Lincoln settlement. This was an acknowledgement that she would have no rights to remain in the house they currently shared. Mary Ivey would also receive two of Lilly's enslaved women, the horse, and the bedstead, bed and sheets. After her death the land, house and enslaved women bequeathed to her were to return to the Lincoln estate under the ownership of their son William. Mary Ivey was not granted an annual allowance which meant she would not be financially independent.

Mary had gained concessions from Lilly but she would have to rely on the men appointed as executors to actually carry out Lilly's wishes: William Dormer, the local attorney who signed the first slave register for the Lincoln settlement; George Harrison Cosens, their neighbour and owner of the Shrewsbury and Elysium estates; and William Downer, of the Portland Parish Vestry. The executors would control the property and they would control William until he was of age. Mary would have heard many stories of how executors, particularly attorneys, abused their power, dissolving estates and selling the enslaved to reap their commissions; she could not depend on Dormer, Cosens and Downer to secure the future of a woman they held in disdain as Lilly's mulatto mistress. She needed an advocate, someone she could marry, which meant a free man of colour, someone who had social connections to planters equal to, or even more powerful than, those of Downer and Cosens, a man who would be a legal pathway to protecting her and her children's rights. There is no record of Lilly's death which must have occurred sometime after he made his will on 24 July, 1811 and before Mary Ivey's marriage two years later.

In 1813, free people of colour as a group successfully petitioned the Assembly for three changes in the law, one of which was the removal of limits on inheritance. That August, Mary consolidated her position through marriage to Edmund Shirley, the doctor, and changed her last name from Mann to Shirley. Edmund was an elite member of the Portland community of free people of colour because he was the 'natural son' of the wealthy planter, Henry Shirley, who, at the time of his death in London in 1813, owned two sugar estates in Trelawny, and a large coffee estate in St George cradled between the east branch and the west branch of the Spanish River above Skibo. Edmund's mother was Sarah Skiers, defined at his baptism as a 'mulatto'.

> EDMUND:
> Our father's love is to the bastard
>   Edmund
> As to the legitimate: fine word,
>   – legitimate!
> Well, my legitimate, if this letter speed,
> And my invention thrive, Edmund the
>   base
> Shall top the legitimate. I grow; I
>   prosper:
> Now, gods, stand up for bastards!
> *King Lear*, Act 1, Scene 2

Edmund Shirley was a young man who had been educated in England and apprenticed to a surgeon in London. His father provided him with an annual allowance for his lifetime and investments from an accumulation of government securities and bonds that he would inherit when he was twenty-one. Edmund and Mary Ivey would not profit from Henry Shirley's sugar estates since those were left to his legitimate nephew in England. However, his mortgaged coffee estates in St George were left in trust jointly for Edmund and the three offspring of colour of Henry's brother, Bernard Shirley. They would inherit the land after debts were repaid with hogsheads of sugar. Henry Shirley referred to his son by his mother's name Skiers, but Edmund claimed the name Shirley for himself. He had returned to Jamaica from London with medical skills that were in high demand on plantations and would have brought with him a variety of medicines as well as, in accord with his training as a surgeon, a set of amputation instruments in a mahogany case.

Mary Ivey was correct in her prediction that following Lilly's death the estate would fall into the hands of an attorney. William Dormer controlled the settlement, but within a few years Edmund Shirley appears in land records and slave registers as the legal guardian of William Ivey Carby and in possession of the Lincoln estate and all who laboured there.

Lilly's death would have caused distress among his enslaved, not because they mourned his loss but because they faced being sold to pay plantation debts and attorney's fees, being separated from those they loved and sent far away from the provision grounds they had cultivated and depended upon to sustain their meagre existences. But it seems that for a while the situation on Lincoln did not change much. William Dormer would have arrived, appointed an overseer, and left carrying the plantation ledgers. The enslaved continued to plant and harvest coffee and arrowroot, they washed and dried the beans and peeled and grated the tubers of arrowroot, they grew food. Then William Dormer would have come back with Edmund Shirley, whom the enslaved knew as the son of Sarah Skiers, the man who amputated fingers, hands and arms when they got caught in the sugar mill on the Shrewsbury plantation. When they heard that Mary Ivey had married and that Edmund, now calling himself Shirley, would run Lincoln, there would have been much speculation about what it meant for them: according to rumour, free people of colour were even harsher masters than white men.

At the time of Lilly's demise, the wealth of the Lincoln settlement lay in its human chattel. The rest of the inventory was worth less than £400: nine tierces (casks) of coffee berries £182.17.04; three mules £75; a horse £12; George Cosens owed £75; household goods, saddlery and clothing £35. There were sixteen enslaved people of whom fifteen were valued at a sum total of £1561.00.00. An enslaved infant, listed as Edmond in the 1817 register, does not appear here. He was the son of Bridget, the most

George 150, Lincoln 112, Smart 135, James 120, Dick 120, Neptune 110 ————£747.00.00
Betsey 112, Nancy 100, Penny 115, Eve 80, Bridget 122, James 60 ————£589.00.00
Edward 45, John 80, Sally 100————£225.00.00

valuable female, whose worth was calculated at £122. When he moved to Lincoln Edmund Shirley would have summoned Bridget to him.

There were two women on the Lincoln estate who carried the name of Lilly Carby's Lincolnshire mother, Bridget. The two Bridgets shared a name but that was all they shared; their lives and their futures diverged, one being property the other a free person of colour. The enslaved Bridget would have understood that it was really Lilly's children, William Ivey and Bridget Ivey, both of whom she had raised from birth, who really owned everyone, including her young son, Edmond. On her way to answer Edmund Shirley's summons the enslaved Bridget would have agonized over the possibility that she might be told that she was to be sold and separated from her son. She was the only one he had sent for.

Edmund hadn't possessed people as his own personal property before taking charge of Lincoln, and now, once the debts on his late father's estate were cleared, he would be running two coffee plantations. He would have seen how white planters, including his father Henry Shirley, treated those they enslaved in Jamaica and in England, so knew what was expected of him. He was two years older than the African woman who stood before him but he did not labour in the fields so would have looked younger than her. Edmund would have recalled the advice of William Downer and George Cosens to assert his authority from the outset.

The enslaved Bridget who wondered anxiously why Edmund had sent for her waited with her eyes lowered, having learnt at a young age not to look directly at whoever owned her. She would have tilted her head just enough to appear deferential while still being able to assess the man and anticipate any move to strike her. Edmund and Lilly must have been quite different in appearance and mannerisms, in addition to their thirty-four-year difference in age. Lilly was working class and because of his years in the Lincolnshire Militia and the British Army was probably blunt and barked orders. Lincoln was no longer being run by an aging white man with callouses on his hands but by someone who looked younger than her, who had light brown skin, wore expensive English clothes, and who tried to intimidate Bridget with his imperious manner. Edmund Shirley might have spoken in a softer tone than Lilly but each word carried weight and authority. Bridget was a young child when she had been stolen but she retained vivid memories of the ship. I think that when she heard Lilly's voice she would have been reminded of the men who climbed down into the hold to push and pull them up onto the deck where they were doused in water. Edmund might have reminded Bridget of the ship's surgeon who announced that her mother was dead, which was not news to her because she had clung to the cold, still body for hours.

Enslaved Bridget would have listened to every word Edmund said but would also have listened to what was not being spoken but was meant. Edmund was talking about Lilly and a will and that she had a new owner, which is what Bridget feared. He was saying that Lilly had 'bequeathed' her and Sally to Mary Ivey. Bridget's thoughts race ahead of Edmund's words. When William Ivey was old enough to run Lincoln himself in a couple of years, she would be separated from her child. Bridget held her breath then heard the words 'instead of Sally' and sighed. Edmund and

Mary Ivey Shirley were taking ownership of her and Edmond instead of Sally.

Two children, two enslaved bodies, Sally and Edmond, one swapped for the other as if they were indistinguishable, interchangeable parts of the plantation economy. Edmund Shirley might have made the change because he considered a young male child a better long-term investment than a young girl, or he might have been persuaded by Mary Ivey to substitute Edmond for Sally because Bridget cared for William Ivey and Bridget Ivey and might be more pliable if they kept her with her own child and less likely to run away. To Bridget all that would have mattered was that she would not be separated from her son, yet: he was too young to survive without her. In the slave register for 1820 Edmund Shirley wrote that he had changed the name of enslaved Bridget's son from Edmond to Providence and registered them both as belonging to him and Mary Ivey. In 1823, when William Ivey reached the age of twenty-one he signed the slave register for Lincoln himself recording nine males, four females and no increase or decrease from the last registration of 1820. Bridget and Providence were not returned to the estate as Lilly's will had stipulated but moved with Edmund Shirley and Mary Ivey to Shirley Castle, land inherited from Henry Shirley's trust.

On the 1st of August 1834, the 'Act for Abolition of Slavery throughout the British Colonies; for promoting the Industry of the manumitted Slaves; and for compensating the Persons hitherto entitled to the Services of such Slaves' became law. Under the terms of the Act owners of enslaved people were to receive £20 million compensation divided between them. Emancipation was a two-stage process. I imagine Bridget and Providence walking to the Buff Bay courthouse to hear the proclamation read aloud. The hundreds gathered there were told they were no longer enslaved but, for another four years, they were tied to labour for their former masters as apprentices for 41.5 hours a week for the 'customary' considerations they had received when enslaved: food, clothing, housing and medical care, insufficient and inadequate as they had always been. They were offered wages for any hours worked in excess of that time, though the amount of the wage was not determined, nor was the length of the working day. This meant that Bridget and Providence continued to increase Edmund Shirley's wealth after the emancipation which did not free them. As a former slave owner, in 1835 Edmund Shirley was compensated for the loss of his property and was awarded 70 pounds, 14 shillings and 3 pence by the Slave Compensation Commission of the British government.

The second Bridget, Bridget Ivey Carby, was nurtured by the Bridget her mother owned. Her future was secured through ownership of human property. The free people of colour, including the Iveys, Manns and Valettes, gathered Mary Ivey's children, their land, legacies and light skin, into the bosom of their community – William Ivey married Margaret Mann and Bridget Ivey married her cousin, Peter Valette Mann.

Following the abolition of the slave trade in 1807, the colonial government passed a number of Amelioration Acts, so named because the intent was to improve the conditions under which the enslaved lived and laboured and encourage planters to prepare them to join a free labour force by giving religious instruction, protecting their marriages and families, limiting the most brutal punishments and encouraging manumission. Such acts were vigorously opposed by the majority of planters. Perhaps William Ivey Carby was persuaded by arguments about the benefits of baptism, for in 1823 he had eight of the twelve enslaved people he owned baptized and given the surname Carby. On the other hand, William Ivey was not convinced by arguments for manumission; rather he passed ownership of his human property to his sister Bridget Ivey and left Portland. By 1829, William Ivey and his wife Margaret lived with their children on a hundred-acre parcel of land adjacent to the Maroon settlement of Charles Town in St George. In dramatic contrast to the enslaved Bridget, who laboured for Lilly and raised Bridget Ivey from birth only to find that in 1834 emancipation did not actually emancipate her or her son, Bridget Ivey inherited all of the most valuable commodity from the Lincoln estate.

In 1832 seven males and three females were registered to Peter Valette Mann (by right of his wife Bridget Ivey Carby). As a former slave owner Bridget Ivey Mann (née Carby) and her husband were awarded 200 pounds, 2 shillings and 4 pence in 1837 by the British government in compensation for nine of these former slaves.

Lilly tried to manage the future with his bequests but futures were not always easy to secure through a will. In 1811, Lilly had specified that he wanted his executors to send 30 pounds a year to his parents in Coleby, Lincolnshire, but his mother Bridget had died in 1804 and his father William in 1807.

His will assumed profitability and continued income for his children William Ivey and Bridget Ivey, but there was only a small amount of coffee berries listed on the inventory of 1816. From the 17th to 19th of October 1815, a major hurricane raged over Jamaica and the northeast of the island was particularly hard hit. Sugar and coffee estates were devastated. All the rivers flowing from the Blue Mountains swelled until they rushed down the hillsides in torrents, including the Swift and Back rivers. Crops, dwellings and people were swept away and the enslaved suffered the worst. After the storm, those that survived had to bury their dead, rebuild their lives, replant the estate and their own provision grounds with the hope that they could grow and harvest in excess of their immediate needs, so they could take the surplus to market to sell. Coffee that had been delivered to the wharfs waiting for shipment to England was completely lost.

Once Edmund and Mary Ivey were in charge of Lincoln the amount of profit extracted from enslaved labour on the plantation increased dramatically; almost 2,000 pounds of Indian Arrowroot flour and over 1,000 pounds of coffee berries were produced annually. Edmund also gained income from renting out 'negroes' for 3 shillings and 4 pence each per day to neighbours, which meant they were sent to the cane fields on the Shrewsbury estate. Edmund and Mary Ivey 'increased' their own investment in human property when their enslaved gave birth but also when they inherited human property from members of Mary Ivey's family. Enslaved infants were placed under the ownership of William Ivey Carby and Bridget Ivey Carby as investments for their future.

What happened to Lilly's 'brown child name [sic] Matthew now a slave belonging to the Elysium Estate' described in his will? Lilly left instructions that Matthew's freedom be purchased when he reached the age of ten by giving 'a negro' from Lincoln to Elysium in exchange. For Lilly, as with Edmund, black and brown bodies were fungible. Lilly also wished Matthew to be apprenticed to a trade and provided with clothing for his apprenticeship. When twenty-one years old, at the end of his apprenticeship, Matthew was to inherit £100 divided into three yearly payments. Lilly did not state how old Matthew was when he admitted to fathering him in his will.

In 1817, Matthew languished among the 310 enslaved men, women and children on the Elysium estate. His name is sprinkled among the youngest of those listed in the slave register as 'Mulatto'. This designation, systematically adopted on the Elysium estate, is a brand of the racialized and racist characteristics of enlightenment thought as rationalized in the economy of chattel slavery. It

Mulatto William Mulatto 16 Creole Son of Annie

Mulatto Matty Mulatto 10 Creole Son of Big Fanny

Mulatto Edward Mulatto 7 Creole Son of Behaviour

Mulatto Alexander Mulatto 4 Creole Son of Mary Cole

Mulatto Joe Mulatto 2 Creole Son of Mary Cole

is also a litany of rape. Both are normalized in the arithmetic of the register. The naming practice identified people who were the offspring of the white men living on, or visiting, the estate: the planter, attorneys, surveyors, overseers, bookkeepers and drivers. These men violated enslaved women on Elysium with impunity. Lilly Carby was one of them.

Matthew, Matty as he was sometimes called, was born in 1807. He was still enslaved beyond the age at which Lilly wished that he be manumitted and apprenticed, as he was among the enslaved that William Ivey took to be baptized in 1823. Matthew was retrieved from Elysium either by his half-brother or by Edmund. I do not know who was 'given' to Elysium in exchange and delivered into the hellish cane fields. Whoever 'exchanged' Matthew did not free him, and in 1832 he is listed among the enslaved owned by Bridget Ivey Carby and her husband Peter Mann.

I find that in 1839 Matthew has moved from Portland to St George and that Sarah Carby, one of the other enslaved people baptized by William Ivey, has gone with him. Like so many black Jamaicans, as soon as full emancipation was granted, ending the apprenticeship system whereby former slaves had to work without pay for their former masters, Matthew and Sarah walked away from the plantation Bridget Ivey Carby owned and settled on a small piece of land they called Lincoln. There is no record that Sarah and Matthew ever married but I find them because a son is born and baptized as William Carby. Matthew was then thirty-two and listed himself as a carpenter on the baptismal record, the trade of his Lincolnshire grandfather William Carby. I do not know if Matthew named his first-born son after his half-brother William Ivey but it is possible that Matthew was leasing his small plot of land from him.

In the search for the descendants of Lilly Carby it has been so much easier to establish lives for William Ivey and Bridget Ivey, the Carbys who were never enslaved, the Carbys who held property in land and in people, the Carbys who enslaved other Carbys and the Carbys and their relatives who received financial compensation from the British government. These Carbys appear in imperial inventories, the officials of Her Majesty's Treasury recorded their full names in the 'Office of Registry of Colonial Slaves and Slave Compensation Commission' and their land holdings were listed in the Jamaican Almanacs which were published annually from 1751 through 1880. These Carbys were not the Sugar Barons or members of the West Indian planter elite, though intimately linked to them through the imperial sexual economy, but these Carbys profited from enslavement too, accumulating just enough wealth to add to the capital of light skin to barter in the marriage market. These Carbys left historical traces. I realized that I had found the roots of the divergence in the Carbys that led to the question asked by

Professor Thelwell early in my career, 'Are you from the black Carbys or the white Carbys?'

Matthew Carby did not inherit. He was owned and enslaved by his half-brother and sister, William Ivey Carby and Bridget Ivey Carby. After emancipation his plot of land was too small to be recorded in the Jamaican Almanacs and, other than in Lilly's will and the baptismal records of his children, the archives are silent about him. His life may be an unfilled space in the imperial inventories but for me Matthew proved to be more than a loose end from Lilly's will. 'Mulatto Matty', Lilly's 'brown child' from the Elysium estate, ties me to Lilly Carby. William, the eldest child of Matthew and Sarah, was my great, great grandfather.

Swift River

The interest of the British government in accounting for Jamaicans of African descent waned after the final slave registration of 1832. The system had been instituted as an imperial inventory to count and keep track of the movements of property and transfers of ownership. Westminster had little interest in recording the actual condition of the people producing British wealth and no care or compassion for the human beings represented by numbers in columns. The process was deeply flawed even by its own measure. The ledgers severely underestimated the level of mortality in children: those who were born and died between registration periods were never recorded; and their totals are proved inaccurate when examined alongside other forms of inventories at the level of a single estate. It is not only difficult but antithetical to attempt to elicit the human out of an inhuman instrument of imperial governance.

The British cared even less about those they had supposedly emancipated. There were only two censuses, one in 1841 and another in 1861, and those counted people only in the aggregate, by sex, colour, occupation and literacy. A full Jamaica census was not undertaken until 1946, after Carl Carby had left the country. In the purportedly 'free' society, the colonial government had little interest in gathering information about Jamaicans as individuals as long as they continued to produce wealth for the metropole. Westminster paid attention only when Jamaicans were in open rebellion.

After the partial emancipation in 1834, and the full emancipation in 1838, some Carbys climbed the hills of Portland and St George to escape their continued indenture on plantations, where they preferred to carve out an existence as cultivators of small plots of land. Others either stayed on, or moved closer to, the few large sugar plantations, like Skibo, that survived the crisis of emancipation. They laboured alongside the indentured workers the British had recently recruited from India and transported to Jamaica in the same ships used in the Atlantic trade in African slavery. There was small growth in what came to be called a Jamaican peasantry, but most land remained concentrated in the hands of the same elite that had controlled it under slavery. Small settlers leased land, often on short term leases, as large landowners were not willing to sell it.

In post-emancipation Jamaica, putatively 'free' labour became subject to new forms of discipline and punishment and limits were imposed on labourers' freedom by criminalizing any behaviour the planters wished to discourage. Immediately after the emancipation proclamation in August 1834, in St George, the members of the Vestry, the large landowners and elite citizens of the parish, feared that their labourers would protest the terms of the new apprenticeship system. In anticipation of protest they decided to increase the number of solitary cells to as many as would fit into the cellar of the Court House. They also resolved to 'surround the premises with a mortar wall ten feet high capped and heaped with broken bottles and to make a foundation for the treadmill'. The treadmill was to be modelled after those found in the Brixton prison in England.

New forms of punishment were introduced all over

AN INTERIOR VIEW OF A JAMAICA HOUSE OF CORRECTION.

the island to ensure the adherence of the apprenticed to the new system of labour. The barbarous brutality and spectacle of physical punishment practised during slavery was supposed to be replaced by a modern regime of punishment, discipline and rehabilitation epitomized by the building of the General Penitentiary in Kingston, opposite which my father was born. Constant surveillance, enforced silence, segregation by gender, and solitary confinement were the operative modern characteristics. But it did not take long before the new systems of labour discipline also incorporated methods previously enacted on the bodies of the enslaved. By 1850, flogging, in addition to imprisonment, was reintroduced for crimes of arson and what were defined as sex crimes, 'bestiality, sodomy and rape'. The 1865 Whipping Bill instituted flogging for the punishment for 'praedial larceny', the theft of crops which were still growing.

The peasant ideal of establishing a community of small settlers to satisfy the desires and needs of the majority of Afro-Jamaicans was never economically or politically supported: they were disregarded and dismissed. In 1864, small settlers in St George organized to send pleas to Governor Eyre complaining of 'badly maintained roads, unemployment, and destruction of the petitioner's crops due to livestock trespass and theft'. Was Matthew Carby among these petitioners? I have no way of knowing, but he was certainly included among those upon whom Eyre placed the blame for their poverty and lack of basic infrastructure. Eyre's response to the problems the petitioners identified was that their condition was their own responsibility, that they only had themselves to blame for their 'lack of morality and civilization'. The remedy, Eyre insisted, lay in the amelioration of their own character and behaviour.

I wish to see them [small settlers] make larger and better dwellings, distribute their families in separate sleeping rooms at night, make provision for medical attendance, pay more attention to their ordinary daily dress ... devote more time to the care and instruction of their children, train them up to habits of industry and honesty ...

Delegations, petitions, marches and protests against injustice and extreme poverty were met not by redress but by violence,

like the march in Morant Bay in 1865 led by Paul Bogle where
seven marchers were shot by the volunteer militia. Anger at
these senseless deaths led protesters to set fire to the Court
House, and by the end of the day there were twenty-five dead.
This caused a peasant uprising throughout the parish of St
Thomas. Governor Eyre declared martial law, sending in troops
who burnt thousands of homes, slaughtered over 400 people,
and arrested and rapidly tried and executed hundreds more. The
violence with which the protest was suppressed, the executions,
the whippings of over 600 and the extremely long sentences
handed down created a vociferous debate in Britain that led to
Eyre's recall as Governor.

Jamaica became a Crown Colony in 1866 and the British
administration had a key role in 'thwarting the attempts of
ex-slaves and their children' to establish a fair system of land
tenure and agriculture. The economic, social and legal structures
which supported the large sugar estates were retained and
extended into banana cultivation, thus excluding the majority
of Jamaicans from land ownership in favour of preserving the
minority, elite planter class. The small settlers who were so easily
dismissed by Eyre were in a precarious position despite their
hard work and productivity. Some cultivators squatted on
Crown lands and many small settlers had to supplement their
income from what they could grow and sell with labour on the
estates for low wages. Whether Matthew and Sarah owned their
small plot of land, or were tenants leasing it for cash payment or
in return for their labour, their situation deteriorated over time.
In 1839, Matthew had been able to describe himself as a carpenter on the baptismal record of his son, William, but, by the time
of the baptism of his third child in 1855, he is recorded as being
a labourer. The struggles of these years of social and economic
injustice would explode into the open rebellions of the 1930s.

Matthew's son William Carby remained in the same area of St
George in which he grew up, and when he and his partner, Mary
Ann, gave birth to my great grandfather, Elisha, William used the
term 'planter' to describe his occupation. My aunt Joyce always
insisted we had ancestors who were planters: the word planter

always sounded so grand because in England Jamaican planters were always represented as white men who owned vast sugar estates. Matthew's and William's holdings, probably leased, would have been small, less than ten acres, because neither of them appear in the Jamaican Almanac's lists of landowners.

V25186 Loading a Fruit Steamer with Bananas for

Elisha returned to the area of the Swift River to marry and there he and his wife Anna deliver my grandfather Wilfred in 1896. The sugar estates and most of the coffee estates in Portland were gone by then, replaced by bananas or livestock. To carry the fruit, the Jamaican railway extension had opened between Bog Walk and Port Antonio with stations all along the coast. Small and large cultivators grew bananas. Individual growers formed themselves into a collective, the Portland Cooperative Fruit Company, to have more power to negotiate terms for their produce with the voracious and aggressive North American market, but the co-op lasted only a few years and was absorbed

by the Boston Fruit Company. By the first decade of the twentieth century, the Elysium, Paradise, Eden and Shrewsbury estates,
and many more, were owned by the United Fruit Company, and
workers experienced the modern form of indenture.

In the late 1920s and early 1930s, the years when my great
grandmother Maria took my father to Swift River in the
summers, they took the train
from Kingston and changed at
Bog Walk. It must have been
an exciting journey for a
young boy, with twelve tunnels
through the mountains and
numerous bridges over spectacular gorges, before reaching the
coast. They visited a flourishing inland market town, one of the
most prosperous communities in Portland. It was a vibrant
commercial, civic and cultural hub which attracted the residents
of Buff Bay, Hope Bay and Port Antonio to its stores and weekend vegetable markets. There were concerts at churches of six
denominations, plays, choral performances and, of course, a
cricket club on whose greens my father learnt to play. The United
Fruit Company had their own fleet of six trucks carrying
bananas from the Shrewsbury and Paradise estates to the tran-
shipment hub at Hope Bay, but there was enough produce from
United Fruit and small growers for independent truckers to
operate an additional seven vehicles out of Swift River. Swift
River was where Carl met his grandfather, Elisha, and a large
extended family. He heard many, many stories of a family and
community that had reinvented itself and, in the process, reinvented a history of which they could be proud: they were never
enslaved, that had happened to Africans not to their ancestors.
Some of these stories my father passed on to me and I took them
into the archives to find out more.

Wilfred, my grandfather, was among the generation who
turned their backs on agriculture. He learnt to be a motor
mechanic and to drive trucks in Swift River, eventually taking
those skills to Kingston and a job at an ice plant. There he met
my grandmother, Millicent Rose Munro, who became Rose

> When I was a child, in the summers, my grandmother took me to Portland, to Swift River, where there were many Carbys. Swift River, Skibo, Hope Bay, and Buff Bay, that was the home of the Carbys.
> Carl Colin Carby to his daughter

Carby. Many young men and women of his generation who did not see their future governed by bananas similarly left and headed for the city.

On the 21st of November 1937, 24 inches of rain fell in 24 hours. The Swift River and its tributaries broke their banks and destroyed everything in their path. When the flooding and mudslides stopped, thirty people were dead, hundreds were homeless, houses, shops and churches were washed away and the three bridges which connected Swift River to Hope Bay were completely destroyed. Without access to markets the town died. People were relocated to other communities while restoration began, but two more floods in 1940 and 1943 added to the disaster, followed by hurricanes in 1944 and 1951. The town my father knew was never resurrected. On my grandfather Wilfred's birth certificate in 1896, Elisha described himself as a 'planter', though I have modified my expectations of what that actually meant. My father told me that Elisha ran a plantation, perhaps meaning he owned his own land and was beholden to no one. He lived a long life in Swift River and died at eighty years old in Skibo. His death certificate states that he was a labourer; Elisha lost everything he had in the Swift River disasters.

It was very easy to find the Carbys in the region of Swift River; I was welcomed and guided through its pathways. Everywhere I went I was told of Carbys in the UK that I had to meet and how to reach them via Facebook. I met Carbys on the side of the road and took their photograph. I climbed to Shirley Castle where Edmund Shirley, Mary Ivey and their enslaved Bridget and Providence had lived. The principal of a wonderful rural elementary school introduced me to six Carby children. She also told me about a genealogy the school had completed on two branches of Carbys. I was invited into the home of one of the senior male members of the family and sat on his porch, which clung to the very edge of a precipitous slope looking down into a valley of coffee bushes. After tea and talk he suggested I go and meet his elder sister. I had the sense that of all the people I had met that day, she was the one who could grant me formal recognition, acceptance into the Carbys of the area.

I descended from the hills to the coast, to Hope Bay at the mouth of the Swift River. There I met the Carby family matriarch, the proprietor of a grocery store. Her younger sister was also there. I sat on her sofa and outlined the history of my father and his family. As I talked I could see my aunt Joyce in the features, the mannerisms and the colouring of these two women and I could hardly contain my excitement. Both of them listened patiently and politely but only one, the younger sister, smiled and nodded in recognition as my stories unfolded.

When I finished speaking there was a moment of silence before I was told the story of two Carby families, one branch of which had left the Hope Bay area. It was the same story I had heard at the Shirley Castle School, but in this version shades of skin were of overriding importance. To the shock of the younger sister, I was not authenticated. I was told that I could not possibly belong to this family matriarch's branch of the Carbys because my skin was much too dark. With that declaration I was dismissed. I had just met a representative of the branch of the Carbys who considered themselves white.

An English Village

My tale could not end with the story of Carbys in the parish of Portland, Jamaica. For almost 400 years black West Indians have carried surnames whose origins lay in Britain. Lilly Carby, however, also repeatedly gave the first names of his immediate family in England to those he fathered (enslaved and free) and to other men, women and children who worked for him and were his property. Through his creation of a colonial simulacra of his Lincolnshire family he established transatlantic threads of kinship between Jamaica and an English village. Lilly surrounded himself with Jamaican resurrections of his English grandfather, parents and brothers: the names of his white parents were carried by his free brown children, that of his white mother was borne by an enslaved African woman, the name of his brother and grandfather was given to Lilly's enslaved son, and men in his enslaved labour force had to answer to the names of Lilly's brothers. This practice of naming bound together what appeared to be different and separate: slave and free, white and black, English and African. I followed these threads of Lilly Carby's imagined and consanguine kinship back across the Atlantic to where he was born to a Bridget and William Carby in Coleby, Lincolnshire, a small English village intimately tied to empire.

Coleby is a village that on its surface evokes a version of Englishness peddled profitably on the international television and film market. I did not feel any intimate connection to the village but I thought it held the key to unravelling the knotty complexities, contradictions and contestations of imperial national belonging. Following Lilly to eighteenth-century Coleby ultimately also led me back to my father during World War Two.

I arrived in 2013 after the UK Independence Party (UKIP), a right-wing populist party, had made significant gains in Westminster by-elections and dramatically increased the number of seats it held in the European Parliament. I drove to Coleby in the midst of the 'history wars' – an intense debate over the teaching of history in British schools. The then Education Secretary, Michael Gove, had proposed a new national curriculum that turned its back on the rest of the world to focus narrowly on the story of an island nation, a celebration of 'the wonderfulness of us'. Such a curriculum was decried by its detractors as imparting a 'tub-thumping English nationalism'. There was much at stake for the present and future of Britain in this political and historical contest over representations of its past: the return of English national-ism with its vehement disapproval and denial of the multi-ethnic nature of Britain, a resurgence of nostalgia for empire, and the reshaping of the politics of national identity.

On my way to Coleby I travelled through land constituted throughout its history by invaders, migrants and settlers. I started in one Roman city, Eboracum (York), to travel to another, Lindum Colonia (Lincoln), both centres of Romano-British urban culture. In York, history seemed upside-down: Norsemen arrived four centuries after the Romans had left, but as I walked about its streets Roman walls and ramparts soared above my head while if I wanted to access Viking remains and remnants I had to go underground. As a society we choose what we exca-vate, decide what is digestible and what we cannot stomach, what we will regurgitate for spectacular international consump-tion, and what we will ignore.

With the city at my back, feet on rubber, tires on tarmac, I drove south searching for a past. I followed the route of a Roman road, Ermine Street, that connected Eboracum to

Lindum Colonia and both these cities to Londinium (London). Generations of Anglo-Saxon immigrants invaded, settled and integrated with the Romano-British, forming multiple contesting Anglo-Saxon kingdoms. By the early ninth century just four Anglo-Saxon kingdoms remained: Northumbria, East Anglia, Mercia and Wessex. The absorption of smaller kingdoms into larger kingdoms is the model that many English historians have used 'to interpret the course of Anglo-Saxon political history as one of progress towards the desired political objective of a single English nation-state'. Instead of trying to establish the singular origins of an English ethnicity, some archaeologists argue that what actually developed was 'a new sort of "international" community'. These debates over interpretations of Anglo-Saxon history are not removed from our contemporary existence, for they highlight what is at stake in how we characterize the identities of people living in Britain today.

Recent genetic studies attempting to define the 'People of the British Isles' assert Anglo-Saxon dominance in their search for genetic clusters. These studies depend upon and recycle racialized genealogical fictions, like 'Caucasian', to determine their control groupings. They also work within very narrow boundaries of geography (rural not urban), and generational population stability (all four grandparents born in the same area), and with only 2,039 subjects. While acknowledging the vast complexities involved in the peopling of the Roman Empire these studies exclude from their analytical frameworks the complexities of the peopling of Great Britain as a result of colonial expansion. As one Cambridge archaeologist asks: 'Is this a country which has always absorbed new peoples and cultures and should continue to do so, or should we defend our national character(s) against Europe and immigrants from around the world?' These studies cannot even begin to imagine what lies outside of their parameters of investigation: that in these 'stable' English villages people like Lilly's parents had black, brown and white grandchildren, enslaved and free, in the isles of the West Indies.

In the late eighth century the four Anglo-Saxon kingdoms faced an external threat from the Vikings. Norsemen made their first sortie into the northeast, landing large armies, and capturing York in 866; by the 870s three of the four kingdoms, East Anglia, Mercia and Northumbria, had been defeated. Raiding turned to settlement and the establishment of Scandinavian dynasties and Viking boroughs. The region become Danelaw, areas in which the laws of the Danes dominated West Saxon and Mercian laws. Some of the settlers carried my surname.

I veered east across the river Ouse and drove through the East Riding of Yorkshire toward the Humber Estuary, where the rivers Trent and Ouse converge at Alkborough Flats. I wanted to enter North Lincolnshire via the Humber suspension bridge, beneath which lies the Viking Way, a footpath marking the influence of the Danelaw in the Eastern counties of Britain, and a path that leads directly to Coleby.

Into a panoramic view of reedbeds, salt marsh, mudflats and a vast expanse of water, I imagined a flotilla of Viking longboats. In 1013 a monk, St Omer of Flanders, described with much poetic licence his impressions of a Scandinavian fleet. I imagined the Norsemen, having made the difficult crossing of the North Sea, resolutely making their way up the estuary, dozens of oars on each ship rowing in unison, or square flaxen sails catching the wind. I felt I could almost hear the sounds of their fast passage through foaming blue water, ropes strained taut, creaking oak boards, the plash of oar, the rhythm of energy expended travelling up through blades pulling against the tide, while I rode inert, strapped into a metal and plastic cage on rubber wheels driving across 2.22 kilometres of curving steel at 50 mph.

On one side lions moulded in gold . . . on the other birds on the tops of the masts indicated by their movements the winds as they blew, or dragons of various kinds poured fire from their nostrils . . . the sides of the ships . . . were not only painted with ornate colours but were covered with gold and silver figures.

St Omer of Flanders

In an island divided into a multiplicity of kingdoms, the Humber Estuary was the boundary between Northumbria and the fluctuating polities of the ancient Kingdom of Lindsey and Mercia. Norse armies assaulted the eastern coastlines, soldiers and migrants sailed up the Humber Estuary, and evidence of settlement is everywhere, if unacknowledged in daily life. Under Danelaw, Eboracum became Jórvík, from which the name York is derived; many of the current names of people, towns, villages and local ecology have Old Norse rather than Saxon or Norman linguistic roots. Some of the names of administrative divisions under Danelaw remain, like 'Ridings' in Yorkshire and 'wapentakes' in Lincolnshire. The derivation of the name Coleby, one of the cliff villages in central Lincolnshire, is a combination of Old Norse *kollr* (top or summit) and *by* (farmstead, village, settlement).

In Coleby I drove around the village to get my bearings. It was very quiet. I tucked my car behind a wall next to an immaculately restored, ivy-covered stone cottage with a wrought iron sign on the wall saying, 'The Blacksmith's House', and I wondered if it marked the site of the village forge in the eighteenth century when Lilly lived here. Coleby was so neat and tidy that leaving my car on the street felt like a major littering offence, an unsightly smudge that could result in the loss of a 'best-kept village' award. Or was this anxiety a displacement of being a brown presence in such a white rural area?

I walked to the end of the road to see the view west from the edge of the escarpment on which the village was settled. Fields bordered with hedgerows, patches of green, brown and the glowing yellow of rapeseed, stretched to the horizon across the valley to the River Witham and into Nottinghamshire, where William Carby and John Carby, Lilly's father and uncle, lived before they migrated to the cliff villages of Lincolnshire. Behind me, on the east side of the village, was a green lane, part of the Viking Way. In 1980, when a service trench for a pipeline was cut, the work was monitored by the South Lincolnshire Archaeological Unit, who mounted emergency excavations when the Roman Ermine Street was revealed in the Jurassic limestone. The road had been constructed in two phases, the team concluded, the first shortly after the Roman conquest.

I turned my back on the Witham Valley and walked back up toward the parish church. In 1907, members of the Leicestershire Archaeological Society published an account of their visit to All Saints in Coleby, which I had consulted hoping to learn something about the architectural features of the church they thought worthy of note.

The tower was the oldest part of the building. As I approached, I could see one of its two original medieval 'key-hole' window openings and its fifteenth-century crocketed spire. The circumspection with which these Leicestershire architectural historians expressed their view of the possible effect of the Norman Invasion on English architecture made me think that they were experiencing their own version of the history wars: 'In our present state of knowledge, this tower . . . may be assigned to a date near the middle of the eleventh century, when Saxon architecture was possibly receiving the impress of Norman influence.' They were hedging their bets.

I was unable to memorize all the architectural terms used to describe the arches, the pillars, the bases and the ornamentation but did remember how mixed it was, what in the newsletter was described as examples of 'transitional' architecture, 'uniting Norman chevron ornament with Gothic mouldings' and, 'in the capitals of the shafts, Norman arabesque sculpture with Gothic foliage'. Many histories conjoin in All Saints Coleby, some well-known and recited by local historians, in tourist brochures and

on Wikipedia. In this tension between Norman and Gothic the architecture embodied a struggle for dominion.

What I wanted to see was the Norman font, decorated with foliage, where Bridget and William brought all their children to be baptized. I turned into the churchyard, walked up the path, and pushed open a pair of iron gates covered in chicken wire to enter the south porch. There I stood, bewildered and frustrated, because the heavily studded fifteenth-century door of All Saints was firmly locked. In the England I had left more than three decades earlier anyone was free to enter a church. I was aware of the irony of being on the wrong side of this forbidding door.

I went to Coleby because of buried and unacknowledged pasts. I did not feel any intimate connection to the village, but I wanted to stand inside the church and imagine its connections to a parish in Jamaica and to enslavement. Inside the porch was a noticeboard on which there was a neatly typed list of the names of persons with access to the key, followed by phone numbers. I dutifully dialled each one and left four messages on four answering machines with my name and number and a request to return my call but, as I hung up, I wondered how many of those who listened to my message would be prepared to bear the expense of making a telephone call to a stranger with a North American phone number. I wrote down the numbers and the names of the people who held a key and determined to keep calling them, which I did, all day, but no one called me back.

I wandered around the churchyard at first aimlessly, then systematically, pacing up and down each row, searching for the Carby name. Some of the limestone headstones stood rigidly upright, resisting the shifting of soil and the force of winter frosts, but most leaned at various angles. I stooped to scrutinize each and every headstone. Inscriptions from the late nineteenth century were easy to read but were too recent for Bridget and William and their children, so I moved on to look for the oldest section of the graveyard. The oldest stones, the most weathered, were no longer leaning but had sunk deep into the earth. Bent double, or on my knees, I peered at indecipherable indentations in flakes and layers of disintegrating stone. I gently brushed surfaces in an attempt to reveal names and dates, but fragments of stone became small chips, particles became dust that adhered to my fingertips. I stared at the dust but it told me nothing.

The headstones and church walls were colonized by different species of crustose lichen, white melding with greys, myriad tones and depths of warm orange and rust. It was exquisite, intricate, indecipherable. Lichen defy conventional understandings of classification. Later that afternoon, in the city of Lincoln, I found beautiful pen and ink drawings in a 1921 handbook of British lichens.

Having been repelled by the rigid classification systems of slave registration it was a relief to turn to an alternative world of observation, where words of approximation dominated the language of identification: '*ish*' qualified colour definitions, 'whit*ish*', 'grey*ish*', 'green*ish*-grey', 'blu*ish*-green', 'redd*ish*', 'redd*ish* brown'; the recurrence of '*or*' linked oppositions, 'simple *or* sparingly branched', 'tubular *or* solid', 'erect *or* decumbent', 'colourless *or* dark-coloured', 'on the ground *or* on walls'; and the adverbs 'sometimes' and 'variously' appeared frequently. Even the pen and ink drawings, acts of visual translation and interpretation, offered multiple perspectives, slices of internal and exterior life simultaneously. With lichens, at least, the poetic qualities of inexactitude remain, capturing the challenges and possibilities of categorization with language that is elastic and pliable, expanding and bending to reach its truths, providing clarity without sacrificing complexity or detail.

Lichens are fascinating models of stable, mutually beneficial associations, models of how entities not only coexist but become something entirely other. They are combinations between two or three organisms, algae and/or cyanobacteria and a fungus. Fungi are unable to produce their own food through photosynthesis and those not existing in a lichenized partnership or other symbiotic relationship break down living or dead organic material in order to survive. But as lichens, fungi benefit from the photosynthesis performed by the algae and cyanobacteria: the algal cells live within the mesh of fungi which stimulate the algal partner to release the energy necessary for survival, growth and reproduction, and protect the alga from extremes of temperature and light, allowing it to survive in habitats where on its own it would not be able to exist. Lichen can survive seemingly everywhere, in any location, including the harshest environments on earth, on any surface, in the air and, as the European Space Agency reported, even unprotected in the vacuum of outer space. Thinking about lichen is liberating as well as instructive in a world in which taxonomies, genealogies and the singularity of lineages, ancestry and origins dominate, circumscribe and limit definitions of humanity. Lichen contain ecosystems, as do humans – we are 'interconnected, interdependent multitudes'.

Lichen can live for hundreds of years, but what counts as living over hundreds of years? A flake of lichen breaks off and reproduces, is this the same life? Or two lichens grow into each other and become one, is this the same life? The lichen I saw in the Coleby churchyard, *caloplaca teicholyta*, would have been there when my father was stationed close to the village at RAF Waddington, but its lifespan could reach 250 years or more into the past, as far back into history as I have sought to travel.

No one returned my calls and I had examined every headstone, so I walked to the local pub thinking that its owners would know exactly who had the key to the church. But the publicans had only recently moved to Coleby. They were strangers, like me, and could not help.

War

The following morning, I decided I had nothing to lose so I knocked on doors and found someone who had access to the key of the church. With a promise to lock the door when I left, I made my way back to All Saints with the key in my hand. I entered and sat in a pew. What had I expected to find? What had I imagined I would feel? I had undertaken a long journey to arrive at this place but I was not on a pilgrimage. What I needed to know I had discovered in libraries and archives and from my father – was he the reason I was here? I was not in Coleby to pay homage to Lilly Carby. I felt angry.

The Parish Register for All Saints Church in Coleby records that *William Carby and Bridget his wife* took their marriage vows in on Thursday, 17 June 1762. This church was where all ten of their children would be baptized and where they would carry one son, nine months old, to be buried in the graveyard. War and the possibility of war would haunt their generation and that of their children.

Five months before their wedding, on 4 January, Britain had declared war on Spain, and on 18 January, Spain declared war on Britain, thus expanding the military conflict referred to in my history school books as the 'Seven Years' War', a label which was easy to remember but was exasperatingly uninformative about where this war was fought, how it began, or what it was about. When I asked these questions I was told something like, 'defending British interests' – the usual vague fog of words behind which imperialism has always crouched. The Seven Years' War (1756–63) was the first of a series of global imperial wars which would take Lilly Carby from this English village to Jamaica and four generations later bring Carl Carby from Jamaica to RAF Waddington, three miles away at the foot of the escarpment.

In 1762, Britain intended to expand its colonial reach in two archipelagos by attacking Havana in the West Indies and Manila in the Philippines. Bridget and William may not have been aware of the international power struggles as Britain, France and Spain sought to carve up the world between them, but they certainly would have felt its effects in Lincolnshire, not least because local militias were raised in response to these declarations.

From August to September 1757, five years before William and Bridget married, Lincolnshire had seen what one historian called 'a complete breakdown of the established pattern of law and order'. Rioting broke out across eastern England against 'the Act for the better ordering of the Militia Forces Recruitment'. The Act had been passed by Parliament the previous June to enlarge the militia so that the regular army could be sent to the various theatres of war and it drastically changed the system by which young men were taken into the militia. Before 1757, 'any person with an annual income from land of fifty pounds or an estate valued at £500' was responsible for providing and equipping an infantry man. However, the new Act shifted responsibility onto the shoulders of all men 'between eighteen and fifty years of age in England, except peers, officers of the militia and regular forces, clergy, dissenting ministers, peace and parish officers, articled clerks, apprentices and seamen'. Recruitment was to be by ballot, and it was 'farmers, labourers and farm servants' who protested against the collection of the lists of names to be placed on the ballot. The rioters declared, 'We will not fight for what does not concern us and belongs to our land-lords: let the worst happen, we can but be tenants and labourers, as we are at present.' Many lists were destroyed and the act was not enforced, but two years later, after corn prices had fallen and a possible French invasion loomed, militias were formed in

North and South Lincolnshire. William Carby and his brother John Carby (Lilly's father and uncle) had recently migrated from Nottinghamshire to Lincolnshire and were in the age group affected by the Act. Were they sufficiently worried about appearing on the ballot that they participated in the protests? Though the war was officially over in 1763, the global conflicts of which it was a part were not resolved, which had effects locally. In 1770, just one month before Lilly was born, the Southern Battalion of the Lincolnshire Militia was called up and William Carby had to participate in twenty-eight days of training. His name still appeared on the muster rolls for the Loyal Welbourn Volunteers in 1803, just four years before he died on 24 October 1807.

On Bridget's wedding day in June 1762, a number of thoughts must have preoccupied her but I doubt that distant wars would have been one of them. It had been a hard winter. In late February there was a 'prodigious storm of snow, hail and wind' and 'snow was piled to a great height'. Many people had died. Up on Burton Ridge a young girl had been buried in the snow at Hobbler's Hole, a place Bridget likely knew well, for she was daughter of a miller and there had been mills up there since the middle ages. The price of wheat had risen from 23s 11d per quarter to 30s 10d, which was good news for farmers and landlords but bad news for everyone else, and come next winter, Bridget would have a baby to care for as well as a husband.

It was a fine warm summer day when Bridget passed under the wooden beams of All Saints and walked up the aisle on her father's arm, past family and friends, to stand next to William. In June 1763, a year after his own wedding, William signed as a witness to the marriage of his brother John Carby to Mary Blackbourn in the same church. Bridget would have been there with their five-month-old daughter, Anne. John and Mary would become the parents of Bryon and Aminadab Carby, who would join the British Army with Lilly and be sent with the 10th Foot to Jamaica.

Thomas Nocton, the Curate, wrote '*Lely*' in the register as Bridget's maiden name on her wedding day. This name suggested a link to ancestors who, if not distinguished aristocrats with 'country seats', were perhaps middle gentry, folks who merited more than a hundred entries in the Lincolnshire County Archives. When searching beyond the history of the English gentry, however, there are many reminders of the power of class and lineage, for Lely, Lily, Lilly and Lillie were randomly and carelessly applied to ordinary villagers, farmers, labourers and peasants. In contrast, the names of men and women of property and reputation, those who possessed estates and even whole villages, those who ruled locally and nationally, were very attentively, carefully and consistently penned into history. The final entries at the bottom of the register of William and Bridget's marriage appear to be in Bridget's and William's own hands. Bridget, in contrast to Nocton's *Lely*, wrote her name as *Bridget Lilly*. Bridget called her sixth child Lilly, after her father's family, even though the baptismal record incorrectly shows Lily. Lilly Carby carried his mother's maiden name.

Bridget's father was Matthew Lilly, a miller in Aubourn. The mill, no longer in existence, was on the banks of the River Witham and Aubourn was connected to Coleby by a well-travelled foot, cart and bridle path across the fields. Visiting Bridget would have been easy for William, but returning home to Coleby was uphill all the way as it is one of a series of cliff villages standing high on the top of Lincoln Edge, an escarpment running through central Lincolnshire on which once stood nine tower windmills. When they married, William and Bridget were already living together in Coleby and Bridget was carrying their first child.

All the Carby children were baptized at All Saints with its imposing part Saxon and part Norman tower and graceful early English arcades and chancel. Bridget and William stood in front of the Norman font ten times holding infants in their arms. As I traced parish records, written by a succession of curates, Bridget's name morphed to Bridgit, Bridgett, Bridit, returned to Bridgit and then, when she was buried in 1804, became Bright.

The Lincolnshire Cliff is a Jurassic ridge, declared 'excellent turnip and barley land, on a bed of limestone, at various depths, from six inches to several feet' by Arthur Young, Secretary to the

Board of Agriculture, in his study of the county. During William and Bridget's lifetime the main crops were barley, turnips and rapeseed with a smaller percentage of wheat; sheep were folded on the turnips, their feet turning the soil and their manure enriching it. William was a carpenter but for those in the family who had to work in the fields it must have been a hard-scrabble life. When I try to imagine what it was like for Bridget harvesting turnips with her children, my mind summons the figure of a young woman named Tess, shivering in a bitingly cold wind blasting across a bleak hillside, undertaking the back-breaking work of hoeing turnips, in Thomas Hardy's novel, *Tess of the d'Urbervilles*.

There were a number of factors which propelled the sons of William and John Carby out of Coleby. An immediate and profound disruption to the lives and well-being of the residents of the parish was not the threat of the militia ballot but the dispossession wrought by enclosure and the loss of the commons in 1760, two years before William and Bridget married. Lincolnshire was characterized by large estates owned by magnate families and a growing minor gentry becoming large landowners. Around these estates the smaller freeholder had been 'swept away'. What made Lincolnshire distinct and similar to Jamaica was its large number of absentee landlords. Many of the parishes south of Lincoln were owned by one landlord.

Coleby Hall lies to the northwest of the main village and Hall Farm to the northeast. Coleby Hall was owned until 1734 by the Lister family who had lived there for generations. Thomas Lister, who was born in 1597 and grew up in the Hall, was probably the most famous member of the family. In August 1642, in the early days of the Civil War, Coleby Hall was raided by Royalist troops and Thomas Lister taken prisoner and dragged before the King's Council. When released, he served as a lieutenant-colonel in Cromwell's Parliamentary Army, then as high sheriff of Lincoln represented Lincolnshire in Cromwell's parliaments. After the Restoration in 1660, Lister was tried as a regicide but was merely banned from holding future office. He had no children and all his estates passed to various family members up to Thomas Scope, who undertook the Acts of Enclosure in 1760.

In 1765, William paid the duty for the indenture of an apprentice, which meant he must have had enough carpentry work to need an extra pair of hands. This was many years before William's sons would have been old enough to be apprenticed and assist him, years during which their future prospects fell. Enclosure was financed by landowners who increased their holdings then immediately sought to recoup this expenditure by raising rents on those who had previously had free access to the commons but were now merely tenants and had no strip of land to till, no village pasture on which a cow could be grazed, or sheep or pigs raised to help support a family. I doubt that William and Bridget owned their own cottage. If they received compensation for the loss of the commons with an allotment it would have been at some distance from where they lived. No compensation would have been as valuable as what was lost. In 1766, there were riots in all parts of England because of the high price of provisions.

These are the dire economic conditions that shaped Lilly's childhood. Like all children who were not sons of the gentry and destined for private schools or tutors, Lilly, his brothers, sisters and cousins would have worked from a young age. Lilly may have acquired basic literacy from his parents and received some religious education, though Sunday Schools were not established in the parishes until 1785 and a parochial school was not built in Coleby until 1854. Lilly would have laboured in the fields of the local squire when he was young, before he was apprenticed to a mason – the skill recorded for him in Jamaica.

In the summer of 1783, when he was almost thirteen, Lilly and his family experienced 'an amazing and portentous summer', one of the most dramatic and disturbing environmental events anyone in England had ever seen. On 23 June, thick clouds of sulphur dioxide gas began to drift over eastern Britain. The sun turned the colour of blood at sunrise and sunset, the corn withered, and people working outdoors found it difficult to breathe, feeling the fog sting their eyes and burn their throats and lungs. Transported in the haze were fine airborne particles that irritated and damaged respiratory systems.

An account from Lincoln: 'A thick, hot vapour had for several days before filled up the valley . . . so that both the Sun and Moon appeared like heated brick-bars.'
Gentleman's Magazine, July 1783

In the evening, 'the aristæ of the barley . . . became brown and weathered at their extremities, as did the leaves of the oats; the rye had the appearance of being mildewed', the leaves of trees 'suffered greatly' and 'vegetable appeared exactly as if a fire had been lighted near them, that had shriveled and discolored their leaves.'

People didn't know that what was causing the acidic and volatile gases that were damaging crops and lungs was the release of an estimated 122 megatons of sulphur dioxide and other gases from volcanic eruptions at the Laki Craters in Iceland, which began on 8 June. The worst affected part of the country was eastern England, where there were two peaks of fatalities: from August to September in the extremely hot summer, and in January and February of 1784, the coldest months on record. There is no record of anyone in Lilly's family being buried in either of these periods, but the impact on human health and the environment was widespread.

> We never see the sun but shorn of his beams, the trees are scarcely discernible at a mile's distance, he sets with the face of a red-hot salamander and rises with the same complexion.
>
> William Cowper

Newspaper circulation and readership was growing in the provinces but word of mouth alone meant that most people would have been aware that highly disturbed weather was occurring across Europe. Very few understood climatology and meteorology so most felt

> 'The naturalist, Gilbert White declared that it was unlike anything known within the memory of man.' Wheat, barley and oats yellowed and withered in 'hot fog', there was a sulfurous stench in the air, intense heat and exceptionally violent thunderstorms.

fear, foreboding and outright alarm when the intense heat was accompanied by a sulphurous stench and, on 2, 4, 7 and 10 July, generated ferocious thunderstorms with lightning that struck barns, churches, houses and livestock and caused fires and floods. Newspapers reported the panic and alarm with graphic descriptions of bodies struck by lightning, the writers reaching for adjectives to adequately describe the extremity of the weather and its effects. I wonder if Lilly thought back to the extreme heat he experienced that summer of 1783 when he stepped ashore, five years later, in Jamaica, as a young man wearing the uniform of the British Army?

In Lilly's lifetime this extraordinary meteorological event may have been exceptional, but it occurred at a time when life was becoming increasingly precarious for the poor in Lincolnshire. The price of wheat continued to rise: in 1783 it stood at 48s 2d per quarter. As food prices increased and people couldn't feed their families, reports of theft of livestock and housebreaking also increased. Punishment was punitive and draconian: public executions on the Lincoln gallows became a regular occurrence. The first bricks for the County Gaol were laid in 1786 and the future looked grim.

Coleby is a very ordinary English village, and the story I tell about its sons is not exceptional. Three young Carby men in one family joined the British Army and were sent to the West Indies. Two returned at the end of the Napoleonic Wars, and one earned an income from harnessing the labour of an enslaved workforce. Lilly and his two cousins left England in 1788: Aminadab was discharged in 1803, blind; Bryon was discharged in 1814, 'in consequence of general debility from long service'; Lilly died being nursed by enslaved women in Jamaica. Similar fates will have been true, not only of this family in this particular village, but of the thousands of other English, Welsh and Scottish families and villages to be found in regimental service registers. Links to colonial exploitation and oppression, to Atlantic slavery and imperial wars, are not the exception, they are our quotidian past.

The last decade of the eighteenth century and the first two years of the nineteenth were dominated by a series of conflicts that historians have named the French Revolutionary Wars, which officially began in 1792, six years after the 10th Foot was dispatched to Jamaica, and which were followed almost immediately by the Napoleonic Wars (1803–15). What these wars were named mattered little to those who fought and died in them, but what they are called makes it appear as if they were being fought just among the European powers: the extent to which they were a continuation of competing imperialisms, colonization and the British policing of slave rebellions in the Caribbean is disguised.

It took me a long time to figure out how Lilly Carby, the son of a Lincolnshire carpenter, ended up in Jamaica. I did not find the answer until I read that if a young man disappears from the records of his town or village in this period, he was in the grasp of the rapidly expanding army. The country emptied of young men. Arthur Young noted in his agricultural survey of

Lincolnshire, undertaken in the last decade of the century: 'the country ... was not so populous as it had been; chiefly founded on the militia lists ... vast numbers have enlisted in the army'. Yet these figures do not reflect the vast numbers of young men who were 'taken up' for service in the West Indies alone, where the death tolls were astronomical. In January 1794 the 81st Regiment of Foot was embodied at Lincoln. It was known as the "Loyal Lincoln Volunteers" because the entire Militia of Lincoln earned their bounty when they volunteered as a body to serve in the British Army. After briefly serving in Ireland they were sent to the West Indies and arrived in 1794 with the aim of assisting planters to restore slavery and repress the rebellion which became the Haitian Revolution. There they lost the equivalent of twice their established strength to disease.

Life in the British Army was brutal and all too short. Being sent to the Caribbean was 'a death sentence; thousands of men perished or were invalided for life by disease'. Yet, even though they were recruited for unlimited service in the army, virtually for life, many militiamen enlisted when discharged from their five-year militia obligation. In the decision to leave in the face of such fears, such 'horror', I find a measure of what these young men imagined would be their fate if they remained in England.

In 1789, the year Lilly landed in Jamaica and encountered Africans for the first time, Olaudah Equiano, an ex-slave who had served in the Royal Navy during the Seven Years' War, published his autobiography, *The Interesting Narrative of the Life of Olaudah Equiano*, and began a book tour of Britain and Ireland. Equiano became 'the first successful professional writer of African descent in the English-speaking world' and a leading figure in the abolitionist movement. In his *Interesting Narrative* Equiano described his first encounter with 'white men with horrible looks, red faces, and loose hair' who he feared would eat him. Lilly did not write an account of the first time he saw Africans disembarked from a slave ship in chains, or how he learnt to claim white privilege and discriminate among human beings based upon their appearance, or about the process of his transformation from soldier, to persecutor, to owner of the enslaved. But Equiano did describe how difference became a refusal to recognize another as human in his reconstruction of a scene on the deck of a slave ship at anchor on the Atlantic coast of the African continent.

In his account of the place where he grew up, Equiano did not describe himself as black or as African; nor when he became a captive or at any point on his journey toward the Atlantic coast does Equiano use the terms black or African. He became black *in the encounter* with the crew of the slave ship who, simultaneously with their refusal to recognize a shared humanity with Equiano, became white. Equiano sought to persuade his readers and those who came to hear him speak that there was nothing inevitable or fixed about concepts of difference that led to discrimination between people based on what their bodies looked like. Rather he showed how the relations of subjugation and exploitation that characterize the colonial encounter produce race as the technology, or mechanism, of differentiation and affiliation.

In this encounter on the Atlantic littoral, Equiano was not only recognized by others and by himself as black, he was simultaneously inducted into capitalist relations as cargo, a double conscription which thrust Equiano into the violent formation of the black diaspora. The lessons that Equiano wanted to impart through his account of becoming a 'black' subject were made relevant to the present of his readers and listeners. For he wrote not only as a 'free' person but also as someone who claimed multiple allegiances and affiliations: he was an African, a Christian, a 'black' person *and* a British citizen. Equiano's narrative spotlighted the 'dilemma of the difference his skin color [made] in the colonial world, and yet he insisted that his mind, feelings and aspirations were similar to those of his readers'. As he travelled between towns and cities in England, Ireland, Scotland and Wales between 1789 and 1794, Equiano wanted 'to convert sympathetic readers into political actors' and persuade the working classes to support the abolitionist cause. In this context the second part of his description of the slave ship is particularly relevant. For Equiano realized that a politics of allegiance, of solidarity, could not be based upon the colour of a person's skin. When he recovered from a faint and saw 'black people' around him Equiano realized that those he turned to were not like him in every respect, for among them were some he recognized as 'those who brought me on board', and 'who had been receiving their pay' and thus profited from his transformation into cargo.

Equiano's constant urge to move beyond the limitations of body politics gestures toward a future in which the parochial, exclusionary national identity of his British readers could become more capacious and more enlightened. Equiano wrote as someone who was not only a member of the African diaspora but also a transnational citizen, and he offered his readers and listeners the possibility of imagining larger, more complex ways of being in the world. If *that* readership had only embraced the possibilities Equiano offered them, they would have been partic255ipants in a future that transcended the racialization of subjects. As Lilly landed with the 10th Foot in Jamaica and began his transformation into a white slave owner, Equiano offered the British public a vision of an alternative: an intuition, a possibility, of broadening and internationalizing what it could mean to be British.

I flew 30,000 feet over the Atlantic Ocean from New York to London thinking about the previous crossings of Carl, Lilly, and many of those enslaved on the Lincoln settlement: Carl in a North Atlantic convoy carrying hundreds of RAF recruits and supplies from Canada to Britain during the Second World War; Lilly in one of the many Royal Navy convoys which transported tens of thousands of soldiers from Britain to the West Indies in the imperial wars of the eighteenth and early nineteenth centuries; and the many millions of Africans captured, chained in the bowels of slave ships and sold in the markets of the Americas and the Caribbean, among whom were those given the names George, Lincoln, Dick, James, Neptune, Nancy, Penny and Big Fanny.

I had travelled to see my father who lived in a residential care home in an English village in North Yorkshire. In northern

Britain, in the summer, late afternoons lengthen into seemingly endless evenings. The sun was in the western sky but the drive-way of the care home lay in the deep shade cast by ivy clad sycamores, Scots Pine and lime trees. I was about to walk past small, brown clods of earth dotting the still damp grass but came to a sudden stop when I realized the mounds were moving. From under the rhododendrons and holly, hedgehogs had emerged and were rootling about. I held my breath. The girl adored hedgehogs; she longed to care for a hedgehog, to sleep and dream with hedgehogs. The girl angered her mother when she found one in her back garden, put it in a box, and smuggled it up to her bedroom and into her bed. When this was discovered, Iris screamed 'fleas!' Box and hedgehog were swept up in a flurry of disgust and deposited outside the back door, while the girl was deposited in the bath for a thorough cleansing. As hedgerows in Britain have disappeared so have hedgehogs. Those in the care-home garden appeared undisturbed by my presence, and I watched them explore, searching for insects, worms or slugs. I listened to the gentle sniffling sounds the girl remembered.

The hedgehogs were the perfect excuse to linger. I longed to see my father but I did not want to enter the building and be among the aged and infirm restricted to shuffling or confined to sitting or lying huddled in layers of clothing and blankets. There was an atmosphere of constant expectation in the building, as its residents were endlessly in wait: waiting for visits from family members who did not arrive or, if they came, were no longer recognized; waiting to be dressed or undressed; waiting to be fed; waiting for the next programme on television; waiting to expel their last breath. I watched hedgehogs instead.

Ninety-one years old and frail, Carl had outlived Iris and all his siblings. He would ask me why he was the only one left, a question to which I had no answer. My father had forgotten I was coming to visit him, but he hadn't forgotten that I was his daughter and he loved me. His entire face lit up when he saw me: sitting in the reflection of a light from a lamp, his rheumy eyes sparkled. He asked if I and my husband were well and then urged me to recount every detail of the life of his grandson: where was he living, how was his progress through his graduate programme, what subject he was studying? My father had no memory of my having answered each of these questions every week on the telephone for more years than I wanted to acknowledge. I answered them again and he instantly forgot what I said.

We sat companionably together, and my father repeated himself again and again while I pretended he was asking questions for the first time. It was easy to lose concentration, to become careless in response, but each time I saw him I was aware of how far I had travelled, how precious each moment together should be, and I desperately wanted to wrest meaning from talk which seemed to have no purpose. I varied the shape of each of my answers and created elaborate versions of each story.

I held my father's hand trying to gauge his health and state of mind. His hands felt cool, almost cold. I traced the structure of bone, muscle and blue vein from his wrists down through his long slender fingers. Once, my father's skin had reflected the warm hues of lightly roasted coffee, but there was no warmth to his colour now, and multiple layers of browns had been scraped away, leaving only a translucent vellum. Soft white down circled my father's almost bald head, his face was cradled in a nest of grey hair, sideburns, moustache and beard: grisaille, a portrait in multiple shades of grey. What constituted flesh, tissue, fat and muscle was gradually disappearing. Instead of being grateful for the presence of my father's life I anticipated and grieved his loss. I feared he would not survive the coming winter.

As I looked up into his face, my father was quiet; his lips were moving but he made no sound. He was working hard to think, but the words he had already spoken he was unable to recall and what he wanted to say escaped his grasp. My father was becoming increasingly distressed and his eyes were urging me to help, to prevent him from slipping, as if I could banish the abyss yawning in his mind. When he became overwhelmed and defeated by the present, I could revive him by talking about the distant past, his childhood in Jamaica or his years in the RAF. My father was able to wander the paths of his long-term memory, though his passage was indirect, circuitous; his ability to narrate in chronological or causal sequence was impaired but he could vividly reconstruct snapshots of particular moments and places.

That afternoon, to fill the void, which terrified both of us, I told my father of my plans to drive south, to the village of Coleby in Lincolnshire. I told him what I had found in the archives and explained why I had to enter the parish church. I did not tell him what I would say when I stood in its Chancel, for I had not yet found the words. Of course, it was too late to tell him the story of Lilly, he could not grasp its significance, but at the mention of the name Coleby stories that I had known for many years spilled from his lips. My father knew and remembered the city of Lincoln and the surrounding area because, from 1944 through 1947, he had served in the 50th Squadron, Bomber Command, stationed at RAF Waddington, a few miles south of the city and north of Coleby.

Today RAF Waddington is the centre of Intelligence, Surveillance, Target Acquisition and Reconnaissance, the eyes and ears in the sky for the RAF and NATO, the control centre for the remote operation of the fleet of armed drones. It is surrounded by tall wire fences topped with barbed wire and patrolled by a contingent of armed security personnel. When I drove past it on my way to Coleby the fences still carried the signs of a recent a mass peace protest. I wondered what my father, who trained as a navigator and radio operator, thought of remote-controlled drones flying and firing missiles thousands of miles away. I wanted to believe that he would sympathize with the protest but doubted he understood what a drone was.

As I watched my father dying I recalled his memory of All Saints Parish Church in the village of Coleby. It was his story that I took with me when I entered that church.

In a Lancaster bomber returning over the English Channel at night, as the early morning glimmer cast a faint light over the waves breaking on shore, or as the flat marshy fens seemed to absorb whatever light the coast had promised was to come, he was searching, searching for a beacon located on the tower of a parish church in the middle of a small English village, a village high on an escarpment below which lay the RAF base, food and a cot on which to collapse exhausted for a few hours, before being awakened for the next briefing and return across the coast and out to sea.

My father could not yet imagine his life as a settler in postwar Britain, had not yet considered that he would never again live in Jamaica; nor would he ever know that the story of his Jamaica began here with a man called Lilly Carby. In 1944 he scanned the sky ahead searching for the beacon on All Saints Parish Church in Coleby. When he saw its light, my father knew he was home, in England.

Acknowledgements

The dismantling of the Welfare State in Britain has broken my heart. I owe my life to the National Health Service and higher education would have been out of my reach had it not been for free access and generous local and state maintenance grants. I would be remiss if I did not acknowledge how crucial the Mitcham and Croydon public libraries were in nurturing a child and transforming her into a thinking being.

I have always believed that scholarship is a collective enterprise, but I have been surprised and gratified by the depth of encouragement and help I have received for the research and writing of this book. I am indebted to Tina Campt and Saidiya Hartman, who have believed in this project and thought it through with me from its first tentative beginnings. They have devoted precious time and intellectual energy to reading numerous drafts and engaging in creative and rigorous critique, as have Anne Anlin Cheng and Vron Ware. I am also indebted to Jessie Kindig, who, while being enthusiastic about the manuscript, also subjected it to close scrutiny and insisted on bringing clarity to my prose.

I did not realize it at the time but the seeds of this book were sown in 1979 at the Centre for Contemporary Cultural Studies in Birmingham, where I began conversations with Stuart Hall about my father's life in Jamaica. He asked me questions that made me realize how little I knew. For forty years Paul Gilroy has been a wise interlocuter and friend whose intellectual generosity and hospitality knows no bounds. Thank you also to Alicia Schmidt Camacho, Anne McClintock, Nancy Cott, Emily Greenwood, Lisa Lowe, Rob Nixon, Caryl Phillips, Ed Rugemer, David Scott, Deborah Thomas, Natasha Trethewey, James Walvin, Laura Wexler and Susan Willis for their intellectual vision and encouragement.

My intellectual horizons have expanded in interdisciplinary Working Groups at Barnard, Columbia and Yale. The scholars, curators and cultural practitioners in the Engendering Archives group enabled me to think more creatively about archives, and I treasure the vision and theoretical rigour of my colleagues in the Practicing Refusal group. I have also benefited enormously from the questions and comments posed by students and faculty in response to sections from the book presented to the Women's, Gender and Sexuality Working Group and to American Studies at Yale and to universities in Canada, the UK and the US.

I have depended upon a variety of institutions for access to research materials. At Yale we have wonderful libraries and art galleries staffed with friendly, knowledgeable people. Thank you to everyone at the Beinecke Library and to Cynthia Roman and Kristen McDonald at the Lewis Walpole Library. I am very grateful to Amy Meyers and the curatorial and library staff at the Yale Center for British Art and have special thanks for the generosity of Gillian Forrester. I have also drawn upon the extensive holdings of the New York Public Library, particularly the Science Industry and Business branch and the Schomberg Center for Research in Black Culture, where the staff were extremely helpful.

Library and Archives Canada is a superb system. Before she retired from the position of Senior Heritage Officer in Moncton, Brenda P. Orr sent me a vast amount of material on the Air Training Plan. The staff at the Moncton Museum, Resurgo Place warmly welcomed me, and Lawren Campbell took time from his busy schedule to find crucial materials and guide me to the one remaining building of the #31 RAF depot base in the city.

I am grateful for the enthusiastic assistance in Jamaica of James Robertson at the University of the West Indies, Mona; Kasiya Halstead and her staff at the Jamaica Archives in Spanish Town; and the staff of the Island Records Office and the National Library of Jamaica in Kingston. In Portland, I was welcomed home by a number of people, including Afton Carby and the principal and pupils of Shirley Castle Primary School. The guidance of Mr White was crucial in wandering the pathways of the Blue Mountains as he made it his mission to locate all the Carbys in the Swift River area.

In London the staff at the British Library, the National Archives at Kew and the Victoria and Albert Museum have patiently and efficiently provided me with vast amounts of material over the years. In the West Country it was a pleasure to work with the staff of the Bristol Archives, and I am indebted to the advice of Madge Dresser, who informed me about their holdings and personally guided me through the city's architectural history and links to the trade in enslaved human beings. Members of the Bristol Radical History group helped me discover the history of the city's workhouses. The staff of the Somerset Archives were on hand to anticipate my every need.

It has been a joy locating parish records in the Lincolnshire Archives and working with the Lincolnshire Family History Society. I am grateful to Dr Peter Chowne and David Cowell who provided me with material from the Society for Lincolnshire History and Archaeology. Mrs Nelstrop in Coleby graciously handed me the key to the Parish Church.

Colleagues, graduate students and staff at Yale, in the African American Studies Department, in the American Studies program and in Women's Gender and Sexuality Studies, have offered constant support. I could not have found smarter or more dedicated research assistants than Jennifer Leath, Deborah March, Rachel Rosekind, Zach Schwartz-Weinstein and Heather Vermeulen. Thanks must also go to Usha Rungoo for her translations and advice.

Michael joined me in my search through the wills and land

records in the Jamaica Archives and together we wandered the streets of Kingston and the hills of Portland. He and Nicholas have offered sage advice, editorial insight and inspiration, and found innumerable ways to make me smile.

Illustration Credits

p. 181 Guinea Street, Bristol, by author

p. 184 Fry's Five Boys Milk Chocolate Advertisement, c. 1910, public domain

p. 185 Former Tramways Electricity Generating Station, Counterslip, Bristol © Stephen Richards, Creative Commons Attribution

p. 190 *West Indies and Guiana*: six lectures prepared for the Visual Instruction Committee of the Colonial Office by Algernon E. Aspinall, Alfred Hugh Fisher Collection, Cambridge University Library Special Collections

p. 191 Home and Colonial Stores on Broad Street, Waterford, May 1910, National Library of Ireland on The Commons

p. 193 Front: 'Cutting bananas in Jamaica', British Empire Series, Cigarette Cards, George Arents Collection, The New York Public Library, New York Public Library Digital Collections

p. 193 Front: 'Jamaica', Arms of the British Empire, Cigarette Cards, George Arents Collection, The New York Public Library, New York Public Library Digital Collections

p. 195 'Empire Day', Courtesy of Bristol Archives, 43207/22/8/6

p. 196 'British immigrant children from Dr Barnardo's Homes at landing stage, Saint John, New Brunswick', Home Children 1869–1930, Courtesy of Isaac Erb/Library and Archives Canada

p. 200 'Bananas two for 11/2d', Alfred Leader, *Through Jamaica with a Kodak*, Bristol: John Wright & Co., 1907, public domain

p. 201 American Slave Troupe, Old Theatre Royal, Bristol, 1869, Courtesy of British Library and Bridgeman Images

p. 202 Jamaican Choir, St George's Hall, Liverpool 1907, Courtesy of Jeffrey Green

p. 207 James Johnston, Castleton Gardens, *Jamaica: The New Riviera*, London: Cassell, 1903

p. 208 'Lily Pond', as above

p. 209 James Johnston, 'Nature's Bounty', Courtesy of of Caribbean Photo Archive

pp. 227–31 Details, Jamaica: Portland, 1817, Slave Registers, Registration, Office of Registry of Colonial Slaves and Slave Compensation Commission, The National Archives T71/151

p. 235 Detail, as above

p. 247 Detail, Jamaica: Portland, 1817, Slave Registers, Registration, Office of Registry of Colonial Slaves and Slave Compensation Commission, The National Archives T71/151

pp. 249–50 John Mair, *Book-Keeping Methodiz'd: Or, a Methodical Treatise of Merchant-Accompts, According to the Italian Form*, Edinburgh, 1763, pp. 276 and 277

p. 253 Detail, Jamaica: Portland, 1817, Slave Registers, Registration, Office of Registry of Colonial Slaves and Slave Compensation Commission, The National Archives T71/151

p. 265 Panel: 'Generals preparing for the defence of their respective districts', from *Martial Law in Jamaica*, Print, London: William Holland, 1801, Courtesy of the Lewis Walpole Library, Yale University

p. 277 Blue Mountain, Portland, Jamaica, by author

p. 281 Jamaica: Portland, 1817, Slave Registers, Registration, Office of Registry of Colonial Slaves and Slave Compensation Commission, The National Archives T71/151

p.285 Coffee plantation, Portland, Jamaica, by author

p. 286 Site plan of Chesterfield, James A. Delle, 'The Landscapes of Class Negotiation on Coffee Plantations in the Blue Mountains of Jamaica: 1790–1850', *Historical Archaeology* 33, no. 1 (1999): 136–58

p. 287 Native Women Washing, Jamaica, published by T. H. McAllister, NY, Courtesy of the Caribbean Photo Archive

p. 308 'An interior view of a Jamaica House of Correction', Courtesy of the National Library of Jamaica

p. 311 'Loading a fruit steamer with bananas for northern markets, Kingston, Jamaica', Courtesy of the Caribbean Photo Archive

p. 318 The Humber Bridge, photo by David Wright, original in colour, CC BY 2.0

p. 321 Tower, All Saints Parish Church, Coleby, by author

p. 322 All Saints Parish Church, Coleby, by author

p. 323 Graveyard, All Saints Parish Church, Coleby, by author

p. 324 Caloplaca teicholyta (Ach.), J. Steiner, Images of British Lichens, lastdragon.org

p. 330 Font, All Saints Parish Church, Coleby, by author

p. 341 All Saints Parish Church, Coleby, by author

Notes

Preface

p. 1 'shared colonial past'. Michel-Rolph Trouillot, *Silencing the Past: Power and the Production of History*, Boston: Beacon Press, 1995. Trouillot argues that 'pastness is a position', that it is 'a temporal relation' which is 'not fixed' (pp. 14–15).

p. 2 'recently deceased'. Jamaica Kincaid, *My Brother*, New York: Farrar, Straus and Giroux, 1997.

Part One: Inventories

p. 8 'people in offices'. An ambitious plan, the Housing Act of 1919 provided government subsidies to local authorities to finance the construction of working-class housing, the 'homes fit for heroes' promised to returning soldiers by the Prime Minister, Lloyd George. Development was slow and the plan, never fully completed, was halted on the eve of the Second World War. By 1945, housing needs were even more urgent. No reference was made to heroes.

p. 8 'night were exalting'. I have revisited and taken liberties with Virginia Woolf's *Orlando*, in which Orlando, becoming bored with slicing the head of a Moor with his blade, turns to his window: 'Orlando's face, as he threw the window open, was lit solely by the sun itself . . . Sights disturbed him like that of his mother . . . sights exulted him – the birds and the trees.' Virginia Woolf, *Orlando: A Biography*, Oxford: Published for the Shakespeare Head Press by Blackwell, 1998, p. 12.

p. 8 'presence of a red fox'. Rob Cowen, *Common Ground*, London: Windmill Books, 2016, p. 23.

p. 9 'could not see'. Ibid., p. 63.

p. 10 'medicinal plants'. Daniel Lysons, *The Environs of London, Being an Historical Account of the Towns, Villages, and Hamlets, within Twelve Miles of That Capital, ... with Biographical Anecdotes [and Plates]*, London, 1792.

p. 12 'wiped clean'. Stuart Hall, 'Racism and Reaction', in *Five Views of Multi-Racial Britain*, London: Commission on Racial Equality 1978, pp. 23–24.

p. 19 'as it represents that past'. Trouillot, *Silencing the Past*, p. 148.

p. 20 'for myself'. Vita Sackville-West, *The Letters of Vita Sackville-West to Virginia Wolf*, Jersey City, NJ: Cleis Press, 2010, p. 56.

p. 22 'a home'. *The Times* (London), 14 July 1930, p. 9.

p. 25 'Wales in 1404'. The last Prince of Wales to be recognized as such by the English Crown was Llywelyn ap Gruffydd, who was overthrown by Edward I of England in 1282. The title fell into disuse until Glyndwr rebelled and made his claim to it.

p. 25 'Caernarfon Castle'. I was taught to spell this as Caernarvon, the Anglicized version of the name of this town in Gwynedd and the version which Microsoft Word insists is the 'correct' spelling. Edward I of England built the castle when he defeated Llywelyn, since when it has been a very visible sign and symbol of English domination. The choice of this site for the investiture therefore resonated with a history of contestation, of Welsh insurgency on the one hand and the maintenance and reinforcement of English claims to the territory and its people on the other. This contestation remains in the choice of spelling, in the selection of the site for such a ceremony, and in the creation of software programs.

p. 26 'Man my son!'. Rudyard Kipling, *Rewards and Fairies*, New York: Doubleday, Page and Company, 1910, p. 181.

p. 26 'trade and civilization'. Paul Richard Thompson, *The Edwardians: The Remaking of British Society*, Bloomington: Indiana University Press, 1975, p. 181.

p. 27 'salute to the flag'. Quoted in ibid., p. 181.

p. 27 'people of the world'. P. D. James, *Time to Be in Earnest: A Fragment of Autobiography*, London: Faber, 1999, p. 24.

p. 27 'Ludlow school'. Ibid.

p. 28 'far-flung Empire'. Jane Madders and Grace Horseman, *Growing up in the Twenties*, Bovey Tracey: Cottage Publishing, 1993, pp. 50, 55–6, 70.

p. 28 'Little Black Englishmen'. Austin Clarke, *Growing Up Stupid Under the Union Jack*, Toronto: Thomas Allen, 2005, pp. 56, 55.

p. 31 'flights to Kingston'. The Jamaica Tourist Board ran a series of campaigns in Britain and North America, 'Come Back to Jamaica', in the mid-1960s, and 'Make it Jamaica, Again' in the 1980s.

p. 32 'marches of the 1930s'. Jamaica became a Crown Colony in

1866 after the Morant Bay rebellion of 1865 and the brutal repression which followed. This meant direct rule through the Colonial Office and a Governor appointed by the Crown.

p. 33 'associated with enslavement'. K. W. J. Post, 'The Politics of Protest in Jamaica, 1938: Some Problems of Analysis and Conceptualization', *Social and Economic Studies* 18, no. 4 (1969): 374–90; Richard Hart, 'Labour Rebellions of the 1930s in the British Caribbean Region Colonies', *Jamaica Labour Weekly*, Caribbean Labour Solidarity and the Socialist History Society, 2002, socialisthistorysociety.co.uk.

p. 33 'starvation wages'. Tate & Lyle made after-tax profits of £14 million between 1924 and 1938. See Philippe Chalmin, *The Making of a Sugar Giant: Tate & Lyle, 1859–1989*, New York: Harwood Academic Publishers, 1990, pp. 204–10. See also Colin A. Palmer, *Freedom's Children: The 1938 Labor Rebellion and the Birth of Modern Jamaica*, Chapel Hill: University of North Carolina Press, 2014.

p. 37 'beggar the imagination'. Patrice K. Morris, 'Imprisoned in Jamaica: An Exploratory Study of Inmate Experiences and Differential Responses to Prison Life in a Developing Country', *International Criminal Justice Review* 18, no. 4 (2008): 435–54.

p. 39 'financial insecurity'. Great Britain Colonial Office, *Jamaica. Correspondence Relating to the Earthquake at Kingston, Jamaica, on 14th January, 1907*, London: Printed for H. M. Stationary Office by Darling & son Ltd., 1907. The table for widows' annuities is on p. 44 of Further Correspondence, a continuation of the above.

p. 41 'Rollington Pen'. Now called Rollington Town School.

p. 41 'support an extended family'. Richard Hart, *Rise and Organise: The Birth of the Workers and National Movements in Jamaica (1936–1939)*, London: Karia Press, 1989, p. 48.

p. 41 'as a pigmentocracy'. Stuart Hall, with Bill Schwarz, *Familiar Stranger: A Life Between Two Islands*, Durham, NC: Duke University Press, 2017.

p. 42 'no hope before 1938'. Oral history of Ken Hill in Karl S. Watson and Patrick E. Bryan, *Not for Wages Alone: Eyewitness Summaries of the 1938 Labour Rebellion in Jamaica*, Mona: Social History Project, Dept. of History, University of the West Indies, 2003, p. 52.

p. 42 'staged a general walkout'. Palmer, *Freedom's Children*, p.43.

p. 43 'standing offshore'. Post, 'The Politics of Protest in Jamaica, 1938'.

p. 43 'all the stores closed'. Oral history of Joseph Kennedy in Watson and Bryan, *Not for Wages Alone*, p. 163.

p. 44 'Kingston Infantry Volunteers'. Palmer, *Freedom's Children*, p. 49.

p. 44 'assistants joined the strikers'. Hart, *Rise and Organise*, pp. 48–60.

p. 44 'need to organize'. Ken Post, *Arise Ye Starvelings: The Jamaican Labour Rebellion of 1938 and Its Aftermath*, Series on the

Development of Societies, v. 3, The Hague: Nijhoff, 1978, p. 99. Post argues that the organization of their work, the routine nature of tasks and lack of responsibility, proletarianized clerical workers.

p. 45 'financial burden'. Darcy Heuring argues that developments in Jamaica 'played a central role in effecting changes to British imperial policy' on the eve of the Second World War, and that an examination of health provides an important way to measure the fall out of imperial policies in the lives of colonial subjects, 'a factor that is essential to better understand the formation and development of Jamaican nationalism and the demise of British imperialism in the twentieth century'. Darcy Hughes Heuring, *Health and the Politics of 'Improvement' in British Colonial Jamaica, 1914–1945*, PhD, Northwestern University, 2011, p. 10.

p. 45 'attacking lungs and bowels'. See Walter Edward Guinness Moyne, *West India Royal Commission Report*, London: H. M. Stationery Office, 1945, chapter VIII, Public Health, Section (b) 'Nature of Ill Health', pp. 139ff. This commission was formed in response to the 1937–38 rebellions. Its investigation into public health begins with a paean to the wonderful climate in the West Indies and the authors try to place the blame for ill health on the shoulders of the black and poor whenever they can. But despite their political agenda to absolve the British government of responsibility the situation they describe is dire and their recommendations include a massive influx of financial support for a medical system.

p. 46 'colony's medical services'. 'In 1921 advice and medicine at a government dispensary cost 4 shillings and surgery was much more.' Heuring, *Health and the Politics of 'Improvement'*, pp. 61–2.

p. 47 'less than human'. For a rather different argument about the dress of clerks and their relation to capitalists, see Post, *Arise Ye Starvelings*, p. 102.

p. 47 'before the price increases'. Ken Post, *Strike the Iron. A Colony at War: Jamaica, 1939–1945*, 2 vols, Atlantic Highlands: Humanities Press; The Hague: Institute of Social Sciences, 1981.

p. 48 'Rob And Flee'. Ibid., vol. 1, pp. 245, 247.

p. 48 'within the UK'. See the letter from the Air Ministry to Harold Moody, 28 June 1940, in Stephen Bourne, *The Motherland Calls: Britain's Black Servicemen & Women, 1939–45*, Stroud: History Press, 2012, pp. 137–8.

p. 48 'to the war effort'. Bourne, *The Motherland Calls*, p. 80.

p. 49 'noble lustre in your eyes'. Shakespeare, *Henry V*, Act 3, Scene 1.

p. 49 'formidable war machine'. David Edgerton, *Britain's War Machine: Weapons, Resources, and Experts in the Second World War*, New York: Oxford University Press, 2011, chapter 3, 'Never Alone', pp. 47–85.

p. 50 'as it was known'. John Terraine, *The Right of the Line: The*

Royal Air Force in the European War, 1939–1945, London: Hodder and Stoughton, 1985, pp. 258–9.

p. 50 'for RAF personnel'. National Archives, AIR/29/697–31 RAF Depot. The Depot was formed at Moncton, Canada in October 1941. In the Operations Record Book for August 1942 the entry for 25th at 15.25hrs notes the arrival of '22 Volunteers from Trinidad in the West Indies', but this group also included Jamaicans.

p. 50 'within a city'. Ed Larracey, 'Moncton Was War Air Center of Canada's Eastern Provinces: No. 31 Personnel Depot Was City Within a City', *The Times and Transcript Moncton Diamond Jubilee Edition*, July 1950, p. 6.

p. 50 'roads recalling London'. Lloyd Alexander Machum, *A History of Moncton Town and City, 1855–1965*, Moncton: City of Moncton, 1965, pp. 344–5. See also *In Transit* the Unit's magazine, sixteen editions of which are in the National Archives, AIR/29/697–31 RAF Depot.

p. 50 'Halifax, Nova Scotia'. 'City Was Great War-Time Air Center: 19 Units Established Here with Thousands of Allied Personnel', *The Times and Transcript Moncton Diamond Jubilee Edition*, July 1950, pp. 5–6.

p. 51 'to fight for England'. Connie Mark quoted in Bourne, *The Motherland Calls*, pp. 65–6. Connie Mark was born in Rollington Town and was recruited into the Auxiliary Territorial Service where she served for ten years working in a British Military Hospital in Jamaica. She moved to Britain in 1954 and was awarded a a British Empire Medal and then and MBE. See also Margaret Busby, 'Obituary: Connie Mark', *Guardian*, 16 June 2007.

p. 51 'joined Coastal Command'. On the Battle of and for the Atlantic see, Terraine, *The Right of the Line*, pp. 401–58.

p. 51 'Admiralty records'. National Archives, ADM/199/2190/63.

p. 51 'attacked by German submarines'. From my father's description of the attack on the convoy this would have been Convoy number SC143 from Halifax to UK, sailing on 29 September 1943 and arriving on 12 October. The convoy was attacked by *Rossbach*, a German Wolfpack of fourteen U-boats. See 'Operation Rossbach', at codenames.info.

p. 51 'sank the following day'. 'ORP Orkan (Polish Destroyer) – Ships Hit by German U-Boats during WWII', at uboat.net.

p. 52 '500,000 miles every week'. British Information Services, ed., *RAF*, New York: British Information Services, 1943.

p. 53 'German cities'. Terraine, *The Right of the Line*, p. 507.

p. 53 'pure and undisguised?'. W. G. Sebald, *On the Natural History of Destruction*, New York: Random House, 2003, pp. 19, 48.

p. 54 'had the right to vote'. This phrase is taken from the title of the study of Jamaica by Erna Brodber. As Brodber states: 'With the enactment of this legislation the exercise of the vote was no longer tied to a property ownership clause which had kept most African Jamaicans outside the formal political process.' Erna Brodber, *Second Generation of Freemen in Jamaica, 1947–1944*, Gainesville: University Press of Florida, 2004, p. 2. Universal adult suffrage was granted in Jamaica in November 1944.

p. 54 'book for the Depot'. National Archives, AIR/29/697–31 RAF Depot, 1941 Oct–1944 Nov.

p. 55 'didn't even have history'. George Elliot Clarke, *George and Rue*, Toronto: Harper Collins, 2005, p. 14. See also 'Author's Note' to the US edition.

p. 56 'dashed against'. Virginia Woolf, 'Professions for Women', *The Death of the Moth and Other Essays*, New York: Harcourt Brace, 1942, p. 241.

Part Two: Calculations

p. 61 'black diaspora'. Stuart Hall, 'Thinking the Diaspora: Home Thoughts from Abroad', Gaurav Gajanon Desai and Supriya Nair, eds, *Postcolonialisms: An Anthology and Cultural Theory and Criticism*, New Brunswick, NJ: Rutgers University Press, 2005, p. 543.

p. 62 'Mother Country'. London is the Place For Me: Trinidadian Calypso In London, 1950–1956, Honest Jon's Records, HJRCD2, UK 2002.

p. 64 'vibrant black British community'. BBC Two's *Windrush*, directed by David Upshal, was broadcast in 1998 and accompanied by the publication of Mike Phillips and Trevor Phillips, *Windrush: The Irresistible Rise of Multi-racial Britain*, London: HarperCollins, 1998.

p. 64 'race in modern Britain'. See Mary Chamberlain, *Narratives of Exile and Return*, London: Macmillan, 1997; Vivienne Francis, *With Hope in their Eyes*, London: Nia, 1998; and Phillips and Phillips, 1998. These are some of the most obvious choices but there are many, many more; among them: Wendy Webster, *Imagining Home: Gender, 'Race 'and National Identity, 1945–64*, London: UCL Press, 1998; Kwesi Owusu, ed., *Black British Culture and Society*, London and New York: Routledge, 2000; James Procter, (ed) *Writing Black Britain 1948–1998: An Interdisciplinary Anthology*, Manchester University Press, 2000; and Yasmin Alibhai-Brown, *Imagining the New Britain*, New York: Routledge, 2001.

p. 65 '*Windrush* in June 1948'. On the question of memory and forgetting, see Catherine Hall, 'Troubling Memories: Nineteenth-century Histories of the Slave Trade and Slavery', *Transactions of the Royal Historical Society* (Sixth Series) 21 (2011): 147–69. For the most recent study, which moves beyond *The Windrush* but also reinforces its iconic status through the title, see John Belchem, *Before the Windrush: Race Relations in Twentieth-Century Liverpool*, Liverpool: Liverpool University Press, 2014.

p. 65 'in the 1920s and '30s'. Laura Tabili, *'We Ask for British Justice': Workers and Racial Difference in Late Imperial Britain*, Ithaca: Cornell University Press, 1994, p.1.

p. 66 'Scotland, for example'. Ian R. G. Spencer, *British Immigration Policy Since 1939: The Making of Multi-Racial Britain*, London and New York: Routledge, 1997, p. 212. Marika Sherwood, *Many Struggles: West Indian Workers and Service Personnel in Britain (1939–45)*, London: Karia Press, 1985.

p. 66 'left an indelible impression'. David Reynolds, *Rich Relations: The American Occupation of Britain, 1942–1945*, New York: Random House, 1996, and Graham Smith, *When Jim Crow Met John Bull: Black American Soldiers in World War II Britain*, London: I. B. Tauris, 1987.

p. 67 'direct business methods'. Reynolds, *Rich Relations*, p. xxv.

p. 67 'most easily absorbed'. Sherwood, *Many Struggles*, p. 58.

p. 67 'was not considered desirable'. Reynolds, *Rich Relations*, p. 217.

p. 67 'proper and adequate employment'. P. B. Rich, *Race and Empire in British Politics*, Cambridge University Press, 1990, p. 162.

p. 68 '*white* engineering regiments'. Smith, *When Jim Crow Met John Bull*, pp. 37–8, 50–1; Reynolds, *Rich Relations*, p. 217.

p. 68 'badly suited to negroes'. Reynolds, *Rich Relations*, p. 217.

p. 68 'foreigners, including negroes'. Ibid., p. 218; Smith, *When Jim Crow Met John Bull*, pp. 190–1.

p. 68 'black men and white women'. 'Politicians reasoned ... that if sexual contacts with indigenous women were to cause the least anxiety, methods of controlling them would have to be found.' Smith, *When Jim Crow Met John Bull*, p. 190.

p. 69 'same town on the same day'. Reynolds, *Rich Relations*, p. 220.

p. 69 'limitation of space and personnell'. Ibid., p. 222.

p. 69 'rebellion in British colonies'. Rich, *Race and Empire,* pp. 150–3. See also the reproduction of documents containing these discussions in T. Hachey, "Jim Crow with a British Accent: Attitudes of London Government Officials Toward American Negro Soldiers in England During World War II, *The Journal of Negro History,* 59, 1 (1974): 65-77.

p. 69 'from July 1942 on'. Smith, *When Jim Crow Met John Bull*, pp. 54–5.

p. 70 'cooperation and acquiescence'. Reynolds, *Rich Relations*, pp. 226–227.

p. 70 'categorial denial'. Ibid., 218–19.

p. 71 'implicated in its enforcement'. Ibid., pp. 224–335.

p. 71 '1945 letter'. Drake Papers Box 63, Folder 1.

p. 71 'empire as a whole'. Quoted in Rich, *Race and Empire*, pp. 154–5. This is one of the few sources I have found that discusses how attitudes toward 'race' during the war are shaped in relation to both US and British colonial policy. Viscount Cranborne, for the Colonial Office, opposed the dissemination of the War Office's 'Notes on Relations with Coloured Troops' and resisted attempts 'to bend to American pressure'. Rich argues that 'Policy on racial discrimination and the preservation of British colonial policy ... were ... for Cranbourne, crucially linked, and for the first time in British government policy there was exhibited a far-reaching understanding of the inter-relationship between race and wider public policy in both Britain and the colonial empire' (ibid., pp. 151, 153).

p. 72 'details of their lives'. See Foucault on the 'capillary functioning of power': 'the point where power reaches into their actions and attitudes, their discourses, learning processes and everyday lives', Michel Foucault, *Power/Knowledge: Selected Interviews & Other Writings 1972-1977*, New York: Pantheon, 1980, p. 39.

p. 72 'half-caste children'. Rich, *Race and Empire*, p. 152.

p. 72 'from the Caribbean'. Stuart Hall, 'Racism and Reaction', *Five Views of Multi-racial Britain*: talks on race relations broadcast by BBC TV, London: Commission for Racial Equality, 1978, p. 23.

p. 73 'London and Liverpool'. See St. Clair Drake, *Value Systems, Social Structure and Race Relations in the British Isles*, PhD thesis, the University of Chicago, 1954; Kenneth Lindsay Little, *Negroes in Britain: A Study of Racial Relations in English Society*, London: K. Paul, Trench, Trubner, 1948; see also Muriel E. Fletcher, *Report on an Investigation into the Colour Problem in Liverpool and Other Ports*, Liverpool: Liverpool Association for the Welfare of Half-Caste Children, 1930. 'In the 1920s and 1930s racial categories and racial subordination were reconstituted on British soil,' Laura Tabili, *We Ask for British Justice*', see also Jacqueline Nassy Brown, *Dropping Anchor, Setting Sail: Geographies of Race in Black Liverpool*, Princeton, NJ: Princeton University Press, 2005.

p. 73 'stories of humiliation'. St. Clair Drake Papers, Box 63, Folder 1, typescript note on looseleaf paper, Schomberg Center for Research in Black Culture, New York Public Library.

p. 73 'pass through its doors'. Robert N. Murray, *Lest We Forget: The Experiences of World War II Westindian Ex-Service Personnel*, Nottingham Westindian Combined Ex-Services Association, 1996, pp. 101–3; 110–12.

p. 74 'purchase a pint'. Ibid., pp. 160–1.

p. 74 'US military bases'. Reynolds, *Rich Relations*, p. 229.

p. 74 'complained to the police'. St. Clair Drake Papers, Box 63, Folder 9, newspaper article retyped on typewriter paper.

p. 75 'British cities and towns'. Sonya O. Rose, 'Sex, Citizenship, and the Nation in World War II Britain', *The American Historical Review*, 103, no. 4 (Oct 1998), p. 1147.

p. 75 'contempt and scathing abuse'. Murray, *Lest We Forget*, p. 106.

p. 75 'the nation's health'. Rose, 'Sex, Citizenship, and the Nation', p. 1164.

p. 75 'Bolero Committee meeting'. Bolero was the code name for the movement of forces from the US to the UK.

p. 75 'possibly, the BBC'. Smith, *When Jim Crow Met John Bull*, p. 195.

p. 76 'peculiar to the English'. William Cobbett, *Cobbett's Weekly Political Register* V, no. 24 (16 June 1804), col. 935, as quoted in Peter Fryer, *Staying Power: The History of Black People in Britain*, London: Pluto Press, 1984, p. 234.

p. 76 'manner of their contagion?'. Laura Ann Stoler, *Carnal Knowledge and Imperial Power: Race and the Intimate in Colonial Rule*, Berkeley: University of California Press, pp. 6, 67-8.

p. 77 'not employ married women'. This marriage bar was ended by the Labour Government in 1946.

p. 82 'Parliament in 1948'. Kathleen Paul, *Whitewashing Britain: Race and Citizenship in the Postwar Era*, Ithaca: Cornell University Press, 1997, p. 9.

p. 83 'definitions of Britishness'. '... balancing several different, competing communities of Britishness within a single empire', ibid., p. 9.

p. 83 'to be British stock'. Ibid., p. 26.

p. 84 'malleability to her unbelonging'. Aihwa Ong, *Flexible Citizenship: The Cultural Logics of Transnationality*, Durham, NC: Duke University Press, 1999.

p. 85 'Harold Moody, March 1946'. Sylvia McNeill, *Illegitimate Children Born in Britain of English Mothers and Coloured Americans: Report of a Survey*, London: The League of Coloured Peoples, 1946, Appendix 6, p. 15.

p. 85 'trace of him there'. Olaudah Equiano, *The Interesting Narrative of the Life of Olaudah Equiano, or Gustavus Vassa, the African, Written by Himself: Authoritative Text, Contexts, Criticism*, New York: Norton, 2001, p. 166. See also the Plymouth City Council website, plymouth.gov.uk.

p. 85 'stretches back for centuries'. Lucy MacKeith, *Local Black History: A Beginning in Devon*, Archives & Museums of Black Heritage, 2003.

p. 85 'ship in the other'. Eric Hemery, *Walking Dartmoor's Ancient Tracks: A Guide to 28 Routes*, London: Hale, 1986.

p. 85 'ashore on Devon's coast'. Pat Barrow, *Slaves of Rapparee: The Wreck of the London*, Bideford: Edward Gaskell, 1998; Vron Ware and Les Back, *Out of Whiteness: Color, Politics, and Culture*, Chicago: University of Chicago Press, 2002, pp. 211–19.

p. 86 'southwest counties of England'. Neil A. Wynn, '"Race War": Black American GIs and West Indians in Britain During the Second World War', *Immigrants & Minorities* 24, no. 3 (2006): 328; Smith, *When Jim Crow Met John Bull*, p. 43. According to David Reynolds, by D-Day there were 130,000 black American troops in the UK (*Rich Relations*, p. 227).

p. 86 'stuff of respectable nightmares'. I am indebted to the work of St. Clair Drake, and his account of this period in his Chicago University PhD thesis, *Value Systems, Social Structure, and Race Relations in the British Isles*, pp. 78–9. The interpretation of the studies of Fleming and Fletcher and their consequences is, however, my own. See also Belchem, *Before the Windrush*.

p. 86 'psychological and "racial" traits'. Drake, *Value Systems*, pp. 78–9.

p. 87 'from the merchant navy'. Fletcher, *Report on an Investigation into the Colour Problem*, pp. 29, 44, 50-55. See Drake, *Value Systems*, pp. 78–82.

p. 87 'boycotts and publicity'. They addressed hotel discrimination, the problems of securing employment for coloured youth, and protests against the use of derogatory terms by the press, on the stage and in the cinema.

p. 87 'West Indian and African'. See the account in Drake, *Value Systems*, pp. 81–8. See also the entry for Harold Moody in 'Making Britain', at open.ac.uk.

p. 88 'our peoples everywhere'. St. Clair Drake Papers, Box 60, Folder 11, 'Draft of the Dissertation, "Blacks in the British Isles"', chapter 4, pp. 158–60. Drake's notes include the following analysis: 'There are a number of contradictory accounts of the origin of the league. Some colored Londoners believe that Moody organized it because he was under pressure from the more radical students to disassociate himself from the Quakers and persons close to the Colonial Office. Those who held to this version say "the League was just a front organization for the Joint Council." Persons more friendly to Dr. Moody say that he was annoyed at the "dilly-dallying" of The Joint Council and its reluctance to move vigorously and dramatically, that he wanted an organization controlled by colored peoples themselves. When they are confronted with the fact that most of the members were English and that John Fletcher of the Joint Council was associated with the new organization form the beginning, they answer that this was a tactical maneuver in the minority strategy and that Moody always intended ultimately to base the organization upon a membership in the colonies. Others say "He was a factionalist and a dictator. He couldn't run The Joint Council, so he set up something he could run. And besides the idea wasn't his, it was the idea of Dr. Nehra, an Indian. He took the idea away from Nehra"' (p. 160).

p. 88 'soldiers and English women'. George Padmore, 'Negro Babies of White Mothers Give Big Headache to Britons', *The Chicago Defender*, 18 November 1944, pp. 1, 4.

p. 88 'Tough Problem for England'. 'Britain's Brown Babies: Illegitimate Tots a Tough Problem for England', *Ebony* 2, no. 1 (November 1946): 19–23.

p. 89 'Christian Veterans of America'. Ibid.

p. 89 'British mothers'. Five cases in 1944, thirty at time of reporting in 1945. League of Coloured Peoples, 'Report of Children's Welfare Work', *Newsletter* XVII, no. 104 (October–December 1948): 110–12.

p. 89 'British and United States governments'. 'President's Letter to Minister of Health', in McNeill, *Illegitimate Children*, Appendix A, pp. 11–13. Harold Moody's arguments were published in the US: see 'Ask Bi-Nation War Baby Plan', *The Chicago Defender*, 6 April 1946, p. 7.

p. 90 'South Side of Chicago'. St. Clair Drake, Richard Wright and Horace R. Cayton, *Black Metropolis: A Study of Negro Life in a Northern City*, New York: Harcourt, Brace and Company, 1945.

p. 90 'University of Chicago'. Drake, *Value Systems*.

p. 90 'a figure impossible to establish'. St. Clair Drake, 'Hand Written Analysis of League of Coloured Peoples Casework on "Mixed Race" Children of African American Soldiers and White English Women', St. Clair Drake Papers, n.d., Box 64, Folder 2, Schomberg Center for Research in Black Culture. See also Drake, Wright and Cayton, *Black Metropolis*.

p. 90 'marriages was quite explicit'. Reynolds, *Rich Relations*, p. 231.

p. 90 'disastrous for their children'. Henry Lee Moon, 'Army Policy Hits Negro Babies of Soldiers and British Mothers', *The Chicago Defender*, 28 April 1945, p. 11.

p. 91 'anxious to have them'. McNeill, *Illegitimate Children*, p. 5.

p. 91 'sometime this year'. 'Ship Tan-Yank Babies to US', *The Chicago Defender*, 12 April 1947, p. 1. This was written in response to an article published in the London *Daily Mail*. Emphasis mine.

p. 91 'feedback in the United States'. Sabine Lee, 'A Forgotten Legacy of the Second World War: GI Children in Post-War Britain and Germany', *Contemporary European History* 20, no. 2 (2011): 165.

p. 92 'US negro families'. 'The Babies They Left Behind Them: From London to Tokyo the Problem of Illegitimate Children Abandoned by Our GIs is Still to Be Solved,' *Life*, 23 August 1948, p. 41.

p. 92 'Holnicote House'. Lee, 'A Forgotten Legacy', p. 165.

p. 92 'Children's Act of 1948'. Ibid. I am indebted to Professor Sabine for her research on Celia Bangham.

p. 93 'Somerset's proposal'. P. L. Prattis, 'British Color Bar is Future

Threat Over Brown Babies', *The Pittsburgh Courier*, 26 February 1949, p. 6. I do not know whether there were responses from other county councils. The records of Holnicote House held at the Somerset Records Office are closed. 'Somerset County Archive & Record Service', www.somerset.gov.uk. See also Lee, 'A Forgotten Legacy', p. 165, fn. 48.

p. 93 'defeat of the scheme'. George Padmore, 'Decides Brown Babies Must Stay in England', *The Chicago Defender*, 23 April 1949.

p. 93 'Mission in Liverpool'. See Pamela Winfield, *Bye Bye Baby: The Story of the Children the GIs Left Behind*, London: Bloomsbury, 1992.

p. 94 'Children, She Asks'. 'Let Me Give a Home to 12 Children She Asks', *The Daily Mirror*, 30 March 1949.

p. 94 'radical circles'. 'In 1988, she was recognized as the founder of Women for World Disarmament by the Women of the Year committee and was one of seventy-two women inducted and invited to their annual lunch at the Savoy in London but little has been written about her since.' '88's Women', *Observer*, 23 October 1988, p. 35. There is also one chapter on Tacchi-Morris in Anne Smith, *Women Remember: An Oral History*, London and New York: Routledge, 1989. This oral history seems to rely heavily on the unpublished manuscript of Tacchi-Morris.

p. 94 'rich and famous'. Including Picasso, Edward, Prince of Wales, and Mrs Simpson, and the socialists, secularists and free thinkers that she met through her father when she was young, such as Annie Besant, H. G. Wells and George Bernard Shaw. See Helen Elliott, 'For Picasso and Peace', *Guardian*, 22 May 1993. She is memorialized in the bricks and mortar of the Tacchi-Morris Arts Center in Taunton, supported by the trust she established in her name.

p. 94 'Acton, London'. She compares herself to Ben Tillett, socialist and union leader, as she stands on a chair rallying the children in her class to strike against injustice. The success of the strike results in the firing of the headmaster and her own expulsion. Typescript Autobiography of Kathleen Tacchi-Morris, Kathleen Tacchi-Morris Collection, Somerset Record Office, DD\TCM/14/1.

p. 94 'eventually known as Taccomo'. Tacchi-Morris was born in South Africa in 1899, where her father worked as an engineer in the goldmines of Johannesburg. Horrified by the company's treatment of African miners he returned home in 1900. She left her first marriage to an officer in the RAF because she despised the provincial narrow-mindedness of the British expatriate community in Malta, where they were stationed. She eventually married Richard Rodham Morris.

p. 95 'clubs in the area'. The Somerset Rotary Club turned her down so she pursued the Business and Professional Women's Club and the

Federal Union Group. Letter from M. Joseph Mitchell to Kathleen Tacchi-Morris, 29 November 1949, DD\TCM\15/14

p. 95 'coloured youth'. Diaries of Kathleen Tacchi-Morris, DD\TCM/13/11–15. The typescript of Mitchell's address, 'Colour Problem Among Juveniles', given on Sunday, 9 October 1949, is in folder DD\TCM/15/14.

p. 96 'children in Holnicote'. Tacchi-Morris to Rickards Esq., 31 March 1949, DD\TCM/15/14.

p. 96 'Children's Committee'. Letter from Harold King to Tacchi-Morris, 6 April 1949 and 1 June 1949, DD\TCM/15/14.

p. 96 'Somerset altogether'. Letter from M. Joseph-Mitchell to Tacchi-Morris, 27 June 1949, DD\TCM/15/14. In November Joseph-Mitchell is still waiting for a reply from the Somerset County Council fixing a date 'for their representative's interview with me'. Joseph-Mitchell to Tacchi-Morris, 29 November 1949, DD\TCM/15/14.

p. 96 'this was also denied'. A letter dated 25 April 1950 from Harold King, headed 'Children Act 1948. Boarding-Out', states that her application to become a foster parent to a child in the care of the County Council has been 'considered by the appropriate Committee at their recent meeting, and I have to inform you that the Committee were unable to approve your application.' 'Minutes of staff meetings, 1949–50, and correspondence with Somerset County Council. DD\TCM/15/9.

p. 96 'efforts to support them'. Letter from M. Joseph-Mitchell to Tacchi-Morris, 27 March 1950, DD\TCM/15/14.

p. 97 'many refugees'. Tacchi-Morris, Typescript Autobiography, pp. 41–2.

p. 97 'arts, drama, music and ballet'. Tacchi-Morris had developed her own method of integrating music and movement which she called 'Kallirhythm', an expansion and elaboration of the system of eurythmics she had learnt from Dalcroze. Prospectus, Taccomo International School, North Curry, DD\TCM/15/14.

p. 97 'everybody in Taunton'. Tacchi-Morris letter to Joseph-Mitchell, 19 November 1949, DD\TCM/15/14.

p. 98 'Exmoor National Park'. HF is the acronym of Holiday Fellowship.

p. 100 'the body which is not ours'. Achille Mbembe, 'The New Global Mobility Regime', Borders in the Age of Networks, The Tanner Lectures, Yale University, 28 March 2018.

p. 101 'overshadows the subject'. Vicki Goldberg, "Finding a Camera and a New Career: [Review]" *New York Times*, 19 November 1999: E, 42:1.

p. 101 'into his dissertation'. This research is to be found in the St. Clair Drake papers, Box 63, Folder 5.

p. 101 'found a brown envelope'. The envelope was marked 'Roosevelt College of Chicago Interdepartment Correspondence.' This was the College where Drake was employed as an Assistant Professor.

p. 102 'writing on coatroom walls'. I have withheld names that could be used to identify people.

p. 105 'greatest camouflage'. Anne Anlin Cheng, *The Melancholy of Race: Psychoanalysis, Assimilation, and Hidden Grief*, New York: Oxford University Press, 2000, p. 73.

Part Three: Dead Reckoning

p. 111 'stories of redemption'. Zia Haider Rahman, *In the Light of What We Know*, New York: Farrar, Straus and Giroux, 2014, p. 307.

p. 112 'in the clouds' W. G. Sebald, *The Emigrants*, New York: New Directions, p. 145.

p. 113 'true nature of life'. Virginia Woolf, *The Death of the Moth and Other Essays*, New York: Harcourt Brace & Company, pp. 3–6.

p. 116 'meaning from another'. Eavan Boland, *Domestic Violence*, Manchester: Carcanet Press, 2007, p. 18.

p. 120 'sites of resistance'. Paule Marshall, 'From the Poets in the Kitchen', *Callaloo* 24, no. 2 (2001): 627–33; Alice Childress, *Like One of the Family: Conversations from a Domestic Life*, Brooklyn: Independence Publishers, 1956.

p. 121 'source of creative friction'. Pierre Nora, *Rethinking France: Les Lieux de Mémoire*, Chicago: University of Chicago Press, 2001; Geneviève Fabre and Robert G. O'Meally, eds, *History and Memory in African-American Culture*, New York: Oxford University Press, 1994.

p. 122 'opportunity of easy credit'. Christine Zmroczek, 'Dirty Linen: Women, Class, and Washing Machines, 1920s–1960s', *Women's Studies International Forum* 15, no. 2 (1992): 173–85.

p. 122 'visit from Princess Margaret'. 'Hoover Washing Machines', at alangeorge.co.uk.

p. 129 'we live in them'. Rahman, *In the Light of What We Know*, p. 271.

p. 130 'history of global telecommunications'. Exeter, CIGH, 'Call for Applications – Beaming the British Empire: The Imperial Wireless Chain, c. 1900–1940: AHRC-Funded Collaborative Doctoral Award', Imperial & Global Forum, 27 February 2017, at imperial-globalexeter.com.

p. 131 'speculation among locals'. 'Beam Wireless', *Evening Post*, 5 January 1927; 'Imperial Wireless Chain', en.wikipedia.org.

p. 131 'ten acres of moor'. John Collinson and Edmund Rack, *The*

History and Antiquities of the County of Somerset, Collected from Authentick Records, and an Actual Survey Made by the Late Mr. Edmund Rack. Adorned with a Map of the County, and Engravings of Roman and Other Reliques, Townseals, Baths, Churches, and Gentleman's Seats, Bath: Printed by R. Cruttwell, 1791, vol. 3, 'North-Petherton', p. 71.

p. 132 'Sir Hugh Popham in 1285'. Sir Hugh served as Commissioner for fixing the boundaries of the royal forests in Somerset for King Edward I. John Burke, Adam Buck, Henry William Pickersgill, Ramsay R. Reinagle, Samuel Freeman and James Thomson, *A Genealogical and Heraldic History of the Commoners of Great Britain and Ireland, Enjoying Territorial Possessions or High Official Rank: But Uninvested with Heritable Honours*, London: Published for Henry Colburn by R. Bentley, 1833, pp. 196–201.

p. 132 'Huntworth Manor'. It eventually became the home of William Portman and his descendants. For the history of the owners of Huntworth Manor, see A. P. Baggs and M. C. Siraut, *North Petherton – Manors and Other Estates*, ed. C. R. Elrington and R. W. Dunning, vol. 6, A History of the Counties of Somerset, London, 1992.

p. 132 'captain of the vessel'. He built a mansion in Wellington, Somerset, held property in Bridgwater and London and, in a dubious manner, obtained the extensive Littlecote estate in Wiltshire in settlement of his legal fees. Details of the life of Sir John Popham and other members of the family are drawn for the most part from Douglas Walthew Rice, *The Life and Achievements of Sir John Popham, 1531–1607: Leading to the Establishment of the First English Colony in New England* (Madison: Fairleigh Dickinson University Press, 2005). See also Charles Nicholl, *The Creature in the Map: A Journey to El Dorado*, New York: William Morrow and Company, 1996.

p. 133 '*Beautiful Empire of Guiana*'. Walter Raleigh and Robert H. Schomburgk, *The Discovery of the Large, Rich, and Beautiful Empire of Guiana, with a Relation of the Great and Golden City of Manoa ... Etc. Performed in the Year 1595*, Reprint ed. Works Issued by the Hakluyt Society, no. III, London and New York: Printed for the Hakluyt society, B. Franklin, 1848.

p. 133 'what is now Maine'. Further inland up the Kennebec River is Somerset County Maine, which is named after Somerset in the UK.

p. 133 'Huntworth to the empire'. Huntworth remained a small community eventually becoming a nucleated hamlet when several large houses were built in the eighteenth century to join the much older Huntworth House and Huntworth Park House. Robert W. Dunning, and University of London, eds, *A History of the County of Somerset: Glastonbury and Street*, The Victoria History of the Counties of England, Woodbridge and Rochester: Boydell & Brewer for the Institute of Historical Research, 2006.

p. 136 'any pity at birth'. William Shakespeare, *Macbeth*, ed., Kenneth Muir, London: Arden Shakespeare, 1997, 1.7, 21–8.

p. 136 'excess baggage, burdens'. William Shakespeare, *King Lear*, ed. R. A. Foakes, London: Arden Shakespeare, 1997, 1.1, 51–3.

p. 136 'To love my father all'. Ibid., 89–104.

p. 137 'wasting body'. The vision of reddish mist on a mirror comes from Sarah Perry, *The Essex Serpent*, London: Serpent's Tail, 2016, p. 234.

p. 137 'exhausting their minds'. Richard Barnett, *The Sick Rose, or, Disease and the Art of Medical Illustration*, New York: Distributed Art Publishers, 2014, pp. 112, 116.

p. 137 'Black Forest'. Linda Bryder, *Below the Magic Mountain: A Social History of Tuberculosis in Twentieth-Century Britain*, Oxford: Clarendon Press, 1988, pp. 23–4.

p. 137 'two sanatoria'. The *Hazell's Annual* for 1907 carried these two advertisements for sanatoria in the areas in Somerset where my relatives lived. *Hazell's Annual*, London: Hazell, Watson & Viney Ltd, 1907, p. 108.

p. 138 'benefit for tuberculosis'. Laming Worthington Evans, *The National Insurance Act, 1911: Summary*, London: National Conservative Union, 1912.

p. 138 'treatment was offered'. L. Bryder, 'The Medical Research Council and Treatments for Tuberculosis before Streptomycin', James Lind Library, at jameslindlibrary.org. From 1921, local authorities were required to provide free sanatorium treatment to all tuberculosis patients in their area, and by 1938 Britain had more than 30,000 sanatorium beds (Bryder, *Below the Magic Mountain*, p. 76).

p. 138 'advanced and chronic'. Bryder, *Below the Magic Mountain*, pp. 293–5.

p. 139 'embodied female achievement'. In the Somerset Archives records for the school are filed under the Bridgwater Grammar or County School for Girls.

p. 139 'academic robes'. Women were not granted Oxbridge degrees until 1920 although they had been allowed to attend classes and sit for some examinations for the previous forty years; for example, see 'Women at Oxford – University of Oxford', at ox.ac.uk.

p. 139 'Somerset Records Office'. See Somerset Heritage Centre: Bridgwater Grammar or County School for Girls, school photographs of all staff and pupils, 1930–39, DD\X\SOM/30; School magazine *Chevron*, 1932–73, C/E/4/362/19; Bridgwater Girls Grammar School, Log book, 1904–44, C/E/4/362/1; Staff Register, 1904–37, C/E/4/362/11; Admission Register, 1931–39 C/E/4/362/8; Miscellaneous papers including speech day programmes and headmistress' reports, concert programmes, photographs, 1910–72, C/E/4/362/18/1 and C/E/4/362/18/2.

p. 140 'ungrateful insolence'. Thompson, *The Edwardians*, p. 24.

p. 140 'Beatrice's illness'. In the 1870s 'Huntworth House was the seat of the Chapmans', see 'Huntworth, Somerset' at visionofbritain. org.uk. In 1911 the residents of Huntworth House were the Petrocochino family often misspelt Petrocockins. 1911 England Census Summary Books, Somerset, North Petherton, District 12. I do not know the name of the family from which the woman my mother referred to as 'lady of the manor', in the 1930s, came.

p. 142 'never wrote a word'. Virginia Woolf, *A Room of One's Own*, San Diego: Harcourt Brace Jovanovich, 1957, p. 117. As Virginia Woolf imagined the life and death of Judith Shakespeare, much of my career has been spent trying to reimagine and reconstruct the lives of the unknown women of this world.

p. 143 Rahman, *In the Light of What We Know*, p. 290.

p. 145 'valley or viaduct'. Frank McKenna, *The Railway Workers, 1840–1970*, London: Faber and Faber, 1980, p. 88.

p. 146 'whence you came'. James Baldwin, *The Price of the Ticket: Collected Nonfiction, 1948–1985*, p. xix.

p. 146 'embossed on a headboard'. British Rail used steam locomotives from 1948, when the railway companies were nationalized until 1968. The Red Dragon was operated by the Western Region of BR from 1950 to 1965. The train was hauled by the Castle class of steam locomotives used by the GWR, which had the brass and copper funnels, remembered here, but later the Red Dragon was hauled by the BR build Britannia class which did not have these funnels.

p. 149 'entered the concourse'. Technically, the man they called their uncle was the husband of a first cousin once removed.

p. 153 'responsible citizen'. Though diligent research could not locate the testimonials themselves.

p. 153 'at their command'. McKenna, *The Railway Workers*, pp. 27–8, 110.

p. 153 'docile countrymen'. See Philip Sidney Bagwell, *The Railwaymen: The History of the National Union of Railwaymen*, London: Allen & Unwin, 1963.

p. 156 'census form'. *A Cultural History of the British Census: Envisioning the Multitude in the Nineteenth Century*, 2016.

p. 156 'the larger truth'. Kei Miller, *The Cartographer Tries to Map a Way to Zion*, Manchester: Carcanet Press, 2014, p. 19, courtesy of David Higham Associates.

p. 157 'impose on persons'. Benedict Anderson, *Imagined Communities: Reflections on the Origin and Spread of Nationalism*, 2nd edn, London and New York: Verso, 1991, p. 173. See also Nicholas Carby-Denning, 'Re-Constituting the Nature of the Nation: Extractivism, Biodiversity and the Rights of Nature in Ecuador', Dissertation, University of Chicago, 2019, pp. 283–294.

p. 157 'life and labour'. Margaret Llewelyn Davies and Virginia Woolf, *Life as We Have Known It*, London: Virago, 1984, p. vii.

p. 157 'lives in poverty'. Carby-Denning continues: 'mapping technologies . . . gloss over the dense thickets, deep swamps, precarious river log-crossings. A world of webs and parasites, of canopy and vines, air filled with the herbaceous taste and smell of fruit and flower. The funky stench of peccaries: wild pigs, which if encountered in part hoards, promptly send a researcher up a tree.' Denning. 'Re-Constituting the Nature of the Nation', p. 138.

p. 158 'town's cure takers'. 'City of Bath', UNESCO World Heritage List, at whc.unesco.org.

p. 158 'measured, capacious, grace'. Alec Clifton-Taylor, *The Pattern of English Building*, London: B. T. Batsford, 1962, p. 94.

p. 158 'St Dorothy parish, Jamaica'. UCL, Legacies of British Slave-ownership, William Thomas Beckford, at ucl.ac.uk.

p. 159 'from 1801 to 1806'. *Northanger Abbey* and *Persuasion*. See also, *Humphrey Clinker* by Tobias Smollett and *The Pickwick Papers* by Charles Dickens.

p. 159 'wealth inequality'. See the analysis of the historical continuity in the geography of mortality in the UK in Sheena Asthana and Dr Joyce Halliday, *What Works in Tackling Health Inequalities?: Pathways, Policies and Practice Through the Lifecourse*, Policy Press, 2006, 'Historical patterns of disease distribution', p. 12; First [and second] Report[s] of the Commissioners for Inquiring into the *State of Large Towns and Populous Districts*, London: Printed by W. Clowes & Sons, for H. M. Stationery Office, 1844-5, pp. 278–9.

p. 159 'locations in Bath'. See 'Back Street, Bath, near Avon Street, c.1920s', Bath in Time: Images of Bath Online' at bathintime.co.uk, which also shows evidence of flooding. The novel is Paul Emanuelli, *Avon Street*, Stroud: The History Press, 2012.

p. 159 'partition of space'. National Library of Scotland, Leabharlann Nàiseanta na h-Alba, SW England, OS 25 Inch, England and Wales, 1841–1952, Somerset VI.2 Surveyed: 1881–1882, published 1896. Historic map layer courtesy of the British Library, Know your Place Project, at maps.nls.uk.

p. 159 'birds of us all'. Cowen, *Common Ground*, p. 1.

p. 160 'out of their sight'. Friedrich Engels, *The Condition of the Working Class in England*, in Karl Marx and Friedrich Engels, *Collected Works*, vol. 4, New York: International Publishers, 1975, p. 353.

p. 160 'no spacious streets'. The description is taken from Emanuelli, *Avon Street*, p. 84.

p. 160 'labyrinths of narrow lanes'. Engels, *Condition of the Working Class*, p. 341.

p. 160 'River Avon'. 'Bath may be regarded, taken as a whole, as a well-built town; the streets generally airy and good, the chief exceptions being in the lower and older part of the town.' Royal Commission on the State of Large Towns and Populous Districts, London School of

Hygiene and Tropical Medicine, and London School of Hygiene and Tropical Medicine. *Report[s] of the Commissioners for Inquiring into the State of Large Towns and Populous Districts*, p. 271.

p. 160 'when the river rose'. 'At Bath, Commissioners under a local Act had power to construct new sewers, and alter and repair old ones, in a district extending over about a fourth of fifth part of that city; no similar power was vested in any body for the remaining districts.' Frederick Clifford, *A History of Private Bill Legislation*, London, 1885, p. 303.

p. 160 'a swarm of misery'. Charles Dickens, *Bleak House*, London and New York: Penguin, 2003, p. 256.

p. 161 'penned in their courtyards'. See bathintime.co.uk for images of the area. Chas E. Goad insurance plans for Bath are available in the British Library Online Gallery.

p. 161 'back of the throat'. Lovis Corinth, *In the Slaughter House*, 1893, painting, oil on canvas, Staatsgalerie, Stuttgart.

p. 161 'poorly ventilated buildings'. Wally Seccombe, *Weathering the Storm: Working-Class Families from the Industrial Revolution to the Fertility Decline*, London and New York: Verso, 1993.

p. 161 'few pence a night'. *Report[s] of the Commissioners for Inquiring into the State of Large Towns and Populous Districts*, p. 272. In the 1871 census nine residents at the Common Lodging House at 19 Corn Street were listed as 'tramps'.

p. 161 'poor neighbourhoods'. See *Report[s] of the Commissioners for Inquiring into the State of Large Towns and Populous Districts*. The section on the City of Bath begins on page 265.

p. 162 'outdoor privies'. City of Bath, UK, National Library of Scotland, Leabhariann Nàiseanta na h-Alba, SW England, OS 25 Inch, 1873–1888.

p. 162 'insect infestation and disease'. For conditions of working-class housing I have drawn upon, Seccombe, *Weathering the Storm*, pp. 42–3.

p. 162 'new construction'. 'Bath City Council and Bath & North East Somerset Council: Planning and Development Control Records, c.1860–c.2000' at somerset-cat.swheritage.org.uk.

p. 162 'the age of five'. The returns of mortality for Frome show that 1 in 5.5 of the total deaths was from phthisis, see *Report[s] of the Commissioners for Inquiring into the State of Large Towns and Populous Districts*, pp. 293, 296, 297.

p. 163 'like spa towns'. The description of the life of laundresses draws upon Patricia E. Malcolmson, *English Laundresses: A Social History, 1850–1930*, Urbana: University of Illinois Press, 1986.

p. 164 'for their expertise'. Ibid., pp. 24–6.

p. 165 'continued into the weekend'. Ibid., pp. 26–7, 33–4.

p. 166 'Carpenter and Builder'. Chas E. Goad Ltd, 'Goad Insurance Plan of Bath 1902, Sheet 5', British Library Online Gallery.

p. 167 'returned to tailoring work'. The GWR kept meticulous employment records all of which are stored in the National Archives, Great Western Railway Company Staff Records: RAIL 264 1835–1962. However, not all of them are open and I could not find a record that matched this Henry Williams exactly.

p. 167 'Cardiff which followed'. Dic Mortimer, *Cardiff: The Biography*, Stroud: Amberley, 2014, chapter 6.

p. 167 'built by the GWR'. Illustration 1e, 'Cardiff in 1883', in M. J. Daunton, *Coal Metropolis, Cardiff 1870–1914*, Leicester: Leicester University Press, 1977, following p. 116.

p. 168 'coal metropolis'. In 1885, coal was 82.3 per cent of total trade. Mined in the Rhondda Valley, coal was transported to the docks in Bute Town for export. See Daunton, *Coal Metropolis*.

p. 168 'lung development in children'. Physicians for Social Responsibility, 'Coal's Assault on Human Health', psr.org.

p. 169 'particulate matter'. Genee S. Smith, Victor J. Schoenbach, David B. Richardson and Marilie D. Gammon, 'Particulate Air Pollution and Susceptibility to the Development of Pulmonary Tuberculosis Disease in North Carolina: An Ecological Study', *International Journal of Environmental Health Research* 24, no. 2 (2014): 103–12; Ting-Chun Lai, Chen-Yuan Chiang, Chang-Fu Wu, Shiang-Lin Yang, Ding-Ping Liu, Chang-Chuan Chan and Hsien-Ho Lin, 'Ambient Air Pollution and Risk of Tuberculosis: A Cohort Study', *Occup Environ Med* 73, no. 1 (2016): 56–61.

p. 170 'in the shops'. See the first three chapters of Adèle Levis Meyer, *Makers of Our Clothes; A Case for Trade Boards, Being the Results of a Year's Investigation into the Work of Women in London in the Tailoring, Dressmaking, and Underclothing Trades*, London, 1909, pp. 1–82.

p. 171 'Tailors and Tailoresses'. The Amalgamated Society of Journeyman Tailors was formed in 1868 and changed its name to the Amalgamated Society of Tailors in 1894. See, 'Amalgamated Society of Tailors and Tailoresses', at archiveshub.jisc.ac.uk.

p. 171 'Britain's imperial future'. Sheila Blackburn, '"To Be Poor and To Be Honest ... Is the Hardest Struggle of All": Sweated Needlewomen and Campaigns for Protective Legislation, 1840–1914', in Beth Harris, ed., *Famine and Fashion: Needlewomen in the Nineteenth Century*, Aldershot and Burlington: Ashgate, 2005, p. 248. Beatrice Webb was also an economist, sociologist and labour historian. Sidney Webb was also an economist and co-founder of the London School of Economics.

p. 171 'Pyle Hill depot'. Alan Godfrey, 'Bristol (SW) & Bedminster, 1902', 1:25, Old Ordnance Survey Maps, Newcastle upon Tyne: Alan Godfrey Maps, n.d.

p. 173 'traumatically, expanding'. The population rose from 3,000 in 1801 to 78,000 in 1884.

p. 173 'had opened large factories'. Anton Bantock and Malago Society, *Bedminster*, Stroud: Chalford, 1997, pp. 7 and 8.

p. 174 'housing area in Bristol'. See ibid., p. 50.

p. 175 'they did not know it'. Michael Ondaatje, *In the Skin of a Lion*, New York: Vintage, 1987, pp. 130–1.

p. 175 '(NAPT), was founded'. This was part of an international movement. See Bryder, *Below the Magic Mountain*, p. 18.

p. 175 'labour camps and educated'. Ibid., p. 19.

p. 176 'existence of capital'. Karl Marx, *Capital Vol. 1*, in Karl Marx and Friedrich Engels, *Collected Works*, vol. 35, New York: International Publishers, 1996, p. 485.

p. 176 'incidents of TB increased'. Helen Bynum, *Spitting Blood: The History of Tuberculosis*, Oxford: Oxford University Press, 2012, p. 111.

p. 176 'usually a man'. Ibid., p. 114.

p. 176 'smell of decay'. Lillian Estella may have had pulmonary tuberculosis or contracted meningeal tuberculosis from unpasteurized milk. See ibid., pp. xix, xxii.

p. 177 'did not pass on'. My Canadian searches resulted in answers from Ontario and I was sent records from the Dr Barnardo's Home where Elsie lived until Barnardo's sent her to Canada. These records confirm that Henry Williams died.

p. 178 'birth to a fifth'. I was unable to find a death certificate for Henry but the information given to Elsie by the Dr Barnardo's Home confirms these events and provides information about George. Dr Barnado's ACS/LFC/MS 17 May 1988.

p. 179 'homes of the workhouse'. These homes were built between 1902 and 1905 as facilities separate from the main workhouse which was no longer regarded as a suitable place for children to live. See 'The Workhouse in Bristol Incorporation, Gloucestershire', at workhouses.org.uk; 'Eastville and Stapleton Workhouses', Bristol Radical History Group, at brh.org.uk.

p. 179 'domestic service'. Bristol had a long history of warehousing the poor in general, and young women and girls in particular, in workhouses; its methods and institutions became models for establishing workhouses in other cities. In 1696, the Bristol Corporation of the Poor was formed and they rented a building for the first workhouse two years later, 'to house a hundred pauper girls', 'The Workhouse in Bristol'.

p. 180 'third of the globe?'. Siobhan Carroll, *An Empire of Air and Water: Uncolonizable Space in the British Imagination, 1750–1850*, Philadelphia: University of Pennsylvania Press, 2015.

p. 182 'rotten bananas?'. 'The Bristol Suffragettes Who Fought Fire with Fire', *Bristol Post*, 17 September 2013.

p. 183 'Temple Meads?'. See Lucienne Boyce, *The Bristol Suffragettes*, Bristol: SilverWood Books, 2013.

p. 183 'happy to supply'. Madge Dresser, *Slavery Obscured: The Social*

History of the Slave Trade in an English Provincial Port, London: Continuum, 2001, p. 100.

p. 184 'numbers of its residents'. J. W. Arrowsmith, *How to See Bristol: A Complete, up-to-Date, and Profusely Illustrated Guide to Bristol, Clifton and Neighbourhood*, 9th edn, Bristol: J. W. Arrowsmith, 1906, p. xviii.

p. 184 'temple to modernity'. 'Bristol Tramways Power Stations 1895–1941', at swehs.co.uk; 'Bristol Tramways', at emep.dsl.pipex.com.

p. 185 'commercial society'. I am indebted to Emily Greenwood for her identification, translation and analysis of the motto on the crest of the Merchant Venturers. 'Indocilis Pauperiem Pati' is an abbreviated Latin quotation from Horace, *Odes*, Book 1, poem 1, line 18. The translation is 'incapable of learning to endure poverty', in this context intended to valorize trade / mercantilism as a means of avoiding poverty / accruing wealth. The quotation and appropriation of the phrase in the crest of the Society of Merchant Venturers to signify almost the opposite of what it signifies in Horace's Ode is typical of the use of Latin quotations as mottoes on flags and crests in the context of the British Empire. In Horace's Ode the adjective *indocilis* agrees with the *mercator* (merchant): [the merchant] is incapable of learning to endure poverty. In the context of the Ode, the phrase *indocilis pauperiem pati* is not an endorsement of a life of mercantile trade; it is part of a priamel where Horace reels off a list of occupations and lifestyles (charioteer, politician, farmer, seafaring merchant, drinker, soldier, huntsman), all of which are ultimately subordinated to his own vocation as poet. Of the merchant, the narrator writes (lines 15–18): 'the merchant, afraid of the African gale brawling | with Icarian waves, praises leisure and the countryside | round his own home town, but soon rebuilds his shattered | ships – he cannot learn to endure poverty'. In the scheme of the poem, the merchant's restlessness, the fact that he cannot endure leisure (*otium*) – one of the marks of the cultivated Roman in the circles in which Horace and Maecenas moved – is not a good thing. In fact, elsewhere in the Odes, Horace will repeatedly suggest (albeit as a literary / philosophical conceit) that the ability to endure poverty stoically is a good thing.

p. 185 'Edward VI in 1552'. 'History – The Society of Merchant Venturers, Bristol UK', merchantventurers.com.

p. 185 'Colston's Girls' School'. 'Education – The Society of Merchant Venturers, Bristol UK', merchantventurers.com.

p. 185 'tobacco they sold'. For the claim that tobacco workers produced this wealth for the university, see 'Women Who Gave Bristol a University', Letters, *Guardian*, 8 April 2018.

p. 186 'Society of Merchant Venturers'. Thomas Garrard, *Edward Colston, the Philanthropist, His Life and Times; Including a Memoir of His Father; the Result of a Laborious Investigation into the Archives of the City*, Bristol: J. Chilcott, 1852.

p. 186 'Augusta National Golf Club'. 'Our Members' at merchantventurers.com.

p. 186 'in the slave trade'. Madge Dresser, 'Remembering Slavery and Abolition in Bristol', *Slavery & Abolition* 30, no. 2 (2009): 223–46.

p. 187 'labour power'. Arrowsmith, *How to See Bristol*, p. 10.

p. 188 'plantation colonies'. 'The Growth of the City', PortCities Bristol, at discoveringbristol.org.uk.

p. 188 'slavery-related activities'. David Richardson, 'Slavery and Bristol's Golden Age', *Slavery and Abolition* 26, no. 1 (2005): 35–54.

p. 188 'exchange with Jamaica'. For an analysis of colonial circuits of exchange, see Brian Larkin, *Signal and Noise: Media, Infrastructure, and Urban Culture in Nigeria*, Durham, NC: Duke University Press, 2008, p. 219.

p. 188 'were landed in Jamaica'. All figures from the 'TransAtlantic Slave Voyage Database', n.d.

p. 190 'British schools'. Alfred Hugh Fisher, 'Fisher Photograph Collection', at janus.lib.cam.ac.uk.

p. 191 'all over the country'. Stephen Humphries, *Victorian Britain through the Magic Lantern: Illustrated by Lear's Magical Lantern Slides*, London: Sidgwick & Jackson, 1989, pp. 34–5, 39, 41, 159–67.

p. 192 'joy and unbounded loyalty'. Press Association, 'The Diamond Jubilee', *The Freemans Journal and Daily Commercial Advertiser*, 23 June 1897, BC3204972870, 19th Century British Library Newspapers.

p. 192 'Greater Britain'. Stephen Constantine, 'British Emigration to the Empire-Commonwealth since 1880: From Overseas Settlement to Diaspora?', *The Journal of Imperial and Commonwealth History* 31, no. 2 (2003): 16–35.

p. 192 'in the UK'. Michael Ball and David Sunderland, *An Economic History of London, 1800–1914*, London: Routledge, 2006, p. 136.

p. 192 'patriotism in children'. John M. MacKenzie, *Propaganda and Empire: The Manipulation of British Public Opinion, 1880–1960*, Manchester: Manchester University Press, 1984, pp. 16, 17, 27.

p. 194 'shows to the schools'. Humphries, *Magic Lantern*, p. 163.

p. 196 'domestic help'. 'Bristol Home Children' at emigrated.bafhs.org.uk.

p. 196 'badly treated or abused'. 'Home Children, 1869–1932', Library and Archives Canada, at bac-lac.gc.ca.

p. 197 'She died in 1989'. Information supplied by her daughter-in-law.

p. 197 'cities and towns'. In 1896, Sir Clifford Sifton, Minister of the Interior, expanded its publicity and immigration programmes with the aim of 'rapidly populating the Canadian Prairies with immigrant farmers and agricultural workers'.

p. 197 'Greater Britain'. Constantine, 'British Emigration to the Empire-Commonwealth since 1880': 23.

p. 198 'southern Europe'. My description of lantern slide lectures is drawn from Ellen Scheinberg and Melissa K. Rombout, 'Projecting Images of the Nation: The Immigration Program and Its Use of Lantern Slides', *The Archivist, Magazine of the National Archives of Canada*, no. 111, 1996, pp. 13–24.

p. 198 'land in the prairies'. Georgina M. Taylor, 'Art Nouveau, Immigration Propaganda, and the Peoples of Saskatchewan', *Saskatchewan History* 50 (Fall 1998): 31–44.

p. 199 'glimpse of paradise'. James Johnston, *Optical Lantern Lectures on Jamaica: 'The New Riviera'*, Bristol: The 'Dunscombe' Optical Lantern and Photographic Stores, 1904, p. 5. Johnston seems to have been lecturing in the UK in May and June 1901. See mention of his lectures in Manchester in 'Current Items', *The Gleaner*, 2 May 1901, p. 7, and in Bournemouth and Cheltenham in 'The Direct Line Enterprise: A Tribute to Mr. Jones', *The Gleaner*, 11 June 1901, p. 2.

p. 199 'island colony?'. Johnston was a long-time resident of Jamaica and represented St Ann as member of the Legislative Council in Kingston. Jeffrey Green, 'The Jamaica Native Choir in Britain, 1906–1908', *Black Music Research Journal* 13, no. 1 (Spring 1993): 15–29. Green refers to the Legislative Council as 'almost powerless' (p. 15). See also Reports from the Legislative Council in *The Gleaner*, 26 March 1903 and 2 March 1905; and 'Death of Dr. James Johnston', *The Gleaner*, 29 November 1921, p. 6.

p. 199 'expansion of empire'. S. B. Saul, 'The Economic Significance of "Constructive Imperialism"', *The Journal of Economic History* 17, no. 2 (1957): 173.

p. 200 'British to Jamaica'. Alfred Jones received a knighthood in 1901. He held considerable financial and territorial interests in West Africa.

p. 200 'market in the UK'. The venture was heavily subsidized by both the imperial and the colonial governments, each guaranteeing £20,000 a year for ten years to develop 'trade and intercourse between Jamaica and England on the basis of the banana trade'. Sydney Haldane Olivier, *Jamaica, the Blessed Island*, London: Faber & Faber, 1936, p. 382. It would appear that Alfred Jones was responding to a direct request from Joseph Chamberlain, so, in my opinion, he should be considered a member of the New Jamaica promoters. John Henderson mentions the link between Jones and Chamberlain in *Jamaica*, London: A. and C. Black, 1906, p. 140.

p. 200 'shops of Bristol'. Dresser, *Slavery Obscured*, p. 117.

p. 201 'London herbalist in 1663'. Michael McCarthy, 'Olde England a "banana republic" banana is discovered', *The Independent*, 16 June 1999.

p. 201 'UK until 1884'. 'Intute Timeline – Social Sciences', at intute. ac.uk.

p. 201 'commonplace sight?'. There are records confirming the presence of black people in Bristol for more than 400 years. See "African-Caribbean people in Bristol," on the Bristol and Transatlantic Slavery section of *PortCities Bristol*. There are no records for the number of black banana sellers in the city.

p. 201 'bunches a fortnight?'. Alfred Leader, *Through Jamaica with a Kodak*, Bristol: John Wright & Co., 1907, pp. 97, 99. The photograph of the Bristol banana seller is from this book.

p. 202 'announcing their performances'. The KCU were called the Jamaican Native Choir in Britain. For an account of their tours see, Jeffrey Green, 'The Jamaica Native Choir in Britain, 1906–1908', *Black Music Research Journal* 13, no. 1 (Spring 1993): 15–29.

p. 203 'photographer from Bristol'. The group also included John Henderson, author of *Jamaica*, illustrated with paintings by A. S. Forrest. On the nature of the material produced in the service of promoting tourism, see Olivier, *Jamaica, the Blessed Island*. It is worth quoting him at length: 'The advertisement of Jamaica ... as a holiday resort for visitors, was resumed ... by another man of imagination and sanguine energy, the late Sir Alfred Jones, Managing Director of Elder Dempster's Steamship Lines, in connection with his enterprise of the Direct Line of fruit steamers between Jamaica and Avonmouth. His efforts promoted interest in and resort to the Island and therewith a multiplication of pamphlets and books and magazine and newspaper articles praising it. Many of these have been, indeed, superficial, conventional and barren of original insight. They too often indulge an unbalanced habit of gushing eulogy – the effect, possibly, of that aesthetic intoxication and derangement of judgement of which I have spoken – a shallow, pictorial, ignorant and vulgar and frivolous fashion of writing about the men women who form the mass of the population, and their reputed psychology, habits and superstitions, and a recurrent unintelligent serving up of old dull legends and antiquarianisms, or references to the exploits of Rodney and Nelson, Henry Morgan, the Maroons, Mrs Palmer of Rose Hall, and so on, which long ago ceased to have any tittle of interest or significance in the consciousness of the Island community. I do not know of any completely truthful and unaffected book about Jamaica, either as a country or as a society' (p. 54).

p. 203 'British imagination'. Producing a landscape as image is not a neutral act of visual representation but an act of social and spatial control, a process Krista Thompson has analysed. I am indebted to her detailed account of the creation of the Caribbean picturesque in a compelling and brilliantly perceptive book. See Krista A. Thompson, *An Eye for the Tropics: Tourism, Photography, and Framing the Caribbean Picturesque*, Durham, NC: Duke University Press, 2006, p. 17.

p. 203 'by US businesses'. Alfred Jones employed the photographer, Alfred Leader, and the lantern slide show lecturer, James Johnston, in this project to remake perception. The travel writer John Henderson dedicates his book *Jamaica* to Alfred Jones but I am unsure if his work was financed by him. Henderson uses the paintings of A. S. Forrest as illustrations not photographs, but his aim is also to change perception of Jamaica. Forrest's paintings work against Henderson's offensive description of Jamaicans: they have a beauty, delicacy and dignity not found in the camerawork of Johnston and Leader.

p. 203 'tour of Central America'. Pacific Mail Steamship Company, Smithsonian American Art Museum, at americanart.si.edu.

p. 203 'attract capital investment'. This account is taken from Jonathan Crary, *Suspensions of Perception: Attention, Spectacle, and Modern Culture*, Cambridge, MA: MIT Press, 1999, pp. 144–5.

p. 203 'Jamaica, West Indies'. James Johnston, *Reality versus Romance in South Central Africa*, 2nd edn, London: Frank Cass, 1969 [1893], pp. 17–18.

p. 204 'for forty-seven years'. See Alan L. Karras, *Sojourners in the Sun: Scottish Migrants in Jamaica and the Chesapeake, 1740–1800*, New York: Cornell University Press, 1992; Alan Karras, 'The World of Alexander Johnston: The Creolization of Ambition, 1762–1787', *The Historical Journal* 30, no. 1 (1987): 53–76. I have been unable to establish if Alexander Johnston is a distant relative of James Johnston.

p. 204 'of African descent'. Johnston, *Reality versus Romance*, p. 18.

p. 204 'adventures in Central Africa'. See James Hooker's informative introduction to the 1969 edition of Johnston, *Reality versus Romance*, pp. vii–xx.

p. 204 'the white man of manual toil'. Ibid., p. 19.

p. 204 'Rev. Elliott in Bechuanaland'. See the letter from W. T. Currie at the Canadian Station, Cisamba to Dr. Johnston, *Reality versus Romance*, p. 328 and the account of Frater and Jonathan's eventual return home to the Jamaica Mission, p.329.

p. 205 'relieved by a visit'. 'Jamaica as a Health Resort: Dr. Johnston Tells of Cures of Consumption', *New York Tribune*, 18 December 1898, p. 12.

p. 205 'foreign landscapes'. Crary, *Suspensions of Perception*, pp. 362–9. Crary's analysis follows his reproduction of a letter Freud wrote to his family giving an account of watching a lantern slide show in 1907 in the Piazza Colonna in Rome, with 'pictures of landscapes' and 'Negroes of the Congo'.

p. 207 'erotic delight'. Johnston, *Optical Lantern Lectures*, p. 13.

p. 210 'British Crown'. Ibid., pp. 12–14, 19, 5–6.

p. 211 'Edwardian era'. Thompson, *The Edwardians*, p. 24.

p. 211 'external market pressure'. For an account of the rise of internal labour markets (ILM) see Peter Howlett, 'The Internal Labour Dynamics of the Great Eastern Railway Company, 1870–1913', *The Economic History Review* 57, no. 2 (2004): 396–422.

p. 212 'gears and motions'. Frank McKenna, *The Railway Workers 1840-1970*, London: Faber and Faber, 1980, p.112-13.

p. 212 'constantly irritated'. McKenna, *The Railway Workers*, pp. 112, 117–19.

p. 213 'Home Rule'. The National Archives, RAIL 786 1911–1926, Great Western Railway Company: Strikes and Civil Disturbances: Records, Subseries LLANELLY RIOTS.

p. 213 'killed two of the strikers'. Neil Prior, "Lanelli's 'forgotten' riot – 100 years ago," BBC New, Wales 16 August 2011.

p. 215 'Homfray family'. The Homfray family, long seated in Yorkshire, came to Glamorgan when Francis Homfray of Wollaston Hall, Worcestershire, married Hannah Popkin of Coytrahen (Coetre-hen), near Bridgend, Glamorgan. Francis, a successful iron-master in Staffordshire and Worcestershire, established an ironworks at Penydarren, Merthyr Tydfil. His third son, Jeremiah Homfray (1759–1833), gave up his share in the Penydarren works to his brother, Samuel, in 1789. In 1813 Jeremiah was declared bankrupt. He fled to Boulogne to avoid paying his creditors. Jeremiah's son, John Homfray (1793–1877), purchased Penllyn Castle in the vale of Glamorgan in 1846. He married Maria, only daughter and heiress of John Richards of the Corner House, Cardiff. The estate then descended in the male line, the present descendant being Major Herbert Franklen Richards Homfray of Newbury, Berkshire. 'Archives Network Wales – Homfray of Penllyn Estate papers.'

p. 216 'working in agriculture'. Thompson, *The Edwardians*, p. 24.

Part Four: Accounting

p. 224 'British Library Reading Room'. Now the British Museum Reading Room.

p. 225 'Colonies from 1812–27'. Sir Bernard Burke and Ashworth P. Burke, *Burke's Genealogical and Heraldic History of Peerage and Baronetage, The Privy Council, Knightage and Companionage*, London: Harrison & Sons, 1910, pp. 184-5. See also cirencester-park.co.uk.

p. 225 'Johnson in his will'. John Ingledew, 'Samuel Johnson's Jamaica Connections', *Caribbean Quarterly* 30, no. 2 (1984): 1–17. See David Olusoga, *Black and British: A Forgotten History*, London: Pan, 2016, p. 84, for speculation on the nature of the relation between Richard Bathurst and Francis Barber.

p. 227 'Commonwealth and Protectorate'. I remember Miss Pym's stories very well, but to confirm facts and dates I consulted the *Oxford Dictionary of National Biography*, online edn, Oxford and New York: Oxford University Press, 2004.

p. 231 'Congo to Angola . . .'. John Hearne, *The Sure Salvation*, New York: St. Martins Press, 1982, pp. 8, 12, 25.

p. 232 '31 December 1969'. Colonial Office: Welfare and Students: Selected Personal Files. Carby CC. 01 January 1946 – 31 December 1969,' National Archives, CO 981/33.

p. 232 'died of disease'. R. J. B. Knight, *Britain against Napoleon: The Organization of Victory, 1793–1815*, London: Allen Lane, 2013.

p. 233 'silenced or unimagined'. Trouillot, *Silencing the Past*.

p. 236 'enrolled in attendance'. Ruby King, 'Education in the British Caribbean: The Legacy of the Nineteenth Century', at educoas.org.

p. 236 '1 per cent'. Shirley C. Gordon, 'Documents Which Have Guided Educational Policy in the West Indies, No. 8: REPORT OF THE COMMISSIONERS MAYHEW AND MARRIOTT ON SECONDARY AND PRIMARY EDUCATION IN TRINIDAD, BARBADOS, LEEWARD ISLANDS AND WINDWARD ISLANDS. 1931 – 32', *Caribbean Quarterly* 10, no. 4 (1964): 3–32.

p. 237 'Second World War'. See Val Simpson, 'The Caribbean Connection', *Spirit of the Air* 1, no. 6 (2006): 20–3. These figures, however, are from 1942 and in his online archive which lists those who served, Cy Grant maintains there were approximately 400; see itzcaribbean.com.

p. 245 'cricket and bowls clubs'. Thank you, Paul, for reminding me that all those cricket scorebooks were ledgers too.

p. 247 '*A-Kitāb al-mukhtaṣar fī ḥisāb al-jabr wa-l-muqābala*'. The al-jabr in the title is the source of the word algebra. Al-Khwārizmī wrote the earliest known work on Hindu mathematics. See Jane Gleeson-White, *Double Entry: How the Merchants of Venice Created Modern Finance* (New York: W. W. Norton & Co, 2012), pp. 38–9, whose spelling I have altered to accord with the entry in Wikipedia.

p. 247 'Sir William Petty'. William Petty, *Several Essays in Political Arithmetick, the Titles of Which Follow in the Ensuing Pages, by Sir William Petty . . .* London: R. Clavel, 1699. I have consulted two editions of Petty's writings: William Petty, *The Economic Writings of Sir William Petty. Together with the Observations upon the Bills of Mortality, More Probably by Captain John Graunt*, edited by C. H. Hull, Cambridge: Cambridge University Press, 1899. See the note in the introduction regarding disputed dates of original publication. The quotation is taken from p. 44.

p. 247 'modern economics'. Ted McCormick, *William Petty and the Ambitions of Political Arithmetic*, Oxford: Oxford University Press, 2009.

p. 248 'Foundations in Nature'. This description of method is to be found in *Several Essays in Political Arithmetick. By Sir William Petty, ... The Fourth Edition, Corrected. To Which Are Prefix'd, Memoirs of the Author's Life*, London, 1755, p. 98.

p. 248 'discourse of creatures'. Paul Gilroy, 'Suffering and Infrahumanity', Tanner Lecture, Yale University, 19 February 2014, unpublished.

p. 248 'matter of historical lineage'. Ibid. See also Rhodri Lewis, ed., *William Petty on the Order of Nature: An unpublished Manuscript Treatise*, Arizona Center for Medieval and Renaissance Studies, vol. 399, 2012, p. 122, as quoted in Gilroy.

p. 248 'accurate way of thinking'. I have been unable to locate a first edition of this text so have used the following, John Mair, 7th edition, Edinburgh, 1763. For an account of the 1936 edition, see M. J. Mepham and W. E. Stone, 'John Mair, M.A.: Author of the First Classic Book-Keeping Series', *Accounting and Business Research* 7, no. 26 (1977): 128–34.

p. 248 'conferred moral legitimacy'. Mary Poovey argues that, 'as a system of writing, double-entry bookkeeping produced effects that exceeded transcription and calculation. One of its social effects was to proclaim the honesty of merchants as a group. One of its epistemological effects was to make the formal precision of the double-entry system, which drew on the rule-bound system of arithmetic, seem to guarantee the accuracy of the details it recorded.' Mary Poovey, *A History of the Modern Fact: Problems of Knowledge in the Sciences of Wealth and Society*, Chicago: University of Chicago Press, 1998, p. 30.

p. 249 'accurate accounting practices'. For a sketch of this history see Gleeson-White, *Double Entry*, pp. 115–31.

p. 249 'eighteenth century'. 'Mair – Book-Keeping Methodiz'd – ICAS – National Library of Scotland', at nls.uk.

p. 251 'commodification as "fact"'. Poovey, *A History of the Modern Fact*, pp. 29–30.

p. 251 '*Broke, Stinking, Dead, &c*'. Mair, *Book-Keeping*, p. 258.

p. 253 'usually called or known'. Additional colonial laws respecting slaves: 1816–1817 viz. 1. Barbadoes. 2. 3. Jamaica.

p. 254 'books without hesitation'. 'The Treatment of Slaves. Jamaica', 1816 (226), 'Colonial laws respecting slaves. Return made in pursuance of an address of the House of Commons to His Royal Highness the Prince Regent, voted on the 12th of July 1815', House of Commons Parliamentary Papers, XIX.259: 77-143.

p. 255 'micropolitics of exclusion'. Steve Hindle, 'Representing Rural Society: Surveyors, Surveying and the Surveyed in Seventeenth and Eighteenth-Century England', Lecture, British Art Center, Yale University, 29 February 2012.

p. 255 'customary rights and dispossession'. 'Enclosure . . . was a plain enough case of class robbery, played according to fair rules of property and law laid down by a parliament of property-owners and lawyers.' E. P. Thompson, *The Making of the English Working Class*, London: Penguin Books, 1978, pp. 237–8.

p. 255 'in the landscape'. Artists almost never represented where the enslaved lived in their paintings of plantations.

p. 256 'the overseer'. Quoted in B. W. Higman, *Jamaica Surveyed: Plantation Maps and Plans of the Eighteenth and Nineteenth Centuries*, San Francisco: Institute of Jamaica Publications Ltd, 1988, p. 81.

p. 256 'enslaved themselves'. Ibid., p. 245.

p. 256 'formerly enslaved'. 'Colonial Laws Respecting Slaves, 124.

p. 257 'health of negroes'. 'Colonial Laws Respecting Slaves, 80.

p. 257 'black existence'. Helena Kelly, *Jane Austen: The Secret Radical*, London: Icon Books, 2016.

p. 258 'remained unresolved'. See James Walvin, *Black and White: The Negro and English Society 1555–1945*, London: Allen Lane, 1973; James Walvin, *England, Slaves and Freedom: 1776–1838*, Basingstoke and London: Macmillan, 1986; Olusoga, *Black and British*.

p. 258 'exploitation and dispossession'. The financial crisis in the novel arising from the condition of the plantation may well have been precipitated by the abolition of Britain's involvement in the slave trade, if not in enslavement, in 1807.

p. 258 'imaginary surface'. See Saidiya V. Hartman, *Scenes of Subjection: Terror, Slavery, and Self-Making in Nineteenth-Century America*, New York: Oxford University Press, 1997, p. 7.

p. 260 'right to grow food'. Higman, *Jamaica Surveyed*, p. 280.

p. 261 'abrogation of their rights'. This was the first in a series of triennial registrations of the enslaved populations throughout the British Empire. Historians of Jamaica diverge in their interpretation of the demand for the registration of the enslaved. Roberts cites increasing colonial revenue by establishing the existence of enslaved peoples not previously entered onto assessment rolls in order to avoid paying a poll tax on them. Colonial legislators were opposed to registration arguing that it violated their right to control internal taxation. See G. W. Roberts, 'A Life Table for a West Indian Slave Population', *Population Studies* 5 (1952): 238–9. However, abolitionists were dismayed to find that abolition did not improve the condition of slaves in the West Indies and they were concerned that planters would continue to obtain slaves through illicit trade. The call for registration was to address both issues. See, B. W. Higman, *Slave Population and Economy in Jamaica, 1807–1834*, Cambridge: Cambridge University Press, 1976, p. 45. In the Act itself the Assembly states as the reason for compliance: 'the Legislature of this Island was anxious to show by every means in its power, the most sincere disposition to guard against any possible infringement of the laws for abolishing the slave trade, for the evasion of which the return of peace may be thought to afford facilities'.

p. 262 'same list or return'. 1817 (338) Additional colonial Laws respecting slaves: 1816–17, 9.

p. 263 'that of England'. The island was divided into parishes and each vestry consisted of twelve elected men. The vestries carried out all aspects of local administration. See Kamau Brathwaite, *The Development of Creole Society in Jamaica, 1770–1820*, Oxford: Clarendon Press, 1971, pp. 17, 20–1.

p. 263 'Jamaica Assembly'. Ibid., p. 22.

p. 263 'signatory on the register'. In the Jamaica Almanack for the Year 1817, the Clerk of the Vestry, Deputy Clerk of the Peace, Collector of the Transient Tax, and the Inspector of Weights and Measures is listed as Richard J. Sherwood, Esq. William T. Downer is listed as a Vestryman. In the Almanack for 1801 he is listed as Col. Wm Downer in the Portland Regiment and as an Assistant Judge in the Jamaica Lists. In 1825 there are five Downers listed as property owners, perhaps his children: Caroline and sisters and George P. M. at Snow Hill, who own 104 slaves; Nicholas P. at Plisham's Hill, who owns seven slaves; and Robert at Downer's Hope, who owns seven slaves. In the 1795 Almanack John S. Downer is listed as Coroner for Portland.

p. 263 'he was getting older'. National Archives, T 71 151.

p. 263 'Jamaica Militia'. As listed in the Jamaica Almanacks for 1799, 1802, 1805 and 1809. The position of judge was unpaid.

p. 264 'different regiments'. John Stewart, who published his *Account of Jamaica* in 1808, complained that 'Anyone, who was a relation of the colonel, or a relation of the colonel's wife; who was in favour with this gentleman, or in favour with any of his friends, required no other merit or pretension to preferment in the militia.' J. Stewart, *An Account of Jamaica, and Its Inhabitants*, London: Printed for Longman, Hurst, Rees and Orme, 1808, pp. 70–1.

p. 264 *'a la militaire'*. Ibid., p. 68.

p. 264 'drunk and debauched'. *Martial Law in Jamaica [Graphic]: Taken after the Life by a Gentleman on the Spot & Dedicated, with Every Assurance of the Highest Consideration, to All Whom It May Concern – Yale University Library.* 1801. Print: etching and aquatint on wove paper, 37.7 x 53.9cm. Prints & Photographs. Lewis Walpole Library.

p. 266 'agent, or otherwise'. Additional colonial laws respecting slaves: 1816–1817: viz. 1. Barbadoes. 2. 3. Jamaica. 4. St Vincent. 5. Antigua. 6. Tobago, 1817 (388) XVII.149, p. 8, 11.

p. 266 'captain of a slave ship?'. Hearne, *The Sure Salvation*.

p. 266 'reasonable living locally'. Brathwaite, *Development of Creole Society*, p. 23.

p. 268 'summit or high place'. George Sidney Streatfeild, *Lincolnshire and the Danes*, London: K. Paul, Trench & Co, 1884, p. 178. Streatfeild also notes that *Kollr* was a common personal name.

p. 268 *'býr* "village"'. *Dictionary of American Family Names*, Oxford and New York: Oxford University Press, 2003.

p. 268 'Bridgit his wife'. *The Register Book for the Parish of Coleby Near Lincoln Bought By Josh Boone Church Warden Oct 1740 Baptisms 1741–1791. Marriages 1742–1753. Burials 1741–1791*, n.d.

Part Five: Legacies

p. 271 'Caribbean literature'. Ekwueme Michael Thelwell is a pioneer in Afro-American Studies and the founding chairman of the W. E. B. Du Bois Department at the University of Massachusetts, Amherst. A Jamaican-born writer, activist, educator and intellectual, he was active in the civil rights and anti-apartheid movements.

p. 273 'parish of St George'. Both parishes lay within the county of Surrey. See the following map which marks the locations of estates: James Robertson and Samuel John Neele, 'To His Royal Highness, the Duke of Clarence, This Map of the County of Surrey in the Island of Jamaica, Constructed from Actual Surveys, under the Authority of the Hon. House of Assembly; by Whom It Hath Been Examined and Unanimously Approved; Is, with Permission, Most Humbly Inscribed.' London: Published 1 November 1804, by James Robertson, A. M., late of Jamaica, 1804.

p. 273 'the Blue Mountains'. I was familiar with the eighteenth-century story of the notorious Thomas Thistlewood from Lincolnshire, but Lilly's class background and the route he took to Jamaica via the British Army was very different to that of Thistlewood.

p. 274 'rebellions of the enslaved'. Daniel Livesay, *Children of Uncertain Fortune: Mixed-Race Jamaicans in Britain and the Atlantic Family, 1733–1833*, Chapel Hill: Omohundro Institute of Early American History and Culture and the University of North Carolina Press, 2018, p. 28.

p. 274 'without armed security'. African Caribbean Institute of Jamaica/ Jamaica Memory Bank, *The Buff Bay Valley: A History*, Kingston: The Inter-American Institute for Cooperation on Agriculture, n.d.

p. 274 'their descendants'. Between 1738 and 1749, John Downer, his heirs and assigns, were granted 800 acres in three parcels. These grants expanded his previous holdings in Portland. The Downers were also granted land in St Thomas. See Return of Land Grants, 1735–1754, CO 137/28, pp. 197–210. JFS Sarah and John Cosens were granted 300 acres in Portland in 1785. Patents, JM JARD 1B/11-1-33, 1774–1786, Island Records Office, Jamaica Archives and Records Department.

p. 274 'without much success'. White Families and Artificers Introduced into Jamaica by Acts of 1749 & 1752, CO 137/28, folios 175 to 180. 'History of Portland', National Library of Jamaica, nlj.gov.jm.

p. 274 'Deficiency Acts'. Livesay, *Children of Uncertain Fortune*, 26.

p. 275 'paid the fine'. The laws were widely broken as it was easier to pay the fines than find white bodies to settle. Brathwaite, *The Development of Creole Society*, p. 170.

p. 275 'British Army'. National Archives, WO 25/1125 1–17 Foot.

p. 275 'West Indies and the Baltic'. For example, Michael Henley & Son was one such shipping company which chartered ships to the government and whose business increased substantially during the French Revolutionary and Napoleonic Wars. See the papers of Michael Henley & Son held at the National Maritime Museum, Greenwich, in which can be found bills for the victualing of soldiers.

p. 275 'expensive undertaking'. Between 1803 and 1815 the Royal Navy lost 317 ships, 223 of which either foundered or were wrecked. David Gates, 'The Transformation of the Army 1783–1815', in David G. Chandler and Ian Beckett, eds, *The Oxford History of the British Army*, Oxford and New York: Oxford University Press, 2003, p. 134.

p. 275 'Guinea ships in the harbour'. Marcus Rediker, *The Slave Ship: A Human History*, New York: Viking, 2007, p. 127.

p. 275 'barracks on the island'. 'Warrant for Regulating the Clothing of Regiments in the East and West Indies', 30 November 1796, War Office: Entry Books of Warrants, Regulations and Precedents', Volume(s), 1817 1670. WO 26. National Archives.

p. 276 'recruit more soldiers'. Richard Cannon, *Historical Record of the Tenth, Or the North Lincolnshire, Regiment of Foot*, London: Parker, Furnivall and Parker, 1847. What is not spoken of in this official history is the large numbers of deserters.

p. 276 'particularly vulnerable'. John Robert McNeill, *Mosquito Empires: Ecology and War in the Greater Caribbean, 1620–1914*, Cambridge: Cambridge University Press, 2010.

p. 276 'was usually fatal'. Roger Norman Buckley, *The British Army in the West Indies: Society and the Military in the Revolutionary Age*, Gainesville: University Press of Florida, 1998, pp. 164–5.

p. 276 'rises to 70 per cent'. R. J. B. Knight, *Britain Against Napoleon:*

The Organization of Victory, 1793–1815, London: Allen Lane, 2013, p. 75.

p. 276 'punishable by death'. Buckley, *The British Army in the West Indies*, pp. 71–2, 164–5, 214–20.

p. 276 'Few deserters were found'. 1st and 2nd Battalions 10th Regiment of Foot desertions/discharges only begin to be listed in 1805. See '1–17th Foot (Return of NCOs and Men Not Actually Known to Be Dead or to Be Totally Disqualified for Military Service Who Have Been Discharged or Have Otherwise Ceased to Belong to the Corps between 1783 and 1810)', n.d. WO 25 1125. National Archives.

p. 276 'Jamaica's plantation order'. Because Lilly did not return to the UK there are no pension or service records for him, unlike for his two cousins, Bryon and Aminadab (alias John Aminadab), who signed up with Lilly. Desertion and discharge rates were very high. If sick, Lilly was no doubt nursed back to health by a black woman. See Buckley, *The British Army in the West Indies*.

p. 277 'were still not free'. Until 1866, the land between Hope Bay and Buff Bay was in the parish of St George, but in a reorganization of parish boundaries the land up until Buff Bay became part of Portland.

p. 278 'which to run'. The Blue Mountains are referred to as a moss forest because of the vast variety of moss and lichens.

p. 278 'inhabited by white people'. S. D. Smith, 'Sugar's Poor Relation: Coffee Planting in the British West Indies, 1720–1833', *Slavery & Abolition* 19, no. 3 (1998): 68–89.

p. 278 'peaked in 1814'. Kathleen E. A. Monteith, 'Boom and Bust in Jamaica's Coffee Industry, 1790–1835', *The Journal of Caribbean History* 47, no. 1 (2013): 1–27.

p. 278 'serving the sugar complex'. Brathwaite, *The Development of Creole Society*, pp. 146–7; Smith, 'Sugar's Poor Relation', p. 84.

p. 279 'directly to the owner'. John Lowandes, *The Coffee-Planter; or, An Essay on the Cultivation and Manufacturing That Article of West-India Produce*, London, 1807.

p. 279 'hundreds of the enslaved'. Jamaica Almanacks, George Harrison Cosens Elysium sugar and rum in 1811 226/11; 1816 (15)312/101; Shrewsbury 1811 454/ 38; 1817 323/81 329(Tot) 178(F) 151(M).

p. 279 'punished and tormented'. Seasoning was a word used to described the length of time it took for a slave to become acculturated to their condition.

p. 279 'conspiratorial spaces'. See Stephan Palmié, *Wizards and Scientists: Explorations in Afro-Cuban Modernity and Tradition*, Durham, NC: Duke University Press, 2002, pp. 137–9.

p. 280 'they were lashed'. Vincent Brown, *The Reaper's Garden: Death and Power in the World of Atlantic Slavery*, Cambridge, MA: Harvard University Press, 2008, pp. 51–5.

p. 280 '335 in Elysium'. These figures are taken from the 1812 Jamaica Almanack and thus refer to information for 1811. In a reorganization of administrative parishes in Jamaica in 1866 the number of parishes was reduced from twenty-two to fourteen, and St George Parish was divided between St Mary Parish and Portland.

p. 280 'beggars belief'. Elysium, 'the supposed state or abode of the blessed after death in Greek mythology', OED.

p. 280 'he renamed some of them'. Trevor Burnard and Kenneth Morgan, 'The Dynamics of the Slave Market and Slave Purchasing Patterns in Jamaica, 1655–1788', *The William and Mary Quarterly* 58, no. 1 (2001): 205–28.

p. 282 'James and Bridget'. This indicates that they were probably part of a single naming event; see Margaret Williamson, 'Africa or Old Rome? Jamaican Slave Naming Revisited', *Slavery & Abolition* 38, no. 1 (2017): 117.

p. 282 'son of Lilly's parents'. A decade later Lilly's parents used the name again for their last child. John Carby was also the name of Lilly's uncle, his father's brother.

p. 282 'younger brother, Matthew'. Carby, Lilly, Will, proved 4 July 1816. JA/1B/11/24/92, LOS Wills 92, Folio 145. Jamaica National Archives.

p. 283 'the eldest child'. Children who were born and died between registrations were not counted.

p. 283 'John Carby was born'. Walter Johnson, *Soul by Soul: Life inside the Antebellum Slave Market*, Cambridge, MA: Harvard University Press, 1999.

p. 283 'were gentlemen, after all'. See the discussion of Edward Long and John Pitney in Simon Gikandi, *Slavery and the Culture of Taste*, Princeton: Princeton University Press, 2011, pp. 177–8.

p. 284 'about the truth'. *The History of Mary Prince*, in *Six Women's Slave Narratives*, Schomburg Library of Nineteenth-Century Black Women Writers, New York: Oxford University Press, 1988, p. 23.

p. 284 'initials of their owners'. Scars and marks of branding were recorded as identification in paid advertisements and lists of runaways taken to workhouses. In 1816, in St George's Workhouse, 'May, an Eboe, belonging to the Eden Estate had the letters RH branded into her right shoulder.' A number of enslaved brought to the Portland Workhouse had been branded. See Douglas B. Chambers, 'Runaway Slaves in Jamaica (II): Nineteenth Century', University of Florida Digital Collections, February 2013, at ufdc.ufl.edu. Did Lilly brand the people he purchased, did they have LC seared into the flesh of their breasts or shoulders? Had Lilly branded initials into the flesh of the enslaved when a bookkeeper on any other plantations? See John Riland, *Memoirs of a West-India*

Planter: Published from an Original Ms. with a Preface and Additional Details, London, 1827, pp. 3, 32, 167, 185.

p. 284 'this enormous crowd'. *The Lincoln Date Book*, Vol. 1, Transcriptions 1761–1802, Lincolnshire Archives DL01 p. 204.

p. 284 'his neighbours permanently anxious'. Brown, *The Reaper's Garden*, p. 153.

p. 285 '[and] an axe'. P. J. Laborie, *The Coffee Planter of Saint Domingo: With an Appendix, Containing a View of the Constitution, Government, Laws, and State of That Colony, Previous to the Year 1789. To Which Are Added, Some Hints on the Present State of the Island, under the British Government*, London, 1798.

p. 286 'by hand in buckets'. Michelle Craig McDonald and Richard Stockton College, 'Sea Change: Coffee and "Plantations for the Poorer Sort"', Library Company of Philadelphia, 2014, librarycompany.org, p. 29.

p. 286 'own provision grounds'. Site plan of Chesterfield and description of coffee works taken from James A. Delle, 'The Landscapes of Class Negotiation on Coffee Plantations in the Blue Mountains of Jamaica: 1790–1850', *Historical Archaeology* 33, no. 1 (1999): 136–58.

p. 286 'seventeen slaves in 1817'. This figure is taken from the 1817 registers. Another small coffee settlement was Sherwood Forest, owned in 1817 by the heirs of William Sherwood, with ten slaves.

p. 286 'to house the enslaved'. Delle, 'Landscapes', p. 150. See also, Higman, *Jamaica Surveyed*; Laborie, *The Coffee Planter of Saint Domingo*; and James A. Delle, 'Women's Lives and Labour on Radnor, a Jamaican Coffee Plantation, 1822–1826', *Caribbean Quarterly* 54, no. 4 (2008): 7–149.

p. 288 'coffee industry in Jamaica'. Monteith, 'Boom and Bust in Jamaica's Coffee Industry'.

p. 288 'and make a will'. 'Carby, Lilly Will'.

p. 290 'like John Carby'. See Brown, *The Reaper's Garden*, p. 110.

p. 291 'Lilly's mother'. The Church of England arrived in Jamaica on the heels of the invasion which ousted the Spanish. The parishes and the Church were under the control of the planter elite until a Diocese was established in 1824. This meant that it did not historically attract the enslaved population who had their own African religious practices. The Baptists during the 1830s were the first Christian missions to become influential.

p. 291 'were also free'. There is an error on the record of Bridget's baptism which reads Bridgend.

p. 292 'three other parishes'. Born in 1707 in the parish of Vere, William Ivey died in 1754 owning a total of 4,532 acres in Clarendon, St Ann, St Mary and St Georges. Quit Rent Books 1754 JFS.

p. 293 '4,000 of them free'. Brown, *The Reaper's Garden*, p. 111.

p. 293 'lobbying as a group'. This account of the community of free people of colour draws on the work of Daniel Livesay, 'The Decline of Jamaica's Interracial Households and the Fall of the Planter Class, 1733–1823', *Atlantic Studies* 9, no. 1 (2012): 107–23. See also, Livesay, *Children of Uncertain Fortune*, p. 42.

p. 294 'when he was ill'. Londa L. Schiebinger, *Plants and Empire: Colonial Bioprospecting in the Atlantic World*, Cambridge, MA: Harvard University Press, 2004, pp. 80–1. See also, Londa L. Schiebinger, *Secret Cures of Slaves: People, Plants, and Medicine in the Eighteenth-Century Atlantic World*, Stanford: Stanford University Press, 2017.

p. 294 'without saying a word'. Lily's cousin Bryon had grey eyes as marked on his army discharge papers.

p. 295 'wring his neck'. There is inconsistency in the Baptismal records. Lovinia Ivey Mann also appears as Lovenia Ivey Mann.

p. 295 'restricted women's inheritance rights'. Carby, Lilly Will; Brown, *The Reaper's Garden*, p. 100.

p. 295 'acknowledgement of their fathers'. Between 1808 and 1813.

p. 296 'fathered children'. They fathered children among the enslaved population on the plantations where they worked.

p. 297 'and her children's rights'. See Brown, *The Reaper's Garden*, pp. 100–13, for an account of the havoc that executors could create in the lives of the enslaved and free people of colour.

p. 297 'limits on inheritance'. Ibid., 113; Brathwaite, *The Development of Creole Society*, p. 70.

p. 297 'Spanish River above Skibo'. Henry Shirley was resident in St George for many years and had once been the owner of the Spring Garden sugar estate on the coast. His son, Edmund Shirley, baptized Edmund Skiers, was born in 1794 in Kingston.

p. 298 'hogsheads of sugar'. Will of Henry Shirley of Saint Marylebone, Middlesex, PROB/11/1543/339.

p. 298 'in a mahogany case'. Acids, extracts, liquors, powders, spirits and tinctures were in common medical use, see ' "List of Medicines Wanted for 1791", Records 1789–1812, Business Records, Slebach Papers, The West Indies: Slavery, Plantations and Trade, 1759–1832', British Online Archives, n.d., Item no. 8456. National Library of Wales.

p. 299 'total of £1561.00.00'. William Dormer made an error when he completed the slave register for Lincoln; Bridget's son Edmund is missing from the final inventory and Eve and Sally were not listed on the 1817 slave register.

p. 302 'the working day'. Thomas C. Holt, *The Problem of Freedom: Race, Labor, and Politics in Jamaica and Britain, 1832–1938*, Baltimore: Johns Hopkins University Press, 1992, pp. 56–7.

p. 303 'suffered the worst'. 'The Storm', *Royal Gazette* XXIVII, no. 43

(21 October 1815); Maxwell Hall, 'Jamaica Hurricane of October 18–19, 1815', *Monthly Weather Review*, December 1907, n.p; William Arnold M.D., 'Answers to Admiralty Queries: Answers from Meteorological Register, 1815', *Jamaica Physical Journal*, November and December 1835, pp. 452–5.

p. 303 'the Shrewsbury estate'. An amount roughly equivalent to that received by an agricultural labourer in the UK at the time, the major difference being that in Jamaica the labour wasn't receiving the wage.

p. 304 'the Elysium estate'. George Harrison Cosens died in 1817 and Elysium was put into the hands of a receiver, William Lambie, Cosens' nephew. There are many other applications of the term, mulatto, these are just examples.

p. 305 'land they called Lincoln'. Settlements under ten acres were not recorded in the Jamaican Almanac for 1845.

p. 307 'had left the country'. Nevertheless, the registers included more information than could be gleaned from the two post-emancipation censuses undertaken, which lacked the detail of nineteenth-century censuses in the UK. For a detailed account see G. W. Roberts, *The Population of Jamaica. A Conservation Foundation Study*, Cambridge: Published for the Conservation Foundation at the University Press, 1957.

p. 307 'wealth for the metropole'. Civil registration of births, marriages and deaths began in 1880 but there is also a trail of parish records for baptisms which include the names of parents and some marriages.

p. 308 'Brixton prison in England'. African Caribbean Institute of Jamaica/Jamaica Memory Bank, *The Buff Bay Valley*, pp. 31–2.

p. 309 'operative modern characteristic'. See Diana Paton, *No Bond but the Law: Punishment, Race, and Gender in Jamaican State Formation, 1780–1870*, Durham, NC: Duke University Press, 2004, chapter 4, 'Penalty and Politics in a "Free" Society', pp. 120–55.

p. 309 'character and behaviour'. Ibid., p. 151.

p. 310 'elite planter class'. Post, *Arise Ye Starvelings*, p. 35.

p. 310 'deteriorated over time'. Patrick E. Bryan, *The Jamaican People 1880–1902: Race, Class and Social Control*, Warwick University Caribbean Studies, London: Macmillan Caribbean, 1991, pp. 131–60.

p. 311 'all along the coast'. On 8 February 1905 Jamaican parishes were reorganized. St George Parish is absorbed into Portland and St Mary's.

p. 312 'out of Swift River'. Hazel Bennett, 'A Community Battered by Disaster', Swift River Jamaica: Background, at e-greenstar.com.

p. 313 'hurricanes in 1944 and 1951'. Ibid.

p. 313 'Carby children'. Commended as a model school in the 2010 Chief Inspector's Report for the National Education Inspectorate.

p. 315 'and an English village'. I am using kinship as the term is used in cultural anthropology: 'recognized ties of relationship, by descent, marriage, or ritual, that form the basis of social organization', OED.

p. 316 'tub-thumping English nationalism'. See Richard J. Evans, 'The Wonderfulness of Us (the Tory Interpretation of History)', *London Review of Books*, 17 March 2011; Daniel Boffey, 'Historians Attack Michael Gove Over "Narrow" Curriculum', *Observer*, 16 February 2013; and Richard J. Evans, 'Michael Gove's History Wars', *Guardian*, 13 July 2013. In 2010, Michael Gove invited Niall Ferguson, an apologist for empire, to be an advisor for the project.

p. 317 'English nation-state'. Malcolm Godden and Michael Lapidge, eds, *The Cambridge Companion to Old English Literature*, 2nd edn, Cambridge: Cambridge University Press, 2013, p. 7. This is the trajectory of Simon Schama's BBC series, *A History of Britain: The Complete Collection*, A&E Television Networks, distributed by New Video, 2002.

p. 317 '"international" community'. John Blair, *The Anglo-Saxon Age: A Very Short Introduction*, Oxford and New York: Oxford University Press, 2000, Kindle loc. 249. See also, Thomas Green, *Britons and Anglo-Saxons, Lincolnshire AD 400–650*, History of Lincolnshire Committee, 2012.

p. 317 'only 2,039 subjects'. See Stephen Leslie et al., 'The Fine-Scale Genetic Structure of the British Population', *Nature* 519, no. 7543 (2015): 309–14; Bruce Winney et al., 'People of the British Isles: Preliminary Analysis of Genotypes and Surnames in a UK-Control Population', *European Journal of Human Genetics* 20, no. 2 (2012): 203–10; and Georgina Ferry, 'Settlers: Genetics, Geography, and the Peopling of Britain', Oxford University Museum of Natural History, oum.ox.ac.uk.

p. 317 'from around the world?'. Catherine Hills, 'Anglo-Saxon Attitudes', in N. J. Higham, ed., *Britons in Anglo-Saxon England*, Publications of the Manchester Centre for Anglo-Saxon Studies, vol. 7, Woodbridge: Boydell Press, 2007, p. 26.

p. 318 'carried my surname'. Godden and Lapidge, *Cambridge Companion to Old English Literature*, p. 9.

p. 318 'Scandinavian fleet'. St Omer, *Encmmium Emmae Reginae*, quoted in Else Roesdahl, *The Vikings*, 2nd edn, London and New York: Penguin, 1998, p. 133.

p. 319 '(farmstead, village, settlement)'. A. D. Mills, *A Dictionary of British Place-Names*, Oxford and New York: Oxford University Press, 2003. See also, Streatfeild, *Lincolnshire and the Danes*, p. 178.

p. 320 'after the Roman conquest'. Peter Chowne, 'The Excavation of Ermine Street at Coleby, Lincolnshire', *Lincolnshire History and Archaeology* 22 (1987): 31–4.

p. 320 'with Gothic foliage'. A. Hamilton Thompson, 'Excursions June

1907 – Notes on Buildings Visited', *Transactions Leicestershire Archaeological and Historical Society* 10, no. 1907–8 (n.d.): 133–90 (144).

p. 324 'exterior life simultaneously'. Annie Lorrain Smith, *A Handbook of the British Lichens*, London: Printed by order of the Trustees of the British Museum, 1921.

p. 325 'cyanobacteria and a fungus'. Frank Dobson, *Lichens: An Illustrated Guide to the British and Irish Species*, 4th edn, Slough: Richmond Publishing Co., 2000. I have drawn my understanding of lichen and the following description from this work. The debates over how to classify them are instructive. Because lichen are a 'dual organism' they cannot be named under the Botanic Code, which recognizes only the fungal partner. One lichenologist insists that 'the field of study is circumscribed by tradition rather than science and a lichen is a biological rather than taxonomic category' (ibid., pp. 5–6).

p. 325 'vacuum of outer space'. European Space Agency, 'Lichen Survives in Space', 8 November 2005, at esa.int.

p. 325 'interdependent multitudes'. Ed Yong, *I Contain Multitudes: The Microbes Within Us and a Grander View of Life*, London: The Bodley Head, 2016.

p. 326 'Thursday, 17 June 1762'. The Register Book for the Parish of Coleby,1741-1791, COLEBY PAR/1/2, Lincolnshire Archives

p. 328 'North and South Lincolnshire'. David Neave, 'Anti-Militia Riots in Lincolnshire, 1757 and 1796', *Lincolnshire History and Archeology* 11 (1976): 21. There were riots in Lincoln on 28 March 1761, associated with the election of Members of Parliament for the city. See *The Lincoln Date Book*, p. 183.

p. 328 'affected by the Act'. It is difficult to determine where William and his brother were born as records are inconsistent. I found a few Williams in Lincolnshire but only one family that had a William and a John who were baptized just eighteen miles away from Coleby in Balderton, Nottinghamshire. William was born about 1736 and John about 1739. In 1743 a George Carby was baptized in the same town and William names his first-born son George. It is my best guess that these are their records.

p. 328 'days of training'. *The Lincoln Date Book*, p. 188.

p. 328 '24 October 1807'. Loyal Welbourn Volunteers, Muster Roll for Coleby, 11th November 1803, Lincolnshire Volunteer Infantry, 1795, 1803–1806, 1813, *Lincolnshire Military Records, Volume 1*, Lincolnshire Family History Society, 2012, p. 80. This record was taken from a copy of the *Lincoln, Stamford and Rutland Mercury*, 18 November 1803, in the Lincolnshire Archives.

p. 328 'as a husband'. Account of weather and prices of wheat for 1762 as recorded in *The Lincoln Date Book*, p. 183.

p. 329 'Lincolnshire County Archives'. People like Robert Lely of the Close, Lincoln, who served as undersheriff to a number of High Sheriffs for the county in the eighteenth century. The Lely family was associated with Oxford and Lincoln's Inn, and a John Lely Ostler would become Mayor of Grantham in the 1850s. There was a Backwell Lely, a surgeon and apothecary, who lived seven miles away from Coleby in the city of Lincoln. Considering the consequences of these class divides in the archives, it made no sense to me that the daughter of a surgeon in Lincoln would marry a carpenter in Coleby, so Backwell Lely was dismissed.

p. 329 '*Bridget Lilly*'. In my navigation of the variety of spellings to be found in the archives I decided to take as definitive the spelling of a name as rendered by the person themselves or one who knew them intimately. In this case, a baptism, Lilly was clearly what Bridget intended to name her son even if his official record contradicts this.

p. 329 'infants in their arms'. Anne in January 1763; William in July 1764; George in November of 1766; Richard in October 1768; John in July 1770 (who they buried the following April); Mathew in December 1773; Mary in May 1775; James in April 1780; and John in July 1783.

p. 329 'in 1804, became Bright'. John Carby, William's brother, and his wife Mary have ten children baptized at the same font: two sons, Brion (Bryon) and Aminadab, and eight daughters, Elizabeth, Mary, Lidha, June, Ales, Susannah, Ann and Sarah. I have used the baptismal records as registrations of births were not yet in existence and it was customary in the Church of England to baptize children soon after birth. There is no baptismal record for Sarah but only a record of her burial, so presumably she died within a week or so of her birth. Errors of spelling and naming abound. The 1764 entry for Elizabeth reads that her parents are John and Elizabeth Carby but it is clearly John and Mary who are the parents and the curate mistakenly wrote Elizabeth twice. The frequency of errors or variations in spelling of names by curates in what was a small parish where everyone knew everyone else makes me wonder about the level of literacy of the curates. In later records Ales becomes Alere, but in the register for Coleby the name Ales can be found in other families.

p. 330 'study of the county'. Arthur Young and Board of Agriculture (Great Britain), *General View of the Agriculture of the County of Lincoln*, printed by W. Bulmer and Co. for G. Nicol; and sold by G. G. and J. Robinson; J. Sewell; Cadell and Davies; W. Creech, Edinburgh; and John Archer, Dublin, 1799, p. 9.

p. 330 'their manure enriching it'. David B. Grigg, *The Agricultural Revolution in South Lincolnshire*, Cambridge: Cambridge University Press, 1966, pp. 2, 104 and Table 13, p. 98.

p. 331 'owned by one landlord'. B. A. Holderness, 'The English Land Market in the Eighteenth Century: The Case of Lincolnshire', *The Economic History Review* 27, no. 4 (1974): 557–76; Grigg, *The Agricultural Revolution*, pp. 33, 104–5.

p. 331 'Acts of Enclosure in 1760'. In the following years Coleby Hall was passed down through various William and Thomas Listers until the estates were inherited by a female, Mary Lister, the last of the Listers of Coleby and Rippingdale (the other Lister estate in the county). Mary's nephew Thomas Scope succeeded to the estates and lived entirely at Coleby Hall. Scope died in 1792 and Coleby Hall passed into the hands of the Tempest family from Yorkshire. Gordon Goodwin and Andrew J. Hopper, 'Lister, Thomas', *Oxford Dictionary of National Biography*, Oxford: Oxford University Press, 2008, oxfordnb.com; Alfred W. Gibbons, *Notes on the Visitation of Lincolnshire, 1634*, J. Williamson, printer, 1898, pp. 26–7, 37.

p. 332 'high price of provisions'. See J. L. Hammond, *The Village Labourer 1760–1832: A Study in the Government of England Before the Reform Bill*, London and New York: Longmans, 1927, particularly chapter 5, 'The Village after Enclosure', pp. 97–105; *The Lincoln Date Book*, p. 184.

p. 332 'Coleby until 1854'. William White, *History Gazetteer and Directory of Lincolnshire*, London: Simpkin, Marshall & Co., 1882, p. 247.

p. 332 'throats and lungs'. Michael Durrand and John Grattan, 'Extensive Respiratory Health Effects of Volanogenic Dry Fog in 1783 Inferred from European Documentary Sources', *Environmental Geochemistry and Health* 21 (1999): 371–6; Th Thhordarson and S. Self, 'The Laki (Skaftár Fires) and Grímsvötn Eruptions in 1783–1785', *Bulletin of Volcanology* 55 (1993): 233–63.

p. 332 'damaged respiratory systems'. BBC News, 'Volcano "Drove up UK Death Toll"', news.bbc.co.uk; John Grattan and Mark Brayshay, 'An Amazing and Portentous Summer: Environmental and Social Responses in Britain to the 1783 Eruption of an Iceland Volcano,' *The Geographical Journal* 161, Part Two (1995): 128.

p. 333 'coldest months on record'. BBC News, 'Volcano "Drove up UK Death Toll"'.

p. 333 'weather and its effects'. Grattan and Brayshay, 'An Amazing and Portentous Summer', pp. 130–1.

p. 333 '48s 2d per quarter'. By 1796 it was 72s 3d per quarter and famine was reported in England.

p. 334 'the future looked grim'. *The Lincoln Date Book*, pp. 200–24. Throughout this period the Lincoln gallows were busy.

p. 334 'enslaved women in Jamaica'. '10th Foot 1 Battalion Statements of Periods of Service of NCOs and Men Liable to Serve Abroad on

24 June 1806', n.d. WO 25/927, National Archives; 'John Aminadab Carby, Certificates of Service, Royal Hospital Chelsea: Discharge Documents of Pensioners', 1803, WO 121/68/220, National Archives; 'Militia, Special Allowance Men, Blind Men and Garrison Sergeants, Aminadab Carby', June 1806, WO 23/140/00120, National Archives.

p. 334 'rapidly expanding army'. The army expanded from 40,000 in 1793 to more than 250,000 by 1813. David Gates, 'The Transformation of the Army 1783-1815', in David G. Chandler and Ian Beckett (eds), *The Oxford History of the British Army*, Oxford: Oxford University Press, 2003, p. 132.

p. 335 'enlisted in the army'. Young, *General View of the Agriculture of the County of Lincoln*, p. 420.

p. 335 'strength to disease'. S. Rogers, Historical record of the Eighty-first regiment, or Loyal Lincoln volunteers; containing an account of the formation of the regiment in 1793, and of its subsequent services to 1872, Gibraltar: Printed by the Twenty-Eighth Regimental Press, 1872, pp.4-8.

p. 335 'if they remained in England'. In 1794, '18,596 soldiers died on active service' and, during the next two years, more than 40,693 were 'discharged on account of wounds or infirmity alone'. These casualty figures continued throughout the Revolutionary and Napoleonic Wars. Gates, 'The Transformation of the Army', pp. 137–9.

p. 335 'Britain and Ireland'. John Bugg, 'The Other Interesting Narrative: Olaudah Equiano's Public Book Tour', *PMLA* 121, no. 5 (2006): 1424–42.

p. 335 'in the abolitionist movement'. Vincent Carretta, *Equiano, the African: Biography of a Self-Made Man*, Athens: University of Georgia Press, 2005, p. 366. While the overwhelming majority of *The Interesting Narrative* is 'remarkably consistent with the historical record', Vincent Carretta, author of the most recent biography of Equiano, states that Equiano's baptism certificate of February 1759 and his naval records of 1773 reveal that he was, in fact, born in South Carolina.

p. 336 'the enslaved'. Being white had been established as a legal privilege in Jamaica by the end of the seventeenth century.

p. 336 'those of his readers'. Roxann Wheeler, *The Complexion of Race*, Philadelphia: University of Pennsylvania Press, 2000, p. 274.

p. 336 'support the abolitionist cause'. Bugg, 'The Other Interesting Narrative', pp. 1431–2.

p. 337 'transformation into cargo'. Equiano, *The Interesting Narrative*, p. 39. See also chapter II, pp. 31–43.

Index